PETER, PAUL AND JACOB

COMMENTS ON

FIRST PETER
PHILIPPIANS
COLOSSIANS
FIRST THESSALONIANS
SECOND THESSALONIANS
FIRST TIMOTHY
SECOND TIMOTHY
TITUS
JACOB (JAMES)

based upon

The Jonathan Mitchell New Testament

BY

JONATHAN MITCHELL, MA

TABLE OF CONTENTS

Introduction

Acknowledgements

Abbreviations and Textual Apparatus

Comments on 1 Peter   1

Comments on Philippians   39

Comments on Colossians   73

Comments on 1 Thessalonians   114

Comments on 2 Thessalonians   134

Comments on 1 Timothy   147

Comments on 2 Timothy   179

Comments on Titus   203

Comments on Jacob (James)   216

New Testament quotes from:
The New Testament, God's Message of Goodness, Ease and Well-Being, Which Brings God's Gifts of His Spirit, His Life, His Grace, His Power, His Fairness, His Peace and His Love
translated by Jonathan Mitchell
Copyright 2009, all rights reserved
ISBN 978-1-4507-0505-9

Cover photo by Caletha Ellis

Cover design by Lynda Mitchell and Joshua Mitchell

INTRODUCTION

This volume is a collection of commentaries on nine letters in the New Testament: one by Peter, seven by Paul, and one by Jacob (also known as James).

Recent scholarship and the continual dynamic of the Spirit have combined to present a clearer view of the original springs from which the faith has flowed. *Ad fontes:* back to the sources! Let us return as close as we can to the primary sources for a clearer understanding as we engage conversations with the ancestors and wrestle with the interpretation of these Scriptures – as they applied to them then, and as they are now appropriate to our time.

Genesis 26 records Isaac digging again the wells that Abraham had dug. The envious Philistines had filled them in with earth, cutting off their supply of water – and thus, of life. Similarly, over the past nineteen centuries of the translation and interpretation of the Greek texts, divergent and partisan views have caused an accumulation of rubble which filled in the wells of the New Testament manuscripts with "earth," cutting off access to the original "springs." The flow of the Living Water from many verses and passages has been blocked. Like Isaac, each succeeding generation must endeavor to re-dig the wells and re-open the providential springs for a fresh release of the Living Word to our land.

The interpretation and comments of this work are based upon *THE NEW TESTAMENT, God's Message of Goodness, Ease and Well-being Which Brings God's Gifts of His Spirit, His Life, His Grace, His Power, His Fairness, His Peace and His Love* – a translation by the author.

My conclusions reflect this expanded translation, and take into consideration the semantic range of many Greek words. Their potential lexical meanings are parenthetically inserted into the text of the translation, along with variant manuscript readings. I have given much attention to the significance of the Greek verb tenses and to the functions of the noun cases, rendering the different ways that each of them could be translated within its context. Each verse is presented in bold face with alternate renderings parenthetically given in light face. The reader should not give preference to one rendering over another, but should thoroughly and thoughtfully consider all the possible combinations. An = sign signifies that what follows is a paraphrase, which means that the literal Greek has been *interpreted* to assist the reader. Bear in mind that such instances are just one studied interpretation of that particular Greek expression.

The main guides for interpreting the original works are the translation and the context, together with careful attention given to the culture and historical setting of the people to whom these letters were written. A concise introduction begins the comments on each letter. I make references to some additional New Testament letters and to the four gospels, as well as occasionally citing Old Testament passages that relate to the context. A few other commentators' quotes are also cited.

In short, this work is intended to shed new light based upon a correct understanding of the Greek texts within the perspective of the local life situations and their first century contexts, and equally important, to serve as a catalyst for critical thinking regarding the impact of these letters upon our lives today.

May God grant us all a deep, refreshing draught from our ancestral wells.

To God be the glory,

Jonathan P. Mitchell

ACKNOWLEDGEMENTS

I want to first thank my wife Lynda for her continued support of this work, for her editorial skills, for her insightful comment throughout the course of this work, and for her creative talents in the design of the cover. Next I want to thank my son Joshua for his technical expertise which has made possible this publication.

I want to thank my sister Rebecca Mitchell and my friend Don Luther for their proof reading and input on grammar and style. I want to thank the following friends and family for allowing me to quote their comments which have added insights in various places in this collection of comments:
John Gavazzoni, Rebecca Mitchell, Dan Kaplan, Don Luther, Lynda Mitchell, Steve Dohse,
and David Byrd for his article "Colossians, Community & the Church's Meal Table."

I want to acknowledge the following scholars whose works have been cited or mentioned:
J.B. Lightfoot, Marvin Vincent, William Barclay, Eduard Lohse, Paul Tillich, Helmut Koester, Jurgen Moltmann, Walter Wink, Ben Witherington III, N.T. Wright, Stacy Wood, Ann Nyland and Lawrence Garcia.

Quotes from the Old Testament have been from the *Concordant Version of the Old Testament* (CVOT), Concordant Publishing Concern, 2005; Joseph B. Rotherham's *The Emphasized Bible*, Kregel Publications; or the Septuagint (LXX), translated by the author.

ABBREVIATIONS and TEXTUAL APPARATUS

ABBREVIATIONS:
MS: manuscript
MSS: manuscripts
LXX: The Septuagint – Greek version of the Old Testament
Gen., Ex., Matt., Rom., etc.: commonly accepted indicators of the books of the Bible
Aleph, A, B, C, D, Ψ, etc., indicate an individual codex or MS
p signifies that the MS is a papyrus MS
TR: Textus Receptus (the "Received Text;" the "Majority Text")
cf. confer and compare

APPARATUS:
Brackets, [ ]'s, have been used for the following situations:
  to give a reading based upon other MSS.
  to insert notes or comments into the text
  to insert words to aid in the reading of the English version
  to indicate the reference of a quote from the Old Testament
  to insert explanations

Parentheses, ( )'s, have been used for the following situations:
  to give other possible meanings of a Greek word
  to give alternate renderings of phrases or verses
  to give a potential idiomatic translations

"=" has been placed before words for the following situations:
  to signifies that the following is a potential idiomatic translation, or paraphrase
  to give another spelling of a name or a suggested equivalent name
  to give a Hebrew equivalent of a word or name
  to give an explanatory note

John A. T. Robinson (*Redating the New Testament*, The Westminster Press, 1976) has put the date of this letter at AD 65. Peter states that he was in Babylon (5:13) when he wrote it through Silas (5:12). It has been suggested that "Babylon" is a code word for Jerusalem, where both Peter and Mark had taken up residence. It is a general letter written to "**selected and picked out exiles** (alien residents, sojourners, expatriates) **of a dispersion**" (1:1), and contains a series of admonitions regarding life in covenant participation. It has in view **a deliverance**, or "a [period of] rescue" which was then "**ready to be unveiled** (revealed; disclosed) **within the midst of and in union with [this] last season** (or: resident within a final fitting situation; in a final fertile moment; on [this] last occasion)" – 1:5.

In 2:12 he speaks of "**a day of inspection and overseeing care**." In 4:7 he says, "**Now the Goal** (or: the end; the final act; or: the finished Product; or: the completion of the plan) **of all people** (and: pertaining to and affecting all things) **has approached and is now near at hand and [He] is close enough to touch** (= has arrived)!," telling them to be sensible and stay sober. Then in 4:17 he tells them, of a "**fitting situation and fertile moment of the appointed season for the result of the judgment** (the effect of the separating for evaluation and decision) **to begin** (to start) **from God's house**." The phrase "God's house" is likely a code word for Jerusalem, and this letter was written just a couple of years before the Jewish revolt against Rome, which resulted in Jerusalem's destruction in AD 70. The visitation, or "day of inspection" is very likely a reference to Christ, the Chief Shepherd (5:4), being made visible in the judgment as Jesus had predicted (e.g., in Matt. 24 and Lu. 21). But what happened in Rome and Jerusalem affected the rest of the Empire as well. So here Peter is giving encouragement for endurance amidst threatened persecution and suffering, as well as steadfastness and covenant allegiance in faith, for their daily living in their current trials (1:6).

As to community organization, we only see Peter showing equal solidarity with them in referring to himself as an older man speaking to the older folks (who were usually the leaders in that time and culture) of the called-out assemblies (5:1). The districts to which this letter was originally sent shows the extent of the missionary activity of the early followers of Jesus. It is significant that there is no mention of questions relating to the Law. It seems apparent that Peter was writing primarily to Gentiles (non-Jews), since in 2:10 he quotes Hos. 2:25,

> [you] who [were] once (or: formerly) **"not a people," but now [are] "God's people;" [formerly] being the ones having "not been given mercy," yet now [are] "folks being mercied** (being given mercy).**"**

Furthermore, this was following other OT references (vss. 7, 8 & 9), showing that the Gentiles had been inserted into the story of Israel. In 4:3 he says that in previous times they had lived according to desires of non-Jews. Peter has here joined Paul in bringing the evangel to the ethnic multitudes.

Chapter 1

1. **Peter, one sent with a mission pertaining to Jesus Christ** (or: an emissary and representative of [the] Anointed Jesus), **to selected and picked out** (elect and chosen) **exiles** (or: alien residents; sojourners; expatriates; strangers residing in a country not your own) **of [the] dispersion** (or: of a scattering; of [the] Diaspora), **temporarily living beside residents of Pontus, Galatia, Cappadocia, the province of Asia, and Bithynia,**

This selected and chosen group of exiles to which Peter is writing is most likely the same group which Jacob (or: James) addresses in his letter, both men using the same term "**dispersion**" or "scattering." They were most likely those referred to in Acts 8:1 or 11:19, that were scattered from Jerusalem in that period. They were not just Jews who were dispersed, but fellow believers, since he calls them "elect." It is the same group to which Paul wrote in Galatia and the other called-out communities in the province of Asia, and to which John sent Revelation.

2. **in accord with and down from Father God's foreknowledge** (or: corresponding to a previous experiential and intimate knowledge possessed by God, who is a Father), **within a setting-apart of spirit** (or: in union with the process of being set apart from common condition and use by [the] Spirit; or: in the midst of a consecration which is a Breath-effect) **into an obedient hearing** (a listening and paying attention with compliance) **and a sprinkling with Jesus Christ's blood** (or: a sprinkling of blood, which is Jesus Christ)**:**
May grace (or: favor) **and peace** [= shalom] **be multiplied into fullness** (or: be brought to fullness) **in you folks** (or: to you folks; for you folks)**!**

Their selection and election, as well as their dispersion, was all in accord with God's plan and foreknowledge. This language suggests: 1) His own prior experience guides His choice, or 2) His prior intimate knowledge of these folks resulted in their being chosen. Their being chosen and their being scattered were both in union with His set-apart Breath-effect (or: Holy Spirit), and the dispersion was within a process of being consecrated. The word commonly translated as "holy" literally means set-apart, with the sense of consecration for God's use. The very choosing by God is what made them set-apart and sacred.

He set them apart into a realm of being: an obedient hearing and listening which required paying attention and then compliance. When He chooses us, there are requirements placed upon us, but as we see above, the sprinkling with the blood of Jesus Christ is what enables us to hear and comply. In the parenthetical expansion I have given a rendering of the genitive phrase in the function of apposition (or: definition). The blood of Christ is also Jesus and His life – for the life is in the blood.

In Peter's greeting we see that both grace and peace can be multiplied to us, and that neither of these is a one-time experience – we can receive more of each, to the point of the fullness of each coming to us, in us and for us (these are three of the functions of the dative case of the pronoun "**you**," each of which makes sense in this context). And since these things may be increased "for" the communities to which he is writing, grace and peace are not limited to nor dependent upon individual relationships with God.

3. **Well-spoken of** (or: Eulogized; Blessed; or: Well-gathered, laid-out with ease, and worthy of praise) **[is] the God and Father of our Lord, Jesus Christ** (or: Who is our Owner, Jesus Christ), **the One [Who], corresponding to and down from His abundant mercy** (or: much-existing mercy which is Him), **[was/is] – through Jesus Christ's resurrection forth from out of the midst of dead folks – bringing us to birth again** (regenerating us; begetting us back up again; causing us to be born again)**:**
       into a progressively living expectation (or: into the midst of continuously living hope);
4.   **into the midst of an incorruptible** (unspoilable; imperishable; unruinable; undecayable), **unstained** (undefiled), **and unfading** (or: unwithering) **inheritance** (or: enjoyment of and participation in an allotted portion as a possession), **one having been kept in view, watched-over, guarded, and which continues being maintained and kept intact within the midst of [the, or our] atmospheres** (or: in union with heavens; = in realms of spirit);
– [which things were/are being birthed and entering] into you folks,

The word "Eulogized" directly corresponds to its Greek counterpart, but the literal meaning of the Greek elements are: well-spoken of, or, well-gathered, laid-out with ease and worthy of praise. Notice that the first two clauses do not have verbs in the text, and I have supplied "**[is]**" to conform to English idiom in the first phrase. The adjective "**Well-spoken of**" is therefore a description of how "**the God and Father**" is regarded by people. Vs. 3 is similar in thought and expression to Eph. 1:3.

Rendering this word "well-gathered... etc." says that these are qualities of God. Peter goes on to tell us that He "**[was/is]**" bringing us to birth again (or: begetting us back up again) through the resurrection of Jesus, which was out from the midst of dead people. Note: His resurrection regenerated us; it caused us to be born again! The Greek is an active aorist participle, so is timeless, but it is tied to the resurrection of Jesus. It happened through His resurrection, and it is existentially happening for each person in his own order or group (1 Cor. 15:23).

Note again that His resurrection is causing people to be born again! God is doing the action, and this is tied to His raising Jesus from the dead.

The phrase "**of our Lord**..." is in the genitive case, and this first rendering means that Jesus has a God and Father. Translating it as a genitive of apposition gives the parenthetical reading "Who is our Owner, Jesus Christ." The "begetting us back up again" is according to and down from "His much-existing mercy." His act of salvation and His causing us to be born again are based upon, and have their origin in, His ABUNDANT mercy. Selah!

Now consider the three prepositional phrases in vs. 3-4 that each begin with "**into**."
1) **into** a continuously and progressively living expectation
2) **into** and inheritance that is incorruptible, unstained and unfading – which has been watched-over, guarded and maintained within the midst of our atmospheres
(or: in union with the heavens – the realms of spirit)
3) and these were through His resurrection being birthed "**into** [us]."

This expectation, this great mercy, is our inheritance which was then, and is now, entering into folks such as described in vs. 5, below.

Recall that Paul tells us that we are saved by and in the realm of expectation (Rom. 8:24). We were caused to be born into a realm of expectation. We are being birthed into an inheritance which from its very character shows that it is God, Himself. Yet, these are birthed into us. What glorious good news!

5. **the ones being continuously garrisoned within** (or: kept under watch and guarded in the center of) **God's power, and in union with an ability which is God, through faith and trust – [and], into a deliverance** (a rescue which brings health, wholeness and a return to your original state and condition; salvation; a [period of] rescue) **[which is now] ready to be unveiled** (revealed; disclosed) **within the midst of and in union with [this] last season** (or: resident within a final fitting situation; in a final fertile moment; on [this] last occasion)

Take note that both we and our inheritance are garrisoned, and this within God's power and in union with an ability which is, in fact, God. In this verse we have another "**into**" phrase, showing that Peter is continuing in speaking of the realm and sphere into which we were being caused to be born, and here we see that it is into a deliverance – a rescue which brings health, wholeness and a return to our original state and condition. This salvation, this inheritance, this expectation was in Peter's day ready to be unveiled within that last season, the closing of the age of the Jewish Law. The deliverance happened in the resurrection of Jesus, but it was not fully disclosed and revealed until the old creation, which was the system of the Law and the old covenant, was destroyed in AD 70. The destruction of the temple was clear evidence that the old had passed away and all had become new (2 Cor. 5:17).

That situation of the transition, from one age to the next, was the fertile moment of the new birth, the new creation. The burial of Jesus was the implanting of the Seed. The revelation of this was coming via Peter, Paul and the other writers of the NT. The time had come to unveil who Jesus was: the Christ, the New Being, the Second Humanity, the Last Adam, who is the life-giving Spirit (1 Cor. 15:45-49). This deliverance and its concurrent unveiling repeatedly comes, individually, to us in a final season of the first Adam within us, at a fertile moment and an appropriate season in our lives.

6. **within which you folks are presently feeling constant joy and happiness and are continuing to rejoice exceedingly – though for a little while, at present, since** (or: if) **it continues being binding and necessary, being pained** (distressed; grieved; sorrowed) **within various tests** (or: different trials and ordeals) **to put you to the proof.**

Those dispersed folks were then presently feeling constant joy and happiness within that "**last season**." It was in union with their deliverance, even though for a little while – since it continued being binding and necessary – they were pained, distressed and given sorrow within the midst of various trials and tests: the goal of which is the proof to themselves and for others.

7. **It [is] to the end that the examined and tested approval of your faith** (of the trust and faithfulness of you folks) **– [being] of much greater value and worth, and more precious, than of gold that constantly loses itself away** (perishes of itself) **despite being progressively tested and examined through fire – might be found [progressing] into praise** (approval; commendation) **and glory** (or: a good reputation) **and honor** (value; worth) **within an unveiling of Jesus Christ** (or: in union with a revelation whose source is, which has the character of, and which is, Jesus, [the] Anointed One; in the midst of a disclosure from [Messiah] Jesus),

This tested approval showed the authenticity, depth and strength of their trust and faith: both personal and corporate. The quality of this faith and trust is, via these tests, shown to be much more precious than gold (which is self-disintegrating) despite its being refined through fire. In 1 Cor. 3:12-15 Paul refers to this same testing of the building being done upon the called-out community. There the fire tests the quality of the construction materials, pointing out that only things of value and worth will survive the fires of this life's testings. Here Peter says that (by comparison) the effects of their faith and trust are worth much more than gold that has passed through the refining process.

Furthermore, it will be found to lead into praise and a glorious reputation (or: a manifestation which calls forth admiration) – as well as honor and value – in union with, or within the midst of, an unveiling of Jesus Christ. This disclosure will reveal the Anointed Jesus, but it also comes from Jesus via the anointing which manifests itself as faith and trust, while showing the character and qualities of Christ, revealed within the called-out community. This unveiling can be of Him to us, or of Him in us. This equates to the manifestation of God's sons (Rom. 8:19). It is what Paul referred to in Gal. 1:16, "**to unveil His Son within the midst of me – and in union with me**."

8. **Whom not seeing** (or: perceiving), **you folks are continuously loving** (experiencing the urge for reunion and acceptance); **into Whom at the present moment you folks are not constantly looking, yet are habitually believing** (or: continuously placing [your] trust and loyalty). **You folks are repeatedly rejoicing and being very happy in indescribable** (or: incapable of being spoken out) **joy which also exists having been made glorious** (or: by unspeakable and glorified joy; in joy [that is] inexpressible and has made a notable reputation; with joy that is glorious beyond words, and which is filled with imagination and good opinion),

Here Peter notes that although these communities never saw Jesus, they continue progressively loving Him, and even though up to the then present time they were still not seeing Him, yet, while continuing in trusting and believing, they are continuing to exult and rejoice in and with a joy which is beyond words and which has been glorified (filled with imagination and good opinion).

I want to first point out one definition that Paul Tillich gave for *agape*, that I parenthetically inserted: the urge for reunion and acceptance. This beautifully describes Christian love, and its intended goal. The expanded renderings of the final clause are also worthy of consideration. Glory (*doxa*) has a broad semantic range, including, notable reputation, good opinion and even "imagination" – something that is often overlooked in theology and Christian teachings. God's or a person's "light" and appearance shine into our hearts and minds, and create an effect.

9. **being ones constantly bringing to, or conveying in, yourselves for provision, attentive care and kindly keeping, the promised goal** (the finished product; the aim and result; the purpose and destiny) **of the** [other MSS: your] **faith and trust: deliverance** ([the] restoration to wholeness and health; a salvation) **of souls** (or: inner beings and selves; or: = people)**!**

Peter describes these folks as having the result of the above love and joy within them, being folks that are in themselves carrying the goal of faith and trust: the wholeness and health of their souls, as well as the deliverance and salvation of other people. The term "**soul**" can refer to either an aspect of our being, our inner beings or self, or can simply be used to refer to people. Each of these applications makes sense here.

10. **Concerning** (or: Round about) **which deliverance** (health and wholeness; rescue; salvation) **[the] prophets, carefully scrutinizing, sought out and then diligently searched out the [Scriptures] prophesying concerning** (or: about) **the grace and favor [directed and coming] into you folks,**

From this statement it would seem that this very deliverance and salvation was the ultimate goal of the OT prophesies – in contrast to the commonly held hopes (such as those held by the Zealots) of a literal Messiah who would deliver the Jews from their oppressors. They apparently searched out other prophesies as well as speaking themselves, of this deliverance which Peter here refers to as "**the grace and favor**" that had also come "**into**" these dispersed Christians. Here let me emphasize that the "**deliverance**" and "salvation" of vs. 9 is the "**grace and favor**" of vs. 10 – showing that Peter is proclaiming the same message of good news as Paul does.

11. **constantly searching into which season or what kind of situation the Spirit of Christ** (or: Christ's spirit; or: the Breath-effect which is the Anointed One), **resident within them, was continuing to point to, making [it] evident and clearly visible, repeatedly testifying** (witnessing; giving evidence) **beforehand about the effects of the experiences and results of the sufferings [projected] into Christ, and the glories** (the manifestations which call forth praise; the good opinions and reputations; the appearances of things) **after these things,**

These same prophets kept on searching into what season, or what sort of situation, or what appointed fertile moment (of the ages) – which the Spirit of Christ (which was within them) kept on witnessing beforehand (previously showing evidence) – it would be, which pointed into the effects of the experiences, and into the results of the sufferings that were to come, with reference to the Messiah – as well as to the manifestations which induce praises that followed these things, and the imaginations which they would inspire in the minds of the new creation.

The Greek word *pathemata* means the results and effects of things (both good and bad) which a person experiences through his senses and feelings. The sufferings which Jesus experienced had effects and brought results: all described as "**glories**" (etc.).

12. **to which folks** (or: in which ones) **it was unveiled** (revealed; disclosed) **that not to or for themselves, but to and for you people, they had been progressively dispensing and serving them – which things are now announced** (or: which tidings were brought back) **to you through those announcing** (proclaiming; bringing and communicating) **the message of well-being and goodness** (or: good news) **to you within** [or, with other MSS: by] **a set-apart Breath-effect** (or: [the] Holy Spirit; or: sacred spirit) **being sent forth from [the] atmosphere** (or: heaven) **– into which things agents** (or: messengers) **are habitually and earnestly desiring** (are constantly in full passion and craving) **to stoop down beside and look in.**

This same Spirit disclosed and unveiled to these prophets that their own and others' prophesies were not talking about themselves, but instead they were dispensing and serving them to the folks (and now, to us) to whom Peter was writing. This means that the prophecies pointed to Christ, and that this included the body of Christ. It was these same prophecies about the Christ that were in Peter's day being announced to them through the people bringing and declaring the message of goodness, ease and well-being to them – by and with the Set-apart Spirit being sent away from heaven (or, the atmosphere). Jurgen Moltmann has stated that with the sending of the Holy Spirit, God now has a history (he also said the same thing about the Father sending the Son). So it follows that God is also a part of the history of humanity, and humanity has thus been unalterably changed. Paul called this "**a new creation**" (2 Cor. 5:17).

These agents (or: messengers) are strongly desiring to stoop beside and peer into these things because they are (I suggest) the prophets of the OT age, as well as the folks then currently bringing the good news, and these things applied to them as well as to us. We have now become God's messengers and agents, and thus do we revisit the OT prophecies to find the Christ in them (*cf* Lu. 24:27).

13. **On which account** (or: Wherefore), **in preparation for work or action, girding up in yourselves the clothes about the loins** (or: waist; i.e., get ready for action) **of your divided thoughts and the things passing through your mind** (or: mental perceptions; intellect and comprehension), **continuously being perfectly** (or: maturely) **clear-headed and sober** (unintoxicated), **direct and set** (or: being constantly sober-minded, completely direct and set) **your hope and expectation upon the grace and favor being continuously brought** (or: periodically and progressively carried) **to you within an unveiling** (or: in the midst of a disclosure) **of Jesus Christ** (or: a revelation which is Jesus [the] Anointed One; or: an uncovering which comes from and pertains to Jesus Christ).

Because of all this, all these communities were advised to brace up (tighten the belts and prepare for work or conflict) their mental perceptions and "batten down" whatever is passing through the midst of their minds – so as to be maturely balanced with clear thinking. We find a similar admonition in Eph. 6:4.

Peter then admonishes them to set their expectations upon the grace and favor that is being brought to them, and borne in them, within the unveiling (or, in union with the disclosure) from the Anointed Jesus (or: which pertains to Jesus Christ) – that revelation which had the character of Jesus, and which brought the qualities of the anointing (and which was, in fact, Jesus Christ: the Risen One). This was a then present (and is a now present) reality – not some future event. The unveiling was the removal of the covering over their hearts and minds, as Paul spoke of in 2 Cor. 3:14-16. It is also the unveiling of their perceptions to see Christ within His brothers (Matt. 25:40).

14. **As children of** (= having the qualities of and characteristics from) **submissive, attentive hearing** (or: Like listening and obedient born-ones), **not being folks repeatedly molding, forming, fashioning or configuring yourselves to and by the former cravings** (the prior over-desires or full passions), **within your ignorance,**

This verse is an echo of Rom. 12:2, "**And stop constantly conforming yourself to** (or, as passive: And quit being repeatedly fashioned or patterned together by) **this age...**" Peter calls them "born ones" who are by nature obediently hearing and paying attention so as to obey. They are not to act or to be as they formerly were, in their ignorance, "fashioning themselves to and by their over-desires." This idolatry continues today, as the masses follow the fashion industry and the media of advertising – both of which focus on the external, which is in opposition to God's reign and the life of Christ. But we should also use caution that our current modes of "praise and worship," which can also slip into external ritual, not become a kind of idolatry which takes the place of intimate communion with Him Who lives within us.

15. **but rather, corresponding to** (down from; in accord with) **the One calling** (or: inviting) **you [being] set-apart** (or: holy), **you folks also let yourselves be made to be** (or: be birthed) **ones set-apart in the same way, in all behavior** (within every conduct; in all turning about or twisting up of [your] way of life),

6

In contrast, we should be conformed to the One calling us, being birthed to be set-apart folks – in correspondence to the set-apart qualities of the One inviting us. This applies to every area of our conduct, and in any turning or twisting of our way of life or the path that we follow.

16. **because it has been written that,**
> **"You people will be** (will exist being) **set-apart** (or: holy), **because I [am] set-apart** (or: holy)."** [Lev. 11:44, 45; 19:2; 20:7]

Peter is saying that what he had said in vs. 15 is because of the promises from the OT, such as this which he quotes, that we WILL be set-apart and sacred – and that this is because He Himself is set-apart and sacred. He is the cause of all; we are HIS workmanship.

17. **And since** (or: if) **you folks are habitually calling upon a** (or: [the]) **Father – the One consistently separating and deciding** (or: judging) **impartially** (without reception of faces, persons, appearances or external circumstances) **according to** (down from; corresponding to) **each one's work or action – let the time of your sojourn** (your temporary stay, dwelling alongside as an alien resident or an exile) **be turned upward, in the fear of reverent living,**

Now since they were repeatedly calling upon this kind of Father, they should continue turned upward to Him in the fear of reverent living – with respect for their alien country and neighbors during this period of living as foreigners within these dispersion regions of what was before considered to be Gentile lands.

We should also note that His decisions about people – His judgments – as well as being fair are also judgments of people's work or action. Peter does not say that the Father judges upon the basis of a person's belief, although it is clear that belief does bring deliverance from our estrangement and the human predicament. Judgment is primarily based upon what a person does, upon his or her works (*cf* 1 Cor. 3:13-15; Rev. 20:12-13). In the OT, Israel was normally judged because of unfaithfulness to Yahweh, and because of injustice to their fellows. God's Fire (which is Himself – Heb. 12:29) does refine (*cf* Mal. 3:2-3), and I suggest that this is the same purpose of the lake of Fire and Deity (which is in the presence of the Lamb, the Sacrifice, in Rev. 14:10). Opinions vary on the significance of the symbol of "**the lake of Fire**" in Revelation, but considering the references that I have just cited, it is my conclusion that this "**lake** (or: pond; or: shallow, constructed pool)" is a place of baptism into God Himself (Fire and Deity), and is for refining, purging and transforming. It is all returning into God (Rom. 11:36 "... **and INTO Him are all things**"). It is a, or the, baptism of Fire and the Holy Spirit, of which John the baptist spoke. It is the second death where death and those who have not yet had their names written in the book of life (each person in his own class and order, 1 Cor. 15:23) have death and other negative characteristics burned out of them (Rev. 20:13-14; 21:8). May He unveil our eyes about this.

18. **having seen, and thus knowing, that you folks were not unbound and released by a ransom of corruptible things** (things that are perishable and subject to spoiling) **– by little coins of silver or gold – from out of your fruitless behavior** (vain conduct; idle and foolish way of life) **handed down by tradition from the fathers** (= your ancestors),

He points out that they are aware that they were not set free by someone paying money. Furthermore, we see that what they were set free from was the fruitless behavior that came to them from the traditions of their ancestors. For those of Jewish ancestry this would be the "works of the Law" to which Paul referred in Gal. 2:16. For the non-Jews it would refer to pagan rites and worship.

19. **but rather by Christ's precious blood** (or: in valuable blood, which is [the] Anointed One; with honorable blood of anointing; by costly blood from [the Messiah]) **– as of a flawless** (unblemished) **and spotless Lamb:**

Peter calls upon their knowledge of the Christ event, in reference to His sacrifice which fulfilled and ended the sacrificial system of the Law. He incorporates into this figure the element of the Kinsman Redeemer (Lev. 25:25) who could (and had the responsibility to) buy a family member out of slavery. However, Christ used His life – symbolized by His blood – to make the purchase. Peter does not say to whom this ransom was paid, but elsewhere (Rom. 6:17, 20) it says that we were slaves to sin and failure, and it was humanity that sinned in the disobedience pictured in Adam (Rom. 5:19). But the central point is the freedom that was purchased – our release from the slavery of the human predicament – and that it was the giving of His life to us that did it.

In the parenthetical expansions we have the range of functions of the dative case of the word "**blood**," as seen in the prepositions "in," "with," and "**by**," as well as the word "**Christ**/Anointed" as the genitive of apposition in "which is [the] Anointed One." This word can also be rendered as "anointing," as seen in the second expansion. This last rendering would then refer to the anointing of the priests (Lev. 8:24), and of the mercy seat on the Day of Atonement (Lev. 16:15).

20. **being One having been foreknown** (previously known by intimate experience), **indeed, before [the] casting down**
> (as of material for a foundation: founding; as of seed in a field: sowing; as of seed of a man: conception [*cf* Heb. 11:11]; as in throwing something down: overthrowing; as in battle = slaying; in politics: abandoning [a measure]; of debts: paying down by installments;) **of [the; or: an] ordered System** (world; universe; a particular order or

arrangement of things), **yet One being set in clear light and manifested upon [the] last part** (or: final; [p72 and others read plural: last things, circumstances or aspects]) **of the times** (or: of the [or: these] successive chronological time periods) **because of you folks –**

Peter tells us that Christ (or, the Lamb) was known prior to the casting down, or the founding, of the ordered system. The word "**foreknown**" implies a previous intimate experience. The question then arises, Who foreknew Him and had intimate experiences with Him? This immediate context goes back to "**the Father**" in vs. 17, but this is not decisive. This word is connected to the context of "[the] **casting down of [the/an] ordered System**." Now if this system that was cast down is the arranged order before Humanity disobeyed in the Garden of Eden, then this foreknowledge may refer to Adam and Eve. Or, it may refer to the prophecy about Christ in the figure of Eve's Seed, in Gen. 3:15.

If we consider the rendering of "**casting down**" to refer to a "founding," then this could refer to the concept of a lamb for a sacrifice (itself a prophecy of the Messiah) that was in the mind of God when He founded the system of the Law which created Israel as a people to whom He related as their God. Or, it could refer back to the establishing/creating of the universe – which would imply a pre-existence of the Christ. See Eph. 1:4 for Paul's reference to "**a casting down of the ordered System**."

This verse continues by referring back to vs. 19 and the Christ, indicating that in contrast to the "**casting down**" this One was set in clear light and manifested at the last part of those Law-controlled times, and this happened for the sake of the called-out assemblies (which also includes us). Those "times" were the end of the age in which Peter was living. They were the times of the transition from old creation to the new; from the old covenant to the new. The ages overlapped in that particular generation, as shown by the sacrifices in the temple continuing on after the cross of Christ – until AD 70 (*cf* Heb. 10:11).

21. **the ones [who] through Him [are] folks trustingly adhering unto God**
> (or: [are] believing ones, ones full of faith, and confiding ones [proceeding] [p 72 & other MSS read the present participle: ones habitually putting trust] into God)**: the One awakening and raising Him up, forth from out of the midst of dead folks** (or: from out of union with dead people), **and giving glory to Him** (a good reputation for Him; a manifestation which calls forth praise in Him). **Consequently, your faith** (trust; confidence; loyalty) **and**

8

expectation (or: hope) **are to continuously exist being [plugged; put; focused] into God** (or: are to be [returned] into the midst of God)!

This verse defines the "**you folks**" of vs. 20: the people who are filled with faith and are trustingly adhering unto God, through means of Him, and through His blood (vs. 19). This manifestation (vs. 20), and the work of His blood (vs. 19), brought humanity back "**into God**" as one by one each is made to believe, made to be filled with faith and then is caused to put this faith into God – He being the realm of being which is the goal and destination of our trust.

God is specified as "**the One awakening and raising Him up**" from out of the midst of dead folks – or, from being in union with dead people – having given glory to Him, or, upon granting Him a good reputation through a manifestation which induced praise.

22. **Having purified your souls** (= inner selves) **within the hearing obedience** (the humble, attentive listening and submissive hearing) **of the Truth and from Reality [which directs and leads] into unhypocritical** (non-hypercritical; non-hyper-separating so as to over evaluate; not determined from below; non-nit-picky; or: unpretended; unfeigned; thus: genuine) **brotherly affection** (= fondness for the fellow believers), **love one another with acceptance in a stretched-out and extended way, from out of a clean** [other MSS: true; genuine] **heart,**

Here we are told to love folks "**in a stretched-out and extended way**" – which pictures a reaching out of our love, from our heart, to others – upon having purified our inner selves within the midst of obedient hearing that comes from the Truth, and submissive attention which pertains to reality. This is the path to purity: being focused attentively on the words from the anointing within us – from His instructions as He sits on the mercy seat of our innermost being.

This in turn leads us into affection for our brothers (= fellow members of the community) which is unhypocritical and not overly-critical. This last word literally means a quality that does not overly separate things so as to evaluate them, and which does not judge from a low position. True friends do not do this. Paul Tillich defines "love" (*agape*) in the following ways: the whole being's drive and movement toward reunion with another, to overcome existential separation; an ecstatic manifestation of the Spiritual Presence; acceptance of the object of love without restriction, in spite of the estranged, profanized and demonized state of the object; – *Systematic Theology III*, pp 134-138.

23. **being folks having been born again** (been regenerated; been given birth back up again), **not from out of a corruptible** (or: perishable) **seed that was sown, but rather of an incorruptible** (imperishable; undecayable) **one: through God's continually living and permanently remaining Word** (or: through a message or expressed thought of [the] continuously living and constantly abiding God; or: through means of a living and dwelling Thought, Idea and Logically laid out Expression and Communication, which is God),

This verse affirms that we have been birthed back up again (note: the Greek *ana* gives this force by conflating its retro and up meanings). This happened via the implanting of an incorruptible and imperishable Seed into humanity via the Word becoming flesh (John 1, prologue), and thence individually through the message that has been heralded throughout the world. This living and remaining Word, and God, has birthed us into the new creation. By using the word "**incorruptible**/imperishable" Peter signifies that the seed will sprout and grow (as in a field), or will conceive and create life (as in a human). Note the final expansion, above, of the last phrase, which gives other definitions of the word Logos, and presents the word God as a genitive of apposition. The adjectives "**living and permanently remaining**/dwelling" can be construed to modify either "**Word**" or "**God**."

24. **because,**
> **"All flesh [is] like grass** (or: vegetation), **and all its glory [is] like a flower of grass** (of vegetation): **the grass is caused to dry out and wither, and the flower falls off...**

25. **"yet the gush-effect of the Lord** (result of what flowed from [Yahweh]; saying, declaration or thing spoken concerning the Lord) **is constantly abiding** (continuously remaining), **on into The Age** (or: the eon)." [Isa. 40:6-8]

He uses this quote from Isaiah to contrast the transitory conditions of our souls – even when purified (vs. 22) – to the gush-effect (Greek *rhema*) that is a declaration from, or concerning, Yahweh. When something flows from Him the result remains and dwells with us, on into the Age of Messiah. Nonetheless, when this gushed-forth impartation (which is His Seed being incarnated within us) becomes one spirit as we are joined unto the Lord (1 Cor. 6:17), we, too, abide and dwell in His new creation Land (figure of His people), on into the new realm/creation of **"The Age."**

Now this continues being "the saying" (the declaration; the gush-effect) **being announced as well-being and goodness to you folks** (or: And this is the thing, and the result of the flow, being spoken into you in the good news).

It should be pointed out that, again, the word "**Lord**" (in the first phrase of vs. 25) can be a genitive of apposition, and can read, "the gush-effect which is the Lord." Thus, we see that in this way, He Himself is constantly abiding and dwelling with us. Remember that He said "**I, Myself, continuously am and exist being with you folks all the days, on until the joint-goal** (or: the conjunction; the end [of all] brought together; the conclusion, consummation and fruition; the combined finished product and actualization) **of the age** (or: which is that Age)" – Matt. 28:20.

This "**saying**" is the announcement of God's goodness, His ease, and His well-being which is brought "into" (Greek: *eis*) us through His heralds.

Chapter 2

1. **Therefore, being folks putting off** (setting away; ridding) **from yourselves all poor quality** (worthlessness; bad character; malice; what is not as it ought to be; wickedness) **and all deceitful bait** (fraud; guile) **and "answers" from perverse scholarship**
     (or: underlying decisions affecting interpretations and judgments made from opinions; or: overly critical behaviors; deficiencies in ability to sift and decide; judgments from inferior positions; legalistic pulling-apart of things for critical analysis; under-assessments) **and envies and all down-talks** (speeches or talks which put people, issues or situations down; backbiting),

The antecedent for being the kind of people that live the way this verse describes, is ch. 1:23 – these folks have been born again through God's incorruptible Seed, His Word. Living now as a part of the New Being (the Last Adam, the Second Humanity – 1 Cor. 15:45-47) and being in union with the Anointed One, they are empowered to put off and rid themselves of all poor quality, deceitful bait (or: guile; fraud), envies, down-talking and **"answers"** from perverse scholarship. What a load to set away from ourselves! But we do this through His life within us and the power of His Spirit.

Recent scholarship has pointed away from the English words "hypocrisy, pretending and play-acting" as the true meaning of the Greek *hupokrisis* in Koine Greek in the mid-first century (*cf* TDNT and The Source NT by Dr. Ann Nyland). As elsewhere I have defined this word from the Greek elements, which are *hupo* (under; below; or, as an intensifier: hyper) and *krisis* (from *krino*: to separate, judge, make a decision, give an answer – especially from scholarship, be critical, pick at minute details, etc., as seen in the expansion, above). This term was most used against the scribes (Jewish scholars and theologians – experts on the Torah) and the Pharisees, in the gospels – folks who did just this.

The other bad qualities speak for themselves, but perhaps we should note "speeches or talks which put people, issues or situations down." Christianity has been, and yet is, full of such – to our shame and disgrace. This broad definition covers a lot of areas in our daily lives. Our speaking should not put people, issues or situations down. We should only edify – build up. At the same time, we are called to evaluate and judge prophesies within the congregation (1 Cor. 14:29). Also, Paul tells us in 1 Cor. 2:15,

> "**the spiritual person** (one dominated by and focused on spirit or the realm of the Spirit, and characterized by the qualities of spirit: the Wind which continuously moves across the land) **is, on the one hand, continuously sifting and re-evaluating** (habitually separating and deciding from above on; progressively holding things up for close examination of) **all things and all humanity, yet, on the other hand, he is being sifted and held up for close examination or decision by no one**."

2. **as recently born infants, intensely yearn** (crave; long) **for the non-baiting** (undeceitful; guileless; honest; unadulterated) **milk belonging to the Word which is pertaining to thought, reason and communication, and which contains the qualities and characteristics contained in the message – to the end that, within it, you folks can** (or: would; may) **grow and increase into health and wholeness** (deliverance; rescued safety; salvation; restoration),

This verifies our new birth, and admonishes us to desire nourishment. The folks to whom Peter was writing were mostly new to this message of Christ, so he compares them to newborns that need to be at the breast of their mother. Peter here is being just that to them (recall: he is part of the Jerusalem which is above, which entity is "**the mother of us all**" – Gal. 4:26).

This guileless, unadulterated milk belongs to God's Word, and pertains to "**thought, reason and communication**." This nourishment also contains the qualities and characteristics that come in the message of the Christ. Its aim is that they (and we) can and would "**grow and increase into health and wholeness**" like young children. This also involves deliverance from the estrangement of our old flesh nature, rescue from our alienated condition, and restoration to what the true human is supposed to be – in Christ. Here you can see how I used the semantic range of the Greek *sozo* which is traditionally rendered "salvation," and which Lawrence Garcia likes to call being "salvaged." This word primarily refers to situations in this life – what He does for us now.

3. **since** (or: if) **you folks,**
> "**by sipping, tasted** (= experienced) **that the Lord** [= Yahweh or Christ] **[is] good, kind and useful** (or: obliging and profitable)**!**" [Ps. 34:9]

Peter shows the continuity and validity of the OT Scriptures, at the same time showing what he means by desiring the milk of the Word. The Word was the central medium for experiencing Yahweh, and was a guide to Israel's experiences and to how they were to live – just as His Word and Spirit now lead us as His sons (Rom. 8:14).

Note the second half of this quote: Yahweh (and, now Christ – consider the correlation of the term "**Lord**" for both) is good, kind and useful (or: obliging and profitable). What a wonderful description of our God. The Greek word used here comes from a word that means "to **use**." This is a predicate adjective, and "**kind, useful**, obliging and profitable" is the semantic range.

4. **Continuously approaching toward Whom – a living Stone, on the one hand being One having been and still being thrown away** (rejected; disapproved) **by mankind** (humans; people), **as the result of a test; yet, on the other hand a Chosen One, a Precious** (Inwardly-valuable; [held]-in-honor) **One, beside God** (= side-by-side with God; = in the presence of God; = in God's view) –

Although the context of Ps. 34:9 would obviously have referred to Yahweh, here the word Whom, whose antecedent is "**the Lord**" of vs. 3, obviously refers to Christ Jesus. First the Jewish

11

leadership tested then disapproved and rejected Him, and down through the centuries many others kept on rejecting Him. But in contrast, to God He was chosen and precious and inwardly valuable. In this last phrase we have the Greek "para" with the dative, and thus the suggested paraphrases which follow the "=" signs.

Peter is also relating Christ to the temple (His body) and as thus being One stone among many, as we see in the next verse.

5. **you yourselves are, as living stones, continuously being erected** (or: progressively constructed and built up), **[being] a spiritual house** (a building with its source being the Spirit, with the characteristics of a Breath-effect), **into a set-apart** (or: holy; sacred) **priesthood to bear up spiritual sacrifices** (or: offerings) **well** (or: most) **acceptable in God** (or: by God; to God; with God), **through Jesus Christ,**

He continues the temple metaphor, now focusing on the individual living stones (the people of the called-out communities, or, the various communities themselves – in relation to each other and to the Messiah). I suggest that in one community, each stone is a person of that community and each community is a spiritual house. But on a macro scale, each community is a living stone (one that displays Christ), and all the called-groups together form His one corporate temple.

Then he changes the metaphor to that of those who serve the temple: a set-apart priesthood which is to bear up spiritual sacrifices and offerings through Jesus Christ – the Chief Priest and Corner Stone of the Temple. Isa. 53:10 speaks of the Messiah making His "soul" a guilt offering for sin. And Jesus speaks of laying down our "soul" for our friends (John 15:13). It is the inward giving of ourselves for others that are the spiritual offerings that are "most **acceptable**" in God and with Him. Ps. 116:17 speaks of "the sacrifice of thanksgiving." In Ps. 27:6 it is "sacrifices of expressed joy," and in Ps. 51:17 it is "a broken spirit along with a broken and crushed heart." Rev. 8:4 seems to associate the prayers of His sacred ones with the altar of incense, which had been as shadow and type of offering spiritual prayer (Greek: *proseuche* – which means "toward having things go well; toward having goodness and well-being").

It should also be pointed out that it is the entire congregations (note the plural "**you**" and "**stones**") that are a priesthood – not just one person per group. Having such a hierarchy is returning to the old covenant order. One of the teachings of the Reformation was a belief of "the priesthood of the believer." Lip service is given to this, but we seldom see this as a practical reality in Protestant Christianity.

6. **so that it continues being contained** (encompassed; included) **in Scripture:**
  "Consider (Behold; Look)**! I am progressively setting** (placing; laying) **within Zion a chosen** (picked-out), **precious** (held in honor and value) **cornerstone lying at the extreme angle, and the one habitually trusting** (relying; believing; investing loyalty) **upon It may by no means be disgraced or brought to shame or be disappointed."**
  [Isa. 28:16]

Peter is giving a reference point for what he had just said – the foundation of Christ in the OT economy – as alluded to in ch. 1:10-12. He quotes Isaiah as his source for calling Jesus the precious, living Stone, in vs. 4, thus, along with the gospel of Matthew, showing Him as being the expected Messiah. And likewise, as we put our trust and loyalty upon Him, we will by no means be disgraced, be disappointed nor brought to shame before our Lord.

That He is called the "**cornerstone**" specifies that He is the One that is the beginning of the whole structure, sets the direction of the walls, and that it is in alignment to Him that the entire rest of the building is to conform. He is our pattern and ultimate reference Point.

7. **Therefore, in** (or: for; with) **you folks – those habitually trusting** (constantly believing and remaining convinced) **– [is] the Precious and Honorable One** (or: To you then, who continue

loyal, [He is] valuable). **Yet for** (or: to; in; with) **those continuing being without faith** (or: being habitually distrustful; being constantly unbelieving or disloyal), **[He is]**

> **"A Stone which those in process of building the house reject** (or: threw away after inspecting and trying) **– this One is brought to be** (or: was birthed) **into [position of] Head and Source of [the] corner,"** [Ps. 118:22]

8. **also [He is]**

> **"A Stone that people strike against and which causes them to stumble, even a Rock-mass which functions as a trap-spring** (designed to be a snare)," [Isa. 8:14]

who, continuing being unpersuaded (unconvinced and thus, uncompliant or stubborn), **are repeatedly stumbling by** (or: in) **the Word** (or: who are constantly stumbling, habitually being disobedient to the message), **into which [situation] they were placed** (= as it was planned).

It is because of what he had just quoted in vs. 6 that he thus begins vs. 7. Note that the bracketed "**[is]**" signifies that there is no expressed verb in the Greek, so the placement of the copula can vary the meaning of the statement. The plural personal pronoun "**you**" is in the dative with no expressed preposition. The first rendering gives either the location of this Precious and Honorable Person, or says that He is Precious and Honorable for and with them. The second rendering also shows His relationship to them, stating that He is valuable to them.

The second statement of vs. 7 would first refer to the Jewish leaders, but also to others who at this point reject Him. Vs. 8 gives another witness from the OT, and describes these same folks as being unpersuaded, unconvinced and thus uncompliant and stubborn. John 3:36 applies to these folks: they remain at this time "**unsalvaged; unrescued**," and yet His inherent, passionate fervor remains upon them, and we see that in His dying He forgives them, for in their rejecting Him they did/do not know what they are doing (Lu. 23:24).

Now take note of the last phrase of vs. 8. This was something that was planned by God: the Jews needed to reject Him and the Romans needed to kill Him (an action of both Jew and Gentile), else we would not have the Life and Deliverance which we now enjoy. God knew that He would be a stumbling stone and a snare rock, and these folks were "**placed**" (passive voice) into the situation of being this way – for His purposes. Recall Paul's revelation in Rom. 11,

> 30. **For just as you folks were once** (or: at one time) **incompliant to God** (or: unconvinced, disobedient, unwilling to be persuaded and stubborn by God), **yet now** (at the present time) **you folks are** (or: were) **mercied** (made the recipients of mercy) **by** (or: in; with) **the incompliance** (disobedience; stubbornness; lack of being convinced) **of these folks.**
>
> 31. **Thus, also, these now** (at the present time) **are incompliant** (stubborn; disobedient; unconvinced) **by** (or: for; to) **your mercy, to the end that they also may now be mercied** (would be the recipients of mercy).
>
> 32. **For you see, God encloses, shuts up and locks all mankind** (everyone; the entire lot of folks) **into incompliance** (disobedience; stubbornness; lack of being convinced), **to the end that He could** (or: would; should) **mercy all mankind** (may make everyone, the all, recipients of mercy)!

What a picture this paints. It was all part of His plan, and it is for this reason that He is "**not accounting to them** (not putting to their account; not logically considering for them; not reasoning in them) **their falls to the side** (their trespasses; their offences), **even placing within us the Word** (the Idea; the Reason; the message) **of the corresponding transformation** (or: the full alteration; the change from enmity to friendship; the conciliation)" – 2 Cor. 5:19b.

9. **Yet you folks [are] "a picked-out** (selected; chosen) **offspring** (family; kin; lineage; race; species; breed) [Isa. 43:20; Deut. 7:6], **a royal** (kingly; palace) **priesthood** [Ex. 19:6; Isa. 61:6], **a set-apart** (holy; consecrated) **multitude** (company; nation; body of people living together; swarm; association; ethnic group; caste) [Ex. 19:6; note: implies a sacred life], **a people constructed**

into an encirclement (made into a surrounding structure; set as a perimeter; made into a performance about [Him]; formed around as an acquisition; gathered into a surrounding [flock])" [Isa. 43:21; Ex. 19:5] **– so that you may tell forth the message of** (or: out-message; publish; declare abroad) **the excellencies and qualities of nobleness** (virtues of braveness, courage, good character, quality, self-restraint, magnificence, benevolence, reliability) **of and from the One calling you out of darkness** (gloomy dimness; the realm of shadows and obscurity) **into the midst of His wonderful** (marvelous; amazing) **light** [p72 reads: into the wonderful Light],

The narrative returns with those of the called-out communities being a contrast to those of vs. 8. Let us put their description in a list for consideration:
1) a set-apart species (race; lineage; family; kin; breed; offspring)
2) a priesthood pertaining to the reign of the Messiah
3) a sacred ethnic group; a holy multitude
4) a people constructed into an encirclement and made into a performance round about Him, gathered into a surrounding "flock."

As such, they and we can announce the message, forth from out of their and our midsts, telling of the virtues and excellencies, etc., of and from the One calling us all from out of the midst of the darkness (of either Judaism or paganism; *cf* Col. 1:13) and into the midst of, and thus to be in union with, His wonderful and marvelous Light (which is God, Himself – 1 John 1:5).

The four descriptions, above, describe the new creation. Number 1 follows the pattern of Israel becoming a set-apart people for Yahweh following their exodus from Egypt. But we are also a new species, breed and race: a part of the Second Human, the Last Adam (1 Cor. 15:45-47), the one New Humanity (Eph. 2:15).

The kingly priesthood corresponds to the new covenant priesthood of Melchisedec as portrayed in the book of Hebrews. The holy multitude (sacred ethnic group) is the new corporate humanity referred to above in 1 Cor. and Eph. This word *ethnos* is the word that was used by the Jews to refer to the Gentiles, but now these have become "holy, **set-apart**" as well, in the one new humanity. The 4th description relates to the figurative picture given to John, in Rev. 5:8-13, of the vast number of agents and messengers surrounding the Lamb's throne, with "**every creature**" in heaven, on earth, and under the earth (figure of those being dead) giving blessing, honor, glory and power unto Him. This is apocalyptic language describing the new creation that resulted from the Christ event.

10. **[you] who [were] once** (or: formerly) **"not a people," but now [are] "God's people;" [formerly] being the ones having "not been given mercy," yet now [are] "folks being mercied** (being given mercy)." [Hos. 2:25]

Here it is clear that Peter is referring to the ethnic multitudes, echoing Paul in Rom. 11:32 and Eph. 2:13-15. This is another picture of Rom. 11:15-17, Paul's analogy of the branches of the olive tree. Note that it is God that does the choosing and the acting in mercy.

11. **Folks that are loved** (Beloved ones)**: I am presently calling you alongside to encourage, aid, comfort and admonish you, as resident aliens** (exiles; sojourners; one dwelling beside citizens in a foreign country) **and temporary residents** (expatriates; strangers) **to continually hold yourselves away from the fleshly over-desires** (passions; full-rushing upon things), **which things are constantly warring** (doing military service; battling) **down against the soul** (the inner self and being),

Peter calls to mind their outward circumstances, recognizing that these folks are living among pagans that could have a detrimental influence upon them through their daily contact with them. He does not here specify particular over-desires or passions which assault their flesh and inner selves, but the following verse gives virtuous behavior as his suggested defense in this conflict.

12. **continuously holding your beautiful behavior** (your fine and ideal turning yourselves back around) **among the multitudes** (the companies; the associations; the ethnic groups; the nations; the castes; the non-Jews, or, Gentiles), **to the end that, within what thing they are continually speaking down pertaining to you folks** (repeatedly speaking against you) **as of ones constantly doing the worthless and things of bad quality** (or: as of evildoers or criminals; as of those repeatedly creating bad situations or forming what not ought to be), **repeatedly looking upon and observing as eyewitnesses the outcome from the beautiful actions** (the fine deeds; the ideal and honorable works), **they may glorify** (or: give a good opinion of) **God, within a day of inspection and overseeing care.**

As with Paul and the other NT writers, there is always the call and admonition to beautiful and ideal behavior as we live among the ethnic multitudes who are not a part of the called-out community. Here he gives the goal for this: observing our lives and the outcome from the fine deeds and honorable works so as to give God glory and so that they would have a good opinion of Him. Jesus taught the same thing in Matt. 5:16,

> **"In this way, let the Light, which you folks possess** (or: which has a source in you folks; or: which you people are), **shine in front of mankind** (before humans), **so that people can see your fine works** (or: the beautiful works that you are; the ideal acts which come from you as a source) **and they can give glory to** (or: and [these deeds; or: these works of beauty] will bring a good reputation for) **your Father – the One in union with the atmospheres [that surround you folks]** (or: within the midst of the heavens)!"

The last phrase draws upon the picture of a general inspecting his troops – which fits the "**warring**/military service" metaphor of the previous verse. This is not necessarily an eschatological statement, for troop inspection speaks of a regular and ongoing activity. God constantly observes us, and in this case, so do those among whom we live our daily lives.

13. **Because of, and by, the Lord** [= Yahweh or Christ], **you folks are to be humbly aligned in and to every human creation and with every societal invention**

> (or: be subordinated to every human framing; let yourselves be arranged under for support of every founding or institution pertaining to mankind which brings order to a state of wildness): **whether to** (or: by; for) **a king, as to** (or: by; for) **one being superior** (or: constantly holding over [others]; = as a prominent cultural institution),

Here Peter sets the scene of God's reign in and through us as we live among the nations. It is for the Lord's sake that we are to be humbly aligned to give support to the society that comprises our local environment. We are to support and align ourselves to the cultural conditions in which we live – including the local governments, for as Jesus said, His kingdom is not of this world order.

14. **or to** (or; by; for) **governors** (government officials; rulers; leaders; guides), **as to** (or: by; for; with) **those being regularly sent** (or: dispatched) **by Him unto a maintaining of right, in regard to doers of worthlessness**

> (or: into a correction from out of the way pointed out pertaining to those creating bad situations; unto an administering of justice, fairness and equity of situations affected by evildoers) **– yet on the other hand, [sent] unto a commendation** (a praise; applause) **of those habitually doing good things** (performing with virtue; constructing excellence).

He goes on to give more specific examples of practical situations. Those who represent God's kingdom are to recognize that He is the One who dispatches governors and those who maintain social order. This is the same message that Paul sent to the Romans in ch. 13:1-6. God's reign supports those whom He sends to be societal leaders, and those whom He establishes to maintain justice and right.

15. **Because thus is God's will** (or: For God's intent and purpose exists in this manner): **folks habitually doing good things** (constructing excellence; performing with virtues; creating goodness) **to repeatedly muzzle** (continuously gag; thus: progressively silence) **the ignorance**

of senseless and thoughtless people (humans without intellect and prudence; unreasonable folks);

This is a very simple and practical statement: God's will is embodied in people habitually doing good things and performing with excellence. The result is the silencing of the ignorant and thoughtless folks who would otherwise lodge complaints against His called-out folks. Religious and pietistic folks tend to think that God's will is something super-spiritual. But recall that the Messiah taught His disciples to pray that God's reign would come to earth (our natural environment) and that His will – that is obviously done in heaven (atmosphere; spiritual realm) – would also be done here among people with whom we live. God has come to live with us in this new heaven and new earth. The Voice from heaven spoke in the present tense to John, in Rev. 21:5, **"Consider this! I am presently making all things new!"** A part of this was stated by this same Voice in vs. 3,

> **"Consider! God's tent** (the Tabernacle of God) **[is] with mankind** (the humans), **'and He will live in a tent** (dwell in a Tabernacle) **with them, and they will be** (will exist being) **His people, and God Himself will be with them** [some MSS add: their God].'"** [Lev. 26:11-12; Isa. 7:14; 8:8, 10; Jer. 31:33; Ezk. 37:27; 2 Chr. 6:18]

His tent, or Tabernacle, is in this age His Temple – His body. We are where He lives. His purposes for the earth and humanity in this age are under the conditions of heaven having come to earth; heaven married to earth. Whoever is joined to the Lord is one Spirit/spirit (1 Cor. 6:16).

16. **as free folks** (those not bound) **– and not continually holding** (or: having) **the freedom as a covering** (or: a veil) **of worthlessness** (bad quality; evil; poorness of situation) **– but still, as God's slaves.**

This reference to freedom calls to mind Paul's reference to freedom from the old covenant in Gal. 4, and his statement in Gal. 5:1. Christ has set us free from all inward and religious bondage, making us citizens of the free woman, the Jerusalem which is above. It was this same Jerusalem that John was shown descending from heaven in Rev. 21:2. We are no longer slave to sin or worthlessness, but to God, our Owner (Lord). We are to live our lives in accord with His will and intent, as Peter points out in the previous verses. Note his description of us as "**God's slaves**," the same term that Paul used of himself in Rom. 1:1.

17. **Value everyone** (Honor all)! **Habitually love** (Practice loving) **the brotherhood** (= the organism of fellow-believers)! **Practice reverence to God** (or: Habitually fear God; Be constantly respecting and revering God)! **Be continuously valuing and showing honor to the king** (or: the One Who reigns).

What a broad and all-inclusive admonition: value and honor everyone. This calls to mind Paul's words in 1 Cor. 13:7,

> **"[Love] continuously covers all mankind; it is habitually loyal to all humanity; it constantly has an expectation for all mankind; it is continuously remaining under and giving support to all people."**

Value, honor, love: these give the Anointed One a good reputation, and give an appropriate picture of God to those not yet a part of the sacred community. Love of the family of believers and loyal ones is how all people will know that we are His disciples (John 13:35).

The second statement, about practicing reverence to God and fearing Him, was a cultural expression of those times that meant living a life that showed respect to God and that was in accord with His expressed will. It means acknowledging His lordship by one's way of living.

The last statement can refer either to the human in charge of the human government under which we live, or to God, referred to in the previous statement.

18. **The domestics** (house servants or slaves; members of a household), **those habitually being subordinated** (being humbly aligned and subjected for support) **by** (or: to; for) **the owners** (masters)**: [conduct yourselves] in all fear and respect – not only to the good and lenient** (reasonable; suitable; equitable; gentle; considerate) **ones, but also to the crooked folks –**

He gives a practical example of how they were to live their lives: with proper respect to those in a position over them, regardless of the kind of person they are. Rebecca Mitchell points to the modern structure of our society citing the example of the employer/employee, manager/worker, governor/governed relationships in corporate entities: respect is still in order, whether those in charge conduct themselves poorly or ethically. We, like God, are to love those that are adversarial to us. In our families and on our jobs we are ministers of reconciliation. But at the same time, "the Way pointed out" to us is justice and relationships that are turned in the right direction: toward goodness and peace (the qualities of God).

19. **for this [is] grace: if through [the] conscience, which is God,** (or: through awareness pertaining to God; or: by means of a joint-knowing with God; or: because of consciousness of God), **someone is continuing to bear and hold up under distress or pains** (griefs; sorrows; anxieties; sufferings), **continuously experiencing it wrongfully** (unjustly; contrarily, in regard to fairness and right relationship; undeservedly)**!**

This gives us another view of grace! It is grace lived out toward other people. It is the life of Christ emerging from hard circumstances and even from injustice. Here we see the call to lay our lives down for our friends and neighbors (which, as Lu. 10:29-37 shows, are more than just our own local group or persuasion).

The phrase "**which is God**," and the parenthetical alternatives, are expressions of the range of function of the genitive case. Conscience, awareness, joint-knowing, and consciousness are words that express the semantic range of the Greek *suneidēdis*.

20. **For what sort of credible report** (honorable rumor; credit; fame; praiseworthy reputation) **[is it] if, being ones habitually doing what is wrong** (failing to hit the target; sinning) **and being repeatedly beaten and struck with a fist** [*p*72 & other MSS: repeatedly lopped-off and pruned], **you folks will be** [*p*72 & other MSS read: you are constantly] **remaining under and enduring [it]? But to the contrary, if while habitually practicing virtue** (doing good; constructing excellence) **and [at the same time] repeatedly experiencing such bad treatment** (or: continually suffering) **you will be** [*p*72 reads: you are constantly] **humbly remaining under, enduring and supporting [it], this [is] grace at the side of** (or: from beside; = in the presence of) **God,**

The second situation is another expression of grace, as the last clause shows, and is a restatement of vs. 19. The next verse says that this is a part of the grace to which we are called. Remember that grace came through Christ enduring bad treatment. We are to do the works that He did (John 14:12) – and this is just one example of such.

The contrast of enduring reprisals for misconduct, to enduring abuse for Christ's sake, clearly points to a faith, trust and loyalty that is lived out as an expression of God's reign amidst contrary circumstances. It is being a light of God's grace within a world of darkness.

21. **for into this you are called** (or: were invited), **because Christ also experienced [this]** (or: suffered) **over you folks** (or: for your sakes), **leaving continuously below** (or: behind) **in you** (or: with and for you) **an underwriting** (a writing under which you are to write or copy; hence: a pattern; a model) **to the end that you could** (or: would) **follow-on in the footprints of Him**

This is the path of the disciple, the one following the Suffering Servant. His life was our pattern for living. He experienced these things for us, and we are to do so for others. This is the increase of His kingdom and reign. We are CALLED to this kind of thing – here in our natural lives – not to just have wonderful spiritual experiences!

22.   **"Who does not make a mistake** (Who did not perform failure; Who does no sin; Who does not construct failure to hit the target), **nor is** (or: was) **deceitful bait** (fraud; guile) **found in His mouth;"** [Isa. 53:9]

23. **Who, being repeatedly reviled** (harshly and bitingly rebuked and insulted), **was not reviling back** (answering insult with insult; taking the position of harsh, biting rebuke); **continuously** (or: repeatedly) **suffering** (experiencing ill treatment), **he was not threatening, but kept on giving [the situation] over to the One at His side: the One constantly sifting, separating and deciding** (or: judging) **fairly** (equitably; following the Path of the Way pointed out, bringing situations to a rightwised condition),

The verbs of vs. 22 are in the aorist tense – the fact form that can either be a simple present or a simple past (scholars differ in opinions on this) – so I have rendered it both ways. Since He remains the same, I lean toward the simple present here. The word traditionally rendered as "sin" is an archery term which means "to miss the target." The extended meanings are "mistake, failure, error," but the underlying idea is that one is trying to hit the target, but does not succeed.

As we follow in His footprints, we, too, should not speak deceit or fraud. We should only speak the truth, in love.

Vs. 23 gives further example for how we are to handle harsh treatment. Keep in mind that "**you folks died, and your life has been hidden** (concealed) **together with the Christ, within the midst of God** (or: in union with God)" (Col. 3:3), and in Gal. 2:20, Paul says,
>   "**I was crucified together with Christ, and thus it remains** (or: I have been jointly put on the execution stake in [the] Anointed One, and continue thus), **yet I continue living! [It is] no longer I, but it is Christ continuously living and alive within me!**"

This outlook and awareness of the new reality is what enables us to follow our Messiah, or with the picture in Isa. 53 – our Suffering Servant, in this way.

Keep in mind that He "**kept on giving [the situation] over to the One at His side**." God is at our sides, as well, going through all our experiences with us. His is also "**the One constantly sifting, separating and deciding** (or: judging) **fairly** (equitably; following the Path of the Way pointed out, bringing situations to a rightwised condition)" – He is constantly making decisions about us, about others and about the situations in life. And we must trust that His decisions are fair and accord with the Way of Christ, turning situations in the right direction that accord with His plans and purposes.

24. **Who, Himself, bore back up again our failures** (our mistakes; our times of falling short or to the side of the target; our sins and errors) [Isa. 53:4, 12] **within His body upon the tree** (the wood; the stake), **to the end that, being folks suddenly coming to be parted away from the failures** (mistakes; errors; sins; misses of the target), **we can** (or: would; may) **live in** (or: by; for; with) **the fairness and equity, in rightwised relationships, in the Path of the Way pointed out** (or: = in covenant participation), **where "you folks are** (or: were) **healed** (or: cured) **in the wound** (or: by the welt; in the bruise of the blow)." [Isa. 53:5]

Peter reminds them of the goal of the Christ event, His cross and resurrection, and the effect it has upon us. He "**parted away**" our sins and mistakes, bearing them up within His body, so that we would live in, by, for and with fairness and equity among other humans, being in relationships that are turned in the right direction, within the path of the Way (Christ) that He pointed out to us (sacrificial love) – the place where we are healed in and by His bruise and wound, for we are healed by being joined to His work, and by coming into union with His life.

Note how Peter is stressing a life lived here, on earth, in rightwised relationships – not away somewhere in a parallel universe, or off in space/spirit. The clouds of the kingdom of heaven have come down to touch the earth, and pour out blessings to humanity. God has made earth His home, bringing the heavens with Him. He is living out His life through us, who are His body, His bride – and the Lamb (Jesus) is within her/us (Rev. 22:3). The nations are walking in the Light of the City (Rev. 21:23-24 –and that Light is Christ, the Lamb, within His called-out communities).

25. **For you folks were continuing to be "like sheep, being habitually caused to wander** (being led astray; or, as a middle: people constantly wandering away)," [Isa. 53:6] **but now in contrast, "you are** (or: were) **turned around and made to return, upon"** [the will of; the herding of] the **Shepherd and Overseer of** (Supervisor of; the One who watches over) **your souls** (your inner beings).

Peter has drawn a lot from Isa. 53, showing both us and Christ to be the subject of that prophecy. Mark well the passive voice in this quote: "**caused to wander**, led astray." But the verb can also be a middle, describing us as "people constantly wandering away," and yet this is due to our flesh, our estranged human nature – something for which we did not ask.

But the good news is that there is a stark contrast in the new creation, with the New Being, as Paul Tillich calls it. And we see another passive voice that shows that we were (and are) turned around and made to return, upon the will and herding action of the Shepherd and Overseer of our souls. We are His flock, the sheep of His pasture (Ps. 95:7). This term Shepherd gives us a tender picture of His loving care and involvement in our lives, as Ps. 23 describes. There He makes, He leads, He restores and then leads again, He is with us, and His staff comforts us. Then He prepares and He anoints, and we have more than enough, with goodness and mercy attending us – as we dwell in, and are, His temple.

Chapter 3

1. **Likewise** (In like manner), **you wives: [Be] habitually with humility aligning yourselves to your own husbands** (or: women: [Be] continually arranging yourselves for support, under your own adult males), **to the end that if any** (or: certain ones) **are habitually unpersuaded by the Word** (or: uncompliant or disobedient to the message; unconvinced with the thought, reason or idea), **they will be profited** (will receive advantage; or: will be acquired as gain) **without a word** (or: message; reason), **through the behavior** (or: conduct; way of life) **of the wives** (or: women),

Having addressed the domestics, in 2:18, he now addresses the wives, or unmarried women of a marriageable age, of the community. Although this is a community of people that have been set free in Christ (Gal. 5:1), and among them there is neither male nor female in the anointed assembly (Gal. 3:28), in their outward relationships of their natural lives they still lived as women and men, as wives and husbands. So it was necessary for Peter to speak to these newly formed communities of faith and loyalty to Christ, that in these areas of their daily living – just as with their relationships to government authorities, or, their owners – they should live as an ordered, structured community within the greater societies in which they resided.

Humility and support were core virtues of the life in Christ, so this was no extra burden being placed upon them. The purpose that he explains is that this kind of loving behavior will profit those who are yet unpersuaded as to the Messiah, remaining uncompliant to the message about Jesus. As for us today, how they lived proclaimed the message, so that without any verbal expression their conduct and way of life will give these outside folks an advantage, and they will be acquired as gain to God's reign.

2. **being eyewitnesses of** (or: looking upon and observing) **the pure behavior** (or: way of life; conduct) **of you folks – which is turned upward in reverence, respect and [sacred] fear and awe –**

These other folks will look upon, and with their own eyes observe, this "**pure behavior**" which is "**turned upward**" to God, in reverence and respect, along with sacred fear and awe – terms that in that culture described the proper deference and relationship of a human to God.

3. **whose world must not consist of the external adornment – of braiding or interweaving or struggling with [the] hair and [the] placing-around of gold ornaments, or of dressing up** (putting on garments) –

No one in the community of Christ should have their "world" consist of external adornment. This is a play on the Greek word "kosmos," as one meaning of this is "an adorned arrangement" – which can refer to one's home, a city, the earth as an ordered interdependent system, or the universe (which God has "adorned"). But a woman's "world" should not consist of her external appearance – else she would then in fact be living an idolatrous life.

4. **but to the contrary, [it should consist of] the hidden person** (concealed humanity; cloaked personality) **of the heart, within the incorruptible and imperishable quality of the gentle** (tender; mild; calm; kind; meek) **and still** (at ease; restful; tranquil; quiet) **spirit** (or: attitude; disposition; or: Breath-effect), **which is** (or: continually exists being) **of great value and very costly in God's sight** (= view, or, perspective).

Here Peter gives what should be the contrasting expression of the reality of kingdom living that is in union with the Messiah – the life of the Age that had been expected. The "**hidden person**" and "cloaked personality" is the New Being (Christ) that indwells us – but yet can be seen by our way of living. This is an expression of Christ within us and among us – the expectation of glory (Col. 1:27), or, a good reputation (which is another meaning of the Greek *doxa*).

It is interesting that Peter uses the adjective "**incorruptible; imperishable**" to describe the gentle and still spirit that is within the hidden person, or concealed humanity, of the heart. Paul uses this same adjective in 1 Cor. 15:52 to describe the dead that are raised up. He also uses it to describe God in Rom. 1:23, and Peter uses it to describe the inheritance into which we have been regenerated (born again), in 1:4 of this letter.

The noun "**incorruption**" is used in 1 Cor. 15:42, 50, 53, and 54 – all verses speaking about the resurrection. Paul says in Eph. 6:24, "**Grace and favor, in union with incorruption** (or: within a state or condition of being unspoiled, and being incorruptible), **[are] with all the people continuously loving our Lord** (or: Owner; Master), **Jesus Christ** ([the] Anointed Jesus)." In 1 Cor. 15:53 he tells us, "**it continues being necessary** (it is habitually binding) **for this perishable and corruptible to instantly plunge** (or: sink) **in and clothe itself with** (or: slip on; put on) **incorruption and imperishability**." Corruptibility is the result of death. But in the next verse he tells us that "**The Death was drunk down and swallowed into Victory** (or: overcoming)" (vs. 54), and in vs. 57 he proclaims that, "**grace and joyous favor [is] in God** (or: by God) – **the One presently and progressively giving the Victory** (or: the overcoming) **to us, in us and for us through our Lord** (Owner; Master), **Jesus, [the] Christ!**" So as Paul said in Eph., above, so here in 1 Cor., grace comes in union with incorruption, and this grace is in the One now giving us the Victory (= Christ) over death through His swallowing down death. It was Christ's resurrection that was His victory and overcoming of death. He has given to us this same victory and incorruption – to our inner humanity, in our spirits, as Peter tells us in vs. 4, above.

5. **For thus, at one time, the set-apart wives** (or: the holy women) – **those being in the habit of placing their expectations and hopes into God – used to normally arrange their world and adorn themselves, constantly being put in humble alignment to their own husbands** (or: continuously being arranged under their own adult males, to give support),

Peter is rehearsing the traditional way of living, exemplified by the Jewish ancestors, while at the same time indicating that these traditions are still wise and appropriate for their then present communities. He is indicating that he is not introducing a new custom – but is using the holy women and set-apart wives of the past as an example. This is a part of the many things that occurred among them that are now examples for us (Heb. 8:5; 1 Cor. 10:11). Again, the basic premise is love, not the specific cultural expressions.

6. **as Sarah used to humbly hear and submissively obey Abraham, habitually calling him "lord"** ("master;" "my owner"), **of which woman you were birthed children** (or: you are become her born ones [= daughters]), **women normally doing good** (performing virtue; creating excellence), **and not being repeatedly caused to fear even one dismay** (alarm; intimidation).

As Paul reached back to Sarah as a type and figure of the freed called-out community (Gal. 4), now Peter does the same thing but drawing upon another aspect of her life, as a specific example of what he has been saying. As Paul used Abraham in Gal. 3:7 (we who have been birthed from faith, trust and loyalty are Abraham's sons), now Peter uses Sarah – as the "mother of us all" (Gal. 4:22-26), and here, specifically, speaking to her spiritual, or in some cases natural, daughters. As Abraham's actions were due to his being a rightwised person, living in the way pointed out (which was obedience to the voice of Yahweh), so women are to be normally performing virtue and creating excellence. This kind of life brings no fear or dismay.

7. **Husbands** (or: Adult males), **likewise** (or: in like manner)**: Continuously dwelling together** (cohabiting; making a joint home) **with [them] corresponding to intimate, experiential knowledge [of them]** (= with a learned insight and an intelligent recognition of the nature and aspects of a married situation), **[be] habitually assigning** (portioning-off; awarding; allotting) **honor** (value; worth) **to the female attributes** (things pertaining to a woman; or: to a feminine one) **as to a person having a disadvantaged position in her living** (or: a weaker livelihood; or: a weaker vessel, utensil, instrument, container, gear, furniture, equipment), **yet as to co-heirs of Life's grace and favor**
> (or: of [the] grace which is life; or, with other MSS: as joint-participants in an inheritance of manifold {diverse; varied; multicolored} grace – of life [p72 adds: pertaining to and having the qualities of the Age {of eonian life}]), **into the [situation where] your thoughts, words and actions projected toward goodness** (or: prayers) **continue not to be hindered or blocked, as if by a trench being cut in their path to impede their progress.**

The first point to consider here is that husbands are instructed to live with their wives in a way that corresponds figuratively to the example of knowing each other in intimate sexual union. This speaks of knowing them very well and having intelligent recognition of what it means to be married, as the parenthetical idiomatic rendering suggests. The Greek word for husband can also mean "adult male." Thus, this admonition can also give an analogy to the men in the community – not in the sphere of physical relationships, but in the sphere of the social and spiritual – to understand the women of the community, and give them honor while in their thoughts and actions "**assigning** [them]" value and worth.   Such insights will also give light to the relationship of the Messiah to His called-out folks (Eph. 5:21-32), and thus benefit the entire community.

He is thus also to assign honor to the female attributes of all folks, as well as to the feminine aspects of a woman. He is to see that, especially in that time and society – but even now still in our own, the woman had a disadvantaged position in her living and way of life. The male-dominated society has always resisted equality. However, in the reign of Christ they are co-heirs of Life's grace and favor – or, of the grace which is Life. Papyrus #72 associates this with "the Age" which was a code term for the new creation that came with the Messiah.

In the last clause I conflate the semantic range of *proseuche* that is traditionally rendered "prayer." Note that he is saying that by living as described in the first part of the verse, a man's thoughts, words and actions that have a view to having goodness will not be hindered or blocked – then he uses a colorful word-picture of a trench cut across a road, to get the idea across.

8. **Now [this is] the goal** (the final situation; the end of the process)**: all [are to be] like-minded** (of the same frame of mind and disposition), **folks sharing and expressing the same feelings** (being sympathetic), **ones being fond of and expressing affection for the brothers** (= fellow believers; = communal members), **people tenderhearted and compassionate, folks of a humble disposition and way of thinking;**
This is what a called-out community should look like. We do not see mentioned here multiple denominations or divisions as there were in Corinth (1 Cor. 1:12-13). This would be a nice group with which to be involved. I think that these characteristics speak for themselves, and exemplify the goal of all called-out communities.

9. **not being ones habitually giving back** (repaying; rendering; giving away) **bad in the place of bad** (or: poor quality in exchange for poor quality; evil for evil) **or abusive language in the place of abusive language** (reviling in exchange for reviling; insulting back against insults), **but just the opposite: constantly speaking things that embody wellness or give a blessing, because into this you are called** (or: were invited), **to the end that you folks may inherit a word embodying wellness** (a blessing; a message of goodness; a thought bringing ease).

The first part expresses the opposite of what it should look like, and then adds to the good qualities given in vs. 8. "**Constantly speaking things that embody wellness or give a blessing**" would flow from what Paul said in Phil. 4:8. Think about only the good and virtuous, and your speaking will follow from the same. And thus, as we sow so shall we reap: an inheritance that is a word embodying goodness, ease and well-being; a blessing; a thought that brings ease.

10. **For you see,**
> "**the person who continues purposing** (willing; intending; wanting) **to be habitually loving life, and to see and experience good days, let his tongue at once cease from [the] worthless and poor of quality** (from [the] bad and evil) **and his lips speak no deceitful bait** (fraud; guile).
11. > "**Now let him bend to incline forth and turn out, away from [the] worthless and poor of quality** (from [what is] bad or evil), **and let him do** (practice; construct; produce) **[the] good** (or: virtue; excellence); **let him seek and try to find peace and harmony; let him also run after it and pursue it,**
12. > "**because [the] Lord's** [= Yahweh's] **eyes [are] upon** (= He looks with favor on) **[the] fair and equitable folks** (the rightwised ones; the just ones who walk in the Way pointed out), **and His ears [directed] into their request pertaining to need; yet [the] face of [the] Lord** [= Yahweh] (i.e., His countenance and posturing) **[is] upon** (= set against) **wrongdoers** (those constantly practicing worthless things, repeatedly constructing bad things or habitually doing evil)." [Ps. 34:13-17]

We should consider how Peter is making his point by quoting from the Bible of his day – in this case, the Psalms. We find this done throughout all of the NT.

Vs. 10 emphasized the importance of the tongue – what we speak, and is a follow-up to vs. 9. Vs. 11 speaks to how we live and our actions. Vs. 12 reminds us of the involvement of God in our lives, of His awareness of and attention to our needs and requests, and that He postures Himself in opposition to those who constantly practice worthlessness. This is a picture of a God that is very involved with humanity, for good or ill, according to His plans and purposes. Yet we should keep in mind that even His wrath (inherent fervor; passion; swelling emotions) come from the Ground of Being which is Love. Isaiah tells us that when His judgments are in our land, we learn righteousness – the Way pointed out to us (Isa. 26:9), and His expressed will is that we be saved/delivered/salvaged and reconciled to Him. His intent is that we treat each other with fairness and love, so our actions are important to Him. They are part of the fruit that He desires and purposes to see from us. The Messiah's complaint against the religious leaders of Israel was that He found leaves (production; activity) but no fruit (that which gives folks health, strength and life) – Mk. 11:13.

13. **And who [is] the person who will be treating you badly** (be causing evil to come to you) **if you folks should come to be zealots in regard to the good** (ones boiling hot from the influence of the Good; enthusiasts of virtue and excellence)**?**
Peter puts this forth as a contrast to the political Zealots of his day, that wanted to overthrow Rome with force and violence. The teachings of Christ were the exact opposite: love your enemies; do good to those who mistreat you; give more than required; etc. We should with "boiling hot influence from the Good (God)" be enthusiasts for virtue and excellence.

14. **But even if you folks might continue experiencing suffering [as well as other things] because of fairness and equity** (justice; walking in the Way pointed out; a rightwised covenant positioning), **[you are] happy and blessed ones. "Yet do not fear their fear** (i.e., what they fear; or, as a subjunctive: Now you should not be afraid of the fear that has them as a source), **nor yet should you folks be shaken** (agitated; disturbed; stirred up) **[by them]."** [Isa. 8:12]

His first statement is a reflection of Matt. 5:10, and in line with this these folks (and we) will be happy and blessed – because "**the reign of the heavens and atmospheres belongs to them** [and: us]." Taking a stand for fairness and equity, for a stance in the Way of Christ, for being pointed in the right direction, will often bring opposition – as history has well shown.

But again Peter draws encouragement from the OT, by his quote of Isa. 8:12. We are not to fear their fear, nor fear that comes from them, neither should we be shaken or disturbed, for our lives are hidden with the Messiah, within the midst of God.

15. **Now "you folks set [the] Lord** [= Yahweh] **– the Anointed One – apart** (or: Yet, let the Lord Christ be set-apart)**"** [Isa. 8:13], **within your hearts!** (or: So, treat the Anointed Owner as holy, in the core of your beings), **always ready** (ever prepared) **toward a defense to everyone – for the one repeatedly asking you for a word** (i.e., a rational explanation and a logical response) **about the expectation within you folks – but still with gentleness** (tenderness; meekness; kindness) **and deep respect** (or: serious caution; reverence; [the] fear [of the Lord]),

I have given two ways of expressing the imperative of the verb "to **set apart**," in the first clause. Each way demonstrates a different perspective in our relationship to the Lord, in regard to Peter's imperative to us. The first brings out how we should regard the Lord, in our hearts. The second emphasizes relinquishing our wills to Him and "letting" (in a relative sense) Him be set-apart, with commensurate deference and honor – in regard to our feelings and emotions. Next I parenthetically restate this imperative using alternative semantic expressions. A further consideration is the fact that Peter has here quoted the next verse in Isa. 8 where in the Hebrew text the word "**Lord**" is actually Yahweh (and thus, my bracketed insertion). We need to keep the relationship between Yahweh and Christ (the Messiah) in mind as we read these OT quotes. I will not here delve into what theological implications should be drawn from this.

The following clause gives an attitude that is joined to the thought of His sacredness and state of being "**set apart**." We should always be ready and prepared to give everyone a verbal "**defense**" about our expectation. The Greek word here is *apologia*, and from this comes the theological expression and function "apologetics." Peter is making this an imperative, and so we should not neglect our preparedness, nor an attitude of being "**ready**," to do just this. This presupposes a learned understanding of just what it is that we expect, which in turn presupposes that we

> "**Make haste, with earnest endeavor and diligence, to place yourself alongside as an approved workman in God** (or: to present yourself to God as a tried and approved workman), **one without cause for shame, consistently cutting a straight and direct [path** {*cf* Prov. 3:6 & 11:5, LXX} **in, to, or with] the Word of the Truth**" (2 Tim. 2:15).

But when we make our verbal or written defense, we must be sure to do it "**with gentleness** (tenderness; meekness; kindness) **and deep respect** (or: serious caution; reverence; [the] fear [of the Lord])," not with arrogance or any negative attitude.

16. **habitually holding a good conscience** (or: having a virtuous joint-knowing, from possessing a clear joined-perception), **so that those, having a habit of spitefully abusing and harassing your good behavior** (or: conduct; way of life) **within, and in union with, Christ, may be brought to shame and disgrace relating to that within which you folks are constantly being defamed** (spoken down against).

This verse adds another component to our response and attitude to others, as we make a stand for the message of goodness, ease and well-being. The purpose for their being brought to shame and disgrace is to present to them a clear picture of their attitudes and actions – so that they can change their thinking and their ways – not simply to put them down. God's purposes are always for the good of humanity, not for their harm. This is an example of His judgment bringing to them a lesson in righteousness.

17. **You see, [it is] a stronger [case, position or reputation] to be repeatedly experiencing harassment, abuse or suffering [while, or, because of] habitually doing good** (practicing virtue; creating goodness) – **if God's purpose** (intent; will) **may be repeatedly willing it – than [because of] constantly doing what is wrong, bad or worthless,**

His logic is clear, and his inclusion of such a situation being in line with God's purpose, intent and will should both encourage and comfort us. To experience harassment or abuse because of doing what is worthless would completely undercut our ability to give a defense for our expectation.

18. **because even Christ** (or: considering that Messiah also) **died** [other MSS: suffered], **once for all, concerning and in relation to failures to hit the target** (about errors and mistakes; around and encompassing sins [some MSS: our failures; other MSS: your failures]) – **a Just One** (a rightwised One; One in accord with the Way pointed out; a fair and equitable individual) **over [the situation of]** (or: for the sake of) **unjust ones** (capsized folks; those out of accord with the Way pointed out; unfair and inequitable people) – **to the end that He at once may bring** (or: can lead; would conduct) **you folks** [other MSS: us] **to** (or: toward) **God. [He], on the one hand, being put to death in flesh** (= a physical body), **yet on the other hand, being made alive in spirit** (or: indeed, being put to death by flesh {or: = the estranged human condition}, yet, being engendered a living one by Breath-effect {or: [the] Spirit}),

So he goes on to give the basis and rationale for the first clause in vs. 17: it is "**because even**, or also, the Messiah **died**," having first received great abuse and suffering, and this was the greatest Good that has ever been done. Then we have the pertinent comparison: He was a "Just Person" – just as they are, because of Christ – Who received the ill treatment "over [the situation – humanity's estrangement and dying situation of] unjust folks (people whose lives were capsized, rather than rightwised; folks that were out of accord with the Way of God; people that were unfair and inequitable)."

Christ's purpose was to bring humanity to God, and this should also be our purpose for enduring harassment and suffering. Our lives poured forth for others is the "laying down of our lives for our friends."

Furthermore, just as He was put to death in and by the flesh, yet made alive in spirit, or "engendered a Living One" by the Effect of God's Breath, so it is with us.

But let us note that this last clause, above, is the first part of the next four verses, which present a context that speaks of His death, what He next did, and then on to the situation that followed His being made alive.

19. **at one point journeying** (going from one place to another; passing on) **within which** (or: in union with Which), **He also proclaimed** (published; preached; heralded) **the message to and for** (or: among) **the spirits in prison** (within a guardhouse)**:**

20. **to and for those being at one time unconvinced** (unpersuaded; disobedient; uncompliant) **within [the] days of Noah, when** (or: while) **he was continuing to be receiving forth, and taking away from, out of God's state of emotional quietness** (taking a long time before rushing or being in a heat of passion; long-enduring patience) **while [the] ark was progressively being prepared and equipped** (constructed to readiness) **– into which a few folks, that is, eight souls** (= people), **were brought safely through [the] water** (or: were brought safely through, by means of water),

Picking up "**being made alive in spirit**," or, "**by [the] Breath-effect/Spirit**" – which is the Greek *pneuma* in the dative case without an expressed preposition – of vs. 18, we see that it was in this same spirit/Spirit that He was journeying from place to place, although Peter does not tell us where. But he does tell us what this "**made alive**" Messiah was doing: "**He also proclaimed** (published; preached; heralded) **the message to and for** (or: among) **the spirits in prison**." But what spirits were these? Vs. 20 gives the answer: "**to and for those being at one time unconvinced** (unpersuaded; disobedient; uncompliant) **within [the] days of Noah**." The implication is that these were all the folks that were killed in the flood, as recorded in Gen. 7, although many people object to what this would mean: that Christ can proclaim the message of good news (the gospel) to people who have died. It would be a precedent for a person who was unpersuaded and disobedient in this life, after death being presented with the gospel by the living Christ. It would establish a pattern.

This verse also tells us that Noah "**was continuing to be receiving forth, and taking away from, out of God's state of emotional quietness**." Part of God's character is "taking a long time before rushing or being in a heat of passion," or, as having "long-enduring patience." Noah was continuing in receiving a gift of the Spirit, while he was building the ark.

Peter moves on to make the point that those who were rescued "**were brought safely through [the] water**." A slightly different point is made by the rendering "were brought safely through, by means of water." The Greek preposition *dia* is used redundantly here (as prepositions often are in Koine Greek), both as a prefix to the verb, and then as a preposition standing alone before the word "**water**." When such cases arise, most translators ignore this redundancy – as I did in the first rendering. But the second rendering is also viable, translating the second *dia* with the meaning of "by means of." The first simply says that they were brought through the water safely. The second indicates that it was the water (which destroyed everyone but the eight) which was in fact the means of their being brought safely through – the vehicle of the ark being assumed.

Now the "**which**" of vs. 21 is neuter, and thus refers to the word "**water**" that ends this verse. With this in mind, let us look at vs. 21.

21. **[into] which, also, an echo of correspondent form** (or: a copy; an antitype; an impress which answers back; in place of the type or pattern) **is now progressively delivering** (rescuing) **you folks** (or: repeatedly bringing you to safety)**: immersion** (submersion and envelopment which brings absorption and permeation to the point of saturation) **– not [the] putting off of [the] filth** (removal of dirt) **away from [the] flesh** (= not baptism or bathing of the physical body, or the removal of the alienated false persona), **but rather – the result of a full inquiry into the midst of God** (or: the effect of an added request unto God; or: = a further quest into "the Divine Mystery" – Paul Tillich) **made by a good conscience** (from an excellent joint-knowing; in relation to virtuous co-knowledge). **[It saves you and it is made] through means of [the] resurrection of Jesus Christ,**

The "**echo**," which is a "**corresponded form**," is "**immersion**." There is a progressive passing through the cross (the echo of the water that brought death to the first Adam in the days of Noah) via the ark of the Christ, moving on into His resurrection. Peter's mentioning that 8 souls were safely brought through may be a symbolic number (as are the numbers in the book of Revelation), 8 being the first day after the sabbath, and thus a figure of the new beginning of God's dealing with humanity, after the flood.

I expanded the meaning of immersion, which can here refer to the immersion of a piece of cloth or a garment into a liquid – and not necessarily the religious symbol of baptism. Paul uses the figure for our having been placed into Christ – into His death, and also into His life. Since Christ, in this sense, is spirit (and we also have the figure of immersion into God's Spirit – Matt. 3:11), if we picture ourselves as permeable (like a cloth) then we can absorb that into which we are immersed (Christ) to the point of complete permeation and saturation.

Now consider Peter's further definition of this "immersion": "**the result of a full inquiry into the midst of God** (or: the effect of an added request unto God; or: = a further quest into "the Divine Mystery" – Paul Tillich)." The Greek word for "inquiry" is *eperotema* which is the word that means to inquire or to ask, with the intensifier *ep-* prefixed (which means fully or added), and the *-ma* ending (which means it is the result or effect of the noun). The phrase which follows this word is "**into the midst of God**." Thus, Peter is not speaking about a physical "water baptism" here. It is a full inquiry into, an interrogation of, and a seeking for the acquaintance with God – that is "**made by a good conscience** (from an excellent joint-knowing; in relation to virtuous co-knowledge)." This speaks of a life in Christ, and this life comes "**through means of [the] resurrection of Jesus Christ**." This immersion into Him – symbolized by the ark passing through the midst of the water – is the correspondent form that is now progressively delivering and rescuing us.

22. **Who continuously exists** (or: is; has being) **within [the place of]** (or: = on or at) **God's right [side, or hand** – i.e., the place of authority and ability to exercise power; the place of receiving**], going from place to place, journeying into [the] atmosphere** (or: heaven) **of those being humbly aligned by Him** (or: pertaining to those subjected, placed and arranged under in Him; which are the folks being set in order for support to Him)**: of agents** (or: messengers; folks with the message), **and of authorities** (or: those who have the right and privilege from out of Being), **and of powers** (or: folks with abilities and influence).

The "**Who**" here is Jesus Christ (Jesus, [the] Messiah), He who now exists is the position of authority, and who Himself is the place of God's acceptance (both of these thoughts being in the figure of a king's "**right** hand"). We are accepted in Him, and He exercises God's power as He is "**going from place to place, journeying into [the] atmosphere** (or: heaven) **of those being humbly aligned by Him** (or: pertaining to those subjected, placed and arranged under in Him; which are the folks set in order for support to Him)." The idea of Him being "seated" (e.g., Eph. 1:20-21, 2:6; Rev. 3:21) is a figure for occupying the position of authority and power, not that He is just sitting there. Here we see that He is on the move, and the word used in Rev. I:8 is a present participle of the verb to come, or to go, and thus can be there rendered "**the One continuously, or repeatedly, or habitually coming and going**."

Peter here tells us where He is journeying: into [the] atmosphere (or: heaven). Now in the Greek text, the next word is a genitive plural of the passive participle which tells us which atmosphere or heaven it is into which He is going, from place to place: it is the one of "**those being humbly aligned by Him**... which are the folks being set in order for support to Him." This can also read "pertaining to those subjected, placed and arranged under, IN Him." As He has placed us "in Him," He also journeys into our atmosphere, our heaven, visiting, being a Paraclete, communing... and judging us.

This is not only limited to us, but we are His agents and His messengers; He has given us authority – the right and privilege from out of His Being (Greek: *ex-ousia*, "from out of the midst of being"); we are folks with abilities to whom He has given the power of His Spirit.
Since the participle is passive present, this is an ongoing process and activity and it reaches beyond us as His sovereign influence bears upon all of creation.

Chapter 4

1. **Christ, then, having undergone experiences and suffering in flesh** (or: being physically and emotionally affected to the point of suffering) **over us** (or: over our [situation] and for our sakes), **you folks also arm and equip yourselves with the same mental inclination** (idea; thought; way of thinking; frame of mind; attitude), **because the person [thus] suffering or going through physical or emotional experiences which affect him in [the] flesh** (or: = by [his] estranged humanity or alienated self) **has in and for himself put a stop to failures, errors and mistakes** (or: sins) [or, with other MSS: has been caused to cease from sin],

This is a word for the disciple, the follower of the Messiah. In Matt. 16:24-25 Jesus speaks of denying ourselves, taking up our execution stake and following Him. Peter here points to His suffering and then tells us to expect the same, but then goes on to give a reason for it: to put a stop to failures, errors and mistakes. This may refer to our own times of missing the target (as the other MSS state), or, as in laying down your life for another, we may by such experiences do the works that Christ did, and bring life to others. Paul said in 2 Cor. 4:

> 11. **For we, ourselves – the continuously living ones – are ever being repeatedly handed over into death** (or: = continuously delivered into life-threatening experiences) – **because of Jesus – to the end that the life, also, of Jesus** (or: so that also the life which comes from and is Jesus; or: so that Jesus' life) **can** (may; could; would) **be set in clear light and manifested – within our mortal flesh!**
> 12. **So then** (or: Consequently), **the Death is repeatedly operating and inwardly working within us, yet the Life [is constantly operative] within you folks.**

2. **[and comes] into the [condition or situation] to no longer live out the additional remaining course [of his] time within [the] flesh** (= in the natural realm) **in the midst of** (or: in union with) **[the] full passions** (or: for [the] over-desires; to [the] rushings of emotions upon things) **of humans** (or: pertaining to or originating in mankind), **but to the contrary, in God's will** (or: for God's intent; to God's purpose).

And here is the second reason: in order to live our lives in God's will, for His intent and to His purpose. We have been set-apart to live a different kind of life: the Christ life – which stand in contrast to following the rushing of emotions and passions characterized by the estranged human condition. As with the wives and women of ch. 3:1, our conduct may win folks over, without our saying a word.

This admonition calls to mind the words of Jesus in John 5:30, "**because I am not seeking my own will** (intent; purpose), **but rather the purpose** (intent; will) **of the One sending Me.**" (*cf* John 6:38). Paul spoke likewise in 2 Cor. 5:15, "**that those living may** (or: could; would) **no longer live for themselves** (to themselves; in themselves; by themselves), **but rather for** (or: in; by; to; with) **the One dying and then being awakened and raised up over them** (over their [situation]; for their sakes)." And in Gal. 2:20 he said,

> "**[It is] no longer I, but it is Christ continuously living and alive within me!** (or: No longer an "I" – now Christ constantly lives in the midst of, and in union with, me). **Now that which I, at the present moment, continue living within flesh** (= a physical body), **I am constantly living within faith, trust and confidence – in and by that [faith] which is the Son of God** (or: in union with the trust and confidence that is from God's Son [with other MSS: in the confidence belonging to God and Christ])."

3. **For the time having gone by [is] sufficient** (= you have spent enough time, in the past,) **to have accomplished** (to have worked down and effected) **the thing desired by** (or: the intention of) **the multitudes** (the nations; the swarms of ethnic groups living together; the non-Jews; the Gentiles), **having gone from place to place in indecent and licentious debaucheries** (deeds of loose conduct), **in rushing passions and over-desires, in excesses bubbling over with wine, in carousing and festive processions, in drinking parties, and in forbidden** (i.e., illegal

in respect to the natural laws of reason, conscience and common decency) **idolatries** (or: being a servant to or worshiping external forms or appearances, phantoms of the mind, unsubstantial or reflected images, or conveyed impressions),

Peter is saying that they had spent enough time in the past living like pagans – and today we might say the same. What he describes is a life void of reverence for life and for God, and wasting ourselves in excesses and lack of control. It is the picture of the "prodigal son" in the parable of the extravagantly loving Father (I take this description from Lawrence Garcia) in Lu. 15:11-32.

4. **within which they, repeatedly speaking abusively, slanderously, injuriously and giving a false image [about you, as well as about other folks], are constantly struck with surprise, thinking it strange and foreign that you folks are not always running together with [them], as a mob, into the same flooding** (pouring forth) **of unhealthiness and lack of safety** (or: dissoluteness of a course devoid of salvation).

This is the common attitude of people who want you to join in with their fun, not understanding why it might not be fun for you. It is inevitable when contrasting cultures (e.g., one of honor, another without honor) and contrasting world views (e.g., one seeing through the eyes of God's reign, another seeing with the eyes of alienated humanity) come together.

5. **Such folks will render an account** (or: be giving back a reason) **to the One readily and continually judging** (separating and making a decision about) [p72: prepared to judge; other MSS: constantly holding {Himself} in readiness to judge] **living folks and dead ones,**

Notice that Peter is saying that God is "**readily and continually judging** – making evaluations and decisions about – **living people and dead folks**." He is not waiting to some future event or situation. He is continually doing it with all of humanity – even those who have died. Now if He is constantly separating and making decisions about dead people, then this would suggest that some sort of existence is still going on with them. It was not a one-time judgment, and that's it. He is actively involved in everyone's life and death, all the time. The present tense which is given in the majority of the MSS suggests an ongoing process, or a situation of repeatedly making decisions about people – even "**dead ones**." He is the same, yesterday, today **and on into the ages** (Heb. 13:8).

6. **for into this [purpose], also, the message of goodness and well-being is** (or: the good news was suddenly) **brought and announced to dead folks, to the end that on the one hand they may at some point be judged** (or: can be separated and decided about) **– corresponding to humans – in flesh**
    (or: according to humans in flesh; or: = in the sphere of people with estranged selves; or:
    = on the level of mankind in an alienated condition that was enslaved by the System), **yet on the other hand, that they can continue living** (or: would be habitually living) **corresponding to** (down from; in line and accord with; in the sphere of) **God, in spirit** (or: by Breath-effect).

This verse may be a parallel of ch. 3:18-20, but Peter gives us no specifics. William Barclay was convinced that "**dead folks**" refers to all the dead, and states in his *Daily Bible Study Series* that he considers it one of the most wonderful verses in the Bible. The tense of the verb "**brought and announced**" is aorist: the fact tense, void of reference to time or kind of action. If this is referring to a state of being outside of time, then it is the appropriate tense to use, and this first clause sheds more light on vs. 5 and His judging of the living and the dead. Some scholars translate the aorist as a simple present (as in my first rendering), which would mean that this is simply something that happens for those who die. Others translate the aorist as a simple past (as in my second rendering), which would suggest this clause as an echo of ch. 3:19.

Some suggest that Peter was referring to those who were only spiritually "**dead in trespasses and sins**" (Eph. 2:1), but that statement includes everybody, and in this context we have a differentiation between the living and the dead.

I have given some parenthetical alternative for the two phrases immediately following the word "**judged**/decided about." I owe the idea expressed in the last expansion on the word "**flesh**" to the writings of Walter Wink.

The last clause "**continue living corresponding to God, in spirit**" is put in direct contrast to "**corresponding to humans – in flesh**," so could lend weight to Barclay's view, but this could also be comparing the first Adam to the Last Adam; the old creation to the new.

7. **Now the Goal** (or: the end; the final act; or: the finished Product; or: the completion of the plan) **of all people** (and: pertaining to and affecting all things) **has approached and is now near at hand and [He] is close enough to touch** (= has arrived)! **Therefore, you folks keep a healthy and sound frame of mind** (be sane and sensible) **and be sober** (be unintoxicated; i.e., be functional and with your wits about you) **into [a state, condition or realm] with a view toward having goodness and well-being** (or: into the midst of prayers).

The semantic range of the Greek *telos* (goal; the end; etc.) lets us ponder the possibilities of what Peter meant in this first clause. In the first rendering I capitalized "**Goal**" (a central idea of the word) to suggest a correspondence to Rom. 11:36, where God is the goal of all things. The word "**all**" is both masculine (= people) and neuter (= things), and thus the two renderings.

I expanded the Greek perfect tense of "**near**..." to show its, or His, continued presence. Christ, or the Age of the Messiah, had arrived and was close enough to touch. Therefore he gives the admonition to them to have a sound and healthy frame of mind, and to keep their wits about them – for the Parousia was there, and His judgment was soon to come (it came in AD 70). The final admonition here is to focus their minds into the midst of prayers – which literally means having a view toward goodness and having things go well.

8. **Before all people** (or: = More than anything), **continue being folks constantly holding the outstretching and extending love** (unambiguous, uniting acceptance) **unto yourselves** (i.e., into each other) **– "because love is constantly covering** (habitually throwing a veil over; progressively concealing; [and with other MSS: will be covering]) **a multitude of failures** (mistakes; errors; misses of the target; sins)." [Prov. 10:12]

The preposition is literally "**Before**," but the plural noun "**all**" is both masculine (= people) and neuter (= things), so I gave the two potential meanings of the phrase: either live a life of mutual love in view of all people, or, make this kind of life your priority. The adjective "**outstretching and extending**" tells us that this is not just a kindly inner attitude or personal emotion, but rather a love that reaches out to others in expressed and practical ways that have an effect upon them. And note the effect of this kind of love: it will be constantly covering, habitually throwing a veil over and progressively concealing a multitude of mistakes, sins, failures, errors, etc. What a witness before the world of mankind. And so we can see that the opposite of love would be to uncover, reveal and expose sin. This quality of God's kingdom is startling to our culture, and even to Christianity. What a message to our media, and to our political campaigns.

9. **[Continue being] those [who are] stranger-loving unto one another** (= friendly, kind and hospitable to strangers, foreigners and aliens [inviting them] into the midst of each other's [homes and/or societies]), **without expressing dissatisfaction** (complaining; grumbling; murmuring),

The plural adjective (used here as a noun) rendered "**those [who are] stranger-loving**," is the Greek *philos* (love, affection, friendliness, and by extension, hospitableness) joined to *xenos* (a stranger, a foreigner, an alien – the opposite of a citizen). Peter does not say that they must have a legal right to be in one's community for his admonition to apply. And if they are with us, we are not to grumble or complain about it – or even express dissatisfaction with the situation.

In fact, it was part of their culture to be hospitable to foreigners and to invite them into their home and see to their needs. Because of fear, this seldom happens in America, unless we already know them or they come with references. But even here, there are some followers of Jesus who practice this.

10. **each one, according as he receives an effect of grace** (or: received a result of favor), **continuously giving supporting service and dispensing it unto yourselves** (i.e., into each other), **as beautiful** (fine; ideal) **house managers** (stewards; administrators) **of God's varied grace** (or: of [the] diverse favor which is God; [as] of a many-colored [tapestry] of grace whose source and character are from God).

This verse is a continuation of the idea in vs. 9, showing how the "alien-loving" is to be dispensed to these folks – as beautiful supporting service that comes from an ideal house manager. And what is being given are various forms and manifestations of God's grace. The Greek *charisma* is normally rendered "gift, or gracious gift," But the *ma* ending signifies that it is the "effect of *charis* (grace)." We each receive the effects of God's grace, and are to pass this on to others in the everyday living of this life. We extend our love, and this creates a loving community that has been called out of the dominant culture (the world, the "dominating system" – Walter Wink) to be set apart as the "Light of the world."

11. **If anyone is normally speaking, [let it be] as God's little words** (= inspired sayings, messages, thoughts and ideas); **if anyone is habitually providing attending service and dispensing, [let it be] as out of [the] strength which God is continually supplying** (furnishing; providing), **to the end that, in union with all people** (and: within all things), **God may be constantly glorified** (may habitually receive a good reputation) **through Jesus Christ, in Whom** (by Whom; for Whom; to Whom; with Whom) **is** (or: exists) **the glory** (the manifestation of that which calls forth praise; the good reputation) **and the strength** (the might), **on into the ages of the ages** (or: into the indefinite time periods of the ages; into the superlative times of the eons).

The first two clauses are cases of "ellipsis" where the predicate is left out, and so I have supplied "**[let it be]**." "**Little words**" is the diminutive form of "logos," God's "little words, thoughts, ideas, messages." I have given a paraphrase which suggests that this phrase may mean "inspired sayings, messages, etc." William Barclay suggest that this is referring to "preaching." However, I suggest that since we house God (He lives in us, who are His temple), and are one spirit with Him (1 Cor. 6:17), that this admonition speaks to all of us: speak the thoughts that come from Him; let our words and thoughts be acceptable to Him (Ps. 19:14); or as Paul says in Eph. 5:

> 19. **continuously speaking** (making vocal utterances) **to** (or: among) **yourselves in psalms and hymns** (or: songs of praise; festive songs) **and spiritual odes** (songs; chants), **continually singing and playing stringed instruments** (making music; psalming; sharply touching or plucking [the strings or chords]) **in** (or: by; with; or: for) **your hearts to** (or: for; by; with: in) **the Lord** [= Christ, or, Yahweh],
> 20. **constantly giving thanks** (expressing gratitude; or: speaking of the well-being that is in grace and favor) **to God, even [the] Father** [*p*46 & others: to the Father, even God] **at all times** (or: always; = on all occasions) **concerning all things** (or: for everything; or: over all mankind), **within the midst of and in union with the Name of our Lord, Jesus Christ.**

Our service, our actions, our works and what we dispense to others should all come from His strength – not our own. This calls to mind the words of Jesus, "... that folks may see your good works and glorify your Father, Who is in heaven."

Note the dative form of "**Whom**" which has the function of location (in Whom), of instrument (by Whom), of the indirect object (for and to Whom), of association (with Whom) – all of which make sense in this phrase which has no expressed preposition.

Both Paul and Peter keep the name Jesus associated with the title/position Christ (or: = Messiah; the Anointed One). We should keep the Person of Jesus connected to our theology of Christ, lest we miss what the Scriptures are presenting to us. Both God's glory and His strength come through Him, and we receive these by being within Him and joined to Him. We do not "evolve beyond Him," since what Peter says here is true, and is the new reality "**on into the ages of the ages**." In the parenthetical expansion of this phrase, the last one gives the force of the Hebrew idiom as we see in "the holy of holies," which equals "the holiest place of all." Paul speaks of "the **ages** to come" in Eph. 2:7. Peter is not specific about what he means by this phrase, but it definitely shows that there is more to come in God's plan and purpose of the ages (Eph. 3:11).

Consider the phrase that translates "**all**" in a form that is both masculine and neuter: "**in union with all people** (and: within all things)." This is part of the purpose clause that begins with "**to the end that**..." and ends with, "**God may be constantly glorified**..." It is saying that God would be glorified IN UNION with ALL people (as well as within all things). Quite an inclusive statement. This is a statement of God's full solidarity with all humanity. His glory is seen in His union with all people. The neuter rendering of all show that He can be glorified in all situations and circumstances – but it takes the eyes and heart of faith and trust to see and accept this word by Peter.

12. **Beloved ones, do not repeatedly feel like strangers to the burning** (= the action of the Fire) **within and among you folks, which is habitually happening to you with a view toward your being put to the test** (or: which is repeatedly coming into being in the face of a proving trial for you; which is progressively birthing itself to an examination in you), **as though a strange or foreign thing [or: occurrence] is repeatedly walking with you folks.**

"**The burning**; the action of the Fire." We are fact-to-face with this within the tests and trials that are birthed in us by God, both to purify us (Mal. 3:2-3) and to temper us as a blacksmith tempers a tool – as well as being faced with ordeals from without. This is a frequent theme in the NT writings, and from the books of Acts and Revelation we see that the followers of Jesus constantly faced these. John the Baptizer spoke of Jesus immersing us in the Holy Spirit, and in Fire. Here Peter tells us that this is normal and that we should expect it, and that it is something that "**is repeatedly walking with**" us. And what is clear is that it is for our benefit. The next verse explains this as "**a common share in the experiences** and **sufferings** of the Messiah." He does not speak to the form that these tests take, but elsewhere we see that they are things that come in opposition to us in our daily lives. Historically, it was probably a different situation within each community to which he was writing.

Paul described these things as persecutions (or: pursuits) and pressures (ordeals; tribulations), but noted that these were,

> "**a display-effect** (result of pointing-out; demonstration) **of God's fair and equitable** (just; in accord with the Way pointed out) **deciding** (separating for an evaluation or a judging), **[leading] unto your being accounted worthy** (deemed of equal value) **of God's kingdom** (or: the sovereign reign which is God), **over** (or: on behalf of) **which you are also constantly having sensible experiences** (or: normally feeling emotions; or: repeatedly suffering)" – 2 Thes. 1:4-5.

13. **But on the contrary, keep on rejoicing and being glad to the extent or degree that you folks are continually participating with a common share in the effects of the experiences and the results of the sufferings of the Christ, to the end that, while continuously exulting and celebrating exceedingly, you folks can** (or: should; would) **also rejoice within the unveiling of His glory** (or: in union with the disclosure of His reputation; or: in the midst of the praise-inducing manifestation which is Him)!

Rejoicing and being glad within this burning seems to be a key element. First of all, we are told here that this means that we are having a common share in Christ's sufferings and are participating in His experiences. But also, while celebrating exceedingly, we can and should also – at the same time – rejoice within the unveiling of His glory. The Fire of God unveils His glory – both in us, and in others, for when other folks observe our remaining under the trials, and giving support to our fellows at the same time, this has an effect in them – to where Christ comes out from behind the veil within them (to use the expression by Stacy Wood). When the Seed of God fell into the ground and died, it was being planted in all of the Second Humanity, the Last Adam. Each one then germinates in his own season and fertile moment, when the Sun warms the soil, and someone – or His rain – waters it.

The uncovering of His glory is the unveiling of His sons (Rom. 8:19). It is God "**revealing His son** (or: Son) **in [us]**" (Gal. 1:16). This is a "now" thing, not just a future event. It also happens when God's true reputation (another meaning of "glory") is disclosed – and all creation rejoices. This happened in Jesus, and then within His body, and continues on day by day.

14. **Since** (or: If) **you folks are constantly being insulted and censured in** (or: [because of] union with) **the Name of Christ, [you are] happy ones** (blessed folks), **because God's spirit of glory and power** (or: the Breath-effect of the reputation and of the ability of God) **is continuously "resting back upon" you folks** [*cf.* Isa. 11:2].

So here we see Peter giving us an example of a trial, and then he proclaims a "beatitude" (*cf* Matt. 5:11) along with an explanation of "**the unveiling of His glory**" of vs. 13, showing that this is in fact "**God's spirit of glory and power**" continuously "**resting back upon**" them. And so it is with us. This is not the usual expectation, in today's Christianity, of the situation of God's glory and power being upon His people, but just as the cross was a demonstration of God's glory, so is our participation in the effects of His experiences, and the results of His sufferings, a demonstration of His glory upon us – they birth resurrection life from Christ within us, and bear the fruit of His Spirit from which others can partake.

15. **Of course let not any one of you folks be experiencing suffering as a murderer, or a thief, or a doer of worthless or evil things, or, as a meddler** (an interferer) **in other people's affairs** (or: one who focuses on things strange, foreign or "other," or involving a place-change). 16. **Yet if as a Christian [s/he is suffering], let him or her not continue feeling shame or embarrassment, but let him or her constantly glorify** (give credit to; enhance the reputation of; bring an opinion of high status for) **God within this Name** (or: in union with this name [i.e., "Christian;" or, referring to "the Name of Christ" in vs. 14, above]),

The reason for suffering as described in vs. 15 is in accord with the natural law of sowing and reaping, because of something wrong that a person has done. But in contrast, vs. 16 shows how suffering can bring glory, credit, an enhanced reputation and an opinion of high status to and for God. How we live our life matters.

The phrase "**within this Name**/name" could have the two references given in the parenthetical expansion. Either way, glory for God should be the focus of our life.

17. **because [it is; this is; now is] the** [other MSS: a] **fitting situation and fertile moment of the appointed season for the result of the judgment** (the effect of the separating for evaluation and decision) **to begin** (to start) **from God's house. Now if first from us, what [will be] the closing act** (the final stage; the end; the consummation; the outcome; the finished product) **pertaining to those continuing unpersuaded and unconvinced by** (or: uncompliant to; disobedient to; stubborn in) **God's message of goodness and well-being** (or: good news)?

The preceding verses have led to this conclusion by Peter. They all had come to "**the fitting situation and fertile moment of the appointed season**" (an expansion of the Greek *kairos*), and this season was one of judgment – the result of God's evaluation and His decision for their world of culture, religion, economy and government. The fall of Jerusalem in AD 70 brought an end to their "world" and the conclusion of that age. Peter says that it was to begin from God's house. This would, in this transition period, have referred to the Jews, the Israel of the old covenant, but note that he includes himself and the called-out communities in the phrase "**from God's house**" by the following phrase "**from us**." There was a change of ages, into a new creation/covenant, but there was also a continuity, a birthing of the new from out of the old. "**God's house**" is a code word for Israel, whose capital was Jerusalem, and it thus begins with Jerusalem and the Temple (His house) and the ramifications continue into the rest of the Empire. The "**from us**" refers both to Israel, and to the people in Jerusalem (where Peter was then living).

At that point in time, Peter did not know what the result would be and how it would affect the Jews or the Romans and the rest of the world of those not yet persuaded or convinced by the message concerning the coming and presence of the Messiah. But he sensed that it would be cataclysmic, and it was.

18.   **"And if the rightwised one** (the fair and just person in right relationships in accord to the Way pointed out) **is repeatedly delivered** (rescued; brought to safety; made healthy and whole) **with difficult labor, then where will the irreverent** (the person without pious awe) **and the failure** (the one who makes mistakes and cannot hit the target; the sinner; the outcast) **make an appearance?"** [Prov. 11:31]

He cites this verse from Proverbs – which describes how it is in the human situation, and from which they could learn, from history – to make his point. Their present situation was serious.

19. **So then, also, let those repeatedly feeling the effects of experiences and of suffering which correspond to, and [are] in the sphere of, God's will** (intent; purpose) **continuously commit their souls to a Faithful Former** (or: Loyal Founder; Trustworthy Creator), **within [the] producing of good** (in union with making of virtue; in construction of excellence; within the midst of performing goodness).

Let us note that our experience and sufferings (presuming that they accord with vs. 16, not vs. 15) correspond to and are in the sphere of God's will, His intent and His purpose. Herein lies peace. In the knowledge of this fact, we can rest in Him. Since it is His will and purpose, we can rejoice and say, "Amen!"

At the same time, we should continuously (the Greek present tense here indicates that this may be for some time, or that there is a process involved) commit our souls (our selves, which include our emotions, feelings, mental processes, wills, being, etc.) to Him that formed and created us and all that is – because He is faithful to, loyal to and trustworthy of His creation.

Furthermore, we are to do this "**within [the] producing of good** (in union with making of virtue; in construction of excellence; within the midst of performing goodness)." So our focus is to be on living our lives with excellence, constantly producing good actions and virtuous works, as we remain with ourselves committed to our Father, knowing that He is loyal to us.

Chapter 5

1. **Therefore, I – the one [being] an older man together with [you]** (or: a fellow elder person) **and a witness of the results of the experiences and of the effects of the sufferings of the Christ, as well as the one [being] a fellow participant** (partner; one who shares in common) **of the glory** (or: manifestation which will call forth praise) **being presently about to be progressively unveiled** (revealed; or: disclosed) **– am repeatedly calling older folks among you to my side, urging, encouraging and being a paraclete:**

Comments on 1 Peter

Peter was performing as a paraclete to the older folks among the communities who would receive this letter. In both Jewish and Greek cultures, the older folks were the natural leaders of the community. For one thing, they normally had the economic power and thus effected the local politics, and for another, with age comes the wisdom of experience. So it is only natural that Peter should make his final appeal to them. He is also reminding them that he, himself, was a witness both to the results of the experiences and to the effects of the sufferings of the Messiah. The Greek *path_ema* means the results or effects of someone being affected by something – whether good or bad. So it can refer both to the results of Christ's experiences, as well as to the effects and results of the things which He suffered. This takes us from His birth all the way to past the cross and on to the resurrection and to the sending of the Holy Spirit, and the creation of the new age of Messiah. Peter witnessed all of this.

Note that the unveiling of "**the glory**," which we discussed in ch. 4:13, was in Peter's day "**being presently about to be progressively unveiled** and disclosed." It was starting to be revealed in the 1st century. That unveiling has progressed through the centuries which followed as His kingdom, which began as a Stone cut out of the mountain of Israel, has grown to itself be a mountain (a figure of a kingdom) which is filling the entire earth (Dan. 2:35).

2. **you folks shepherd** (i.e., lead to pasture, feed, tend, protect, care for) **God's little flock [that is] among you folks, constantly watching over [them], not in a forced manner** (not by exercising compulsion or constraint; or: not unwillingly), **but to the contrary, without compulsion** (engendering volunteering; yieldingly; or: voluntarily; willingly), **in accord with** (or: in line with and corresponding to; in the sphere of) **God; neither with eagerness for dishonest gain** (greedily; for the low reason of what you can get out of it), **but rather, readily rushing toward it with passion.**

So the older folks are to be the shepherds – which means that they were to lead the younger folks to places where they could be fed; to tend, protect and care for these people in their community. Peter here uses the same metaphor that Jesus did with Peter himself, in John 21:15-17, and which Jesus applied to Himself in John ch. 10. They were to constantly watch over the younger ones.

There was to be no force, compulsion or constraint. This care was to be in accord to the character of Yahweh (our Shepherd – Ps. 23), and in line with God. They were not to have any agenda of personal gain, but to eagerly and readily rush toward this community service fore-spiritedly, with passion.

3. **Nor yet as ones constantly exercising down-oriented lordship** (acting as owners or masters, bearing down with demands) **of the members of the inheritance** (of those who are the allotments of the heritage; or: of those considered to be small objects to be used in assigning positions or portions), **but to the contrary, progressively becoming beaten models** (types made by the strike of a hammer; examples) **for the little flock,**

Peter did not want the leaders, the older folks, to be controlling. They were not to act like owners who bore down with demands upon others. There was to be no "**down-oriented lordship**" over the members of God's inheritance.

The contrast for these "leaders" of the community was to become "**beaten models**" for the little flock. This literal rendering gives a much richer picture than the more common translation "examples." As you see in the expansion, it means a model that has been formed by the strike of a hammer. This hammer is God shaping us into His image. It is the clay being put through all the processes required to make it to be suitable for the wheel in the hands of the potter – and then the fires of the kiln. Even in this we see that it is all God, and nothing of us. Furthermore, with the "**little flock**" seeing the work of the Spirit upon the "elder folks," this very necessary process becomes an appropriate "example" for them.

4. and so, with the Chief Shepherd (or: the Original and Ruling Shepherd) **[thus] being made visible** (being shown in clear light), **you folks will be bringing to yourselves – with care and kindly keeping – the unwithering and unfading wreath of the glory** (or: the enduring recognition of achievement which comes from this good reputation).

It is the process implied in vs. 3 that makes the Chief Shepherd visible – in them, and now in us. The good reputation is that Christ is being observed in the lives of these folks. As they "shepherd" their little flock, the Life which is Christ is being shown in clear light. And as Paul said in Phil. 4:1, the wreath, which signifies success in the metaphor of the stadium games, is actually the little flock that they are tending. It is "the enduring recognition of achievement" in the lives now being lived in those whom they have been serving. It is Christ in them, the expectation which is the glory (Col. 1:27).

5. Likewise (or: In like manner), **you younger people be humbly placed, arranged and aligned by** (or: subjected for support to) **older folks. Yet all of you folks** (or: everyone) **tie on yourselves, as an outer garment** (like a slave's apron), **the humble attitude** (the lowliness of thinking) **to one another** [other MSS add: continuously being ones that are humbly aligned], **because**
> **"God habitually sets Himself in opposition, being resistant to those who try to appear conspicuously above others** (to haughty and proud ones), **yet He constantly gives grace and favor to humble** (or: lowly) **folks."** [Prov. 3:34]

Here he turns his admonitions to the rest of the community, the younger people. They are to be supportively aligned by the wisdom and experience of the older folks, yet this wisdom was for each person to "**tie on**" themselves, as with a slave's apron, a humble attitude toward each other (including the older folks).

Then, again, Peter cites an OT aphorism as the basis for what he is saying. This is what God is like and how He responds to people. We see this demonstrated in the ministry of Jesus. He set Himself in opposition to the scribes and Pharisees, and gave grace and favor to the outcasts – the lowly ones and the people of low social standing.

6. Let yourselves be made humble (or: lowly), **then, under God's strong hand – so that He can** (or: would) **at some point lift you up** (or: may elevate or exalt you folks) **within a fitting situation** (or: in [the] proper appointed-season; in the center of a fertile moment) –
7. while throwing (or: tossing) **your entire concern** (whole worry; every anxiety) **upon Him, because He constantly cares about and takes an interest around you folks!**

The verb of the first clause is imperative, passive. He is telling us not to resist what God is doing in His bringing us low. We are to toss our entire concern for ourselves and our lives upon Him, the Loyal Father, because He constantly cares about us and takes an interest around our situations. We, His loyal children, are to be without anxiety as we await the fitting situation and proper season for Him to at some point lift us up and elevate our position. We see an example of this whole process in the humbling and later exalting of Nebuchadnezzar in Dan. 4.

I also give Paul Tillich's definition for the Greek *kairos* in the phrase, "in the center of a fertile moment." God waits until the time is right for us.

This is also a picture of God's plan of the ages, in the humbling of humanity – through Adam's disobedience – and then our exaltation through the obedience of Jesus (Rom. 5). And through it all, He cares about our concerns.

8. Be sober (or: clear headed)! **Be awake, alert and watch! Your barrier in the Way pointed out** (your road hazard; your opponent at court; the one "in your face" opposing your fairness and equity), **one who casts or thrusts something through the midst of folks**

(e.g., like a soldier casting a javelin or thrusting a sword through someone, or a person throwing an issue through the midst of a group, causing division; or: a slanderer), **as a constantly roaring lion, is continuously walking about, incessantly seeking to drink something or someone down** (or: searching to gulp and swallow [someone] down),

[comment: this path-hazard and road barrier may have been local religions, cultural or political opposition, or a spirit of contrariness]

This verse should not be taken out of context and made to be a description of the works of "the devil," as has been the tradition. It flows out of vs. 6-7, describing the situation in which "**God's strong hand**" will humble us. Jacob/James 4:10 tell us, "**You must be made low** (humbled; demoted) **in the Lord's sight** (= in [Yahweh's, or Christ's] presence), **and then He will lift you up** (elevate you)." We see God's strong hand in Ex. 3:20 where Yahweh "put forth [His] hand" to smite Egypt. The "rod of God" (Moses' staff) brought victory to Israel in Ex. 17:9-12, but it had become a snake in Ex. 7:10-12, and brought plagues on Egypt in vs. 19-20. In ch. 10:3, Yahweh says to Pharaoh through Moses, "How long will you refuse to humble yourself before Me?"

Recall the story of Job, and how in ch. 40 and 42 he responded humbly to Yahweh. In ch. 2:10 he said, "Indeed, should we receive good from the One, Elohim, and should we not receive evil? In all this Job did not sin (err, miss the target) with his lips" (Concordant Version; my expansion). This last statement says that Job was right, that we should receive evil from God. But we see in the first two chapters that God used an adversary (the Sabeans; the Chaldeans), or adversarial situations (lightning; a great wind) and personal affliction (boils) – and Job was humbled. But later, Yahweh raised him up, as we see in ch. 42.

In Hos. 5:14-15 (LXX) we see Yahweh describing Himself:

"**Because of this, I Myself am like** (or: exist being as) **a panther to** (or: for; in) **Ephraim, and like a lion to** (or: for; in) **the house of Judah: thus I Myself will tear, and then journey on; I will take** (grasp in [My] hand; seize), **and there will be no one to be rescuing and dragging [folks] out of [My grasp].**
I will journey on and return into My place until they will be caused to disappear, and then they will search for My face, and seek My presence."

Now in vs. 9, below, he tells us that "**these same experiences and suffering**," which they had observed as having come upon others in the brotherhood, were "**to repeatedly and progressively bring the goal**" that God had in mind, and in vs. 10-11 he says that it is God and His strength that will do this. These experiences are the same things that he spoke of in ch's. 1:6 and 4:12-14. Paul, in 2 Thes. 1:4-5 says,

"... **all your pursuits** (or: chasings; or: persecutions; harassments) **and the pressures** (squeezings; constrictions; contractions; tribulations; oppressions; ordeals) **which you habitually have again** (or: sustain hold up). **[This is] a display-effect** (result of pointing-out; demonstration) **of God's fair and equitable** (just; righteous; in accord with the Way pointed out) **decision** (separation for making a distinction and an evaluation or a judging), **unto your being accounted worthy** (of equal value) **of God's kingdom** (or: the sovereign reign which is God), **over** (or: on behalf of) **which you are also constantly having sensible experiences** (or: normally feeling emotions; or: repeatedly suffering)."

This being the case, they were nonetheless admonished to "**Be sober** (or: clear headed)! **Be awake, alert and watch!**" As the Messiah was delivered to the Romans "**by the specific, determined, bounded** (limited) **plan** (intended purpose, design and counsel) **and foreknowledge** (intimate knowledge which was experienced beforehand) **of God**" (Acts 2:23), so were they delivered into these tests and trials. As Jesus told His disciples to "watch" and "pray" in Gethsemane, so Peter advises these folks, and us. Paul in Eph. 6:10-18 told them to put on God's armor and to take a stand (as in vs. 9, below).

Dr. Ann Nyland (*The Source NT*, Smith and Stirling Publishing, 2004) points out that the Greek *diabolos* means "slanderer," and thus translates in a similar way the idea expressed by my expansion "opponent at court," seeing this as a legal metaphor. What I rendered "**Your barrier in the Way pointed out** (your road hazard; your opponent at court; the one 'in your face' opposing your fairness and equity)" she sees as a figure of a lawyer in a court of law, and a legal suit. The entire clause refers to opposition against the called-out community. There are folks or forces that are trying to thrust slander, legal suits, or whatever, to defame and discredit the community of faith, and as Saul did against the early church, these folks are operating as a roaring lion, wanting to devour this move of God. We face similar oppositions in our day, and history is replete with examples. Also see 2 Tim. 4:17c.

9. **to whom take a stand against** (withstand; set yourself in opposition), **[being] strong** (firm; compact) **ones in** (or: by) **the faith, trust and loyalty – [being] folks having seen and thus knowing about these same experiences and sufferings [that] are to repeatedly and progressively bring the goal upon** (bring perfection upon; accomplish maturity upon) **your brotherhood within the dominating arrangement of the System** (or: in the midst of the secular realm; or: in the ordered world of religion, economy, culture and government).

Jesus said in John 16:33 that we would have tribulation and pressures within the systems of our cultures – those systems that endeavor to dominate and control folks. But again, this is part of His plan: to use these religious, social, economic and political forces to refine and purify us. His plan is always: death, and then resurrection to a higher realm and state of being. Although His work of the cross brought the new creation, we, in following Him, must existentially take up our own crosses (Matt. 16:24) – and do the works that He did (John 14:12). These experiences and sufferings bring this goal upon us.

10. **Now the God of all grace and favor** (or: the God whose character and quality is all grace and favor; the God Who is every grace and joyous favor), **the One calling** (or: inviting) **you folks – ones experiencing a little and briefly suffering – into His eonian glory** (His glory and reputation which has the quality and characteristics pertaining to the realm of the Age and which continues on into an unseen and indefinite time) **within Christ Jesus** [with other MSS: in union with the Anointed One (= the Messiah)], **the Same One** (or: He) **will get [things, or, you] down and prepare [them, or, you]** (or: repair [them; you]; fit, knit or adjust [them; you] thoroughly), **will set [things; you] fast and establish [them; you], will impart strength** (will make [things; you] strong), **will set a base upon which to ground and found [things and you]:**
11. **the strength** (or: might) **[to do these things is] in Him** (and: by Him) **on into the ages. It is so** (Count on it)! [other MSS: the glory and the strength {is} in Him, on into the superlative times of the ages (or: the ages of the ages)]

The God Who humbles us is a God of all grace and favor. He brings us low in order to raise us up to a higher place. He is calling us into the glory – the manifestations which call forth praise – of the Age of the Messiah. This glory is within Christ Jesus, Who will get us and things down in order to prepare us and them. Then He will set us and them fast and establish us and them. He will impart strength and set a base upon which to ground and found us and situations.

The strength and might to do all this is in Him, and by Him, and this carries on into the ages. We can count on it. As there were ages in the past (Col. 1:26; Eph. 3:5), so Paul also tells us that there are ages to come – Eph. 2:7.

12. **Through Silvanus** (or: Silas), **the faithful and loyal brother who is full of trust, as I continue logically thinking and considering, I write through means of a few** [thoughts, lines, or, words; *p72* reads: through a short {letter}], **persistently calling [you] alongside to encourage, comfort and aid [you], as well as constantly bearing a full witness and adding evidence of this continuing to be God's true** (and: real) **grace and favor, into which you folks should set yourselves to take a stand** (or, as an imperative: into which, [enter] and stand firm!).

Peter is sending this letter through Silvanus (thought to be the same person, Silas). I have expanded the adjective *pistos*, that describes this brother, to give its semantic range. Peter is using this short letter of a few thoughts to be a paraclete for them – to call them to his side, to encourage, comfort and aid them – as well as to bear full witness and give added evidence of this message continuing to be God's true grace and real favor. They are to set themselves, and we are to set ourselves, into this message and favor, and take a firm stand therein.

13. **The jointly-chosen** (selected-together) **called-out community** (assembly; congregation; ecclesia) **within Babylon constantly embraces and greets you folks; also Mark, my son.**

Scholars differ in their opinions as to what the name "**Babylon**" refers. Some suggest Rome, others the city in the east to where the Jews had been taken in captivity (some remained there, and it became a center of Jewish scholarship which resulted in the "Babylonian Talmud"). Still others suggest that this was an enigmatic reference to Jerusalem, where both Peter and Mark had taken up residence. The name became a metaphor for corruption and idolatry and it was given to John as a symbol in Rev. 17 and 18. The figure there is of a prostitute, and calls to mind Isa. 1:21 where Jerusalem is thus described. Prostitution was a metaphor that the prophets of the OT used to describe Israel's unfaithfulness to Yahweh. Jerusalem has been shown by numerous scholars to fit the descriptions of Babylon in Rev. 17-18, and the beast upon which she rides speaks to her association with Rome (beasts in the book of Daniel represented empires).

14. **Embrace as you greet one another within love's expression of affection** (a kiss from participation in the transcendent unity of the unambiguous life, and affection which is the urge toward accepting reunion that overcomes existential separation – a synthesis from Tillich's definitions of *agape*). **Peace** (and: harmony; = shalom) **[is] in** (or: [is] by; with) **you folks – all those within, in union with, and centered on, Christ** [other MSS add: Jesus]! **It is so** (Amen: Count on it)!

The phrase "**within love's expression of affection**" can refer to the middle-eastern form of greeting, which was a hug and a kiss on the cheek, or, it could speak to the kiss of the love of God, within which we exist. As elsewhere, I have added the verb "**[is]**" to the last clause, making it a statement, rather than adding the verb "[be]," which would make it a wish. Note that the phrase "**you folks**" is in the dative, so it can be "**in you folks**," or "by you folks," or "with you folks." His peace is within us, but now it also comes through us who are within, in union with, and centered on, Jesus, the Anointed One (= the Messiah). As with Jesus, Paul, Jacob (or: James) and John, Peter makes it clear that those who have been called out to be a community of Christ are also called to be a community of covenant love. Their messages are the same.

John A T Robinson (*Redating the NT*) gives the date of this letter as AD 58. Philippi was a Roman colony, and as such its citizens were also citizens of the city of Rome itself. It was located in Macedonia on a main road that led from the East to the West at a pass through a mountain range that divides Asia from Europe. There were apparently not enough Jews there to establish a synagogue, and we see no quotes of the OT in this letter. *Acts* 16 tells of Paul's visit to this city and of his persecution there.

Philippians is a personal letter in which he thanks them for their material support and gives admonitions and encouragement for Christian living and for unity. Scholars have termed this a letter of joy and of excellent things. The passage of ch. 2:5-11 contains a profound Christology.

Chapter 1

1. **Paul and Timothy, slaves of Christ Jesus for** (or: to) **all the set-apart folks** (the holy ones; the saints) **within and in union with Christ Jesus, to those being in Philippi, together with care-givers** (folks keeping a watchful eye upon [people and situations]; those noting and being concerned for others; overseers) **and attending servants:**

Note that, using Paul's and Timothy's examples, we are not primarily slaving for God, but for people. We belong to God and represent Him, but our work for Him is as He is within human beings. Recall the parable by Jesus about the sheep who ministered to Him by ministering to those in need (Matt. 25:35-40). The kids (immature goats) missed where He was living, so did not do anything for Him – even though they probably had lots of ritual "praise and worship."

Keep in mind that our sphere of existence is "**within Christ Jesus**," and that our relationship with Him is "**in union with**" Him. This is what makes us "**set apart**," and holy (no longer profane). Our relationship is not one of a vassal on his knees before a feudal king, but seated together with Him in His throne (Eph. 2:6), or joined in intimate union with His as His bride/wife (Rev. 19:7), to then produce the fruit of His Spirit. Yet we regard Him as Lord, which also means Owner, Master. And recall that He calls us "friends" (John 15:14, 15).

Paul addresses this letter to those whom I have rendered as "**care-givers**" and "**attending servants**." Others, coming from an institutional and hierarchal mindset render these words "overseers and deacons" (NIV, NASB), "bishops and deacons" (NRSV, Berkeley Version, KJV), "those who are in charge of the congregation and those who are engaged in its service" (Barclay), "overseers and ministers" (The New American Bible), "pastors and helpers" (Beck: An American Translation), "presiding elders and deacons" (The Jerusalem Bible), "superintendants and assistants" (Goodspeed) – to cite a few. Now the folks serving in these functions may have been "congregation leaders, and those serving the congregation" as David Stern terms them in his Jewish NT, but I wanted to emphasize the "ground level" functions of these terms as Jesus described the work done in Matt. 25:35-36.

Recall that Jesus told his students to not be called Rabbi (= teacher) or father (Matt. 23:7, 8), and He chided the Pharisees for loving "the uppermost seats in the synagogues" and distinctive greetings (which indicate their position in society) in the market places (Lu. 11:43; 20:46). Here Paul refers to himself and to Timothy as slaves: the lowest position in their society. So I doubt that he was addressing this letter to people of high status in the called-out community or to people of an "office" or "position of authority," but rather to the "care-givers" who oversaw to the needs of the needy, and gave attending service to others (Acts 6:1-2 uses both the noun and the verb of this last word in reference to serving food to folks).

The phrase "within and in union with Christ" is central to the good new which Paul brought. William Barclay (*The Daily Bible Study Series, the Letter to the Philippians*, p. 11) says, "*In Christ Jesus* occurs 48 times, *in Christ* 34 times, and *in the Lord* 50 times.*" He further mentions that Marvin Vincent states that "when Paul spoke of the Christian being in Christ, he meant that the Christian lives in Christ as a bird in the air, a fish in the water, the roots of a tree in the soil" (ibid, p. 11).

2. **Grace and peace** (or: Favor and harmony [= shalom]) **to you folks from God, our Father and Lord, Jesus Christ** (or: from God, our Father, and [the] Lord, Jesus [the] Anointed One).

Paul's greetings to these folks is also his central message, the over-arching subject of this letter: grace and peace. He often ends his letters with a similar statement. Barclay says that "peace" means "total well-being, everything that makes for a man's highest good" (ibid, p.12). Strong sates that it probably came from the verb *eiro*, which means "to fasten together in rows; to insert and string together." Barclay suggests that it is "connected with the Greek word *eirein*, which means *to join, to weave together*" (ibid, p. 12). Thus do we get the sense of "harmony."

In the Greek text there is no definite article before the word "**Lord**," so I have given two possible renderings of the phrase which follows the word "**God**" – you may choose according to your theology.

3. **I constantly give thanks** (or: habitually speak of the goodness of grace) **to my God upon every memory** (or: recollection; or: mention) **of you folks,**
4. **at all times** (or: always) **in my every request** (or: petition) **over [the situation of] you all** (or: on behalf of all of you folks), **habitually making the request** (or: petition) **with joy**
5. **upon [the awareness of] your participation** (partnership; communion; common share; fellowship; contribution) **into the message of goodness and well-being** (or: good news), **from the first day until the present moment** (now),
6. **being persuaded and convinced of this very thing: that the One inwardly beginning** (making an inward start; inciting; inwardly originating [note: in the context of sacrifices, this word meant "to begin the offering"]) **a good work, a virtuous action or an excellent deed within you people** (or: among you folks; or: in union with you [all]), **will fully bring it to the goal** (will be bringing perfection upon it; shall continue upon it to the final act and finished product: its completion; will bring upon its destiny; [note: this was a technical term for the ending of the sacrifice]) **– until** (or: right up to) **[the] Day of or from Christ Jesus** [with other MSS: as far as a Day which is Jesus Christ]**! –**

I give in vs. 3, parenthetically, the meaning of the verb "**give thanks**" from the meaning of the elements which make up the word. This presents a deeper insight into that for which Paul is "giving thanks." He goes on, in vs. 4, stating that he does this "**at all times**" and also makes request to God concerning their situation – making his petition "**with joy**," not with concern or worry.

His joy comes from his awareness of their solidarity with the message of Christ, the good news of God's goodness and the well-being which Christ brings. They have shared in and partnered with this from the time they first heard it.

Vs. 6 declares a wonderful promise: first that it is God (the One) Who begins the work in us, and births good works from us, and second that He is the One Who will bring it to the goal – He will bring us, and our works to the perfection and finished product, and will continue upon it to the final act! The function of the Greek preposition *en* as "in union with" give the sense of God working with us, in union with our works to bring them to a finished product. Note the technical implications of the terms "**beginning**... **goal**," when used in the context of the sacrifice: here we have a picture of the cross, the work of Christ. The "**good work**" was begun and finished "in Christ." As we are "in Him" so is that work finished "in us," even though we experience it as a process of growth and maturation. The Seed proclaims the Fruit.

In Paul's day, he was looking ahead to "**[the] Day of Christ Jesus**" which is another way of saying "the Day of the Lord" – which was an Old Testament term for God coming in judgment, and which we can look back in history to see such a coming in AD 70.

But note that there is no definite article before "Day" in the text, so it can read "a day of or from Christ Jesus." This could refer to an eschatological day in a metaphorical sense that we are children of the Day (Christ – 1 Thes. 5:5), referring to the coming of the Light in Christ and the new day of the new creation. Or, it could refer to a day in our lives when He personally visits us with an evaluation and a decision for us. When any work in us or through us comes to completion, our work may be judged by His fire, as in 1 Cor. 3:12-17, where in vs. 13 he says,

> "**each one's work will make itself to be visible in clear light** (or: will become apparent), **for the Day will make [it] evident** (show [it] plainly). **Because it is being progressively unveiled** (continually revealed) **within the midst of Fire, and the Fire, Itself, will test, examine and put to the proof** (or: prove by testing) **what sort of work each one's exists being.**"

Paul does not say here that this happens only at the end of our lives. I suggest that in our daily lives we repeatedly come to times of fiery trials that prove our deeds and actions. And in the expansion, with other MSS, rendering the genitive as apposition shows us that the Day IS Jesus Christ.

7. **just as** (or: correspondingly as) **it is fair for me** (or: it is right in me; it accords with the Way pointed out to me) **to habitually think this regarding all of you folks** (or: to continuously have this opinion and disposition over you all), **because of the [situation for] me to constantly hold** (or: have) **you folks within my heart, both within my bonds** (fetters; chains) **and within the verbal defense** (a word spoken from and on behalf of) **and legally valid confirmation** (the placement on a good footing to establish and make firm and steadfast) **of the message of goodness and well-being – you all being my co-participants** (common partners; fellow-sharers together) **of the grace and joyous favor!**

> (or: ... to continuously possess you people in the midst of the core of my being – you all being my joint-partners of this grace, both in union with my imprisonments and in verification of the good news!)

Paul continues his thoughts about those in Philippi, from vs. 6 into vs. 7, saying that it is fair and right for him to thus think about them since he constantly holds them in his heart. I have given two readings of the Greek syntax; translators take one of these two interpretations, as either makes good sense: 1) he has them in his heart both within his confinement and as he makes verbal defense and confirmation of the message, since they are co-participants of grace; 2) he holds them there because they are his joint-partners of this grace in both aspects: in his imprisonments and in the verification of the good news. The first emphasizes them being in his heart as he endures imprisonment and makes a defense of the message of goodness; the second emphasizes their participation with him in these two things.

8. **You see, God [is] my witness** (or: evidence), **how I continually long** (or: yearn) **for all you folks within the inner seat of Jesus Christ's tender emotions** (upper internal organs – heart, liver, lungs; = compassions).

Here Paul states that his own emotions are immersed within the tender emotions of Jesus – showing his union with Christ, being "**one spirit**" with the Lord (1 Cor. 6:17). This of course shows that Paul is thus also expressing Christ's emotions toward the called-out communities. The Lord also longs for us.

9. **And this I habitually think and speak toward having things be well** (or: pray)**: that your love may continually grow with excess and would progressively encompass [you and your world] with surpassing abundance still more and more, within full and accurate experiential and intimate knowledge and all insight and sensible perception,**

The goal is for our **LOVE** to continually and progressively encompass people and situations (as expressed in vs. 10), "**WITH SURPASSING ABUNDANCE, still MORE AND MORE**"! But wait, there is more! This is to happen "**within full and accurate experiential and intimate knowledge and all insight and sensible perception.**"

Paul Tillich gave these two definitions to **love** (*agape*): 1. the whole being's drive and movement toward reunion with another, to overcome existential separation; 2. acceptance of the object of love without restriction, in spite of the estranged, profanized and demonized state of the object; – *Systematic Theology III,* pp 134-138.

Such can only be accomplished by His Breath-effect and ability. This is an example of vs. 6: the good work that Christ undertook in us, and will be bringing it to completion.

10. **into the [situation for] you folks to habitually test, examine, distinguish and determine** (or: make sure by proving) **the things that carry through and are thus of consequence or make a difference, so that you may constantly be** (continually exist being) **folks judged by the light of the sun** (thus: clearly sincere and with integrity) **and ones [that are] not stumbling or jarring against [anything] nor striking toward [someone] and causing trouble, on into the Day of Christ,**

With the growing and encompassing love together with intimate personal insight and knowledge, we are equipped to live a life that habitually tests and examines (note: the Greek word was used for testing metals) concepts and situations so as to make a determination about what is significant and important – things of consequence that make a difference in life. In doing this we are also brought into the Light of God where He evaluates us and makes a judgment about our growth, while directing our steps so that we do not jar or offend others or cause trouble – on into the Day of Christ. Note that Paul expected them to live on into this Day, which if seen as a day of judgment came in AD 70. But if seen as a sphere of existence (Christ, Himself), then it speaks of continuing deeper into the depths of God (1 Cor. 2:10).

11. **being folks having been filled full with [the] Fruit of fair and equitable dealings which bring right relationship within the Way pointed out** (or: = from covenant inclusion): **the one [that is] through Jesus Christ [that is] leading into God's glory** (good reputation and manifestation of that which calls forth admiration) **and praise** (approval and commendation)
> (or: being those filled full of fruit of a rightwised nature through Jesus Christ, which proceeds into glory and praise that belongs to and pertains to God; or: ... through Jesus Christ, with a view to inhabiting the qualities and characteristics of God's reputation and praise).

Here Paul points out the condition that results from His Light evaluating us and leading us in His path: we grow and become filled (passive voice – this happens to us due to our union with Christ, who is the One evaluating and directing us) with the Fruit of living a rightwised life that is in right (equitably joined) relationships. All this comes "**through Jesus Christ**" being within, and in union with, us. This Path (the Christ-life) leads us into His glory and praise. Note the parenthetical expansions. The final parenthesis gives two other options for rendering this last clause. Each gives its own insight, and each presents a magnificent picture of where He is leading us: farther into Himself and His glory.

12. **Now I am constantly intending** (purposing and deciding for) **you folks to habitually know through intimate experience, brothers, that the affairs pertaining to me have rather come, and yet remain, into an advancement** (a progression; a striking ahead) **of God's message of goodness and well-being,**
13. **so that my bonds** (prison fetters) **[are] clearly seen** (visible; apparent; illuminated so as to be widely known) **to be within Christ, within the whole of the praetorium** (the living quarters of the emperor's guards), **and among all those left over** (the rest; the remaining ones),

14. **and by my bonds most of the brothers** (= the majority of the fellow believers), **having become persuaded and now being confident in the Lord, [are] to a greater degree** (or: more exceedingly) **courageously daring to be fearlessly continuing to speak the Word of God** (or: God's thoughts and message)**!**

As elsewhere, Paul's predicaments effect an advancement of God's message. Barclay tells us that the verb here was used "for cutting away the trees and the undergrowth and removing the barriers which would hinder the progress of an army" (ibid, p. 20). May it be so with us. Thus it is evident that his bonds (and whatever restraints we may have) are clearly seen to be in Christ. His life is a witness to those about him; His very predicament and hard circumstances are giving courage to the majority of the fellow believers, and they, despite seeing what has happened to Paul, are fearlessly continuing to speak God's word and message. We see how God works all into good (Rom. 8:28) as we observe that Paul's being restrained and detained made other folks more confident and courageous in proclaiming God's Idea: the Christ who dwells in us, and His message of love and conciliation through the new creation within Him.

15. **Certain folks** (or: Some), **indeed, are also habitually proclaiming** (or: are even heralding, publishing and preaching) **the Christ through** (or: because of) **envy, jealousy and rivalry, as well as strife** (discord; debate); **yet also, certain ones** (or: some) **through delight** (or: because of a good disposition and a good opinion [about it]; or: through thinking well [of it and/or people]; because of approval [of the message]; or: = because they are pleased to do it).

In vs. 14 he has just said that his bonds gave the majority of the believers confidence to fearlessly speak God's message, but we see that their hearts were manifested, for they were doing it for different reasons, which vs. 16 & 17 define. The word "**delight**" has a fairly broad semantic range, as indicated in the expansion, so I suggest that those doing it for positive reasons also varied in these reasons.

16. **These, on the one hand, forth from out of love – having seen and thus knowing that I am constantly lying into** (or: repeatedly located with a view to; habitually being laid down, and thus set into the midst of) **a defense of the news of well-being and message of goodness.** 17. **Yet those, on the other hand, from out of faction** (partisan purposes; contentiousness; or: from self-interest, or from a motive of financial gain, or to enhance their careers) **are habitually announcing in accord with the message of the Christ, not purely** (= with pure motives) **– being ones habitually presuming** (or: supposing) **to be repeatedly arousing and raising up squeezing** (pressure; affliction; tribulation; oppression) **to** (or: for) **my bonds** (or: in my imprisonment).

As to vs. 16, we could today say that Paul was repeatedly "lying in prison," and "**lying**" is the core meaning of this word, but he is using it in its more figurative sense, as the expansion shows. His position was that of defending the message of God's goodness. We see elsewhere that much of this defense was against the attacks of the Jews and their religion.

I find it interesting that Paul recognized that some fellow believers had either factious motives, or motives for personal gain (the Greek word here for **faction** originally meant "working for pay," but later came to also mean seeking an office for a career, or having a partisan motive), and that their jealousy made them preach all the more just to bring greater affliction upon and oppression to Paul's situation. Still for these negative motivations they kept on "**announcing in accord with the message of the Christ**!"

18. **For what?** (or: So what?; = What difference does it make?) **That moreover, in every direction** (or: by every turn; by every method), **whether in pretense** (as a cloak for other purposes) **or in truth** (reality; essential essence), **Christ is continually being correspondingly announced, and in this I constantly rejoice.**

Paul saw that God was working even the negative into good (Rom. 8:28), and that Christ is being correspondingly announced in every direction, on every turn, and by every method. Let us also rejoice with Paul as we see the same today.

19. **For I am aware** (have seen and thus know) **that this will step away into deliverance** (rescue; health and wholeness; salvation) **for me** (and: in me) **through your request and the supply** (support; provision) **of the Spirit of Jesus Christ** (or: from the attitude pertaining to and having the characteristics of Jesus Christ; of the Breath-effect which is Jesus, [the] Anointed),
20. **in accordance with my looking away – with my head stretched out to watch – and [the] expectation** (or: hope) **that within nothing will I be put to shame** (disgrace; embarrassment), **but to the contrary, within all freedom of speech** (boldness and public openness which comes from being a citizen) **– as always, even now** (at the present moment) **– Christ will be made great** (be magnified; be enlarged) **within my body, whether through life, or through death!**

The last phrase of vs. 20, "**or through death**," shows that Paul had a broad understanding of the concept of "**deliverance**," of which he spoke in vs. 19. The increased proclaiming of the message would bring some sort of climax – either his freedom from prison, or his death. Nonetheless, he had confidence in both the request on his behalf by those at Philippi, and the supply, support and provision from the Spirit of Jesus Christ. Our supply can be from the attitude of Jesus, which He has placed within us, or from the effect of His Breath as He breathes fresh anointing into us. These would combine to cause a stepping away into deliverance for him, and in him. They gave him an expectation, for which he was eagerly watching. They brought him all freedom of speech, and he knew that Christ would be made great within his body. May we all view our predicaments in this way.

21. **For you see, to me, to be living [is] Christ** (or: For the [situation] in me and for me, life [is the] Anointed One), **and to be dying [is] gain** (advantage; profit).

What a profound statement that describes life in the Spirit, participation in His reign, union with Christ. This, too, should be our mindset and our world-view. It applies both literally and figuratively. Both renderings of the first clause paint a clear picture of a disciple of Jesus. This is the "attitude" of the new creation, of the New Being.

22. **Yet since** (or: Now if) [p46, D: Whether] **the [situation] is to continue living within flesh** (= in a physical body in the natural realm), **this for me** (or: in me) **[will be] a fruit from work** (produce relating to [my] action) **– and so what** (or: which) **I will** [p46, B: I should and could] **choose** (take to myself in preference) **I am not presently making known.**

It would seem that Paul regarded himself as having a part in this decision, and for him to "**continue living within flesh**" was related to the result of someone's work, or perhaps his own action. But he was not saying what his choice would be.

23. **So I am being continuously held together** (or: caught; squeezed) **from out of the two: constantly having the craving** (holding the strong desire and impulse) **into the [situation] to untie and loose back up again** [as in loosing tent pins and ropes when striking camp, or loosing moorings to set sail], **and to be** (to exist being) **together with Christ – for [that is] rather to a much higher rank** (a more advantageous situation; a more profitable thing; [it is] much better)!

On the one hand he wanted to move on – pull up his tent pegs and continue down the trail in the next realm, for he knew that this meant being together with Christ, which would include His body in that realm, and he regarded that as a more advantageous situation. He expressed similar sentiments in 2 Cor. 5:

> 1. **For we have seen, and thus know, that if our house, of the tabernacle which is pitched on the land, would at some point be dismantled** (or: that whenever our house, which is this tent upon the earth, should be loosed down), **we constantly have** (continuously hold; presently possess) **a structure** (a building) **forth from out of the**

midst of God: an eonian house (a house having the qualities and character which pertain to the Age; a house for the ages) **– not made by hands – within the midst of the heavens** (or: resident within the atmospheres).
2. **For you see, even within this one we are continuously groaning, utterly longing and constantly yearning to fully enter within and to clothe upon ourselves** (to dress upon ourselves) **our dwelling-house** (habitation) **– the one [made] out of heaven** (or: the one from, or made of, atmosphere; the [dwelling-house, or habitation] from out of the midst of [the] sky) **–**
3. **since, in fact, also being folks at some point entering within and clothing ourselves** (or: being dressed, also), **we shall not be found naked.**
4. **For we also, being** (continually existing) **within the tent, are continuously groaning, being the ones constantly weighed down** (burdened). **Upon which [situation] we are not wanting to go out from** (to unclothe; to strip; to undress) **but rather to fully enter within and to add clothing upon ourselves, to the end that the mortal** (or: this mortal thing) **may be drunk down and swallowed under** (or: by) **The Life.**
5. **Now the One working this down, producing and fashioning us into this very [situation is] God, the One giving to us the down payment** (earnest; pledge; first installment) **of the Breath-effect** (or: which is the Spirit and the Attitude).

24. **Yet the [situation] to be staying** (remaining-on) **in the flesh [is] more necessary** (indispensable; a more forced constraint) **because of you folks.**

Yet he loved and felt solidarity with the called-out communities in this present realm, and realized that they needed him.

25. **So, having been persuaded and still being convinced of this, I have seen and thus know that I will remain on, and shall be abiding** (dwelling so as to be ready to give aid) **together alongside with** (or: among) **all you folks – on into your progress** (or: cutting or striking a passage forward; advancement) **and joy that comes from, belongs to and has the characteristics of the Faith** (or: which is the trust, conviction and loyalty),

So now he goes on to tell them the decision, and he did remain – on into the next decade – and although he apparently remained in custody, he likely had continued contact with them as they cut their passage forward, and he continued in their joy that comes from the faith, and which belongs to and is trust, conviction and loyalty. The expansions of the last phrase present the possibilities of the Greek being either an ablative or a genitive, along with its potential functions and the semantic range of the noun "**faith**/trust/conviction/loyalty."

26. **to the end that, in me – [that is], through my presence again face to face with you – your loud-tongued exultation-results** (or: your justification for boasting) **in Christ Jesus** (or: in union with [the] Anointed Jesus) **may surround [you] in excessive abundance.**

His hope was that he would see them face-to-face, and that this would surround them with an exceeding abundance of exultation. Here we see Paul's heart, and the loving solidarity that he had with these folks. Notice that he wanted to see the effects, or results, of their exultation – or, the reason for their boasting.

27. **Only, by habit live** (or: continue living) **worthily, as citizens with behavior corresponding in value to Christ's good news** (message of goodness), **so that whether coming and seeing to become acquainted, or continuing absent, I may go on hearing about you folks** (the things concerning you)**: that you are constantly and progressively standing firm within the midst of and in union with one Breath-effect** (or: = steadfastly united in spirit and attitude), **continuing to be corporately striving in one soul** (by one inner life competing side-by-side as in the public games) **by the faith that comes from the good news** (or: in the conviction that

belongs to and pertains to the message of goodness and well-being; or: by the trust which is the message of wellness and ease),

As usual, Paul turns to practical admonitions. They are to live as worthy citizens – and I suggest that he means citizens that bring a good reputation about Christ to their city and region, as well as citizens of the Jerusalem which is above (Gal. 4:26) that correspond to the message of the goodness of God's kingdom, being appropriate representatives of God, Who is love. This would also have spoken to their privileges and responsibilities of being Roman citizens, as well. God's kingdom is a life that is lived here on earth that is joined to the Spirit of God within the heavens. This is why Jesus told us to pray that our Father's will would be done here, even as it is in heaven.

Paul also wants to hear that they are constantly and progressively standing firm in the Spirit, living in union with God's Breath-effect. This could also refer to the entire community of called-out folks being "steadfastly united in spirit," this last rendering leading into their corporately contending for the kingdom, as having one soul (= mind, will, purpose, feeling).

The ability to be "as one" comes by the faith that is inherent in the message of goodness and well-being, as well as in the trust which in fact is this wellness and ease in Christ.

28. **even constantly being folks [that are] in nothing startled, intimidated or frightened by** (or: under) **the opponents** (the ones continuously lying in the opposing position) – **which is a public indication** (a pointing-out as of display; or: a showing within) **of loss** (ruin; destruction) **for** (or: to) **them, yet of deliverance** (wholeness, health, rescue and salvation) **to, for and among you folks** [other MSS: in and among us; other MSS: of your deliverance], **and this [is] from God,**

They are not to be frightened, startled or intimidated by those who oppose them – whether they be the Jews, or folks from pagan religions, or the Roman government. This lack of fear and failure to be intimidated publicly displays God's deliverance of both the individuals and their community, while at the same time showing that their opponents have lost ground in their attempts, as well as indicating their moral ruin and the destruction of community solidarity. Individual loss and ruin is the current state of being of those who oppose Christ. The Light of the called-out folks stands in stark contrast to the darkness of lifeless religions and dominating social systems. This deliverance, rescue, wholeness and salvation comes from God. It is Christ within and among us.

29. **because to you folks it is given by grace** (or: He graciously was given in you people, as a favor for you people), **over the [issue] of, and on behalf of, Christ, not only to be progressively believing and habitually trusting into Him, but further, also, to be repeatedly having sensible experiences over Him** (or: to constantly experience feelings and impressions on behalf of Him; to habitually suffer and be ill used for His sake; to be continuously affected on account of the things pertaining to Him) –
30. **constantly having** (or: continuously holding) **the very** (or: the same) **contest in the public games** (or: race in the stadium; agonizing struggle in the gathered assembly) **such as you saw** (or: perceive) **within me and now are presently hearing in me** (or: and at this moment are repeatedly hearing [to be] in me).

The deliverance and salvation spoken of in vs. 28 brings the gift of grace and favor to them, as well as the ability to progressively believe and continue trusting over the issue of, and on behalf of, Christ. This is a key understanding of how the proclaiming of the Word of God works upon the souls of those who are blessed because of having ears that are presently and habitually hearing (Matt. 13:16).

Note, however, that the syntax of the first clause in vs. 29 allows the parenthetical reading, speaking of Christ being given in us and for us, through the death and resurrection of Christ, and then the outpouring of His Spirit, so that His body would both believe and have experiences via their senses, in regard to Him.

Vs. 29 next tells us, via the first rendering, that we are graced and favored for the following, giving the semantic range of the Greek expression (*paschein* – present infinitive):
1) to be repeatedly having sensible experiences over Him
2) to constantly experience feelings and impressions on behalf of Him
3) to habitually suffer and be ill used for His sake
4) to be continuously affected on account of the things pertaining to Him.
These are all expressions of the Christian life, and we are "graced" to have these experiences as they relate to Him, and we need this gifting of grace in order to go through them.

In vs. 30 Paul uses the metaphor of the stadium games, and the race course there, to give his readers an analogy for the things which in vs. 29 he said that they would experience. He used his own life and experiences as a point of reference for them, and for us. Sometimes it would be an agonizing struggle.

Chapter 2

1. **If, then, [there exists] any calling-alongside to receive relief, aid, encouragement, consolation, comfort or supporting influence** (or: any receiving of the work of a paraclete) **within Christ or in union with [the] Anointing, if [there is] any spoken comfort and consolation of love** (belonging to love; having a source in love; or: which is love), **if any communion** (common participation; fellowship; partnership; sharing) **of Breath-effect** (or: belonging to spirit; having spirit or Breath as its source), **if any tender emotions** (literally: upper internal organs) **and compassions** (or: pities),

Note all the qualities and personal emotions, as well as gifts and supports, that are supplied in Christ and His Anointing:
1) the work of the Paraclete: relief, aid, support, comfort, encouragement, etc.
2) spoken comfort and consolation from love
3) communion of spirit, sharing of [the] Breath-effect, partnership from the Spirit, common participation from the Spirit
4) tender emotions
5) compassions

Do we avail ourselves of these things, or are we aware of them in our lives? They can often come through His body, or from within us – from wherever there is Christ, or the Anointing.

2. **fill my joy full, so that you folks may be continually having the same frame of mind** (may be mutually disposed; may have the same opinion; may mind the same thing), **habitually holding** (or: having) **the same Love: folks joined together in soul** (inner life of feelings, will, heart and mind), **continuously minding The One** (or: habitually holding one opinion; constantly thinking one thing; regularly disposed to one [purpose]; [other MSS: the same]) –

Having "**the same frame of mind**," or a mutual disposition and opinion, or even focusing on the same thing, describes a unity of spirit and purpose. Holding the same Love (Christ's love; the Love which is Christ) will mean that they are joined together in soul (the inner self; the feelings; the will; the existential being), for the love of Christ holds us together (2 Cor. 5:14). Minding The One, means keeping our focus on God. Or, it can mean the group having one thought, idea, purpose, etc. – repeating what was said in the first clause. All this made Paul's joy full.

Barclay comments, "No man can walk in disunity with his fellow-men and in unity with Christ" (ibid, p. 33). That is a strong statement. How then can we be at-odds, or at war? In the same passage he further says, "It means an unconquerable good-will even to those who hate us, to those whom we do not like, to those who are unlovely."

3. **nothing down from** (or: along the line of; corresponding to; or: descending to) **party interests** (hireling-like contention; faction; self-serving; or: from a motive of financial gain, or to enhance one's career) **nor down from** (or: along the line of; corresponding to; or: descending to) **empty reputation** (futile opinion; vainglory; fruitless appearance) **– but rather, in humility** (or: by an attitude of being in a low station; in humbleness of disposition and way of thinking) **constantly considering one another** (or: each other) **[as] those habitually holding [a position] above themselves** (or: [as] being superior in regard to yourselves),

Here Paul gives two characteristics (given with each word's semantic range) of behaviors that are in contrast to what he has just said in the last clause:
1) party interests, hireling-like contention, faction, self-serving, from a motive of financial gain, or to enhance a career
2) empty reputation, futile opinion, vainglory, fruitless appearance.

All of these are opposed to the spirit and attitude of Christ. My wife Lynda pointed out that folks who operate from these motives are similar to those in Corinth who aligned themselves with one teacher in opposition to the teachings of others:

> **"each of you is habitually saying, "I, myself, am indeed [a follower] of Paul," yet [another], "I, myself, belong to Apollos," and [another], "As for me, I [am] of Cephas' [group]," but [another], "I, myself, [am] from Christ." Christ has been parted and remains divided into fragments!** (or, as a question: Has Christ been fragmented into divided parts?) – 1 Cor. 1:12-13.

Don Luther comments, "'Nothing down from... party interests...' I see this as a lofty position that we assume toward others. It is our unassailable castle down from which we dispense grace... or not. Christ had a legitimate place from which to give us gifts... the Father. But He did not serve us from there. He came into our low estate and became the servant."

Paul goes on to give the appropriate alternative for their mutual behaviors and attitudes: being in a humble spirit with an attitude of someone who is in a low social station; being folks who as a way of life consider each other as being in a higher position than themselves, therefore always giving honor and showing respect.

4. **not each one continuing to attentively view** (keeping an eye on and noting) **the things pertaining to themselves, but to the contrary, each one [viewing] even the things pertaining to others** (or: different folks).

This is another call to love – to not be self-centered nor focused on our own concerns or our own group, but rather to focus on the needs and concerns of other folks and those outside our own circle: those outside our own family, group of friends, culture and country. It's about being in community – it was for this that we were "called-out" from elitism, sectarianism, and exclusivism.

5. **You see, this way of thinking** (this attitude and disposition) **is continuously within and among you folks** (or, as an imperative: So let this minding be habitually within you folks) **– which [is] also within Christ Jesus,**

The spelling of the verb is either indicative or imperative, thus the two renderings. But the main thing is that this mindset and attitude, as described in vs. 4, is Christ's way of thinking, His disposition toward people. He is more concerned about us than about Himself.

6. **Who, starting and continuing as inherently existing** (or: beginning under; subsisting) **within God's form** (or: in an outward mold which is God), **He does not consider the [situation] to be equals in God a plunder** (or: a pillaging; a robbery; a snatching; or: a thing or situation seized and held),

> (or: Who, [although] constantly humbly and supportively ruling in union with an external shape and an outward appearance from God, did not give consideration to a seizure: the

[situation] to continuously exist being the same things as God, even on the same levels in God, or equal [things; aspects] to God,)

This verse has caused much theological discussion, but we should first of all consider the context of the five previous verses, and especially vss. 4-5, for the subject of vs. 6 is a way of thinking. Paul is using Jesus as an example of the kind of thinking that he is recommending – more than making an ontological statement about Him.

Again Don Luther makes a good observation on this verse, "As Christ was the conduit of the divine life to His creation, He was not taking a position of power and authority from which He could dispense the Father's heavenly gifts to His subjects, but rather a position of servitude. So should we, as His members, continue the 'work' of dispensing God's Grace to all. This is the real foot-washing service."

Grammarians have differing views regarding how Paul is using the Greek participle *huparchon*, which I rendered first as "**starting and continuing as inherently existing**" and then inserted the expansions, "beginning under; subsisting," and finally, in the second rendering of this verse, as "constantly humbly and supportively ruling." The first element of the word is *archon* which is often translated as "ruler," but which comes from *arche* whose basic meaning is "beginning." Prefixed to *archon* is *hupo*, whose basic meaning is "under." *The Concordant Greek-English Keyword Concordance* gives the elements as meaning "under-originate."

Most translators render this word as a verb of being, as this seems to fit most contexts and is an easy solution. I have done the same, while also presenting for our consideration of this enigmatic verse more information concerning its makeup and potential meanings.

Now Paul does not tell us when or under what circumstances He was "under-originating." It is usually presumed that this refers to before His incarnation, because of what follows. Full consideration of vs. 6-8 is a subject for its own study, and, because of the required length, is beyond the scope of this present work. But I will here point out some things for your consideration. First note that the word "**equals**" is in the plural. Consider the expansions which define what Paul means in regard to "**plunder**/seizure": "the [situation] to continuously exist being the same things as God, even on the same levels in God, or equal [things; aspects] to God." Whatever all this means, the point is that Christ did not have this mind-set. He was not focusing upon His own concerns but rather upon ours, as vs. 4 admonishes.

Barclay points out the two meanings of *hurpagmos*: 1) to snatch, and 2) to clutch, as if to hug, and says "...Jesus did not need to snatch at equality with God, because he had it as a right..." nor "hug it jealously to himself" (Barclay, ibid, p. 36).

In line with my first rendering of the last clause of this verse, we should not consider being "equals in Christ" a plunder, but should simply accept the fact that He has made us to be members of His body – He being the Source and the Head, and thus always having preeminence.

7. **but to the contrary, He empties Himself** (or: removed the contents of Himself; made Himself empty), **receiving** (or: taking; accepting) **a slave's form** (external shape; outward mold), **coming to be** (or: birthing Himself) **within humanity's** (mankind's; people's) **likeness.**
8. **And so, being found in an outward fashion, mode of circumstance, condition, form-appearance** (or: character, role, phase, configuration, manner) **as a human** (a person; a man), **He lowers Himself** (or: humbled Himself; made Himself low; degrades Himself; levels Himself off), **coming to be** (or: birthing Himself) **a submissive, obedient One** (one who gives the ear and listens) **as far as** (or: to the point of; until) **death – but death of a cross** (torture stake)!

The verb of the first clause of vs. 7 is in the aorist, so I give both a simple present, and a simple past rendering. He did this, but through us – His body – He still does this for folks. Jesus received a slave's form both in coming to be a human being, and in placing Himself under the Law (see my article, What is the "Form of a Servant"? at the end of the comments on this letter). In birthing Himself in humanity's likeness, I suggest that He took to Himself everything that belongs to the Adamic race, and then became the Last Adam, the Second Human Being (1 Cor. 15:45-47), and included us all in this new creation – what Paul Tillich calls "The New Being." But coming to be in mankind's likeness is also here equated to having "**a slave's form**." This would seem to suggest that humanity's estranged condition was indeed slavery. But this was temporary, as we see our new condition as being freedom; it was existential, but not ontological. Then vs. 8 tells us the He lowered Himself even further, all the way to becoming obedient to the death (the result of the first Adam's sin), even the death as if He were a criminal and outcast of society – the death of a cross. This death Paul calls submissive obedience: obedience to the Father, and this specific obedience Paul discusses in Romans ch. 5, especially vs. 19,

> "**For JUST AS through the unwillingness to listen, or to pay attention, resulting in disobedience** (or: the erroneous hearing leading to disobedience) **of the one person THE MANY** (= the mass of humanity) **were rendered** (established; constituted; placed down and made to be) **sinners** (failures; ones who diverge and miss the target), **THUS – in the same way – ALSO through the submissive listening and paying attention resulting in obedience of the One THE MANY** (= the mass of humanity) **will be rendered** (placed down and established as; constituted; appointed to be) **just ones** (folks who have been rightwised; people in the Way pointed out; righteous ones who are free from guilt; folks in right relationship and who are fair and equitable)."

He yet humbles Himself by coming to dwell in us, His temple, even allowing us to sometimes crucify Him afresh (Heb. 6:6).

9. **For this reason, God also lifts Him up above** (or: highly exalted Him; elevates Him over) **and by grace gives to Him** (or: joyously favors on Him) **the Name – the one over and above every name! –**

Paul continues using the aorist with "**lifts**/exalted." This fact tense applied to the past, in history, but also to the present in the realm of spirit/heaven. He also does this through the imparted knowledge of the Truth which He repeatedly plants within each successive generation.

By giving Him the Name, we see that,
> "**All authority** (or: Every right and privilege from out of Being) **is** (or: was at once) **given to [Him] within heaven and upon the earth** (or: in sky and atmosphere, as well as on land)!" (Matt. 28:18).

10. **to the end that within The Name: Jesus!** (or: in union with the name of Jesus; in the midst of the Name belonging to [Yahweh-the-Savior]), **every knee** (= person) **– of the folks upon the heaven** (of those belonging to the super-heaven, or [situated] upon the atmosphere) **and of the people existing upon the earth and of the folks dwelling down under the ground** (or: on the level of or pertaining to subterranean ones; [comment: note the ancient science of the day – a three-tiered universe]) **– may bend** (or: would bow) **in worship, prayer or allegiance,**

Paul continues from soteriology (the topic of salvation) to eschatology (the topic of things of the end), here giving us a picture of the final act of the ages: every knee (a figure of every person) bending to bow in worship, prayer and allegiance. A picture that shows that He has conquered all, and that all belong to Him, and that all bow in reverence and allegiance to Him. He includes all the realms of the 1st century Hellenistic/Jewish world-view: heaven (the skies), on earth, and even under the ground/earth (figure of what was then considered the realm of the dead). This statement excludes no one. Barclay says of this last clause, "It made certain that some day, soon or late, every living creature in all the universe, in heaven, in earth and even in hell, would worship him.... Worship is founded not on fear, but on love" (ibid, p. 38). Bowing in allegiance speaks of respect and gratitude. Bowing in prayer speaks of reverent relationship.

11. **and every tongue** (= person) **may speak out the same thing** (should and would openly agree, confess and acclaim) **that Jesus Christ [is] Lord** (Master; Owner) – **[leading] into [the] glory of Father God** (or: unto Father God's good reputation; [progressing] into a manifestation which calls forth praise unto God [the] Father)!

This is a work of the Holy Spirit, for,
> "**no one is able** (normally has power) **to say, 'Jesus [is] Lord** (or: Lord Jesus; perhaps: = Jesus [is] Yahweh)!' except within and in union with [the] Holy Spirit** (or: in a set-apart and consecrated spirit; in [the] Sacred Breath)" (1 Cor. 12:3b).

Furthermore, it is this kind of statement and confession of allegiance that brings glory to the Father, and leads into Him having a good reputation. Then He will give a manifestation which will bring praise to Him from all of creation. What a scene that will be! When we, as individuals, bow and express allegiance to Christ, it brings glory to God, our Father, at each occurrence throughout the ages.

Barclay posits that this verse "is one of the most important verses in the NT," and then states that "These four words [*Jesus Christ is Lord*] were the first creed that the Christian Church ever had" (ibid, p. 39). The creed of the Roman Empire was "Caesar is Lord," so Paul is making a revolutionary claim which contradicted the Roman Caesar cult. This universal proclamation of the complete and total victory of Christ has one aim, goal and destiny: the glory and majestic reputation of the Father!

12. **Consequently, my loved ones, according as at all time** (or: as always) **you folks submissively listened, paid attention and humbly obeyed, not as only in my presence, but further, now** (at this moment), **much more in my absence – in company with fear and trembling** (or: = earnestness and concern) **– be habitually working commensurately with the deliverance** (or: be constantly producing on the level and sphere of the wholeness and well-being which are the outcome of the rescue and salvation) **of, or pertaining to, yourselves,**

With the above view in mind – of all ultimately submitting to Him – Paul now asks those at Philippi to prefigure this by continuing to submissively listen and humbly obey by habitually working commensurately with their deliverance – or, "be constantly producing on the level and sphere of the wholeness and well-being which are the outcome of the rescue and salvation" that pertains to them. In other words, live according to the new creation and new being that you are!

The words "**fear and trembling**" could be taken at this extreme, for those who do not yet know the heart of love which is our Father. Or, it can also mean "in earnestness and concern" which comes from respect and reverence. These folks had "**humbly obeyed**" the message from Paul, and they should continue with this disposition as they "constantly produc[ed] on the level and sphere of their wholeness and well-being..."

13. **for you see, God is the One habitually being inwardly active, constantly working and progressively effecting [results] within you folks – both the willing** (intending; purposing; resolving) **and the [situation] to be continuously effecting the action and inward work – above the thing that pleases** (or: over [the situation of] well-thinking and delight; for the sake of [His] good pleasure).

Ah, what a comforting promise: it is God that is doing the work in us – and this includes both our wanting and willing, intending and resolving, as well as our actually "**effecting the action and inward work**!" So it is not up to our will, but His. Barclay emphasizes this, saying, "... it is always *the action of God*.... The desire for the salvation of God is not kindled by any human emotion but by God himself.... The work of salvation is begun, continued and ended in God" (ibid, p. 41, 42).

Now note that His work superabounds "**above the thing that pleases**." His work is super wonderful.

Now if we take the second rendering, we see that His working has in view "well-thinking and delight." So this could be either His, as I suggest in the last version of this phrase, or ours. But not to worry, His delight is always a good pleasure for us.

14. **Be habitually doing** (accomplishing; constructing; producing) **all things apart from grumbling complaints** (or: murmurings) **and reasoned considerations** (or: designing thoughts; divided reckonings unto the settlements of accounts; arguments which permeate the environment or go in every direction),

Grumbling complaints: about the weather, about our health or energy level, about our town, about the climate (dry or humid), about bugs, about neighbors, about the president, about the other political party, about our economy, about having to wait – in lines, in traffic, for our spouse to be ready to go, etc. – *ad infinitum!* We have become a culture of complaint rather than a culture of gratitude. We resemble the Israelites in the wilderness.

But the admonition here is to be HABITUALLY doing ALL THINGS **APART FROM** "**grumbling complaints**." Keep in mind that he is speaking to followers of Christ here. We would not expect this from folks outside the called-out community – those not yet born into His kingdom. Yet my paragraph above describes many "Christians" these days.

Paul is then speaking of "**reasoned considerations**" that come from wrong motivations, as shown in the parenthetical expansion. We are to do all things from singleness of mind and purity of heart – because it is good and just and worthwhile to do them, not because we have ulterior motives or self-serving designs. Notice the last rendering of this phrase: "arguments which permeate the environment or go in every direction." This is from the force of the prefix *dia* which indicates "permeation" as it passes through the midst and into every corner of our world.

15. **so that you folks may come to be blameless ones** (those without defect), **even unmixed** (unblended; artless and sincere) **children of God – unblemished** (flawless) **people in the midst of a crooked and distorted** (as having been misshaped on the potter's wheel) **generation** (or: a twisted family which has been altered and turned in different ways so as to be dislocated), **within which** (or: among whom) **you folks are continuously shining** (giving light; or: appearing; made visible by light) **as illuminators** (causes of light; or: luminaries) **within [the] ordered System** (world of secular culture, religion, economics and government),

In vs. 15, cause for blame and defect come from practicing the things cited in vs. 14. We become "mixed bags" (to use a current idiom) when we blend these things into our character and way of living. We cease to be pure and sincere when ulterior motives enter into our relationships. They bring blemishes and flaws to the image of Christ. But we are to remain "**unmixed**" by things of the religious or cultural world in which we live, so that we can be folks that are continuously shining – amidst a crooked and distorted generation – and be illuminators of the system in which we live. Or, as Jesus said it, "the light of the world." But in consideration of the above potential negative qualities that can come into us, we must remember that,
> "**the blood of Jesus, His Son, keeps continually cleansing us** (or: is progressively rendering us pure) **from every sin** (or: from all error, failure, deviation, mistake, and from every [successive] shot that is off target [when it occurs])" (1 John 1:7).

16. **constantly holding upon** (or: having added; keeping a good grip on) **Life's Word** (or: a message which is life), **[leading you] into loud-tongued exulting-effects** (boasting; vaunting) **for me** (or: in me), **on into Christ's Day** (a day of [the] Anointed; or: a day which is anointed), **because I do not** (or: did not) **run into emptiness** (that which is without content), **nor do I** (or: did I) **become weary or struggle in labor into emptiness** (that which is without content).

This verse just adds to our being "**illuminators**." We are indeed just that when we hold upon a message which is life – having Life's Word added to us.

Paul's expression of "**loud-tongued exulting-effects**" and "boasting" seems out of place in our culture, but it was apparently an appropriate way of expressing joy and victory in his time and culture. He was looking ahead to the same Day that he has referred to elsewhere, Christ's Day of making decisions about things and people. Paul was seeing the Philippian community as a success in Christ, and this was to bring Paul great joy and exulting because of them – because it will mean that he had not run his race into emptiness, or into a situation with no content. His weariness and struggles in labor would not have been in vain – there is a reality which contains fullness, into which he is proceeding.

17. **But even more, since** (or: if) **I am also repeatedly poured out as a drink offering upon the sacrificial offering and public service pertaining to your faith** (or: which comes from your trust; in regard to the faithful loyalty which comprises you people), **I am constantly rejoicing** (or: glad) **– even continually rejoicing** (glad) **together with all of you!**
18. **Now in the same way, you yourselves also be constantly rejoicing – even continually rejoicing together with me.**

In vs. 16 Paul planned to glory in the fact that he did not run for nothing. In 17 he continues on, noting that he has been repeatedly poured out as a drink offering (metaphorical language for suffering hardship and expending his life) on their behalf – in regard to the growth and health of the faith and trust in their lives. But still he is constantly rejoicing – rejoicing with them in their growth. Furthermore, he wants them to be constantly rejoicing with him in his joy. He repeats the last clause of vs. 17 in vs. 18, but switching who is doing the rejoicing with whom. With Paul it is total solidarity.

19. **Now I continue expecting – in the Lord Jesus – to quickly send Timothy to you folks, so that I also may continue well in soul** (in good cheer; in good spirits), **knowing the [situations and circumstances] concerning** (or: the things about) **you folks.**

Paul is so joined in spirit with them that he plans to send Timothy to them so that he can learn of their situation and circumstances, and thus continue well in soul (be in good spirits) himself! No wonder he taught the Corinthians about Christ being one body of many members.

20. **You see, I presently have no one equal-souled** (of the same soul; = equally sensitive) **who will legitimately** (or: genuinely) **divide his mind so as to have his thoughts anxious about your interests and to care for the [circumstances] concerning** (or: the things about) **you folks.**

He refers to Timothy here, one of whom Paul knows no one of equal soul, who will so devote his heart to their interests and care. Timothy seems to be in the image of Paul, who is in the image of Christ, as like produces like.

21. **For all those [others] are constantly concerned with** (looking out for; are seeking) **their own interests** (or: things), **not with the interests and things pertaining to and belonging to, or having the qualities and characteristics of, Jesus Christ.**

Other folks are not like Timothy, but are doing such things as those which he spoke against in vs. 3 and 4, and now again here: being concerned with their own interests, not with the interests of Jesus Christ – and in this case, with Him in His body at Philippi. These others were looking out for their own thing, not things that pertain to, belong to, or have the qualities of Jesus Christ.

22. **Yet you folks continue knowing by experience his proof by scrutinized examination and testing, that as a child for a father, he slaves** (performs as a slave) **together with me, into the message of goodness, ease and well-being.**

23. **I continue expecting, indeed then, to send this one immediately** (out of the very time or situation) – **as soon as I can look away from the things around me** (or: see-off the [situations and] things concerning me).
24. **So I have been persuaded and am confident within [the] Lord** [= Christ or Yahweh] **that I myself, also, shall quickly come to you folks.**

In vs. 22 Paul returns to speaking of Timothy, and of their acquaintance with him and his work with Paul, pouring himself into the work of Christ. Paul tells them that he expects both to send Timothy to them, and then to come, himself. This would both encourage them and give them joy in the expectation of Timothy being with them, and then later possibly Paul himself. But now, in the following verses, he turns to speaking of the man who we presume is the one that will bring this letter to them. He had been sent to serve Paul (on behalf of the Philippian congregation), but Paul has decided that it was necessary that he should return home.

25. **Now I consider it necessary and pressing to send to you Epaphroditus, my brother and co-worker** (joint-operative) **and fellow soldier, yet your envoy** (representative; emissary; sent-forth agent), **and a public servant of my need,**

Paul is returning Epaphroditus with the highest of recommendations: brother, co-worker (not just his servant), fellow soldier, their own emissary to him, and public servant with regard to his needs. Paul's use of the word "**envoy**" gives us a clear understanding of the Greek *apostolos* which unfortunately is usually transliterated instead of translated. Epaphroditus was an agent of the called-out congregation in Philippi; he was sent-forth from them, as their representative, to minister to Paul's needs. This word should not be used as a "title" or to signify and office or position in Christ's body: it is a function.

The last word was used of folks who at their own expense arranged for and funded public events (e.g., sponsored plays or paid for certain civic needs) and were considered benefactors of the state.

26. **since he had been continuously having great affection and longing to see all of you folks, even being repeatedly dejected and deeply troubled because you heard** (or: hear) **that he fell sick** (or: is ill).

Here Paul is now thinking of the personal feelings and needs of his fellow worker, and would rather send Epaphroditus home than keep him around just to benefit from his help. He is doing what he had in vs. 3 and 4, above, admonished them to do: keeping in sight the concerns of another, rather than of himself.

27. **For he even fell sick** (or: also is ill) **as being a consort near alongside of death. But contrariwise, God had mercy on** (or: mercies) **him – yet not only him, but further, me also – to the end that I should not have pain and sadness upon pain and sadness** (or: = major and added sorrow).

It has been suggested that he may have contracted a serious flu or fever that tended to plague Rome during this period. Yet God had mercy on him, and Paul tells us that this also gave himself mercy in not having to bear the pain of losing this dear brother to the illness. Here we see the importance of relationship to Paul – it is not just about doctrine, but about care for one another.

28. **More diligently** (earnestly; eagerly), **then, I send** (or: sent) **him, so that in seeing him again, you may be glad and rejoice – and I may be more relieved of pain and sadness.**

Paul's concern for Epaphroditus' need to return home brought Paul pain and sadness. He also wanted those in Philippi to be glad and to rejoice, via his return.

29. **Be focusing on him, then, to welcome and continue receiving him within the Lord with all joy, and be constantly holding such people in honor and value,**

Paul here promotes what some have called a "culture of honor." We are to value people and show them honor: they are members of the Christ; they are children of our Father.

30. **because through Christ's work** (with other MSS: on account of [the] Lord's Act) **he drew** (or: draws) **near, as far as death, with [his] soul casting himself to the side** (or: in [his] inner being handing himself over and risking [his] life; = throwing self aside, he gambled [his] life), **so that he might fill back up your deficiency** (your lack; your coming too late; = what you were unable to do) **in the area of public service toward me** (= civic sponsorship and funding me).

Here Paul gives reason for the special honor due to Epaphroditus: his courage and valor and total commitment to the work of Christ. It is significant that Paul takes this much time and space in his letter on behalf of one individual. His teachings of the work Christ are usually in universal terms, but the message also involves solidarity with each individual.

Chapter 3

1. **As for the rest** (or: For what remains), **my brothers** (= family; = fellow believers), **continue rejoicing** (be habitually glad and delighted) **within [the] Lord** [= Christ or Yahweh]. **To be repeatedly writing the same things to you** (or: To continue writing these very things for you) **[is] surely not troublesome for me** (or: delaying me or causing me to hesitate), **and for you [it is] something to secure you from stumbling.**

To be rejoicing is a familiar call from the NT writers. I suggest that this is more than saying "Keep a positive attitude in all the pressures that you face." I think that rejoicing is both a defense mechanism and an offensive tool, for it both protects our way of thinking while keeping depression at bay, and it also changes our very atmosphere.

Paul is repeating himself to them, but we all need to be reminded of where to focus and how to respond. As he says, it secures them from stumbling over offenses along their paths.

2. **Constantly keep your eyes on and be aware of the dogs** (= impudent, shameless or audacious people; scavengers without a master); **habitually be observing so as to take heed of worthless workers** (craftsmen of bad quality; laborers who are not as they ought to be); **keep on seeing so as to continually observe and be aware of [the party of] the down-cision** (the mutilation; the incision; the notching or cutting-into; the sacrificial meat-hacking; the wounding or maiming; or: = people who cut things down or off).

Here is one of the focuses: watch out for dogs. The amplified definition on this word gives the best that scholars have come up with for its metaphorical use in this time and culture, and this seems to fit the following context. We are told that the Jews called the Samaritans "dogs," and William Barclay says that there is a Rabbinic saying that classified the nations of the world as such. Paul's reference to "worthless workers" would, I suggest, be about those within the called out community who are "building upon the foundation" of Christ. Recall what he said in 1 Cor. 3:11-17 when he used the figure of "wood, hay and stubble."

In the next warning I have coined a word to express the literal elements of the Greek word, and to show the pun that Paul makes in Greek. He is referring to the Jews who were in the flesh "the circum-cision," but the word that he uses to describe them would mean "the mutilation" (such as castration), or the other meanings given in the parenthetical expansion. The meaning of "cutting off" could be a reference to his olive tree metaphor in Rom. 11:17, or the meaning of the meat-hacking could refer to animal sacrifices. He is telling them to be aware that the Jews may infiltrate them and try to turn folks back to the old covenant, or the Jewish Christians who hold to also keeping the Law may try to mix Law in with grace.

3. **For you see, we ourselves are** (exist being) **The Circumcision: the people** (or: those) **continuously rendering sacred service in a spirit of God** (or: by God's Breath-effect; to God's Spirit; with God's breath; [some MSS: service to God in spirit; *p46* omits "God," so simply: serving in spirit]) **and constantly making our boast** (being loud-tongued, vaunting and exulting) **within, and in union with, Christ Jesus; even folks** (or: those) **being people having been persuaded and thus continuing to put no confidence within flesh** (= having no reliance upon what is physical: e.g., religious works or natural heritage; or: the estranged human nature; [comment: this could be a reference to animal sacrifices]).

This is a statement of the new reality, the new covenant, the Last Adam, the New Being. We of the ethnic multitudes have been grafted into the olive tree to be producers of oil – the anointing (Rom. 11). All nations and people groups who have been born into Christ's reign are now "**The Circumcision: the people [that are] continuously rendering sacred service in a spirit of God**, or, by God's Breath-effect, or, in God's breath and to His Spirit." Paul said the same thing in Rom. 2:

> 28. **For you see, the Jew is not the one in the visibly apparent or outwardly manifest** (or: For not he in the outward appearance is a Jew), **neither [is] circumcision that [which is] visibly apparent** (outwardly manifest) **in flesh** (= in body),
> 29. **but rather, a Jew [is] the one within the hidden [place]** (or: [that which is] in the concealed [realm]), **and circumcision [is] of [the] heart in union with Breath-effect** (or: within [the] spirit), **not in letter, whose praise** (applause; full recommendation; [note play on words: Jew is a derivative of "Judah," which means "praise"]) **[is] not from out of mankind** (humanity), **but rather from out of God.**

Our boast is in Christ Jesus, not in our race or lineage – we "**put no confidence within flesh**," whether it be our nationality, our religious works, our human attributes, or (speaking of the Jewish and pagan religions) in animal sacrifices.

4. **Even though I, myself, continue holding** (or: having) **[grounds for] trust and confidence also within flesh, if any other man is in the habit of thinking** (or: is constantly seeming) **or presuming to have come to a settled persuasion, thus having confidence within [his] flesh, I to a greater degree** (more so; for a better reason; rather more):
5.   **in circumcision, on [the] eighth day;**
       out of race (from posterity; by birth; as to class or species), **of Israel;**
       of Benjamin's tribe; a Hebrew out of the midst of [the] Hebrews
       (or: = a supreme Hebrew);
       in accordance to Law, a Pharisee (or: down from custom, a Pharisee);
6.   **in accordance to zeal, one constantly pressing, pursuing and persecuting the called-out community;**
       in accordance to fairness and equity in the way pointed out in the Law, one coming to be, of myself, without defect (one becoming blameless).

In vs. 4-6 Paul lists all the things of the flesh in which he could have put confidence – in this list he demonstrates that he was an elite of the elite among Israel – but in vs. 7-8 he repudiates all this:

7. **But to the contrary, whatever things** (or: things which) **were being gains** (advantages; assets) **to, for or in me, these things I have esteemed and now consider** (or: regard) **as a loss** (a penalty; a forfeit; disadvantage; a bad bargain; a detriment) **because of the Christ** (or: on account of the Anointed One [= the Messiah]).

Here we should stop and consider: Paul had everything that many Christians today wish that they had – all the Jewish things: traditions, heritage, rituals, temple, etc. And Paul considers all this as a loss, a disadvantage, a detriment!

8. **But further – indeed, then, as a matter of fact – I even am habitually considering** (or: regarding) **all things** (all; everything) **to be a loss** (a disadvantage; a bad bargain; damage; a forfeit; a penalty) **because of** (on account of; for the sake of) **the thing that is constantly holding things above and thus having all-surpassing value and superiority: that which pertains to and comes from the experience of the intimate knowledge of my Lord, Jesus Christ** (or: of Christ Jesus, my Owner) **– on account of and for the sake of Whom I undergo loss of** (experience the forfeit of; receive as a disadvantage) **all things** (everything; the whole life-experience, environment and possessions) **and I continue considering** (or: regarding) **them to be [either] a lot of refuse and filth** (pieces of dung; a pile of manure) **[or] things that are cast away from the table to the dogs** (garbage), **to the end that I may have the advantage of Christ** (or: could maintain the gain of the Anointing; enjoy the assets of or make a profit from [Messiah]),

And why did he consider all old covenant things to be loss and a disadvantage? Because of "**the thing that is constantly holding above**" all those things: "**that which pertains to the experience of the intimate knowledge**" of Jesus Christ. Let that sink in: all outward religion, tradition and heritage are a bad bargain and a disadvantage when compared to KNOWLEDGE of Jesus Christ! And not just "head knowledge," but intimate, experiential knowledge.

Note that Paul not only considers all the Jewish things a loss to him, but as being REFUSE, filth, dung, manure, excrement – things to be cast away! The real advantage, gain, profit and asset is CHRIST!

9. **and may be found within Him** (or: in union with Him) **– not continuing having** (or: holding) **my pointed-out way** (my fairness and equity; my relationships; my basis for what is right; my own righteousness) **from out of the Law or custom, but to the contrary, the [fairness and equity which accord with the Way pointed-out] through means of Christ's faith** (or: the trust-conviction which is Christ): **the [covenant] fairness and equity in right relationships from being rightwised within the Way pointed out [which is] forth from out of the midst of God as a source [and is placed and thus based] upon that faith, confidence and trust –**

And so now having Christ, then to be "**found within Him**, and in union with Him" (where the experiential, intimate knowledge is given), and thus have nothing to do with the Law. Contrary to having the Law, is Christ's faith (or, as a genitive of apposition: the trust and faith which IS Christ) and the right relationships, fairness, equity of being rightwised (turned in the right direction) which come from the midst of God – that which is based upon Christ's faith and lives in a sphere of trust, and not upon keeping a law. This is the new Reality.

10. **to intimately and experientially know Him, and the ability – even the power – of His resurrection and also the [other MSS: a] common sharing** (participation; partnership and fellowship) **of the results and from the effects of His experiences** [note: these include good times/feelings and passions, as well as sufferings] **– being a person that is being continuously conformed to** (being progressively brought together with the form of; being habitually configured to) **His death,**

Paul returns again to what he said in vs. 8 about knowing Him, but here he adds, "**and the ability – even the power – of His resurrection**." Then he also speaks of having an experiential partnership in His experiences. These come from our union and solidarity with Christ, our being a part of Him (being His body), but also infers that He is in partnership and common sharing of our experiences as His body. Furthermore, I suggest that this union with Christ is the only way in which we can be progressively conformed to His death. It relates to our having been crucified in Him and buried with Him (Gal. 2:20; Rom. 6:4), but that spiritual reality is now existentially being lived out in our lives as we pour out our lives for others.

11. **since in some way I would arrive and meet down face-to-face unto**

(or: if somehow I can attain the level [to be] into the midst of; or: if by any means I may meet with the corresponding sphere [leading] into) **the out-resurrection** (or: the arising and standing back up again from out of the midst) – **the one forth from out of the midst of dead folks.**

It would seem that Paul is speaking of a special or different resurrection, for he adds the prefix "**out**" to the normal word for resurrection. Perhaps he was anticipating his death before the coming of a, or the, "general resurrection," and perhaps he had in mind what he had mentioned in his 1st letter to the Thessalonians, in ch. 4:14-17. Perhaps he wanted to "rise first." This may also have been what John referred to as "the first resurrection" in Rev. 20:5-6 and the symbolic reigning with Christ "a thousand years." See my comments on this passage of Rev at greater-emmanuel.org/jm. We cannot be sure, here, for he gives no explanation. However, he has brought it up in the context of being conformed to His death and the power of His resurrection, so perhaps it is unwise to stress the importance of this prefix "out." Yet, if he was referring to the spiritual resurrection that we all now experience through union with the risen Christ, why would he not also have been experiencing that at the time of writing this letter?

In a discussion with Don Luther and Steve Dohse on vs. 10-11, I was reminded of what Jesus said in John 12:24. He had just said, in vs. 23, that the hour had come when the Son of man could be glorified – referring to His death and resurrection. Then He says, "... **unless the grain of wheat** (or: kernel of corn; = seed of an agricultural crop), **falling into the earth** (the ground; the field), **should die, it, by itself, continues remaining alone. Yet if it should die, it proceeds to bear much fruit** (= it produces a harvest of many grains, or, seeds)." This is a picture of an "**out-resurrection**," where the plant arises and stands back up, out from among the other dead, or dying seeds. It is a resurrection that yields a harvest. The power and ability of His resurrection (vs. 10, above) is that it produces life for others. Paul wants his death, and ensuing resurrection, to produce a crop – the seed of Life in many others. And so it has! His words via his letters have given life to, and in, countless millions for almost 2000 years.

12. **Not that I already take it by the hand** [*p*46 & D add: or already have been rightwised and made to be one in accord with the Way pointed out with fairness and equity] **or have been already brought to the purposed goal and destiny** (matured unto perfection and finished), **yet I am consistently pursuing** (running swiftly in order to catch), **since I would** (or: if I could) **take down by the hand** (seize; forcefully grasp and gain control over) **even [that] upon which I also was** (or: am) **taken down by hand** (seized; forcefully grasped and taken control of) **by and under [the control of] Christ Jesus.**

Paul wanted to continue growing in the Life of Christ until his seeds were fully ready for harvest. His focus was to push on to the goal. He had been apprehended by the fullness of Christ, and now he wanted to apprehend that same fullness. Christ had taken Paul down, by His hand, forcefully grasping him, and taking control of him. This had freed Paul, so that now he could in turn run swiftly in order to catch hold of Christ and the full Anointing. He returns here to the stadium games metaphor. This is how Paul viewed living a life in Christ. Because of being within Him and in union with Him, there is more to be gained. The life in Christ is not static.

13. **Brothers** (= Fellow believers; = [My] family)**! I am not** [other MSS: not yet] **calculating** (logically considering; reckoning) **myself to have taken it down by hand** (seized, grasped or gotten hold of it in order to have it), **yet [there is] one thing: habitually forgetting, on the one hand, the things behind** (or: in the back), **and on the other hand constantly reaching and stretching myself out upon the things in front** (or: ahead),
14. **I am continuously pursuing down toward** [the; or: an] **object in view** (a mark on which the eye is fixed): **into the prize of God's** (or: the award which is God's) **invitation to an above place** (or: an upward calling having the source from, with qualities and characteristics of, God) **within the midst of and in union with Christ Jesus.**

Vs. 13 seems to repeat vs. 12, though with some different expressions and the addition of forgetting the past and reaching for the future. He was forgetting everything listed in vss. 4-6, above, as well as the former covenant and the Law. Then in vs. 14 he specifies what he is reaching for: the prize which is God's invitation to an above place, etc., and this place is "**within the midst of, and in union with, Christ Jesus**."

But with the genitive of the word "**invitation**" not rendered in apposition, "**the prize of God's invitation**" may be seen as the result of God's invitation, and be the same prize that Paul refers to in 1 Cor. 9:24 (the only other place where this word is used in the NT),

> "**Have you folks not seen, so as to know, that those progressively running, on the race-course within a stadium, are indeed all progressively running** (or: constantly and repeatedly racing), **yet one normally** (= each time) **grasps** (takes; receives) **the prize** (victor's award)**? Be habitually running** (progressively racing) **so that you folks can** (may; would) **seize and take [it] down in your hands**."

This prize may well be the fruit of his ministry, those to whom he gave himself, or as he says elsewhere, "**[his] glory**" (1 Thes. 2:20), and below in ch. 4:1 he refers to them as his "**winner's wreath**."

15. **Therefore – as many as [are] people who are mature** (ones who have reached the goal, being finished and complete) **– we should constantly be of this frame of mind** (have this attitude and opinion; think this way; be minding and paying attention to this). **And if you folks are habitually thinking differently** (are continuing differently minded; are continually having a different attitude or opinion), **God will also unveil this to you** (or: uncover and reveal, or disclose, this in you).

Paul is saying that we should think just as he did – as expressed in the previous verses. We should be pursuing down toward the object in view: whatever we perceive the goal to be, the prize of God's upward call in Christ Jesus. He is addressing this admonition to folks who are mature in Christ, who are aware of the finished and complete work of Christ. He encourages us to have the attitude and mind-set that he described in vss. 13-14. He is also confident that God will eventually bring everyone to this opinion so as to be minding this. Their hearts and minds will at some point be unveiled (*cf* 2 Cor. 3:14-16 for a parallel example).

16. **Moreover, into that which we precede [others]** (or: into what we went before in; into what we come ahead so as to arrive at; = unto whatever stage we have reached) **in the very same thing [our goal is] to be habitually drawn into a straight line and consistently advance within our ranks**

> [Aleph2 and other MSS add phrases to read as follows: Besides, into what we outstrip {others}, by the same standard (measuring rod; rule) {it is for us} to habitually advance in line (i.e., frame our conduct in an orderly routine; or: consider the elements and observe the rudimentary principles by the same standard) – to constantly be intent on and keep thinking of the same thing (or: be of the same frame of mind and attitude)].

I suggest that Paul is continuing to use the racecourse metaphor here, especially in the first text. Wherever we are in this race, to whatever lap around the track we have attained, or mile marker we have reached, stay in your lane. Within whatever group you are moving, be consistent, stay with it and advance in your proper position.

In the Aleph 2 text he first seems to be advising competing by the rules, which include staying in your own line and be orderly while keeping in mind the elements of the game. The last part speaks to keeping your focus and being single-minded. Our thinking and our attitude, or frame of mind, are oft-repeated topics in Paul's writings. How we think, and what attitude we entertain is an important aspect of kingdom living.

17. **Brothers** (= Fellow believers; = My family), **be progressively birthed to be joint-imitators of me** (or: unite in becoming my imitators), **and continually keep a watchful eye on and take**

note of those habitually walking about thus (i.e., those who thus live their lives), **according as you folks continue having us as a pattern** (model; example; type).

Here he advises using him as a role model and pattern. Do the same with other believers who live their lives in this same manner – learn from them and become as they are. This would include: to consider things of the flesh and religion (vs. 4-6) to be a loss and as dung (vs. 7-8); to gain Christ and be found in Him (vs. 8-9); to know Him and the power of His resurrection while being progressively conformed to His death (vs. 10) and then arrive at the "**out-resurrection**" (vs. 11) and apprehend that for which they are apprehended (vs. 12); to continuously pursue the prize of His calling in Christ (vs. 14) – and to continue with this mind-set (vs. 15), while playing by the rules of the kingdom (vs. 16).

18. **For many – I was often telling you about them, yet now I am also presently weeping** (lamenting) **in saying it – continue walking about** (i.e., are living their lives) **as enemies of the cross of the Christ** (the Anointed One's execution-stake),

We might think of many examples of such lives, but for Paul I think the main enemy was the person who tried to get people to return to Judaism – to the Law and the old covenant – or, as vs. 19 says, people that are focused on the carnal rather than the spiritual.

19. **whose goal** (eventual end; closing act; final stage; result; finished discharge) **[is] ruin and loss** (or: waste and destruction), **whose god [is their] cavity** (or: belly) **and [whose] reputation** (or: glory; opinion) **resides within their shame** (disgrace; embarrassment) – **people continually thinking about** (habitually being intent on; constantly minding) **the things existing upon the earth** (or: = folks whose minds are earthbound).

If in vs. 18 he was referring to Judaizers, then he may here be saying that their eventual end will be the same as Jerusalem: waste and destruction in AD 70. Instead of focusing on the Jerusalem above – the freewoman – they were focused on the then existing earthly Jerusalem and Mt. Sinai, the Law (Gal. 4:22-31).

20. **For you see, our citizenship** (result of living in a free city; or: commonwealth-effects; political realm) **continues inherently existing** (or: continues humbly ruling; continuously subsists; repeatedly has its under-beginning) **resident within the midst of [the] atmospheres** (or: heavens), **from out of where** (or: which place) **we also continuously receive and take away in our hands from out of a Deliverer** (a Savior; One restoring us to the health and wholeness of our original state and condition)**: [the] Lord** (or: a Master), **Jesus Christ,**

This first clause corresponds to Gal. 4:26, the free city "which is above." This is a figure of the called-out community, and it is from within these folks that we are able to "**continuously receive and take away in our hands from out of a Deliverer**," our Savior, Jesus Christ, who lives with His people, who are His temple. We constantly receive life, health, healing, deliverance and sustenance from Him through His community. They perform as a paraclete to those in need.

John saw our present situation pictured in a vision of the new heaven, the new Jerusalem, in Rev. 21:1-4 and our current ministry to others, described in 22-27. See my article "A New Heavens and A New Earth" at www.greater-emmanuel.org/jm.

21. **Who will be actively transfiguring** (progressively refashioning and remodeling; continuously changing the form of) **our body from the low condition and status** (or: the body of our humiliation; or: the body which is us, pertaining to this lowliness) **into the [situation] for it to be birthed conformed to the body of His glory** (or: be brought into existence having the same form together with His body, from that which calls forth praise; [with other MSS: joint-formed by and with the body of His good reputation]), **down from** (or: in accord with; in the sphere of; along the lines of; to the level of; following the pattern of; stepping along with; commensurate with; following the bidding of; as directed by) **the inward operation** (energy; in-working) **of the**

[conditions or situation for] Him to be continuously able (or: with power) **also to humbly align The Whole to and in Himself** (or: to subject and subordinate all things for Himself; to arrange everything under so as to have full control and to support [it] by and with Himself).

Christ, by His Spirit (Who/Which also dwells within His called-out folks) and by His Word, will be progressively refashioning, remodeling and transfiguring our body from the humiliation, to be conformed to the body of His glory. This is what happens as we walk the Path within Him who is the Way. We have much to anticipate as we live our lives here. Now the first question that we need to ask is, What body is it to which he is referring? Is it our individual physical body, or is it the corporate body of Christ? Reading the personal pronoun as in the genitive of apposition, it reads "the body which is us." His body is a corporate body (1 Cor. 12:12) and this is the body of His glory (Christ in you the expectation of glory – Col. 1:27). Recall John 17:22,

> **"And I, Myself, have given to them** (or: in them), **and they now possess, the glory** (the notion; the opinion; the imagination; the reputation; the manifestation which calls forth praise) **which You have given to Me, and which I now possess, to the end that they may continuously exist being one correspondingly as** (just as; according as; on the same level as; in the same sphere as) **We [are] one."**

That glory was not an outward glory, but an inward one, just as His working is an inward one. It was the glory that the Father had given to Him, which He then possessed, but could not be seen outwardly.

The words "**down from**" is the Greek *kata*, which as you see has a broad semantic range. If we use the meaning of "in the sphere of," this corresponds to His inward working – where the transfiguration and remodeling takes place. The meaning "along the lines of" says the same thing. It is not an outward, physical transformation, but an inward one – of which he is here speaking.

In vs. 10, above, Paul made reference to having the power of His resurrection. Let us look in 1 Cor. 15 where he also speaks of bodies, resurrection and Christ:

> 42. **Thus also** (or: In this way too) **[is] the resurrection of the dead people. It is habitually** (repeatedly; presently; one after another) **being sown within corruption** (or: in union with decay and ruin; in perishability); **it is being habitually** (or: presently; repeatedly; one after another) **awakened and raised up within incorruption** (non-decayability; imperishableness).
> 43. **It is constantly being sown within dishonor** (in union with lack of value; in the midst of worthlessness), **it is being habitually** (or: repeatedly; constantly; one after another; progressively) **awakened and raised up within, and in union with, power and ability.**
> 44. **It is habitually** (continually; repeatedly; presently) **being sown a body having the qualities and characteristics of a soul** (a soulish body; or: = a body animated by soul); **it is habitually** (repeatedly; constantly; presently; one after another) **being awakened and raised up a spiritual body** (a body having the qualities and characteristics of the Breath-effect). **Since there is a soulish body** (or: = body animated by soul), **there also is** (or: exists) **a spiritual one** (or: = one animated by spirit).
> [comment: note the germinal connection between the two – they are a progression of the same body]
> 45. **Thus also** (or: In this way also), **it has been written, "The first human** (or: man), **Adam, came for existence** (or: was birthed) **into [being] a living soul"** [Gen. 2:7]; **the Last Adam into [being] a continuously life-making** (life-engendering; life-creating; life-giving) **Spirit** (or: Breath-effect).

Now note the connection of resurrection with power, in vs. 43. Next, in vs. 44, we see that it is "**being awakened and raised up A SPIRITUAL BODY.**" Then he tells us that there is a natural body that pertains to the soul – the one which is sown – and there is a spiritual one – the one that is resurrected, and consider my note that this is a progression of the same body. It is like the seed that fell into the ground that I referred to, above (vs. 11 comments). Note also the present tense of the verbs: habitually, repeatedly, constantly, presently, one-after-another. This, again, is an ongoing process that was happening in Paul's day, as it has ever since the resurrection of Jesus.

Now note vs. 45 which Paul is relating both to resurrection and to the two bodies. We have the first human, Adam (the soulish person) and we have the Last Adam Who is a continuously life-making, life-creating, life-giving Spirit. The resurrected person is a spirit. This is the spiritual body (the "**afterwards**" person of vs. 46). The first Adam was corporate humanity, in this context; the Last Adam is the corporate spiritual body of Christ, with Jesus as its Head.

Now let us look further in 1 Cor. 15,

47. **The first human** (person; man) **[was/is] forth from out of the earth** (land; ground; soil; dirt), **made of moist soil and mud** (or: having the quality and characteristics of moist dirt that can be poured; soilish), **the Second Human** (Person; Man) **[is made] of heaven** (or: sky; atmosphere).

48. **As [is] the person made of and having the character and quality of moist soil or mud** (pourable dirt; soil), **of such sort also [are] the people [who are] made of and have the character and quality of moist soil or mud** (soilish folks); **and likewise, as [is] the Heavenly Person** (or: the one made of and having the quality and character of the supra-heaven), **of such sort also [are] the supra-heavenly people – those made of and having the quality and character of the supra-heaven** (or: finished and perfected atmosphere).

49. **And correspondingly as we bear and wear the image of the dusty person,** [p46 adds: doubtless] **we can and should** [B reads: will] **also bear and wear the image of the supra-heavenly One** (or: the One having the quality and character of the finished and perfected atmosphere).

Vs. 48-49 describe humans transfigured to be conformed to His body of glory, and vs. 47 tells us that they are "[**made] of heaven**/atmosphere," this latter being parallel to the "**made of moist soil and mud**" of the first clause. The "**made of heaven**" is a figure for the spiritual. Having the quality and character of the supra-heaven and wearing His image is equivalent to being conformed to the body of His glory.

And then there is 1 Cor. 15:51, which answers to vs. 10, above,

51. **See** (Look and consider)! **I am progressively telling you a secret** ([the] mystery)! **We, indeed, shall not all be laid to sleep [in death], yet we all will be changed**
> (or: On the one hand, not all of us will be made to [die], but on the other hand, we all will be altered; or: We all shall not be put to repose, and so we all shall be transformed; or: All of us shall not sleep, but we all will be rearranged to be another or made to be otherwise),

And then,

53. **For it continues being necessary** (it is habitually binding) **for this perishable and corruptible to instantly plunge** (or: sink) **in and clothe itself with** (or: slip on; put on) **incorruption and imperishability, and for this mortal** (one that is subject to death) **to instantly plunge and sink in and clothe itself with** (or: put on; slip on as a garment) **immortality** (deathlessness; undyingness).

This sounds very much like 2 Cor. 5:

1. **For we have seen, and thus know, that if our house of the tabernacle, which is pitched on the land, would at some point be dismantled** (or: that whenever our house, which is the tent upon the earth, should be loosed down), **we constantly have** (continuously hold; presently possess) **a structure** (a building) **forth from out of the midst of God: an eonian house** (a house having the qualities and character which pertain to the Age; a house for the ages) **– not made by hands – within the midst of the heavens** (or: resident within the atmospheres).

> 2. **For you see, even within this one we are continuously groaning, utterly longing and constantly yearning to fully enter within and to clothe upon ourselves** (to dress upon ourselves) **our dwelling-house** (habitation) **– the one [made] out of heaven** (or: from, or made of, atmosphere)**.**

Consider in vs. 1-2 here, that we continuously and presently have and possess this house/clothing. But looking at a couple more verses in 1 Cor. 15, we see another interesting aspect of what we now possess.

> 54. **Now whenever this mortal instantly plunges and sinks in and then clothes itself with** (or: slips on; puts on) **the Immortality, then will come into existence** (will be birthed; will take place) **the word** (the thought; the idea; the message; the saying) **which has been written,**
> **"The Death was drunk down and swallowed into Victory** (or: overcoming)**!"** [Isa. 25:8]

And then,

> 57. **But grace and joyous favor [is] in God** (or: by God) **– the One presently and progressively giving the Victory** (or: the overcoming) **to us, in us and for us through our Lord** (Owner; Master), **Jesus, [the] Christ!**

So we now have and possess the Victory – God has given it to us – that drank down and swallowed the Death. This is the final way of being conformed to His death (vs. 10, above), which ended in victory (the "out-resurrection" of vs. 11, above). Now this was a corporate event that coincided with His resurrection – and this was all the result of "**the inward operation** (energy; in-working) **of the [conditions or situation for] Him to continuously be able** (or: have power) **also to humbly align** (or: to subject; to subordinate; to arrange under so as to have full control of and support) **The Whole** (or: all things; everything) **in Himself** (to Himself; for Himself; by and with Himself)."

He is able to align the whole of humanity – as well as the whole universe – "in Himself, to Himself, for Himself, by Himself, and with Himself!" He refashions the whole body of humanity, as well as the universe (the new creation in Christ), to be birthed conformed to the body of His glory.

John Gavazzoni has shared this insightful summation on this topic:
"In my opinion, when we get into Paul's head, we find that he considers there to be only 'one body,' and proceeding from that premise, he understands our individual bodies to be members of that one body. Our individual transformation can come about in relationship to the corporate body.

"I'm with you also on the matter of the relationship of the natural body to the spiritual body as one of procession. The spiritual body lies within the natural body as its intrinsic constitution. As I've pointed out a number of times, the corruptible 'it' that is planted in death, and the incorruptible 'it' that emerges in resurrection life, are the same 'it.'

"The natural body is not discarded in favor of the spiritual body, the spiritual body emerges out from within the natural, even from within its darkness. The body of Jesus of Nazareth, and the body of Christ, are the same body.

"The body of Jesus, would then be the Seed/DNA form of the ultimately emerged corporate body of Christ. All that He is becomes finally the reality of us all together united in Him."

Chapter 4

1. **Consequently, my brothers** (= fellow believers; family) **– loved ones and longed-for folks** (people missed with a craving), **my joy and winner's** (or: festal) **wreath – thus** (in this way) **you**

constantly stand within [the] Lord [= Christ or Yahweh]**: [as or being] loved ones!** (or, as an imperative: be habitually standing firm in thus manner: in [the] Lord, [B adds: my] beloved!)

The word "**Consequently**" refers back to what Paul had just been saying in the last part of ch. 3. Remember that this was a letter, and chapter breaks are an artificial addition to the text. Here, again, Paul expresses his emotional connection with those in Philippi, and here reveals that they themselves are the prize (winner's wreath) to which he referred in 3:14. He spoke of those in Thessalonica as his "glory and joy" (1 Thes. 2:20).

The form of the verb "stand" is either indicative or imperative, so I have given renderings as both. Paul is either affirming that fact that their stand is in the Lord, and thus by the Lord, or he is admonishing to stand firm in Him, as beloved ones. Either text makes sense in reference to their continued relationship to Him.

2. **I am calling Euodia alongside, and I am calling Syntyche alongside, admonishing** (entreating; begging; assisting) **[you two] to be habitually thinking about the same thing** (minding and being intent on the same thing; disposed in the same way; = agreeing and maintaining a common mind), **within, and in union with, the Lord.**

Here he calls for union of thought, disposition, and focus, or he is calling for these two women to be in agreement. This may be in reference to a situation, or some "drama," of which he was aware but did not mention here, or to the fact that he knew that they often had different points of view and he is admonishing unity between them.

3. **Yes, I am asking you, too, O genuine and legitimate yokefellow** (or: O loyal Synzugus; O Suzugos, one born in wedlock; O paired star who rises as I set; O joined and united one belonging to [my] birth group), **be consistently taking these women together to yourself to aid and assist them – which women toil together with me** (or: compete [as] in the public games along with me, and contend on my side) **within the message of goodness and well-being** (good news), **with Clement and the rest of my fellow workers, whose names [are] within Life's Book** (or: in a book of life; a book which is Life; [comment: = participation in life]).

The word normally translated "**yokefellow**" could also have been the name of a person (Barclay notes that some have suggested that this "helper," who was a "genuine or legitimate helper," could have been Paul's wife, to which he was yoked [ibid, p. 74], but the word is in the masculine form), so I have also rendered it as such since he had just referred to these two women in the previous verse and uses the word "and/also" just before this phrase. He is asking Synzugus (or: Suzugos) to be consistently giving these women help, especially since they "contend and compete, [as] in the public games" (Paul's sports metaphor to characterize the life in Christ as a striving for excellence, as is used in ch. 2:16, 3:14, and the "winner's wreath" in vs. 1, above, as well as in 1 Cor. 9:24, 26; Gal. 2:2; 5:7; Heb. 12:1) alongside of him and the other "fellow workers" (now changing metaphors), in the work of the good news. It is worthy of note that these women are on a par with the men in the work of the message of goodness, as well as in the striving for excellence.

Life's book, or a book of life, or a book which is Life, is most likely a metaphor for participation in the life of Christ. In those days cities had a registry of those who were their citizens, and since Paul has used the metaphor of "the Jerusalem which is above" as being the mother of believers (see Gal. 4), this is likely a reference to such.

4. **Be constantly rejoicing within, and in union with, [the] Lord** [= in Yahweh or in Christ], **at all times** (or: always)! **Again, I will declare it, Rejoice** (or: You folks be habitually rejoicing)!

The fact that he emphasizes that they should be constantly rejoicing within Christ, and in union with Christ, suggests that they may have had constant reasons for which a carnal person would be depressed or complain. Here he is not saying that they are continuously happy, but rather he is admonishing them to be rejoicing in Christ, even if their situations or conditions are hard.

5. **Let your gentle fairness, lenience, considerateness and suitable reasonableness be intimately and experientially known to all mankind** (or: by and for all humans). **The Lord** [= Christ or Yahweh] **is near** (close by – at hand, close enough to touch, and available)**!**

What a picture of Christ we are to show to the world: gentle fairness and suitable reasonableness – which is to be intimately and experientially made known to them. This means through personal interaction with everyone with whom we have contact. Through means of this, they will know that the Lord is near – that they can touch Him by touching us, and that He is available to them.

6. **Do not be habitually worried, anxious or overly concerned about anything! On the contrary, in everything** (and: within every situation), **by thinking and speaking toward goodness and having things go well and with ease** (or: in prayer) **and in expression of need – together with thanksgiving – repeatedly let your requests be made known to** (toward; face to face with) **God,**

Within every situation, and in every area of our lives, by thinking and speaking toward goodness and having things going well we can avert worry and concern. In expressing our needs to Him, we can rid ourselves of anxiety. Expression of gratitude to our Father should flavor our moods. We have direct access (*pros*, which also means "fact to face") to God and we can repeatedly make requests of Him, and express to Him our need. We are in conciliated relationship to our Father.

7. **and God's peace** (= shalom; or: and so the harmony which is God), **which is continuously having a hold over** (is habitually holding sway over; or: is constantly being superior and excelling by having it over) **all mind and inner sense** (or: every intellect; all power of comprehension; or: all process of thinking), **will garrison** (guard; stand sentinel over) **your hearts and the results of thinking** (thoughts; reasonings; understandings; effects from directing the mind on something; or: dispositions; designs; purposes; effects of perceptions; [*p*16 adds: and bodies]), **within, and in union with, Christ Jesus** [*p*46: {the} Lord Jesus].

By following Paul's advice in vs. 6, God's peace – which continuously has a hold over our mind and inner senses – will garrison our hearts and reasonings, and will stand guard over our designs and purposes. His peace habitually holds sway over us, because we are within Him. Our union with Jesus guards the core of our being and His peace is superior to the effects of our thinking and perceptions. Once again, it is our relationship to Jesus that gives us this – not just our awareness of who we are. And as *p*46 reads, it is a relationship of Him being Lord.

8. **In conclusion** (or: Finally; or: What [is] left), **brothers** (= fellow believers; [my] family), **as much as is true** (or: as many things as are genuine and real), **as many as [are] awe-inspiring** (serious; respectable; noble; dignified by holiness), **as much as [is] rightwised** (put right; fair, equitable; just; in right relationship within the Way pointed out), **as many as [are] pure and innocent, as much as [is] affection-inducing** (friendly; directed toward what is liked; lovable or lovely; agreeable; well-regarded; winsome; engendering fondness; attractive; kindly disposed; loveable), **as many as [are] well-spoken-of** (commendable; reputable; of good report; the effect of fair speaking; renowned), **if [there is] any excellence and nobleness** (virtues of braveness, courage, good character, quality, self-restraint, magnificence, benevolence, reliability) **[in them] and if [there is] any praise applied** (expression of high evaluation; honor paid; approval or applause) **[to them], be habitually thinking about these things in a logical way** (repeatedly make these things the focus of careful consideration and analysis; continuously take these things into account)**!**

What an admonition for life! These things should be our focus – and on such things we should make careful consideration and analysis, habitually thinking logically about the following:

1) things that are true, real and genuine
2) things that are awe-inspiring, serious, noble and dignified
3) things that point in the right direction (toward Christ, Who is the Way pointed out), and are in relationships that are fair, equitable and just
4) things that are pure, having no mix of ulterior motive
5) things that induce affection, are friendly and loveable, etc.
6) things that are commendable and have a good reputation
7) things that are excellent and noble, along with the virtues parenthetically listed
8) things that evoke approval and high evaluation

We see nothing negative in that list. These things engender peace and love, and keep us in a healthful mind. May we clothe our minds and hearts with the soldier's equipment which is God, of which Paul spoke in Eph. 6:11-17, as a defense against all the negative which the world systems throw at us.

9. **Keep on practicing and accomplishing these things which you folks both learn and accept** (or: learned and received alongside) – **even [what] you heard and saw within me. And, the God of the Peace** (or: And God, the source and quality of peace [= shalom]; Then the God which is harmony) **will enter into an existence in company with you folks – and will be with you folks.**

The "**practicing and accomplishing**" simply speaks of a way of life, a mode of being. It refers to the teaching, the message, becoming internalized. When this happens, "**the God of the Peace** (Christ) **will enter into an existence in company with [us] – and will be with [us]**."

10. **Now I greatly rejoice** (or: rejoiced) **within the Lord** [= in union with Christ or Yahweh] **that now, at last, you folks shoot up to flourish to the extent to be constantly focusing your thinking over me** (to continuously have my concerns intently in mind; to repeatedly take thought on my behalf) **– upon which, also, you folks were progressively thinking, yet you continued without a fitting situation** (you were being out of season; you kept on lacking the opportunity).

Paul rejoices to see their growth in the Lord, to the point of focusing their thinking away from themselves – and in this case upon Paul's needs. He notes their progress, but is also aware of their lack of opportunity to express it.

11. **Not that I am suggesting a need, for I learned and so know to be self-sufficient** (to be contented by warding-off my own [needs]; or: to have independent provisions) **within whatever circumstances or situations [that] I am.**

In speaking of being "**self-sufficient**," I suggest that Paul is not here saying that he does not depend upon God, but rather that he is not relying upon others when he can be "warding-off [his] own [needs]." The phrase was used of those who had "independent means," but I think that Paul is using the word to mean working at a "side job" or finding ways or situations in which to secure food and shelter, especially considering the next verse.

12. **I am aware of [what it is like] to be repeatedly made low [on provisions], as well as aware of [what it is like] to be continuously surrounded by more than enough**
(or: I have seen, and thus know, both to be humbled, and I have seen, and thus know, to be constantly and excessively abounding). **I have been instructed to shut the mouth, and I am initiated into the secret** (or: mystery): **within everything and within the midst of all things** (or: among all people), **both to be** (or: [how] to be) **habitually feeding until satisfied, and to be** (or: as well as [how] to be) **habitually hungry; both to be** (or: [how] to be) **constantly and excessively abounding** (continuously surrounded by more than enough), **and to be** (or: as well as [how] to be) **repeatedly in need** (or: lacking).

There are two possible thoughts in the Greek of the first couplet. The first refers to the opposite situations of being low on provisions or having more than enough, in way of provisions. The second thought, expressed in the parenthetical rendering, would refer to the experience of having been humbled, as contrasted to having everything go well, and be continuously abounding in spirit and good reputation.

He goes on in the next couplets explaining **the secret** which he had learned (a technical term which means to be initiated into the "mysteries," or "secrets") about life, and these apply to every situation and to being among all people:
1) to experience being habitually feeding until satisfied – and what that is like
2) to experience being habitually hungry – and what that feels like.
With both extremes a person can also learn how to handle the moral pitfall of the one, and how to deal with the realities of the other.

3) to experience having excessive abundance – and what that is like
4) to experience being repeatedly in need, or having constant lack – and what that is like.
With #3 it takes wisdom and a moral compass to successfully handle wealth, and be aware of what such can do to a person.
With #4 it takes both wisdom to know how to survive, and fortitude to deal with the emotional stresses that this condition brings. Paul knows how to handle both the calm and the storm, both the feast and the famine.

13. **I constantly have strength for all things among all people, [from being] in union with and within the midst of the One continuously enabling me** (empowering me; infusing me with power and ability)**: Christ!**

Christ is the One that was continuously enabling and empowering Paul to handle all of the extremes that he noted in vs. 12, and all things in between. This was because he was both in union with Christ, and lived within the midst of Him, and this gave him strength for all.

14. **Moreover you folks performed beautifully** (acted ideally; did virtuously; produced finely), **sharing** (partnering; participating; having common association) **together with me in my pressure** (squeezing; tribulation; trouble; oppression).

Paul commends their performance and behavior in being a part of that through which he went. He calls them his partners, etc., of his squeezing oppression, trouble and tribulation. And they had acted ideally and virtuously through these situations.

15. **Now you Philippians have seen, and thus are aware** (or: know), **that within the original period** (or: the beginning) **of the message of goodness, ease and well-being** (good news), **when I went** (or: came) **out from Macedonia, not one called-out community shared** (communicated; participated; partnered; held common association) **with me** (or: for me), **[leading] into a discourse** (or: with regard to an account or a matter of discussion; = injecting a thought) **of giving and of receiving** (or: of getting; of taking), **except you folks, alone** (or: only), 16. **because even in Thessalonica both once, and twice!, you folks sent [provision] into my need.**

Paul gives recognition of their sharing with him by giving support and sending provision, from the beginning of his ministry – and that they were the only community that did so. They thus became his partners, and had brought up the practical thought of giving to him, and of his receiving assistance.

17. **Not that I am in the habit of really seeking the gift! But rather, I am in the habit of really seeking the constantly abounding fruit which is overflowing into your discourse** (or: your account; your word; your matter of discussion; your message; your thought).

He gives a disclaimer, and then points out his goal. He uses the same phrase here that he used in vs. 15 about a "**discourse** (Greek *logos*), account or matter of thought." This can be considered a metaphor for what in our day we call a "bank account," but I suggest that Paul is seeking the fruit of "giving and receiving" in all areas of their lives, which includes their "thoughts, ideas and communications," as well as in their sharing the "message" of Christ. His goal is abundant fruit of the Spirit in their lives – as well as provision and sustenance.

18. **But now I am continually holding possessions from** (collecting; or: = receiving payment for what is due me from) **all things and from all folks; I am even constantly superabounding** (being surrounded by more than enough). **I have been filled full, receiving from beside Epaphroditus the things from your side: an odor of a sweet fragrance** (a fragrant aroma), **an acceptable sacrifice, well-pleasing to God** (or: with God; for God; in God).

Recall that Epaphroditus was sent from Philippi with provisions for Paul. So now he has been receiving from all people, and from all situations, and he possesses a superabundance. He sees their gifts as comparable to offering incense or a perfumed sacrifice, as in the days of religious ritual, but now in the new reality. He affirms that this is "**well-pleasing to God**, or in God."

19. **So my God will fill to the full your every need** (or: will make full all lack which pertains to you folks) **down from His wealth [being] within [the] glory [that resides] within Christ Jesus**
  (or: that accords to His wealth that resides within the opinion or imagination [which is] within Christ Jesus; to the level of His riches, within a manifestation of splendor which calls forth praise, within Christ Jesus; down through His abundance, within the reputation [arising from] within the midst of Christ Jesus; in the sphere of and in line with His riches [which are] in union with a glory resident within an anointing from Jesus).

Even as they have been so faithful in their giving, Paul assures them that, just so, God, down from His own wealth, will supply for all of their own needs. The three prepositional phrases that conclude this verse are presented in the parenthetical expansion, in their multiple possible renderings. Consider the nuances of the semantic ranges which both the prepositions and the nouns offer.

20. **Now in our God and Father [is] the glory**
  (or: Now for our God and Father [is] the reputation; Yet by our God and Father [is] the manifestation which calls forth praise; So to our God and Father [is] the good opinion; But with our God and Father [is] the imagination) **on into the indefinite and unseen time periods of the ages! Count on it, for it is so!**

Paul is referring to the glory that he spoke of in vs. 19. It is resident in God, but it is also for God and to God. It also comes by God. These different prepositional renderings come from the possible functions of the dative case, and I have given them all since they all make good sense, and there is no expressed preposition in the text.

Note also the semantic range of the Greek *doxa*, which is normally only translated as "**glory**." When joining this verse to the promised supply in vs. 19, consider the affirmation that "with our God and Father [is] the imagination" for creating this supply. Imagination is often an overlooked gift, but it is a part of "**the glory**."

Also keep in mind that Christ is God's glory... on into the ages of the ages, and we can count on this, for it is so (an expanded rendering of "Amen.")

21. **You folks gladly greet and embrace as a dear one every set-apart person** (every holy one; every saint) **within Christ Jesus. The brothers** (= fellow believers; = the family) **with me are habitually greeting and warmly embracing you folks.**

The word Paul uses for "**greet**" (sometimes rendered "salute"), means to give a warm and affectionate embrace, as to someone who is very dear to us. Those with Paul are by this word, and in their spirits, embracing those at Philippi. It is an expression of love, not just a "greeting."

22. **All those set-apart are habitually greeting and warmly embracing you folks – yet especially those of Caesar's house** (= household).

Paul had brought the message of goodness to the household of Caesar, where he was imprisoned, in Rome. Through his ministry to them, they had apparently come to have a great love for the faithful folks in Philippi. Such goodwill coming from Caesar's household speaks much in regard to the influence of Paul on the city of Rome.

Another thought that comes from Paul mentioning this is that this could also be showing Paul's attitude of solidarity between himself, along with those assisting him, and those of Caesar's staff – considering himself and those with him to be a part of the group with whom he lived, although being in chains.

23. **The grace of** (or: The favor belonging to and having its source in; The grace which is) **our Lord** [with other MSS: the Owner and Master], **Jesus Christ, [is] with the spirit of you folks** (or: [is] with your corporate breath-effect; or: [is] with the character and attitude manifested through you folks; [other MSS: {is} with all of you]). **It is so!**

As elsewhere, Paul affirms to them that the Lord's grace is with them, giving a characteristic exclamation with the word "**It is so** (Amen)!" It is interesting that he says "**with the spirit of you folks**." He notes and acknowledges that their community has a spirit of grace, a "character and attitude" which manifests favor towards others.

I am here inserting a short study on ch. 2:7 for a metaphorical consideration of:

WHAT WAS "THE FORM OF A SERVANT"?

In chapter two we read:
7. **but to the contrary, He empties Himself** (or: removed the contents of Himself; made Himself empty), **receiving** (or: taking; accepting) **a slave's form** (external shape; outward mold), **coming to be** (or: birthing Himself) **within humanity's** (mankind's; peoples') **likeness.**
8. **And so, being found in a present condition and outward appearance** (or: fashion) **as a human** (a person; a man), **He lowers Himself** (or: humbled Himself; made Himself low; degrades Himself; levels Himself off), **coming to be** (or: birthing Himself) **a submissive, obedient One** (one who gives the ear and listens) **as far as** (or: to the point of; until) **death – but death of a cross** (torture stake)**!**

There is much to ponder and consider in this passage, but I want to focus on the phrase "a slave's form," or, as the KJV reads, "the form of a servant." My question is: was this an ontological statement referring to His incarnation, or was it a functional statement referring to social status and realm of operation?

When Jesus washed the feet of His disciples He was doing the work of a slave (John 13:4-17). In Lu. 22:27, Jesus said, "**Yet I Myself am in your midst as the person constantly giving attending service.**"

Yet in John 13:13 Jesus said "**You address me 'The Teacher,' and 'The Lord** (Master; Owner),' **and you folks are speaking ideally, for thus I am** (exist being)." So if He was existing being Lord, Master, Owner, was He existing being – was His ontological existence – a slave?

The social and relational existence of humanity was "dominion" and of being a subjector – Gen. 1:28. And then there is Ps. 8:5-6, "... crowned him with glory and honor and set him over the works of Your hands. You have put all things under his feet." So for Jesus to become human, via incarnation, was not necessarily to "take the form of a slave." To what, then, did this phrase refer, in regard to Jesus and His life here on earth?

Did it mean that He was in a place of less glory when living as Jesus? From what He said about His former glory with the Father (John 17:5), and what He asked His Father to give Him (vs. 1, 5), and from what was seen in Him as the resurrected Christ, then I would say, Yes, prior to resurrection He lived having less glory than before and after that incarnation. But in vs. 22 He also said that He had given to the disciples the same "**glory which You gave to Me**." So this was not necessarily a factor of His ontological existence – as differing from the rest of humanity.

So to what was Paul referring, about a slave's form, in our opening passage?

In Gal. 4:25, Paul says,
> "**Now this Hagar is** (= represents) **Mount Sinai, within Arabia, and she continuously stands in the same line** (row; rank; = corresponds to; or: is habitually rudimentary together) **with the present Jerusalem, for she continues in slavery** (or: bondage) **with her children**."

Mt. Sinai is a figure for "the Law." Those who lived under the Law were "slaves," according to what Paul has just said here, and he used the "present Jerusalem" as a figure for those under the Law.

Since Paul goes on to say in vs. 31,
> "**Wherefore, brothers** (= fellow believers; family), **we are not** (we do not exist being) **children of the slave-girl** (the servant girl; the maid), **but, to the contrary, of the freewoman**,"

it is evident that the freedom versus the slavery is not in reference to the inherent humanity of people, but to a situation and condition under which humanity exists. Paul had been the offspring of the "**present Jerusalem**," i.e., of the Law, but since his conversion he was now a "**child of the freewoman**" – the Jerusalem which is above (vs. 26).

Paul further clarifies this by saying that the two women in his allegory represented the two covenants (vs. 24). So, to be a part of the 1st covenant was to be a slave. He had made this analogy in the first part of this chapter when he compared being a child to being like a slave (vs. 1), and then says in vs. 7,
> "**So that, you are** (you exist being) **no longer a slave, but rather, a son, and since a son, also an heir** (a possessor and an enjoyer of the distributed allotment) **through God** [other MSS: God's heir through Christ]."

What he is saying regarding sonship (here, meaning maturity and adulthood) is the same as his later analogy of belonging to the freewoman, in vs. 31. Now considering our opening question about the form of a slave, consider vs. 4-5 in this chapter that has reference to Jesus,
> 4. **Yet when the fullness of the time came** (or: that which was filled up by time reached full term), **forth from out of a mission** (or: from out of the midst of [Himself]), **God sent-off His Son as an emissary** (envoy; representative), **being Himself come to be born from out of a woman, being Himself come to be born under** [the rules, authority and influence of] **Law,**
> 5. **to the end that He could** (or: would) **buy out** (ransom; redeem; reclaim [from slavery]) **those under [the] Law – so that we could** (or: would) **receive and take away into possession the placement as a son** (an adult child placed with rights and responsibility within the household; the conferred sonship).

Note Paul's terms here, "**born from out of a woman**" and "**born under Law**." This latter made Him a slave. I suspect that when Paul made reference to the birth from a woman, here, he was

70

setting the stage for his following analogy of the birth metaphor which begins in vs. 19 and continues through the rest of the chapter. In vs. 21 he addresses those "**constantly wanting or intending to be under Law** (or: exist [controlled] by a legalistic custom or system)." Thus, in vs. 19, the "**progressing, again, in childbirth labor** (travail; labor pains), **until Christ may be suddenly formed** (= until the Anointing would be at some point birthed) **within you folks**" would refer to their being birthed from out of the Law and into the new covenant, or, to being born (again; from above – John 3:3) from the free Jerusalem which is above.

So from Gal. ch. 4 we see that Paul regarded the Law, the 1st covenant, as slavery. And from our passage in Phil., above, we see that Christ was under this form of slavery until – to the extent of – "**lowering Himself**" to the death of a cross. This was because the Jewish authorities said, "**We, ourselves, are continuously holding** (or: having) **a Law, and corresponding** (or: according) **to the Law, he continues bound** (indebted; obliged) **to be dying away**" (John 19:7).

He took on the form of a slave (the structure of the Law), and as that structure's Lamb, He became the outcome, the goal, the inescapable end of the Law: a sacrifice. He took the form, or role, of being Yahweh's Servant (also means: slave) as we see prophesied in Isa. 52:13-53:12. He subjected Himself to a "**form of godliness**" (2 Tim. 3:5) that had only the power of death (Rom. 7:9-10) so that Christ, and the new covenant/kingdom, could be "formed" in us.

He took on the outward form of a religious system (the Law) which was the form of a slave/servant, in order to put an end to outward religious form and bring us into the freedom (set free by the Son – John 8:36) of spirit and truth (John 4:23), "**the freedom of the glory and splendor of God's children** (or: into the liberty of the manifestation of that which calls forth praise and a good opinion, which pertain to God's born-ones)" – Rom. 8:21.

Paul also said in Rom. 8:
> 2. **For the principle and law of, and which is, the spirit of 'The Life within Christ Jesus'**
>> (or: For you see, the Law of Life's spirit, joined with [the] Anointing of Jesus; or: For the Spirit's law of life within Christ Jesus; or: the Law of the Breath-effect, which is Life in union with [the] Anointed Jesus)
>
> **frees you away from the Law of the Sin** (or: the principle of failure and the missing of the target; the code of behavior that produces error; the principle of deviation from the goal) **and the Death** (or: immediately set you [other MSS: me] free for the law that deals with and has the character of sin and death).

Freedom ends slavery. We were enslaved to the tree of the knowledge of good and evil, which was exemplified by the Law. The spirit and truth of "**The Life within Christ Jesus**" freed us from this slavery. He took on this form, the form of the servant/slave, to do this for us. So Paul ends Gal. 4 and moves on to the glorious conclusion in ch. 5,
> 1. **For the [aforementioned] freedom, Christ immediately set us free** (or: [The] Anointed One at once frees us in, to, for and with freedom)! **Keep on standing firm, therefore, and do not again be habitually held within a yoke of slavery** (or: a cross-lever [of a pair of scales] whose sphere is bondage)
>> (or: Continuously stand firm, then, in the freedom [to which the] Anointing sets us free, and let not yourselves be progressively confined again by a yoke pertaining to servitude)!

Christ's yoke is easy, and His burden is light – it is the yoke of spirit/breath and reality. But to do this He Himself had to become a submissive One, One that was obedient to the Law, taking on "**the form of a Servant**." And so we read in Rom. 15,

71

8. **For I am saying [that] Christ has been birthed and remains a Servant** (an Attendant; a Helper; a Minister) **of and pertaining to Circumcision** (= God's covenant people), **over God's truthfulness** (or: Circumcision's Servant for the sake of a truth from and about God, and a reality which is God), **into the standing to confirm** (stabilize; make good; cause to stand by stepping in place on a good footing; or: to guarantee the validity of) **the promises which pertain to and belong to the fathers** (the patriarchal promises),

9. **and on the other hand [to place on good footing and confirm the standing of] the ethnic multitudes** (the nations; the non-Israelites; the pagans), **over mercy** (for the sake of mercy), **[are] to glorify God** (to enhance the reputation of and the opinion about God), **just as it has been written,**

> **"Because of this I will openly profess and acclaim You** (speak out of the same word for and to You; agree and promise) **within ethnic multitudes** (among nations that are pagans and Gentiles), **and I will play music** (strike the string; make melody; sing with musical accompaniment) **to, for and in Your Name."** [2 Sam. 22:50; Ps. 18:50]

10. **And again he is saying,**

> **"Be of a good frame of mind** (Be merry and glad; Have thoughts of wellness), **you ethnic multitudes** (non-Jews), **together with His people."** [Deut. 32:43]

In conclusion, I suggest that the "form of a servant" refers to function and societal role – and in this case a definite reference to His place under the Law – and not as a reference to His ontological essence.

Robinson (*Redating the New Testament*) has assigned circa A.D. 58 for the year of Paul and Timothy's letter to this called-out community. Colosse was in the Roman province of Asia, near Laodicea and Hierapolis. While many Jews lived in this area, William Barclay describes the called-out community there as "mainly Gentile" (*The Daily Study Bible Series; the Letters to the Philippians, Colossians and Thessalonians*, 1975, p. 94). Additionally, Eduard Lohse cites their "estranged" condition (1:21) and their "uncircumcision" (2:13), supporting this view (*A Commentary on the Epistles to the Colossians and to Philemon*, p. 2, *Hermeneia – A Critical and Historical Commentary on the Bible*, Fortress Press, 1971).

In his classic commentary (*Epistles to the Colossians and to Philemon*, MacMillan and Co., Ltd., 1897), J.B. Lightfoot describes what he sees as doctrinal error that subsequent teachers had introduced into the community, and that became the central reason for this letter to be written. He calls that error "the Colossian heresy" and devotes his first chapter to tracing its history from the Essene branch of Judaism to what he identifies as first century "Gnostic Judaism" (p. 91). Barclay says that "no one can tell for sure" just what their heresy was and refers to it as "one of the great problems of NT scholarship" (ibid., p. 95). On the other hand, on p. 97 he gives a general description of the Gnosticism of that time and place, and states that it was a "tendency of thought" which would include all the problems that Paul and Timothy have addressed here. Ben Witherington III, however, thinks that Paul is "dealing with some sort of ascetic Jewish piety," or "esoteric and mystical Jewish philosophy," citing the references to "circumcision (2:11-13; 3:11), observance of Sabbath (2:16), and food rules (2:16, 21)" which were "boundary markers for Jews" (*The Letters to Philemon, the Colossians and the Ephesians, A Socio-Rhetorical Commentary on the Captivity Epistles*, William B. Eerdmans Publishing Co., 2007, pp. 109-110).

Lohse sees the first two chapters as an "unfolding of the universal scope of the dominion of Christ," and points to the "lordship of Christ" in the lives of the community as the main theme of the last two chapters (ibid., p. 3). Colossians contains a wealth of beauty and truth, and Witherington suggests that it shows "some development in Paul's thought" (ibid., p. 111). That neither the noun "salvation," nor the verb "save" nor the title "Savior" appear here seems significant. Both ethical implications and the necessity for virtue are found in the admonitions for covenant living in the section from 3:5 to 4:6. Such admonitions are often referred to as "Paul's imperatives." However, these are based upon the content of the message presented in the section from 1:5 to 3:4, which is an example of "Paul's indicatives." These "indicatives" present the new state of being, and in them we see Paul's theology and his understanding of a realized eschatology.

This commentary will discuss what I consider to be the highlights of the letter, and the implications of each verse.

Chapter 1

1. **Paul, one sent with a mission pertaining to Christ Jesus** (or: an envoy of [the] Anointed Jesus; an emissary who has his origin in Christ Jesus) **through God's will, and Timothy, the brother** (or: = fellow believer; or: the brother Timothy),

In verse 1, he identifies himself as "**one sent with a mission pertaining to Christ Jesus** (or: an envoy of [the] Anointed Jesus) **through God's will**..." This was his personal mission statement, the life-path which God had chosen for him. The Greek word *apostolos* is normally transliterated into the word "apostle," instead of being translated: one sent off with a mission (or: an envoy; an emissary). The institutional church made this word a technical word signifying an "office" in their hierarchy, but as Paul elsewhere styled himself as a "slave of Jesus Christ" (Rom. 1:1), and even though he elsewhere presented his credentials in defense against those who would repudiate him (e.g., Phil. 3:5-6; 2 Cor. 11:5), I doubt that he was describing himself with this word in any way other than the function which it indicates. Through God's will he had become a person with a mission that had its origin in Christ Jesus [*cf* John 15:16, "**You yourselves did not choose Me, but to the contrary I, Myself, selected and picked out** (or: chose) **you folks and placed** (or: set) **you** ..."]. He was mandated by Jesus, on the road to Damascus. Each of us can likewise receive direction from God to perform some function in His reign.

2. **To the set-apart folks** (the holy ones; the sacred people) **within Colossae – even to ones full of faith** (or: to faithful and trusting people) **– to [the] brothers within Christ** (or: and to loyal fellow believers [who are] in union with [the] Anointed [other MSS add: Jesus]):
Grace and joyous favor (or: The act that produces happiness, which was granted [to all] as a favor), **as well as peace and harmony** [= shalom], **to you folks from God our Father** [other MSS read: from God, our Father and Lord, Jesus Christ].

Note that Paul speaks on behalf of the Father, sending God's grace, favor, peace and harmony to the set-apart folks in Colossae. I suggest that this was not just a nice formality, or a well-meaning wish, but an impartation to those folks, and now to us who read this – for it is God's Word, to them and to us. The Spirit of those words brings the content into our spirits. We should speak to others in the same way. Our words should also be spirit and life (John 6:63). The parenthetically inserted definition of grace/favor derives from Jim Coram, writing in "Unsearchable Riches" vol. 102, number 5, p. 201. I appreciate that he has designated grace as an act, which we understand to be the Christ event of His death, resurrection and now the giving to us of His life. Through his words, Paul is extending this life, the Word, unto the folks in Colossae.

In regard to the phrase "**within Christ**," Lohse suggest that this is a reference to the Christ-event, and describes those whose existence in "in the dominion of the exalted Lord" (ibid., p. 10). This would tie them to the historical event, as well as point to the new spiritual-political realm of this covenant community.

Now look at Paul's and Timothy's relationship to them, and his affirmation of them in vs. 3-5:
3. **We habitually express gratitude for the goodness in grace, and give thanks to God, the Father** [other MSS: to the God and Father] **of our Lord, Jesus Christ, at all times continually thinking and speaking goodness and well-being concerning** (or: praying about) **you folks,**
4. **upon hearing of your faith, loyalty and trust [being, resident, or having its source] within Christ Jesus** (or: in union with [the] Anointed Jesus) **and the love which you folks habitually have and hold [which is extended and given] into all the set-apart folks** (or: holy ones; saints; sacred people)
5. **because of the expectation** (or: expectant hope) **– the one continuously lying stored away as a reserve – resident within the atmospheres** (or: heavens), **which you folks already heard** (or: heard before) **within the word** (message; discourse; or: Logos) **concerning the Truth** (or: the word of truth; the idea belonging to and having its source in Reality; the message which is truth and reality) **which originates in and pertains to the message of ease, goodness and well-being** (or: which belongs to the good news).

In vs. 3 I have expanded the phrase normally rendered "**give thanks**" to show the literal meaning of the Greek from its elements: to express gratitude for the goodness in grace. Grace and God's goodness were the heart of the good news which Paul proclaimed. The plural verb shows the solidarity between himself and Timothy. The word normally rendered "praying," in the latter part of this verse, means literally to "think and/or speak goodness and for having things to be well." Consider Paul's attitude toward the folks to whom he was writing: goodness and grace (or: favor), peace and harmony. What better context is there from which to speak? What better forces to send forth, from his spirit, toward those folks?

The term "Father" was a frequent term for God, even in Hellenistic writings. Israel was called Yahweh's son in Hos. 11:1, so Paul may here be placing Jesus as into Israel's story, as its representative figure, and also be combining the referents of both Jew and Gentile into one new history of a new humanity. The alternate MSS readings which insert "and" may have derived from a copyist's desire for clarification, or may have come from a different MS tradition.

Consider what is said in the first clause of vs. 4: the faith and trust which they had was faith and trust that existed within Christ Jesus. It had **its source** or was **resident within** (the meaning of the preposition *en*) Christ Jesus. Another way of rendering this phrase is: in union with Christ Jesus. The source of their faith was Christ, and the actualization of it was union with Him. Lohse rightly mentions that the faith mentioned here "does not refer to the content," but rather to the realm of existence within which they live (ibid., p. 16). Compare Acts 17:28-29a.

Paul has also heard of the love which they constantly had and which was continuously extended into all the set-apart folks (vs. 4b). This was "**because of the expectation** [that was] **resident within the atmospheres** (or: heavens)," and this was an expectant hope which had come to them within the words, or message, concerning the Truth (Christ) and Reality (the New Being that was brought through Christ). This Word is a new revelation from God to humanity.

The location of this expectation also speaks to "the kingdom, reign and sovereign activities of the atmospheres/heavens" of which Jesus taught in the Gospel of Matthew. It is a higher realm of existence, and points to the risen Christ as the enthroned Ruler and Lord of this new reality that has invaded the earth. This was the good news, or literally: the message of ease, goodness and well-being (vs. 5).

The message that Paul (presumably) had proclaimed to them brought them trust (or: faith), love and an expectation concerning Truth and Reality. It was not the message of a heavy burden, as brought by the Pharisees – of all the things which must either be done, or not done. It was a message of ease, goodness, and well-being. It was in their "bank account," continuously stored away as a reserve, resident within the atmosphere which surrounded them: the realm of God's Spirit, also known as "heaven."

So look at the next verse, and what Paul stated as fact:
6. **This [Word; Logos] is being continuously present alongside [and proceeding] into you folks, just as it is also continuously existing within all the ordered System** (within the entire world of culture, secular society, religion, economics and government; or: in the entire universe; or: = the entire Roman Empire), **repeatedly bearing fruit of itself and constantly being grown and caused to be increasing, just as also within you folks, from [the] day in which you heard and at once fully experienced – in intimate knowing and accurate realization – the grace of God, within Truth** (or: God's favor resident within [the] truth; God's grace in the midst of reality; or: the favor which, in reality, is God).

That word, or message, "**is being continuously present alongside [and proceeding] into you folks.**" What a wonderful thing of which to be aware! But look at the next clause: "**just as it is also continuously existing within ALL the ORDERED SYSTEM** (or: within the entire world of culture, religion, economics and government)"! The Word, Christ, His message, is continuously existing in our atmosphere (resident, with expectation) – alongside us. It is available for us and for the whole world.

Not only this, it is "**repeatedly bearing fruit OF ITSELF** (middle voice), **and [is] constantly being grown and caused to be INCREASING**," and it is "**the grace of God, within Truth** (= Christ)," or, "the favor which, in reality, IS God!" Lightfoot says concerning this verse, "The Gospel is essentially a reproductive organism, a plant whose 'seed is in itself'." (ibid, p. 133) Lohse sees in this clause a reference to Gen. 1:22, 28. He also cites 4 Ezra 9:31, "Today I sow my law in you and it shall bring forth fruit in you..." (ibid., p 20). The message of goodness, this Logos which they heard and experienced with intimate, full and accurate realization, was the favor from God and the Grace which is God. It exists within the new reality where He dwells within us!

What an opening for his letter! And Paul says that they had heard it and at once fully experienced it, in intimate knowing and accurate realization. They realized that the new creation had come in the New Being that was in Jesus Christ, and that they were a part of it.

7. **Just in this way, you folks [were taught and] learned from Epaphras, our beloved fellow-slave, who is full of faith and loyal, an attending servant of the Christ on our** [other MSS: your] **behalf** (or: who is a faithful dispenser of the Christ [who is] over us [or: you folks]), 8. **the person also clearly showing and making evident to us your love in spirit and attitude** (or: your love within [the] Breath-effect; your love in union with [the] Spirit).

Epaphras was a Colossian who was currently under arrest with Paul (ch. 4:12), and it was he who had brought the message of the Messiah to Colossae. Note that Paul put him on a par with himself, a "**fellow-slave**" – they both having the same Owner/Lord. Epaphras was not just Paul's assistant, but "**an attending servant of the [Messiah]**." Conflating the MS readings, he was obviously serving Christ in those there with Paul, and also in the Colossians, and because of this, even serving Him now, in us who read this witness.

I amplified the Greek *pistos* into "**full of faith and loyal**" so as to color in the semantic range of this word which Paul applied to Epaphras. Vs. 8 shows us that he had brought the witness regarding the Colossians to Paul.

Consider the possible renderings of the phrase first given as "**in spirit and attitude**." This can mean "in the sphere or realm of spirit/attitude," or "within/in-union-with [the] Spirit/Breath-effect" – this latter referring to God's Spirit. The Greek *pneuma* literally means the effect or result of a breath, or of breathing. Normally rendered "spirit," I have chosen in my translating to also render it "breath-effect" in order to present the Greek way of thinking in this word that can also mean "wind."

9. **And because of this** (or: So that is why) **we, from the day on which we heard, are not ceasing constant praying** (thinking and speaking toward having things being well) **over your [situation] and asking** (or: making a request) **on behalf of you folks, to the end that you may** (or: would) **be filled full with the entire contents of the accurate, full, experiential, intimate knowledge and insight of His will** (His design, purpose, plan and intention; or: so that you may know and experience all that He wants you to know and experience) **within the sphere of all wisdom and spiritual understanding** (comprehension; a junction of that which is sent together; discernment; being able to make the pieces fit together).

Here we see that this new creation involves a process, in solidarity with which Paul was not ceasing to constantly think and speak with a view to having things go well for them: "**to the end that [they] may** (or: would) **be filled full with the entire contents of the accurate, full, experiential, and intimate knowledge and insight of His will**..." Then he expands this thought, praying that this knowledge and insight would be "**within the sphere of all wisdom and spiritual understanding.**"

Paul did not want them to just know the basics, and be satisfied with a simple knowledge of the Christ event. Consider those words: "**all wisdom and spiritual understanding!**" He did not want them to be satisfied with the milk of the message (1 Cor. 3:2). This may seem beyond us, but recall that Paul also said in 1 Cor. 2:16 that "**we have the mind of Christ.**" It is important to have insight into His design, purpose, plan and intention. The Greek can also read, "so that you may know and experience all that He wants you to know and experience," viewing the meaning of "His will" on a personal level. We need insights into both: His will for us and what He wants us to know, as well as His plan of the ages – understanding where He is leading humanity. All of this spiritual understanding is resident within Christ, into whom we have been placed. The immediate goal of which Paul is speaking is our being "**filled full with the entire contents of the accurate, full, experiential, intimate knowledge** (*epi-gnosis*)" concerning His will and intention. As to the word wisdom, Lightfoot says, "*Sophia* is mental excellence in its highest and fullest sense," while understanding implies "a tentative, partial approach to *sophia*" (ibid, p. 136-7).

The next verses continue his thoughts with a further end in view:
10. **[Thus we pray for you] to walk about worthily** (i.e., to live your life with corresponding value) **with regard to the Lord** (the Owner; [= Yahweh or Christ]) **[progressing] into all pleasing** (or: into every desire to please; into the midst of entire pleasure) **within every good work or virtuous action, while habitually bearing fruit and constantly being folks [that] are being progressively caused to grow and increase in the full, accurate, experiential and intimate knowledge of God** (or: with God's full experience of intimate knowledge and insight; or: by the added insight and experiential knowledge which is God),
11. **being continuously empowered in every ability** (being ones progressively enabled within all power) **corresponding to the strength of His glory**
> (or: down from and in the sphere of the might pertaining to and having its source in His reputation or His manifestation of that which calls forth praise; or: = the strength coming from His manifested presence [= His *Sh'khinah*]) **[leading] into every [situation of] persistent remaining under [difficulties] to humbly give patient support** (or: unto all relentless endurance) **and long-waiting before rushing into emotions** (or: long endurance; a long time before breathing violently with passion; or: perseverance; tolerance towards others), **accompanied by** (or: together with) **joy.**

Now Paul adds in a practical side of this new reality: that we should live our lives in a manner that is worthy (or, of equal value) with regard to the Lord, our Owner. In regard to vss. 9-19, Lightfoot says, "The end of all knowledge, the Apostle would say, is conduct" (ibid, p. 137). And he sets the bar high: it is to be walking into all pleasing (or: into entire pleasure) WITHIN every good work or virtuous action, while habitually bearing fruit. This sounds like a hard task, if you try to do it on your own, but read on, you will come to vs. 13, and you will see that all has changed – our position and standing has been transferred: we are in the midst of His reign, and vs. 16 tells us that the whole new creation is now within, and in union with, Him, and you will see that vss. 19 & 20 confirm the matter.

The phrase "**into all pleasing** (or: into every desire to please; into the midst of entire pleasure)" in vs. 10 can be taken to refer to God, to the covenant community, to the society at large, and/or to the sphere of the members existence. The next phrase, "**within every good work or virtuous action**," calls to mind the letter from Jacob (or: James). Lohse cites the Qumran *Community Rule* (1 QS I, 4f) as saying "cling to all good works" (ibid., p. 29). Paul gives more insight to this in Eph. 2:10,
> " **for you see, we are** (we continually exist being) **the effect of what He did** (or: His creation; the thing He has constructed; the result of His work; His achievement; His opus; the effect of His Deed)**: people being founded from a state of disorder and wildness** (being framed, built, settled and created), **within and in union with Christ Jesus, upon good works** (virtuous actions; excellent deeds) **which God made ready** (prepared; or: prepares) **beforehand, to the end that we may walk about** (= live our lives) **within and in union with them.**"
God prepared beforehand the excellent deeds and virtuous actions which we are purposed to do in union with Him, and within Him. These are not self-works. Their performance arises from Him.

Next, I want you to notice the voice of the verb "grow" in the second half of vs. 10: "... **and constantly being folks [that] are BEING progressively CAUSED to grow and increase**..."
That is the passive voice, and it means that God is doing the work, causing the growth, so that we are able to live our life in an equal value, with regard to the Lord. Good news! Nonetheless, we should never forget or disregard His purpose for this growth: it is not to build the ego; it is to live a life worthy of Him, attended by good works and virtuous actions. It is His life in us that makes all this possible. We bear fruit and grow as a branch by remaining in the Vine (see John 15:1-13, and heed the warning, but also keep in mind that He said these things to make our joy full – it's all good news).

Notice that Paul again brings up knowledge: "**the full, accurate, experiential and intimate knowledge of God** (or: with God's full experience of intimate knowledge and insight; or: by the added insight and experiential knowledge which is God)." This is the *epi-gnosis* that is God's knowledge, as well as knowledge about God. I have also expressed the genitive as apposition in the phrase "knowledge which is God." No wonder Paul said, "**to intimately and experientially know Him, and the ability – even the power – of His resurrection**" (Phil. 3:10).

As we look at vs. 11, note that this is a continuation of vs. 10, and that once more the passive voice is used, "**BEING continuously EMPOWERED in every ability**..." And this "every ability" is "**corresponding to the strength of HIS glory.**" So it is by His power, His ability and by the strength of His glory. Still, again we see that Paul is not just loading us with blessings for nothing: it is "**[leading] into every [situation of] persistent remaining under [difficulties] to humbly give patient support**," and into "**long-waiting before rushing into emotions** (etc.)," but then we see that this is "**accompanied by joy**!" Recall that His joy is our strength.

Lohse point out the recurring use of "all/every" in vss. 4, 6, 9, 10 and 11 (ibid., p. 24). Paul sees the permeation of God's Spirit and the activity of His Sovereignty as affecting everything within this called-out community.

We now begin a passage that focuses on the Father and the Son, and which speaks to the work of the Father, to whom we constantly give thanks (vs. 12), and of the relationship of the Son to all of creation. Here Paul presents us with one of the most universal and all-inclusive pictures of the new Reality, the new creation that is within the Christ of the universe.

12. **[We are folks who are] constantly giving thanks to the Father: the One calling you** [other MSS: us] **– as well as making [you; us] competent** (sufficient; qualified; fit; suitable) **– into the divided share of the lot of the inheritance** (or: into the part and portion of the allotted possession) **of the set-apart folks** (or: pertaining to the holy ones; belonging to the saints; from the sacred people) **within the Light;**

Note that it is the Father that calls us and that makes us competent, sufficient, fit, qualified and suitable. He is the Actor, the One doing the deed, in both vs. 12 and 13. These verses give the human no place in what is done: it is the work of God. The calling is for us to be a partaker of the inheritance that pertains to and belongs to His sacred folks, those set-apart unto Him. The location, or sphere of existence and relevance, of this allotted possession is within, and in union with the Light – a figure of Christ and the Life which brought knowledge and understanding to mankind (John 1:4-5) – but the inheritance itself is the ethnic multitudes, unto the boundaries of the earth (Ps. 2:8). This was given to the Son, but the Father invites us to have a part, to be God's fellow-workers (1 Cor. 3:9) in "**enlightening every person**" (John 1:9). In 1 Cor. 1:9 Paul phrases it, "**through Whom you folks were called and invited into a participation** (a common partnership; fellowship; a sharing) **of His Son, Jesus Christ, our Lord** (Owner; Master)." As the Levites had God as their inheritance, under the old arrangement (covenant), so we have His Son, Jesus Christ as our inheritance and enjoyment of the allotment.

13. **He who drags us out of danger** (or: rescued us) **forth from out of the midst of the authority of the Darkness** (from Darkness's jurisdiction and right; from existing out of gloomy shadows and obscure dimness; = the privilege of ignorance), **and changes [our] position** (or: transported [us], thus, giving [us] a change of standing, and transferred [us]) **into the midst of the kingdom and reign of the Son of His love**

 (or: into the midst of the sovereign influence of the Son Who has the characteristics and qualities of His accepting love; into union with the sovereign activities of the Son Whose origin is His love; or: into the sphere of the reign of the Son of the Love which is Him; into the center of the kingdom of the Son, which is His love),

Recall what Paul said in Eph. 2:1, "**And you folks [who were] continuously existing being dead ones by** (or: to; with; in) **the results and effects of your stumblings aside** (offences;

wrong steps) **and failures to hit the mark** (or: mistakes; errors; times of falling short; sins)." It is because we were dead that He had to DRAG us out of danger. And where were we? In the midst of the authority of the Darkness. Darkness represents ignorance, lack of Light. Mankind was like dead bodies that had to be dragged out of the lake of sin and death. He first breathed into us the breath of life, and then we truly became LIVING souls. He gave birth to us from above, and gave us faith and the ability to believe. Lightfoot states that Paul "regards them as already rescued from the power of darkness, as already put in possession of their inheritances as saints" (ibid, p. 140).

But what was this "authority, jurisdiction and privilege of the darkness" from out of which we had been existing? What had the authority over Israel and the Jews? The Law. It contained that which was a shadow (darkness) of the impending good things (Heb. 10:1). The religious beliefs and superstitions of the pagans held authority over their lives. In both cases it was ignorance of the Truth, of Reality – which is Christ – and absence of the Light (which also is Christ), vs. 12.

The Father changed our position, transported us, from out of the midst of Darkness's jurisdiction, into the midst of the kingdom and reign (the sovereign influence and sphere of activity) of the Son, which is His love (genitive of apposition). It is a kingdom of Love, which is God. Paul does not say that it was our decision, or the implementing of our wills, to do this. God just did it. That, my friends, is grace. The sphere of His kingdom and reign is the sphere of... the Son of the Love which is Him (an alternate translation of the last phrase of vs. 13). Lightfoot suggests that *exousias* (authority; jurisdiction; etc.) here implies delegated, but unrestrained or arbitrary tyranny, while *basileia* (reign; kingdom) describes "a well-ordered sovereignty," and states that Chrysostom also seems to have this idea (ibid, p. 139).

14. **in Whom** (or: in union with [which Son]) **we continuously have and hold the redemption** (the release and liberation procured by payment of a ransom) **[which results in] the sending away of the failures** (or: the dismissal of the errors pertaining to falling short and straying to the side of the target; the flowing away of the sins; the divorce from mistakes),

Now it is being within Him, by being placed in union with the Son, that we have and hold the redemption, which is the release and liberation which He procured for us. Now look at what this bought: the sending away of our failures (no more guilt); the dismissal of our errors (no more carrying the burden or the results of our lacks of attainment); the flowing away of the sins (we are now clean and turned in the right direction); the divorce from our mistakes (we are no longer bound to what we did that was wrong). This, my friends, is freedom! This is all because the Father transferred us into the Son, the Second Humanity (1 Cor. 15:47).

Lightfoot remarks that *apolutrosis* (redemption; ransom) has changed the metaphor "from the victor who rescues the captive by force of arms (vs. 13, *erusato* [drags out of danger; rescues]) to the philanthropist who releases him by the payment of a ransom" (ibid, p. 140).

15. **It is [this Son] Who is the Image** (portrait; the Exact Formed Likeness; the Figure and Representation; visible likeness and manifestation) **of the not-seen God** (or: the unable to be seen God; the invisible God), **the Firstborn of all creation**
>   (or: of every creature; or: of every framing and founding; of every act of settling from a
>   state of disorder and wildness; or: pertaining to the whole creation; or: = the Inheritor of
>   all creation Who will also assume authority over and responsibility for every creature),

Recall that Jesus said to Philip, **"The one having seen Me has seen, and now perceives, the Father!"** (John 14:9). And now we, too, can reflect the Father as we are changed from glory to glory (2 Cor. 3:18). Lightfoot notes that *eikon* involves the idea of "manifestation," as well as likeness and representation (ibid, p. 143). Furthermore, Jesus is the One in whom God reveals Himself. But not only was Christ "the Exact Formed Likeness" of God, whom we do not see, but He is the Firstborn of all creation. This is an all-inclusive, universal statement.

Eikon is the word used in Gen. 1:26-27 (LXX), in speaking of God making humanity in His image. So here, Paul is reaching back to the creation story, associating Jesus with Adam as he does in Rom. 5:12-21 and 1 Cor. 15:45. But here, Christ is the end of that story (the last Adam) and the beginning of the next (the Second Human).

But what does it mean to be the firstborn? The first one? Yes. The preeminent one? Yes. But in the Hebrew culture, to be a firstborn son meant something more: he was the one who had the duty and responsibility to assume authority over and responsibility for the rest of the family, if need be to be the kinsman redeemer. He was also next in line to receive the inheritance, when the father died. Being "**Firstborn of all creation**/every creature" means that He has the duty and responsibility to redeem the whole creation; to set free every creature. And this He will do.

Lightfoot says that the "appellation, 'the first-begotten, the eldest son,' are given to the Logos, by Philo..." He further states that, "it is interpreted by R. Nathan in *Shemoth Rabba* 19, fol. 118.4, 'God said, As I made Jacob a first-born (Ex. 4:22), so also will I make king Messiah a first-born (Ps. 89:28).' Hence 'the first-born'... became a recognized title of Messiah" (ibid, p. 144). "God's 'first-born' is the natural ruler, the acknowledged head, of God's household" (p. 145).

As you see from the parenthetical expansion, the Greek *ktisis* (creation) can also refer to the "act" of bringing order out of chaos, and the "founding" of a society. Or, this phrase can speak of "every creature," either individually or as an "aggregate of created things."

In Prov. 8:22 (LXX) we read,
> "The Lord created (formed) Me [= Wisdom] [as; to be] a Beginning (*arche*) of His Ways (Paths) [leading; injected] into His acts and works."

Lohse footnotes C.F. Burney, "Christ as the 'ΑΡΧΗ of Creation (Prov. 8:22, Col. 1:15-18, Rev. 3: 14)" JTS 27 (1926) where Burney gives the various meanings of the Hebrew *reshith* (used in Gen. 1:1) as meaning "beginning; head and first-fruits" (ibid., p. 46-47). The first two definitions are also the meanings of the Greek *arche*, which is used in Gen. 1:1 in the LXX.

16. **because within Him was created the whole** (or: in union with Him everything is founded and settled, is built and planted, is brought into being, is produced and established; or: within the midst of Him all things were brought from chaos into order) – **the things within the skies and atmospheres, and the things upon the earth** (or: those [situations, conditions and/or people] in the heavens and on the land); **the visible things, and the unseen** (or: unable to be seen; invisible) **things: whether thrones** (seats of power) **or lordships** (ownership systems) **or governments** (rulers; leadership systems; sovereignties) **or authorities – the whole has been created and all things continue founded, put in order and stand framed through means of Him, and [proceeds, or were placed] into Him** (or: = He is the agent and goal of all creation).

Now the first phrase in vs. 16 is shocking – so much so that many translators decide to translate the Greek *en* by the word "by." But the core meaning of the word is "in; within; within the midst of; or: in union with (where one is actually also within another)." So the whole of creation (all things – nothing left out!; "*ta panta* is nearly equivalent to 'the universe'" – Lightfoot, p. 149) was created, built, caused to be planted and settled and is produced and established WITHIN HIM. I am reminded of Rom. 11:36,

> "**Because, forth from out of the midst of Him, and through the midst of Him** (or: through means of Him), **and into the midst of Him, [is] the whole** (everything; [are] all things; or: = Because He is the source, means and goal of all things – everything leads into Him)!
> **By Him** (In Him; To Him; For Him) **[is] the glory** (the manifestation of that which calls forth praise; the reputation; the notion; the opinion; the credit; the splendor) **on into the ages. It is so** (Amen; So be it)!"

Again, there is Acts 17:28,

"**For you see, within the midst of and in union with Him we continuously live** (or, as a subjunctive: could be constantly living), **and are constantly moved about and put into motion, and continue existing** (experiencing Being)."

1 Cor. 8:6 gives us another declaration:

> **to us** (or: for us; with us) **[there is] one God, the Father, from out of the midst of Whom [is] the whole** (or: [are] all things) – **and we [directed and proceeding] into Him – even one Lord** (or: as well as one Owner and Master), **Jesus Christ: through Whom [is] the whole** (or: [are] all things) – **and we through means of and through the midst of Him!**

The list of all that is included in vs. 16 is quite inclusive: all that exists. Then Paul proceeds to say that this whole of the universe "**has been created and continues founded through means of Him**," and also "**[proceeds, or was placed] INTO Him**," or, as the parenthetical paraphrase words it, "He is the agent and the goal of all creation." The universality of this verse is inescapable. We also have here an echo of John 1:3, "**All things** (or: All people; [The] whole) **come to be** (or: are at some time birthed; occur; or: came to be; were birthed; or: suddenly happened) **through and by means of It** (i.e., the Word; or: Him), **and apart from It** (or: Him) **not even one thing comes into being** (occurs; was birthed; came into being; happens) **which has come into being** (which has occurred; which has happened)." Note the aorist verb tenses, which I have rendered here in John both as simple present tenses, and as simple past tenses, since the aorist is simply a fact tense with not expression of time or kind of action.

The subject of vs. 13b-22 is the Son, the Christ. The divinity and deity of the Son, and the cosmic reference to Him, are clearly seen in the first clause of this verse, which begins with *hoti en auto*: because within Him. His instrumentality in creating "all things" is seen in the next to the last phrase of this verse, where Paul used *di' autou*: through means of Him. The final phrase expresses the goal of all, similar to Rom. 11:36, above, *eis auton*: into the midst of Him. Rendering *eis* as "for" misses the central idea of these three Greek prepositions, which all speak of "location": within, through the midst, into the midst. He is the sphere and place where all creations exists and resides. Here Lightfoot says, "All the laws and purposes which guide the creation and government of the Universe reside in Him, the Eternal Word, as their meeting-point" (ibid, p. 148).

So how are we to understand the list that follows "**unseen things**"? I suggest that they are here speaking of things – like the wind – of which you can see the effects, but not the things which produce the effects. A "throne," even though a visible chair, speaks of rulership and sovereignty. A "**lordship**" (ownership system; system of domination) is a position and a relationship to that which, or those whom, are owned. You can see the effect and the manifestation, but not the "lordship." Likewise "government" and "authority" are ideas of domination, rule, and privilege of action. All these things are as unseen as the wind, but they are realities within our world.

Lightfoot ends his comments on this verse, "The Eternal Word is the goal of the Universe, as He was the starting-point. It must end in unity, as it proceeded from unity: and the center of this unity is Christ" (ibid, p. 153). Lohse quotes Marcus Aurelius, speaking about Nature, "... out from the midst of You [come] all things; within the midst of You [exist] all things; into the midst of You [proceed] all things" (M. Ant. 4.23.2, my translation, ibid. p. 49). This closely mirrors Rom. 11:36.

17. **And He is before** (prior to; or: maintains precedence of) **all things and all people, and the whole has** (or: all things have) **been placed together and now continues to jointly-stand** (stands cohesively; is made to have a co-standing) **within the midst of and in union with Him,**

This shows that He was prior to the "**all things**" which He created, and He maintains the preeminence over **all people** (note: the form of the first all, *panton*, is both neuter and masculine, this latter function indicating "people;" the second, which I rendered first "the whole," has the neuter article and thus means "all things"), and then Paul uses the perfect tense to show that it was a completed action and now so exists, restating that "all things" continue jointly-standing within the midst of, and in union with Him! What solidarity; what union!

Lightfoot points out from "**He is**," "... the present *estin* declares that this pre-existence is absolute existence. The *autos estin* here corresponds exactly to the *ego eimi* in St. John..." (ibid, p. 153).

18. **and so He is the Head** (or: Source) **of the body – which is the called-out community** (the ecclesia; the summoned congregation) **– Who is the Beginning** (or: the Ruler; the Originator and Ruling Principle; the Beginning Power and Ability of the process), **a Firstborn forth from out of the midst of dead folks, to the end that He would be birthed** (may come into existence; or: could come to be) **within all things and in all people: He continuously holding first place**
> (or: constantly being preeminent; or: habitually being the First One; or: continuing being the First Man [note: this phrase has in Greek literature been used as a title for a person]),

So we can logically see that He is the Source and Head of the body, since He is the Source and Head of all things! He is the beginning power, as well as the power of continued existence. He is also the Firstborn from out of the midst of dead folks – referring both to His resurrection, and to His place as Originator of the new creation. Then note the purpose statement: "**to the end that He would be birthed, may come into existence and could come to be WITHIN ALL THINGS and IN ALL PEOPLE!**" [note: the Greek *pasin* is both neutral and masculine] Paul goes beyond himself here to make his point clear and beyond question. The purpose clause that begins with, "to the end that" shows the goal and destiny of all creation and all people.

The responsibility to and for dead folks is again present in the title "Firstborn" since a father's legal role and responsibilities were passed on to his firstborn son. For this reason he was given a double portion of the inheritance (Deut. 21:17). Lightfoot points out that the *pro* ("before, prior to, all things and all people") of vs. 17 should be interpreted by the *pro*'s (in firstborn and first place/preeminence) in this verse, along with the *pro* in vs. 15. And because of this, He (the Creator of the world) is the Head and Source of His body, the ecclesia. *Cf* Heb. 12:22-24, where in vs. 23 we find the statement,
> "**[that is] in** (or: to) **an assembly of an entire people** (or: an assembly of all; a universal convocation) **and in** (or: to) **a summoning forth** (or: a called-out and gathered community) **of firstborn folks having been copied** (from-written, as from a pattern; or: enrolled; registered) **within [the; or: various] atmospheres** (or: heavens)..."

The covenant community is made up of "firstborn folks" who are His body, members of Christ, Who is "**the Firstborn among, within the center of, and in union with many brothers!**" – Rom. 8:29.

19. **because WITHIN Him all – the entire contents** (the result of that which fills everything; all the effect of the full measure [of things]) **– delights to settle down and dwell as in a house** (or: because He approved all the fullness [of all existence] to permanently reside within Him)

Again, he expresses the inclusiveness and universality of all existence dwelling within what we might call the "Cosmic Christ." This is a statement of God's purpose of the ages. Jesus said something similar in John 17:21,
> "**to the end that all mankind may** (or: everyone would) **continuously exist being one, correspondingly as You, O Father** [other MSS: Father], **[are] within the midst of Me, and I [am] within the midst of You – so that they, themselves, may and would also continuously exist being within the midst of Us...**"

Lightfoot says that *to pleroma* was "a recognized technical term in theology, denoting the totality of the Divine powers and attributes" (ibid, p. 157). However, vs. 20 again uses the phrase *ta panta* (the whole; all things) that was used in vss. 16 and 17, so the antecedent of Paul's thought in this verse is the same of that of the entire passage: the entirety of creation.

20. **and THROUGH Him at once to transfer the all** (the whole; = all of existential creation), **away from a certain state to the level of another which is quite different**

(or: to change all things, bringing movement away from being down; to reconcile all things; to change everything from estrangement and alienation to friendship and harmony and move all), **INTO Him – making** (constructing; forming; creating) **peace and harmony through the blood of His cross** (execution stake): **through Him, whether the things upon the earth** (or: land) **or the things within the atmospheres and heavens!**

So vs. 20 makes a beautiful summation of Paul's presentation here: "**THROUGH Him at once to transfer the all** (the whole; = all of existential creation), **away from a certain state to the level of another which is quite different** (or: to change all things, bringing movement away from being down; to reconcile all things; to change everything from estrangement and alienation to friendship and harmony and move all), **INTO Him.**" This is the work of the cross. Anything less simply devalues that work. "The whole universe of things, material as well as spiritual, shall be restored to harmony with God" (Lightfoot, p. 158). "Now the universe is again under its head and thereby cosmic peace has returned... through Christ..." (Lohse, p. 59).

He is the Way of peace and harmony. This peace exists within Him in all realms – on earth, as it is in heaven. He is the expression of God's kingdom come, and nothing exists outside His reign of sovereign action and influence.

The first rendering of the Greek infinitive of *apokatallasso* is a core meaning of the verb, "to transfer... different," and is the primary lexical definition. But the root, *allasso* means to change, alter or transform, make different or other than it was. The prefixed prepositions *apo* & *kata* signify a movement away from being down, so this would imply an upward movement. I have included the traditional definition "to reconcile" and thus also added the resultant idea of a "change from estrangement and alienation to friendship and harmony." But the central idea is a movement away from where humanity was, and what had been established, to be placed **INTO** (*eis*) **Him**.

Paul then uses two *dia* phrases to confirm that this all happened "through" the work of Christ: "**through**" the blood of His cross, and then "**through**" Him. There is no place in this for religious works, or even our belief in Him. It is all THROUGH HIM. The last two phrases of this verse are a common expression of the totality of their view of the universe: upon the land/earth, and within the heavens/skies. Thus Paul points to the universality of the work of the cross. Nothing is excluded.

21. **And so you folks, being at one time people having been alienated away** (being estranged; being rendered as belonging to another; = having been put out of the family) **and enemies** (or: hated ones) **by the divided thoughts** (in the dualistic perceptions and things going through the mind in every direction) **within** (or: in the midst of; in union with; or: = in the performance of) **the miserable deeds** (gushes of wicked actions; laborious and painful works) –

Here he describes the human condition (*cf* Rom. 1:18-32) as it is before being made alive in Christ (1 Cor. 15:22). The folks at Colossae had been such folks, having been "**dead people in and by offences and failures to hit the goal**" (Eph. 2:1). Consider the two aspects of our estrangement and enmity: divided thought with dualistic perceptions (*dia-noia*, the prefix having the root idea of dividing in two, or going throughout in every direction; these perceptions may have arisen from the influence of Gnostic Judaism, which was dualistic in nature), and the gushes of miserable activities. The term "alienated" may indicate the predominantly Gentile makeup of the group (*cf* Eph. 2:12-14). He has just painted a black back-drop for what he is about to say in the next verse:

22. **yet now He at once reconciled** (or: changed and transferred to a different state; [*p*46 & B read: you folks were reconciled]) **within the body of His flesh** (= His physical being), **through His death, to place you folks alongside, down before Him and in His sight: set-apart** (holy) **folks and flawless** (unblemished; blameless) **ones, even people not accused, with nothing laid to your charge** (or: unaccusable ones; unimpeachable ones; folks without reproach),

A great change has taken place. These folks are now reconciled (*apokatallasso*), which literally means that they were suddenly "changed and transferred to a different state of being; moved away from an established condition of being down, and changed to be other than they were." This was done through the work of the cross, for it says that it happened within the body of His flesh. His death and resurrection transferred them from the old creation into the new, placing them alongside Him and in His sight. It was this transfer that set them apart from the rest of the alienated mass of humanity. It also transformed them into being other than they were, for now they are "**flawless** (unblemished; blameless)" – through His blood (1 John 1:7). He does not "account to them their offences" (2 Cor. 5:19) and so they are "**people not accused, with nothing laid to [their] charge**." No one can accuse them! What a turnaround from how they were formerly described in vs. 21! This is the good news. The "**now**" indicates the "present [order of things]" (Lightfoot, p. 159), i.e., the new creation. Witherington sees this verse as echoing both Rom. 5:10 and 2 Cor. 5:18-20 (ibid., p. 139), and here cites A.T. Lincoln ("Col.," in *The New Intepreter's Bible XI*, Abingdon, 2000, p. 606) as pointing out "that the physical body of Christ was the means of reconciliation..." It was true that His body and life was the vehicle, but Paul makes it clear that it was "God, within Christ" that was doing the reconciliation (2 Cor. 5:19), and it was a reconciliation of "the world" – of the universe (?), or of the aggregate of humanity, and not just the covenant community. Or, as we see in 1 John 2:2,

> " **And He Himself exists continually being a cover around our mistakes and errors, sheltering us from their effects so that we can be in peaceful and rightwised relationships** (or: being the act by which our sins and failures are made ineffective, effecting conciliation [to us]), **yet not only around those pertaining to us** (or: having their source in us), **but further, even around the whole ordered System** (secular realm and dominating world of culture, economy, religion and government; or: cosmos; adorned universe; or: = all mankind)!"

The infinitive *parastesai* is commonly rendered "to present," but it literally means "**to place or set alongside**." *Katenopion autou* means "**down before Him and in His sight**." So we must ask, "Where is He?" He is present within His temple: us. So Paul is not speaking of some future event, but of a reality that existed at that time – and now. This was accomplished "**within His flesh**" – which means, on the cross. The work has been accomplished, and is finished. And we are not only at His side and down before Him in His presence, but He also

> "... **jointly roused and raised** (or: suddenly awakens and raises) **[us] up, and caused [us] to sit** (or: seats [us]) **together within the things situated upon** [thus, above] **the heavens within and in union with Christ Jesus**" (Eph. 2:6).

23. **since in fact** (or: inasmuch as) **you folks are continually remaining on** (or: are constantly persisting) **by trust, in the faith and for loyalty, being ones having been provided with a foundation so as to continue grounded, even seated so as to be settled ones, and not people being repeatedly moved elsewhere** (shifted; removed; or, as a middle: shifting yourselves) **away from the expectation** (or: expectant hope) **pertaining to, belonging to and having its source in the message of ease, goodness and well-being of which you hear** (or: heard)**: the [message] being heralded** (announced; publicly proclaimed and preached) **within all creation which is under the sky** (or: heaven) – **of which I, Paul, am myself come to be a herald, an emissary, and an attending servant** (or: a dispenser).

Vs. 23 continues with their happy condition, noting that they are in fact continually remaining on and constantly persisting by trust and in faith with loyalty, "**being ones having been provided with a foundation so as to continue grounded**..." Look what Christ has done for them (and us!)! The foundation is Christ Himself. He provided Himself (via His word and spirit) so that they would "continue grounded." What a firm promise from God.

Paul goes on to say that they are "**even seated so as to be settled ones**," – seated where? "**Upon the heavens, within and in union with Christ Jesus**" (Eph. 2:6) – and now they are "**not people being repeatedly moved elsewhere**, or shifted, or even shifting themselves, **away from the expectation that pertains to**, belongs to, and has its source in, **the message of ease,**

goodness and well-being." Then he assures them that this same message is being publicly announced and proclaimed WITHIN ALL CREATION under the sky (or: heaven)! Witherington observes that this "bold claim" is an example of the Asiatic rhetoric of this letter (ibid., p. 112). This message is universal, for everyone. Paul was a dispenser of this good news. He was a herald. The news came from and was about the King and His present reign over all creation. Jesus was his Authority for preaching it, as he was His emissary and attending servant.

24. **I am at this moment continuing to rejoice within the effects of experiences and the results of my sufferings over your [situation] and on your behalf, and I am progressively filling back up in turn – so as in [His] stead to replace, supply and balance out, within my flesh** (or: = with the means of my natural situation) – **the deficiencies** (or: results from what is lacking; effects from need) **with regard to the pressures** (or: from the squeezings, tribulations and tight spots) **that pertain to the Anointed One** (or: that belong to and affect Christ; or: from the Christ) **over [the situation of] His body, which is the called-out community** (which exists being the summoned-forth congregation – the ecclesia)

> (or: Now I am progressively filled with joy – in union with the feelings coming from passion over you folks – and am habitually filling up again, to bring balance, the effects of what is lacking, resulting from the distresses of Christ – resident within my flesh – concerning His body, which is the invited-out assembly),

What an attitude to have for our fellow members of the body: constantly rejoicing in our sufferings (or, other experiences) over their situation. And here Paul reveals that this suffering is actually **supplying what is lacking and creating a balance**, within his flesh (both his body, and his human nature), in regard to whatever is lacking with respect to the pressures and tight spots that the body of Christ was presently going through. This is solidarity; this is being a fellow worker with Jesus, and with His body – the called-out folks. Where there is a lack, or an imbalance, even at a distance we can make a difference, for we are joined in spirit as one body. Our experiences and any suffering which we may undergo have a positive effect upon the rest of the body. From what Paul has said here, there must be a need for the body to have pressures and squeezings, and there is a need for us to be joined with others as they, and we, go through this. *Cf* Eph. 3:13.

The "**filling back up in turn... to replace, supply, and balance out**" is the only place in the NT where the more usual word *anapleroo* (to fill up) is prefixed by *anti*. "It signifies that the supply comes *from an opposite quarter* to the deficiency" (Lightfoot, p. 163). One picture of *anti* is that of someone taking hold of an object, from the other side, to assist in lifting or managing the item. This word was used of creating balance in situations, by filling in areas of lack.

The second rendering of this verse presents a different picture, giving another meaning of *pathēma* (feelings coming from passion) and treating *ton thlipseon* as an ablative (resulting from), instead of a genitive. *Thlipseon* is rendered "distresses," which is modified by "of Christ," and *en te sarki mou* is seen as modifying "Christ," so we have, "resulting from the distresses of Christ – resident within my flesh – concerning His body..." With this, we see Christ, Who is within Paul, as being distressed over the situations of His body, the called-out covenant community. But Paul's joy and feelings of passion bring a balance to the distress of Christ Who lives within him – for there had been some problems in Colosse. Recall how Jesus was distressed over the situation of Jerusalem (Lu. 13:34).

25. **of which I am come to be an attending servant** (or: a dispenser), **corresponding to** (or: down from; in the sphere of) **God's household administration** (or: God's directives for the tasks of a household manager; the stewardship whose source is God and pertains to His house; God's economy; God's scheme and arrangement which He planned for His household) – **the [detailed plan] being given by me unto you** (or: to me [and infused] into you) – **to fulfill God's Word** (or: to make full the message pertaining to God; to make a full presentation of God's message; to deliver God's thought and idea in full; or: with a view to you fulfilling God's idea):
26. **the Secret** (or: sacred mystery) **having been hidden away and remaining concealed away from the ages** (or: from [past] eons), **as well as away from the [past] generations, yet**

now (at the present time) **is set in clear light in His set-apart folks** (or: was manifested to His holy ones; is caused to be seen by His saints; is shown for what it is, for His sacred people),

In these two verses Paul first sets himself as an example of this solidarity, for he views himself as an attending servant and a dispenser in the sphere of and commensurate to God's household and its administration. He sets himself in line with the directives from God with a view to the tasks of the management of God's house, and the purposes of His economy. This plan was given to the folks at Colossae by Paul, and he infused it into them, so as to fulfill God's Word and to deliver God's thought and idea in full to them. The last parenthetical presentation for the final clause of vs. 25 renders the infinitive *plerosai* as giving a purpose statement, rendering *eis* "with a view to": God's economy and scheme is for Paul to dispense into the Colossians so that THEY would fulfill God's idea. This is expressed as "the expectation from glory" in the next verse.

God's idea and message is described as "**the Secret**" – a plan and an arrangement (the new covenant) that God had hidden away and concealed from those that lived in the past ages (*cf* 1 Cor. 2:7; Lightfoot points out the "the ages" were made up of many "generations" – p. 166), but in Paul's time was NOW (vs. 22) set in clear light for His set-apart folks, and manifested in His sacred people (of whom the saints of Colosse were a part). This is a strong statement against Gnosticism which was characterized by "secret knowledge" that is revealed only to the initiated. There is no intellectual exclusiveness here, it is manifested in all His people.

27. **to whom God wills** (or: at one point purposed; or: intends) **to make known by intimate experience, what [are] the riches of the glory of this Secret** (or: the wealth which has it source in this sacred mystery's manifestation which calls forth praise) **within the multitudes** (among the nations; in the Gentiles; among the swarms of ethnic groups), **which is** (or: exists being) **Christ within you folks, the expectation of and from the glory**
> (or: which is [the] Anointed in union with you people: the hope of the manifestation which calls forth praise; or: which is [the] Anointing within the midst of you folks – the expectation which is the glory),

Note that in vs. 27 that is to them, as well as the rest of the multitudes (ethnic groups among the nations) and to us, that God purposed, wills and intends to make known – by intimate experience – just what this Secret entails, and the riches of the glory which has its source in that manifestation (Christ) which calls forth praise. Then he explains that it is "**Christ within [them], the expectation of the glory**." The term *christos* is a noun that can either mean "Christ," or "the anointing," and it is through the anointing from His Spirit that He dwells within us, and among us. Christ Himself, and the flow of His Spirit, is in union with us: that is the glory, which was the expectation of the Promise (the Secret), from ages past. Christ within, and among, the Gentiles (the ethnic multitudes) was "the Secret." Christ brings a "manifestation which calls forth praise" (or: glory) to the nations now, whereas before the glory (along with the sonship, the arrangements and the promises) belonged only to Israel (Rom. 9:4).

Rendering the last phrase, *tes doxes*, as an ablative (from the glory) gives the meaning that the expectation comes from the manifestation which calls forth praise, and that manifestation is Christ. Thus, Christ is the source of the expectation – which is Christ within and among them (the ethnic multitudes). The "glory" has now been set in clear light "**in His set-apart folks**" (vs. 26), the covenant community in Christ.

28. **Whom** [other MSS: Which] **we ourselves habitually proclaim down the line** (or: announce in accord with the pattern), **constantly putting [Him] into the minds of every person** (or: human) **and repeatedly teaching every person** (or: human), **within the sphere of all wisdom, to the intent that we may place every person** (or: human) **finished** (mature; perfect with respect to purpose; complete; as having reached the goal of destiny) **by [our] side, within and in union with Christ** [other MSS add: Jesus],
29. **unto which [goal] I habitually work hard** (or: progressively toil on) **and become weary, constantly struggling as in a contest, corresponding to** (or: down from, yet on the level of)

His inward working (or: energy and operation)**: the One continuously operating** (energizing and inwardly working) **within me – within power and in ability.**

Thus it is, as he says in 28 & 29, that this Secret – both His anointing, and Christ Himself – was being habitually proclaimed: in accord with the pattern (the directives of His household administration). Paul was putting this plan and purpose into their minds; he was inserting Him into their minds, repeatedly teaching every human. The sphere of his teaching was wisdom; the intent and scope of his announcing was to "**place every human**" by their side as a finished, mature and complete person that had reached the goal of their destiny (along with the firstfruits) – and this was to place them "**within and in union with Christ**."
This was the goal of his continuous work, his progressive toil. He related it to being in a contest, but his struggle corresponded to, and was on the level of, Christ's inward working (His energy; His operation) Whom he acknowledged as being that continuous operation and powerful ability. As with Paul, it is Christ, and His power and His ability, inwardly working within us: this is the glory; these are the riches of the Secret; this is God's reign and kingdom within and among us, which Paul proclaimed (Acts 20:25; 28:23). The "**power and ability**" are the influence and activity of His reign in us. He is "**continuously operating within [us]**."

Chapter 2

1. **You see, I continue wanting you folks to have seen and thus perceive** (realize; know) **[the] size of and how extensive a contest I am having and how intense a struggle I constantly hold** (or: continue to have) **over [the situation of] you and the folks in Laodicea, and as many as have not seen my face in [the] flesh,**

Here we see Paul's actual solidarity with the folks to whom He ministers Christ. He compares it to a contest in the games in the arena, perhaps a wrestling match in which he is struggling along with them as they encounter opposition in their lives. He does not say what it is that he struggles with, on their behalf, but that it is intense, and that perhaps, in his spirit, he is facing off many of those who oppose them. In his spirit he is right there with them, as he was with those at Corinth, "present in spirit" even if "absent in body" (1 Cor. 5:3). Those in Colosse were benefitting from Paul's strength in the Lord, even though he had apparently not met them (*cf* Lightfoot, p. 170). He was having an effect upon their situation, just as if he were physically there. He was wrestling with them against the Domination System that was hostile to them, and perhaps against false teachers who brought legalism, dualism or ascetic Jewish mysticism in among them. But as to the last clause of the verse, Lohse suggest that this actually means, "all who are among you and do not yet know me personally" (ibid., p. 80).

2. **to the end that their hearts may be called near, alongside, for comfort, relief, aid and encouragement – being joined cohesively** (jointly knitted; welded together; literally: mounted together in copulation) **and united in love and acceptance – even into all the riches** (or: wealth) **pertaining to the state of having been brought to fullness** (or: of the full assurance and conviction) **from the comprehension** (or: which is the joint-flow of discernment; of the junction of that which is sent together for a person to be able to catch on and understand) **[leading] into full, accurate, intimate and experiential knowledge and insight of God's Secret: Christ**
> (or: of the secret of the God who is Christ; or: of the secret from God, which is [the] Anointing; [with other MSS: of the sacred mystery of the God and Father, in relation to the Christ {or: having its source in [the] Anointing; or: belonging to Christ}]),

His performing as a paraclete for them (as expressing in the first clause of vs. 2) was actually giving them aid, relief, comfort and encouragement. The end in view was for their hearts to be joined cohesively (welded or knitted together, in union as lovers) **in love and acceptance** (*agape*). This would bring them into all the riches that come with the condition of having been brought to fullness through comprehension – where things just fall together to give understanding – which leads into full, accurate, intimate and experiential knowledge of and insight into (*epi-*

gnosis) God's Secret, which is Christ. As you see above, this last phrase can also be rendered: "the secret from God, which is [the] Anointing."

So where in 1:27 the focus of the Secret was Christ within and among those within the nations, here the Secret is put more simply, and I have given three functions of the genitive: 1) of possession: that Christ is God's Secret; 2) of apposition: the secret of the God who is Christ [note: with both God and Christ being in the genitive, this could read "of the God-Christ"]; and 3) instead, rendering God as ablative (or, genitive of source): "the secret from God," and *christou* as apposition and translating it "which is [the] Anointing." Lastly, I inserted other MSS readings, with *christou* rendered as a genitive of relation, and then as a genitive of source, and finally as a genitive of possession. Each of these functions work and make sense within the context. Perhaps all these options will create a more complete picture of the Secret.

Now consider: This beautiful result comes from their being intimately joined together as a unit. The fruit of the knowledge of Christ comes from such solidarity in spirit. Such wealth and fullness ensues from bonded loving relationships.

3. **within Whom** (or: in which) **are** (continually exist) **all the hidden-away** (or: concealed) **treasures** (or: treasure chests or vaults; storehouses) **of the wisdom and experiential, intimate knowledge and insight.**

Here, the antecedent of the first phrase is either Christ, or, the secret (thus: Whom/which). In this, in Him are ALL the hidden-away and concealed treasures (or: storehouses) of Wisdom and experiential Knowledge/intimate Insight. What an inclusive statement! It is an amplification set in parallel to vs. 2. You can leave behind all the wisdom literature, all the Gnostic writings, all the mystic religions, even all the Law of Moses and the Prophets: the riches from all of these (and they all do have some riches of insights – Father is gracious and bountiful to all) are now manifested in Christ. The goal has arrived, folks: just abide in Him (John 15:4).

I have here read *apokruphoi* (nom. pl. adj.: hidden-away; concealed) as modifying *thesauroi* (nom. pl. noun: treasures; etc.). Paul is here contrasting the riches of Christ, Whose Light reveals all, to the Gnostic "hidden knowledge" that is kept secret from the masses. But all those "**hidden-away vaults of the wisdom and knowledge**" that the Gnostics claimed to have are now revealed to be within the Messiah, and are manifested through Christ: they are not "hidden" in Him any longer. Paul spoke of the treasure in 2 Cor. 4:7, " **Now we presently and continuously hold** (have and possess) **this treasure within containers** (jars; pots; vessels; equipment) **made of baked clay** [e.g., pottery; bone ware]." This is because the Christ, within Whom these treasures of wisdom and insightful knowledge exist, lives within us!

4. **Now I am presently saying this so that no one may be derailing you in a persuasive discourse or reasoning, by logic and reasoning that are off to the side and thus cheats by false reckoning,**

Don't be bumped off the Track by legalistic thinking from the old creation, the old covenant. Don't be lured off the Path by fascinating trinkets from some hidden source, or by plausible arguments from philosophy. These will cheat you by their false reckoning: stay with Jesus Christ! Recall what He said to the "sheep and the kids" in Matt. 25 – this is a real life, meeting real needs in the lives of the lost and the dead (who, incidentally, He regards as being Himself – even if they are in prison, or destitute). Keep in mind those with whom He spent His time – the outcasts!

False reckoning can cheat us from the fullness of the knowledge of Christ and the benefits of being lovingly joined, as described in vs. 2. Wherever we are not cohesively joined in love for others we are derailed from the realities of Christ, and fall short of His glory.

5. **for though** (or: even if) **I am presently absent** (or: being away) **in the flesh, nevertheless I continue being together with you folks in the spirit** (or: by the Spirit; in union with the Breath-effect), **constantly rejoicing and seeing** (or: observing) **your arranged succession** (or:

drawing up of rank and file for an ordered disposition in battle array; or: post and place in line; also: = a body of soldiers or militia) – **as well as the solid body having a backbone which is the result of strengthening unto firmness – of your trust and faith** (or: pertaining to your faithfulness and loyalty; which have the qualities of confidence and conviction of you folks) **[which is being placed] into Christ** (or: [which flows] into [the] Anointing).

Again he is affirming his actual solidarity with them, his being a part of them, in union with the Breath-effect – by the Spirit and in his spirit. Note that although he has been intensely struggling (vs. 1), he is "**constantly rejoicing**" as he sees their arranged succession, post and place in line, which "**as the solid body having a backbone**" shows strengthening unto firmness (part of this due to Paul's participation with them). Now note the last clause where he defines this strength and firmness: their trust and faith; their faithfulness and loyalty which have the qualities of confidence and conviction! But is this their own good qualities? No, it is the fact that their disposition of strength, compared to a battle array, and their backbone is due to all of this having been placed into Christ, flowing into the Anointing. It all comes from our awareness of the Secret: our participation in the knowledge of Him, and our union with Him. Placing our trust into Him, where He guards and keeps this faith and trust, is also the secret.

6. **Therefore, as you folks take along and receive** (or: took to your side and accepted) **the Christ – Jesus, the Lord** (the Owner; the Master) **– continue walking about** (i.e., ordering your life) **within Him** (and: in union with Him),
7. **being people having been rooted** (or: having been caused to take root) **– even ones being constantly and progressively built upon The House** (i.e., added to the structure) **– within Him; also being folks repeatedly made steadfast and progressively stabilized with good footing within the faith** (or: confirmed by the conviction; made secure for trust and loyalty), **just as you are taught** (or: were instructed), **continuously superabounding** (being surrounded by more than enough) **within it – within gratitude and thanksgiving** (or: in an expression of the ease and goodness of grace, as well as the well-being of favor).

Now note in vs. 6 how specific Paul is when he speaks of their receiving the Christ and of their taking Him to their side. He does not just say "the god in you; the Christ-consciousness in you," he says "**Jesus, the Lord, Owner and Master**." It is within Him, the Person of God, within Whom, and in union with Whom, that we are to continue walking about, ordering and living our lives. He remains our Source and Head; He is our Owner and Master! We cannot leave Him behind as though we have advanced beyond what the Scriptures show us. Note also that the Greek construction used here suggests the term "the Christ," which equals "the Messiah," as a title, not part of a personal name. The additional title, "the Lord," speaks to His position as Ruler – in contrast to Caesar being lord – of the creation, and Owner of all as slaves, for this was the primary meaning of *Kurios*.

Vs. 7 combines two metaphors: agriculture/vegetation, and construction. We have been caused, by the Spirit of the Life of Christ, to take root down into Him (He is the Ground of our being); we are His planting, His vineyard, His crop of grain. At the same time we are being "**constantly and progressively**" built upon the House of God (God's Temple); we are an added room on the Father's House (John 14:2). Note the expressive changes in the verb tenses in these metaphors: first the perfect, "**having been rooted**;" next the present, expressing being constantly and progressively built. These are two aspects of the work of God upon, and in, us. And all this "**within/in union with Him**." Lightfoot points out "The rapid transition of metaphor... the path [vs. 6], the tree [or plant], the building..." (Lightfoot, p. 174; my additions).

Paul goes on to emphasize that they/we are folks that are repeatedly **made steadfast** (in case we slip or stumble) and **progressively stabilized with good footing within the faith** – confirmed by conviction; made secure for trust! He does it all. As well as this being a picture of solidarity, Lohse see in it a "consolidation" of the community (ibid., p. 94). Note that this came through instruction and teaching, within which they were continuously superabounding. Consider what this means concerning the importance of teaching. Many want to say, "Just having Christ is enough for me," but Jesus spent years of intensive instruction to His disciples, and then they continued to learn by the teaching of the Holy Spirit. (In the natural life you do not become a doctor just by knowing one.) And all this "**within gratitude and thanksgiving** – or in an expression of the ease and goodness of grace, as well as the well-being of favor." We have come into such good news! Here, Lightfoot says, "Thanksgiving is the end of all human conduct, whether exhibited in words or in works" (ibid, p. 175). Amen.

8. **Keep watching out for and beware that someone will not be the one progressively** (or: repeatedly) **carrying you off captive** (after stripping you of arms and seizing your goods, proceed in kidnapping you as booty or a prey) **through the philosophy and empty seduction** (or: a deceitful trick having no content) **being handed down from and being in line with the tradition of the people** (or: corresponding to the thing handed along from humans), **down from** (or: in line with and corresponding to) **the elementary principles** (or: rudimentary teachings and fundamental assumptions) **of the organized System** (the world of culture, religion, government, secular society or economy), **and not down from Christ** (or: in accord with the sphere of and in line with Christ; corresponding to an Anointing),

This vs. begins by repeating the caution given in vs. 4; it must have been a real concern to Paul. History shows us how real a threat it was. Here he shows how "**the philosophy and empty seduction** from **the tradition of the people**" can take us into captivity – which means that we lose our freedom. Witherington points out the human tradition and philosophy which Paul is addressing in this community is deceptive, and that "Paul is speaking into a rhetorically and philosophically saturated environment" (ibid., p. 154). Lightfoot says that "Philo speaks of the Hebrew religion and Mosaic law as *the philosophy of the fathers*," and that "Josephus speaks of the three Jewish sects as *three philosophies*," and refers to what Paul says in this verse as speaking of philosophies that are "hollow and misleading" (ibid, p. 177). 4 Macc. 5:11 exhorts, "Will you not awake from your trifling philosophy? and give up the folly of your notions...?" This is the state of the institutional church today. Their minds are held captive to church traditions; they are afraid to think for themselves or be led by the Spirit into all truth. It is "**the elementary principles** and rudimentary teaching and fundamental assumptions" (*stoicheia*) of both society and the organized church (the world of which Paul warns us not to be conformed to – Rom. 12:2) that is their captors, their adversaries. Lightfoot paraphrases this, "They enforce an elementary discipline of mundane ordinances fit only for children. Theirs is not the Gospel of Christ" (ibid, p. 175). Witherington states that "there is no lexical evidence" that *stoicheia* meant either the "heavenly bodies composed of the basic elements" or "the elementary spirits of the universe (e.g., demons, angels and spirits)".... "before or during NT times," but that there is much evidence for it meaning "elementary teachings" (ibid., p. 155).

It is the instruction and teaching of Jesus and the Spirit (vs. 7) which come to us via His Word and His Spirit/Anointing – and which are in accord with the sphere of Christ, and in line with Christ – to which we are to adhere. This was also a contrast to the initiation into the "mystery rites" which were the traditions of pagan religions, or to the "**traditions of men**" (Mark 7:8).

9. **because within Him all the effect of the fullness of the Deity** (the result of the filling from the Godship and feminine aspect of the Divine Nature) **is bodily settling down and taking up permanent residence** (= is continuously dwelling in person),

This is a foundational statement. Who is the Him of this verse? Vs. 6 told us: "Jesus, the Lord." Not just the "cosmic Christ," but the individual, Jesus, Who is our Owner and Master. This is a critical concept, for Jesus is God having become human and taking up permanent residence in this solidarity with humanity. He is the Second Humanity, the Last Adam (1 Cor. 15:45-47). He is both an individual, and corporate humanity. As a human, in Him "**all the fullness of the Deity continues bodily settled, in permanent residence.**"

But let us remember that we are joined to Him. He and the Father have taken up residence in us (John 14:23). When we think of fullness, in this verse, we should not think quantity, but quality.

90

All that He is, is within us – and thus are we His body, the organism within which He lives and moves and has His Being. Can we receive this? Just keep in mind, it is Him, not us, for Paul tells us elsewhere that we/he no longer live(s), but Christ lives within us (Gal. 2:20). Yet, we are not obliterated by His presence in us – we are joined to Him and are now one spirit/Spirit with Him (1 Cor. 6:17).

You may be wondering why I rendered the word "Deity" also as "Godship and the feminine aspect of the Divine Nature." That is because the Greek word *theotēs* is feminine.

So we are not to be captured by the assumptions and teachings of organized religion, or of society, BECAUSE all God's fullness dwells in the Christ: He is the source for what we are to believe, and for how we are to live our lives – He is the Way.

10. **and you folks, being ones having been filled up** (or: made full), **are** (or: exist) **continuously within, and in union with, Him, Who is** (or: exists being) [other MSS: the One being] **the Head of** (or: the Source of) **all government and authority** (or: of every beginning and right; of all rule and privilege which comes from being),

Oh, now what is Paul saying? All the fullness is within Him, yet WE are folks that have been filled up! Filled up with what? With Him. Yet, we continuously exist WITHIN Him. This is immersion (baptism), to the point of saturation (think of a cloth that is immersed into a bowl of dye). But I also expanded the meaning of *en* (within), conflating with it the meaning "**in union wit**h" which give the full picture of our relationship to and with Him.   This verse should not have been broken away from vs. 9 – it is a continuous thought.

Next he gives us another clue: Christ is the Source (like the head of a river) and Head of ALL government and authority. Wow! Sounds like His kingdom has been actualized. His sovereign reign is in place here and now. The buck stops with Him. Can you accept this?

11. **within Whom you folks were also circumcised** (or: in union with Whom you are cut around and off) **by** (or: in; to; with) **a circumcision not done by hands** (not handmade)**: in the sinking out and away from** (or: the stripping off and undressing of; the going out and away from) **the body of the flesh**
      (= the corporate body of the Jewish religion and national heritage; or: = the natural body, or, the body pertaining to the natural realm; or: = the estranged human nature and alienated self) **– in the circumcision of the Christ** (in Christ's circumcision; in the circumcision which was done to Christ; or: in the circumcision which is the Anointing),

By being placed into Christ, even the non-Jews (goyim; Gentiles; ethnic multitudes) become the true Circumcision, as Paul stated to the called-out in Phil. 3:3,
      "**For you see, we ourselves are** (exist being) **The Circumcision: the people** (or: those) **continuously rendering sacred service in a spirit of God within, and in union with, Christ Jesus; even folks** (or: those) **being people having been persuaded and thus continuing to put no confidence within flesh**" (this last phrase referring to either being a physical Jew, or to the old covenant religious system of flesh sacrifices – in contrast to the new covenant of the Spirit). Paul is using a metaphor that symbolized those who were set-apart to, for and in Him – to be His People. These non-Jews are now figuratively Israel, and the seed of Abraham – the only folks in the Scriptures to whom circumcision belonged. It is the same as being God's Temple – a figure taken from the shadow of the old covenant.

Now the last part of this verse gives pause for thought (as if every verse did not!) – "**in the sinking out and away from the body of the flesh in the circumcision of the Christ**." He is obviously not speaking of physical circumcision here, but metaphorically speaks of His death on the cross. I have offered three different paraphrases, parenthetically, at the end of the verse:
a) that this body refers to the corporate body of the Jewish religion and culture;
b) that this has in view our natural body or the body which pertains to the natural realm;

c) that "flesh" here refers to the estranged human nature and the alienated self.
Any or all of these may apply. And in the last phrase of this verse, I particularly like the idea expressed in the rendering "the circumcision which is the Anointing."
It was both a work done by Christ via His cross – once for all – but also, switching metaphors, the progressive work of the Spirit within us as His fire "purifies the sons of Levi" (Mal. 3:3).

But primary to the whole figure of circumcision is: covenant inclusion and participation. Through the crucifixion of the Christ, the Adam of the new humanity was circumcised – His one act of obedience being the representative which stood on behalf of the Many (Rom. 5:8-21), or, all humanity. Thus were the Colossians, and all mankind, circumcised in Christ's circumcision – and were thus made to be included in His covenant with the Adamic race of humans.

12. **being buried together in Him** (jointly entombed with Him) **– within the placing into** (in the immersion and saturation, and its result; in the plunging for permeation; within the overwhelming; in the dipping into; within the baptism) **– within the midst of Whom you folks were awakened and caused to rise up together through the faith which is** (or: belonging to; coming from) **the inward operation of God** (or: the trust belonging to the effectual energizing from and which is God)**: the One awakening and raising Him up, forth from out of the midst of dead folks.**

Here Paul focuses on the work of Christ: His death and burial, figured by immersion (baptism, which involves a "**placing into**;" [note: some MSS read, "the result of baptizing," rather than the act]) which here we see also included us, and then His resurrection within which we were awakened to life and were caused to rise up together "**through the faith having its source in** (or: coming from) **the inward operation of God...**" This echoes 2 Cor. 5:19, "**God was within Christ, progressively and completely reconciling the world to Himself...**" The faith and trust both belong to "the effectual energizing from" God, and it is the "energizing which is God," this latter being the genitive of apposition. God was the One awakening and raising up Christ, and is the One who did the same for us, we being within Christ and having been buried together with Him. Jesus was speaking of His death when in Lu. 12:50 He said, "**I have an immersion** (a baptism) **[within which] to be immersed** (baptized)."

This is also an echo of 1 Cor. 2:2, where Paul said to them, "**for I decided not to see or know anything among you folks, except Jesus Christ – and this One being one having been crucified** (executed on a stake)!" Paul wanted to see the crucified Jesus (which also implied the work of the cross) within them, where the Love of laying down one's life for another was being manifested among them. Here he calls to mind the whole process, from the cross to the burial and then the resurrection. It is this resurrection life that raises us up in union with Him, and which energizes us as He lives within us.

Take note of the passive voice of the verbs in the next to the last clause of vs. 12: "**were awakened and caused to rise up...**" This was the work of God, not the work of our "believing." Note also that it was through "the faith [resident within] the effectual energizing – which is God."

13. **And you folks – continuously being dead ones within** [other MSS: by] **the results and effects of falls to the side, and in** (or: by) **the uncircumcision of your flesh** (= physical bodies or national heritage; or: = estranged human nature and alienated self) **– He makes** (or: made) **alive together: you** [other MSS: us] **jointly together with Him, gracing us and granting favor to us [for; in] all the effects of the falls and stumbling to the side** (= false steps),

Here he continues the metaphor by contrasting their "uncircumcised flesh" to the life in the spirit, i.e., in Christ – "**alive together: you/us jointly together with Him.**" In their physical bodies they were still dying; in their national heritage they were "the uncircumcision" – with regard to the "olive tree" of Rom. 11; they were dead as far as the estranged human nature or the "alienated self" was concerned (as Paul suggests, in Rom 7). Yet He made, and makes, them/us alive together with Him and gives them/us grace in and for all the effects of our false steps and of our falls and stumbling to the side of the path. Being filled up with Him, we yet find ourselves stumbling and falling to the side. But His favor continues, and we find grace for the failures. Once again, it is HE that makes us alive. When we were dead, we could not believe or do anything. When He makes us alive, then we believe – because He has made us alive. Quite simple, really.

14. **anointing and wiping out the handwriting in the decrees** (bonds; bills of debt; ordinances; statutes) **put down against** (or: with regard to the effects of the thoughts or suppositions, and the results of the appearances of what seemed [to be], corresponding to) **us, which was continuing to be under, within and set in active opposition to us, and He has picked it up and lifted it from out of the midst, nailing it to the cross** (or: on the execution stake),
This is another description of the work of the cross, and its effects for us. He became the Law personified, and the Law was nailed to His cross, in His body. Here is where He became sin for us (2 Cor. 5:21), for it was the Law of sin and death (Rom. 8:2) that He nailed to His cross: He put the Law to death, in His body, nailing it to the execution stake. Thus was He in this way the end of the Law for us (Rom. 10:4). Paul uses the preposition *kata* to show that the handwriting was "**down against**" us. From the imperfect tense of the verb we see that these decrees and ordinances were persistently active, and from *hup-en-anti-os* we see that they were close and direct in their opposition to us. *Hupo* has the root meaning of being under, thus this law was our foundation. *En* signifies within, and call to mind the law in our members (Rom. 7:13-23). *Anti* shows that it took the opposite position against us. This adjective intensifies what he had said in *kata*, which in itself means against. However, as *kata* also means "corresponding to" or "in alignment to" or "in the sphere of," this handwriting could also refer to any of the Words of God that were written down, including "dying you will die" in the garden of Eden story.

Furthermore, the word "**decree**" (*dogma*) is from *dokeo* which means "to appear; to seem; to think; to suppose." The *–ma* ending signifies "the effect" or "the result." Thus have I given the inserted parenthetical rendering for your consideration, along with the alternate meaning of *kata*.

But note that He "**lifted it from out of the midst**." He took it out of the midst of our being, replacing it with "**the principle and law of, and which is, the spirit and attitude of 'The Life within Christ Jesus'**" (Rom. 8:2). But He also removed it from the midst of our society, from out of the midst of the creation which He was making new. The cross changed everything.

He also freed us from slavery to sin, wiping out the bonds and bills of debt, as well as the ordinances and statutes (i.e., the necessity for keeping the Law). "In the case before us the Jewish people might be said to have signed the contract when they bound themselves by a curse to observe all the enactments of the law (Deut. 27:14-16; comp. Ex. 24:3); and the primary reference would be to them" – Lightfoot, p. 185. Lightfoot further points out that the non-Jews, "**not having a law** (or: [the] Law), **are in and among themselves a law**" (Rom. 2:14b), would thus also be included in this.

This picture could also be a metaphor for a philanthropist (in this case our Kinsman-Redeemer) paying the debt of a slave (us) and thus "erasing" the bond that was standing against us. He gave His life over our situation. With His death the old heaven and earth passed away; with His resurrection the new heaven and earth were birthed into existence.

15. **after Himself causing the sinking out and away of** (or: stripping off and away [of power and abilities]; undressing [them of arms and glory]; putting off and laying away [of categories and classifications]; or: divesting Himself of) **the governments and the authorities** (or: the ruling folks or people of primacy, and the privileged folks). **And then He made a public exhibit, in a citizen's bold freedom of speaking the truth, leading them in a triumphal procession within it [i.e., the cross].**
>(or: Undressing Himself {or: Stripping [them] off from Himself}, He also made a public display of the rulers and the authorities, with boldness leading them as captives in His victory procession in it {or: in union with Him}.)

The base verb of the beginning participle is *duno* and means "to sink, go down; to set (as the sun)." This in itself points to the ending of the age, before the arising of the new day. The voice being middle is expressed in the reflexive "**Himself**" as being the Actor. But it could also give the picture of Christ having taken all upon Himself all governments and authorities, as the representative Human, and then via the cross stripping off Himself, and us. Christ took the old to the grave, and stepped out of it, leaving the former clothing in the tomb. Lightfoot points to the force of the double compound formed by prefixing two prepositions to this word. The first is *ek*, and thus makes *ekduo* which strictly means "to sink or go out from, and thus, to take off, strip or unclothe." To this is prefixed the preposition *apo* which signifies "off; away." Lightfoot says that this word "appears not to occur at all before St. Paul, and rarely if ever after his time..." (ibid, p. 187).

So notice here what happens to the governments and ruling folks (this could refer to the Sanhedrin, the priests, the scribes, etc., as well as secular governments and rulers), as well as those folks of privilege (this could be a reference to the Jews), they were caused to sink out and away, or, put in other words:
a) He stripped off and away their [power and abilities]; He took the kingdom away from the Jews;
b) He undressed them [of their arms and glory]; He divested priests of their robes and position;
c) He put off and laid away [categories and classifications]; He made Jew and Gentile to be one;
d) He divested Himself of folks that rule others, as well as the People (Israel) who had been in the position of primacy (Greek: *archas*), and those who had lived with privilege from out of who they were (Greek: *ex-ousia* – out of being). A prophetic picture of this can be see in Zech. 3, where Joshua the high priest is clothed with filthy garments, but was stripped and given a change of vestments with a pure (LXX) miter on his head.

Through their killing Him, He publically exhibited both who they were, and the Domination System [Walter Wink's term] out of which they operated. The parenthetical optional renderings at the end of this verse speak for themselves. Through the cross He triumphed over the systems of government, society, religion and culture, and took possession of them, as expressed in the picture of the triumphal procession. He is now King of kings and Lord of lords. He speak Truth boldly, as the First Citizen of the New Jerusalem. He now took them and made all things new – a new heaven and a new earth, wherein dwells fairness and equity, in rightwised relationships. He stripped off and put the lordship and privilege of sin away from us (Rom. 6:14) and swallowed up its ensuing death in Victory, removing the strength of sin – the Law (1 Cor. 15:54-57).

Lohse points out the repeated use of the preposition *en* (within) in vss. 7, 9, 10, 11, 12 and 15 with the pronouns "Him," "Whom" or "It." And vs. 13 has *sun* (with; jointly together with) with "Him." The idea of the sphere of His existence and of Himself, together with union and solidarity, are strong concepts in Paul's presentation of our association with Him. It is all "**in Him**."

16. **Therefore, do not let anyone habitually pass judgment on you** (or: make decisions for you) **in [matters of] eating and drinking, nor in a part of a festival, or of a new moon, or of sabbaths** (= concerning things that are of a religious nature),

This is a beautiful statement demonstrating the freedom that Christ has brought (*cf* Gal. 5:1). These are examples that represent being free from religion: freedom from dietary laws, freedom in regard to participating in special functions or to setting certain days apart as holy, and freedom from the Law of Moses, of which sabbath-keeping was a symbol. Recall that this was one of the most frequent complaints of the Pharisees against Jesus. He was a free Man, even though living under, and bringing to an end, the Law. Here, Paul is hinting, "Don't let anyone intimidate you or bring their rules on you. Love them but don't let their religion bring you under their dominion." Lightfoot suggest that the idea "in matters of" (*en merei*) "seems originally to mean 'in the division or category'..." (ibid, p. 191). These are the things that create a religion, and doctrines. These were characteristics of the former arrangement (or: covenant), the old order. "Under the new, they have ceased to have any value.... [and are] alien to the spirit of the New Covenant" (ibid, p. 192).

See the article "Colossians, Community and the Church's Meal Table," by Dr. David Byrd at the end of this chapter.

17. **which things are a shadow of the things being about to be** (or: of the impending), **yet now the body belongs to the Christ**
>(or: So we see, the body is Christ; or: Now the body has its origin in the Christ; or: Yet the body has the character and qualities of [the] Anointed; [note: A.T. Robertson sees in this construction "the body" {figure of: "the substance"} as casting the shadow; Vincent is similar]).

That they are termed by Paul "**a shadow**" calls to mind the references to the Law, as being such, in the book of Heb. See Heb. 8:5, and also 10:1, which says:
>"**For the Law** (= Torah), **having and holding a shadow of the impending good things**..." – which is almost the same as what is said here.

The contrast could also be between the body – which signified people, and is that which actually matters – and religious behavior, which has no substance and is really insignificant.
I have set the last clause with four of the functions of the genitive case. The body was created as the new creation in Christ, so it is set in contrast to the Law. Consider the what Robertson and Vincent laid out in the parenthetical note, above. As to the last clause, Lightfoot states, "As the shadow belonged to Moses, so '*the substance belongs to Christ*'; i.e. the reality, the antitype, in each case is found in the Christian dispensation" (ibid, p. 193).

18. **Let no one be acting as an umpire, or an arbiter in the public games, so as to decide down against you, or to disqualify you, in regard to the prize** (or: to award the prize [to you] unjustly – Eduard Lohse) **– in lowness of understanding, intellect, frame of mind and deportment, continuously wanting [you] also [to be] in ritual-relating to the agents**
>(or: constantly delighting in religious activity originating from the messengers [note: e.g., old covenant rituals]; or: repeatedly taking pleasure by cultic religious service about, or external worship of or through the "angels"), **while continuously stepping randomly and rashly into** (or: entering purposelessly, thoughtlessly or feignedly into; or: = being initiated into) **things which he has** [other MSS: he has not] **seen** [note: this may refer to being initiated into cultic secrets or mysteries], **progressively being made natural and instinctual by the inner senses and perceptions of his flesh**
>(or: habitually being puffed up under [the influence of] the mind of his flesh [= his natural abilities and conditions, or by his alienated self, or by the human nature that has been conformed to the System]),

Paul here speaks against some general categories of religious involvement, beginning by using participation in the stadium games of his day as a metaphor for not letting anyone detract them from the goal of life (Christ, God's will for them, living in love, etc.), which he represents as "**the prize**" of winning the games. Note that this word could also apply to being told that you "won the contest" when in fact you did not. This is the other side of an "unjust award," and would speak to people promoting you to a position for which you did not qualify, due to their lack of discernment.

Those who pay special attention to a person's way of understanding (in this case, selecting against use of the mind and intellect to understand the things of God, or stressing humility), or to maintaining a specific frame of mind (e.g., detachment, or an attitude of "warring" in the spirit), or to the specific manner in which one is to conduct himself, or to doing some kind of ritual which relates to the agents (in religion, called "angels") – these folks are to be ignored and not followed in their ritualistic behaviors. Note in the parenthetical expansion that the genitive *ton angelon* can read "about 'angels,'" to use the common term. Apparently the "Colossian philosophy" brought teachings of this nature into the covenant life of the community – and Paul here warns against it. Ideas of "intermediate agents" are not an integral part of the good news about Jesus as Lord, and about His establishment of His body in the earth. Such ideas were characteristic of Gnosticism. The reports of interactions with messenger-agents from the spirit realm are incidental to, and are certainly a peripheral part of, all the NT writings.

Lohse suggests that the phrase *en tapeinophrosune* (which I first render: "**in lowness of understanding, intellect, frame of mind and deportment**") can also mean "fasting" – a cultic conduct for preparing one's self to receive mystic experiences (ibid., p. 118).

As to the clause "**while continuously stepping randomly and rashly** (or: to no purpose; thoughtlessly; feignedly) **into things which he has** [other MSS: he has not] **seen**," some scholars (e.g., Lohse; the translators of the New World Translation) consider this a quote. Witness Lee (*Recovery Version of the NT, notes, p. 931*) suggests that it refers to " the heretical teachers [who] lived in the realm of sight, in contrast to the faith mentioned in vs. 12." The verb is used only here in the NT, and some scholars have suggested that it infers approaching something so as to examine it, or to investigate a matter. From this it has been considered to refer to initiation into a mystery cult. See the notes on Merkabah Mysticism (a Jewish variant of Hellenistic mysticism) by Dr. Ann Nyland (*The Source NT*, Smith and Stirling Publishing, Aus., 2004, p. 390-391). Lohse (ibid., p. 119-120) points out that this verb was found in inscriptions that were excavated at the sanctuary of Apollo at Klaros, which suggests its use with regard to initiation into that mystery religion. The MSS that insert the word "not" in this clause suggest a copyist's desire to debunk the supposed experience – or else these copies came from a source that was earlier to those of my first rendering.

He also warns against rash religious behavior or random participation in that which comes from visions or spiritual experiences (things that someone has either seen, or pretends to have seen), which behavior and participation leads to a life that is more and more concerned with natural things rather than truly spiritual concerns – even as far as just leading a life from instinct, rather than being led of the Spirit, and following "**perceptions of his flesh**" or the conditioning of the System, rather than discerning by the Spirit. The alternate parenthetical rendering of the last clause describes the fruit of a mind that is natural, as opposed to spiritual (resulting from the new birth, having been joined to God's Spirit), and which "puffs itself up, without reason."

19. **and thus not continuously** (or: terminating the continuum of) **getting strength from** (or: apprehending and becoming strong by) **the Head** (or: the Source), **from out of Whom all the body** (or: the entire body) **– being constantly fully furnished and supplied to excess with funds and nourishment, and progressively joined cohesively** (welded together; knitted and compacted together; united and made to go together as in mounting for copulation) **through the instrumentality of the joints** (connections; junctures; fastenings) **and links** (things bound together, as by ligaments) **– goes on growing and increasing God's growth**
> (or: the growth of God; the growth having its source in God; the growth pertaining to God; the growth and increase which is God; or: the growth from God).

The involvements of vs. 18 are here contrasted to being strengthened by the Head and from the Source (Christ) and being in proper relationship to the rest of the body of Christ, each member receiving nourishment through its connection to other members in a continuum of flow (as with a circulation system) and being "**progressively joined cohesively through the instrumentality of the joints** (connections in the body) **and links**." Paul uses a human body as a metaphor for the knitted and compacted union of each person to Christ, and to each other person, with the desired end being continuous "**growing and increasing God's growth** (the growth of God, and the individual's growth from God)." These final parenthetical options represent different function of the genitive case in the last phrase of the verse, "from God" being sometimes called the ablative case, all having the same spelling in Greek.

"The increase and growth of God" is a startling concept, and even more so since it happens through people, the "body" of Christ. Here we see a certain fluidity and expansion in the aspects of God. In Himself there seems to be a kind of openness which He creates as He expands and directs His own creation – all, I suggest, in accord with His purpose (Eph. 1:9-11).

MS D* (noted for its additions which add clarifications) and a few others add the word "Christ" after the word "Head."

20. **Since** (or: If) **you folks died together with Christ, away from the world's system of elementary principles** (or: the rudimentary teachings and fundamental assumptions of the organized System [e.g., world of religion, secular society, education or culture]), **why, as living in [the] world** (in an organized system), **are you constantly being subjected to** (or, as a middle: submitting to; binding yourself to) **rules** (decrees; commands; or: effects of thoughts or results of imaginations; "dogmas" [of the system])**:**
21. **"You should not** (or: may not) **touch** (handle; light or kindle), **nor yet should you** (or: may you) **taste by sipping** (= partake of or enjoy), **nor yet should you** (or: may you) **come into contact!"**

In 20 and 21 he gives more arguments for staying away from religion and the teachings of the organized System, in its various forms. The examples he chooses are primarily from the Law, but we can see the same in institutional Christianity (most of which has adopted much from the Law as their particular rules of behavior, within the various sects). All such things are contrary to the freedom which we have in Christ and a life of growth which He characterized as being organic (e.g., as with the Vine and His branches). We should not be subjected to "**rules**," or decrees, or commands, or "effects of thoughts or imaginations," and especially to "dogmas" of the System.

Note the clear and firm statement of vs. 20 that we "**died together with Christ**." This is a central concept of Paul's theology. We need to affirm this in our own thinking, and take on his own point of view, and attitude, "**that** [some MSS add: since] **One Person** (or: Man) **died over [the situation of] all mankind** (or: for the sake of all); **consequently all died** (or: accordingly, then, all humanity died)" – 2 Cor. 5:14. Can we accept that all humanity died in Christ? Believe it! Paul repeats the fact that the Colossians are dead below, in ch. 3:3. And our personal outlook and view of ourselves should be,

> "**I was crucified together with Christ, and thus it remains** (or: I have been jointly put on the execution stake in [the] Anointed One, and continue thus), **yet I continue living! [It is] no longer I, but it is Christ continuously living and alive within me!** (or: No longer an "I" – now Christ constantly lives in the midst of, and in union with, me). **Now that which I, at the present moment, continue living within flesh** (= a physical body), **I am constantly living within faith – in and by that [faith] which is the Son of God** (or: in union with trust and confidence that is from God's Son [with other MSS: in the confidence belonging to God and Christ]), **the One loving me and giving Himself over to another for the sake of me** (or: even transmitting Himself, over my [situation and condition]; or: also passing Himself along for me)." (Gal. 2:20)

Vs. 21 describes things which the Pharisees would demand, as well as some sects of Christianity. However, it also spoke against any "asceticism" of whatever sort of teaching was disrupting the covenant community. The "do not touch" also echoes Eve's response to the serpent in the garden of Eden, and that was in reference to that which gave knowledge and experience (*gnosis* in the LXX) of good and evil. Such prohibitions produce restriction, not freedom.

22. **– which are all things [that are proceeding] into decay and ruin** (thus: corruption) **by consuming and being used up or misused – down from and corresponding to the effects of commands** (or: on the level of the results of purposed directives and imparted instructions), **as well as teachings and trainings, of humans** (whose source is mankind; from people)**?**
23. **– which things, indeed, having a message** (a word; an expression; may = a promise or reputation) **of wisdom in self-imposed observance of ritual or self-willed form of worship, and in humility** (= self-abasement), **even in asceticism** (unsparing) **of [the] body, [yet are] not of any value or worth [and lead] toward a filling up of the flesh to the point of satiation**

> (= a gratification of the alienated self; = a satisfying of the estranged human nature; or: = a bringing of religious works to the full; or: [and have] no honor, facing a fullness and plenty which are flesh; or: = are worthless, with a view to having enough in the natural realm)**!**

In 22-23 he shows the transitory aspects of such behaviors, as well as their legalistic and human characteristics, which simply come from traditions (*cf* Isa. 29:13, LXX). Their so-called virtues are **"not of any value or worth, and lead toward a filling up of the flesh to the point of satiation**." As such they are contrary to the Spirit of Life. I have offered five possible paraphrases, parenthetically above, as potential interpretations of what Paul is saying in the final clause of vs. 23. I think that his message is clear: stay away from religion and a legalistic lifestyle.

Barclay sums this up by saying, "... freedom comes not from restraining desires by rules and regulations, but from... Christ being in the Christian and the Christian in Christ" (Barclay, ibid., p.146). Lohse sees this section (vss. 16-23) as a detailed refuting of what the philosophers in Colosse were trying to promote (Lohse, ibid., p. 114; for an in-depth discussion on this, which includes consideration of syncretism with Jewish elements, see pp. 129-131).

Chapter 3

1. **Since, therefore, you folks were awakened and are raised up together in the Christ** (or: If, then, you are aroused and raised with the Anointed One), **be constantly seeking and trying to find the upward things** (or: the things being above), **where the Christ is** (exists being), **continuously sitting within the right [side]** (or: at the right [hand]; = at the place of receiving, and in the place of honor and the power) **of God.**

The verb "**raised**" is in the aorist tense, so could either be a simple past tense in English, or a simple present. – thus the two options. Either way, we are aroused and raised. When? When Christ was raised. It was "together with Him." We have been a part of the first resurrection (the Corporate Christ, the Firstfruit from among dead folks). Therefore we are seated with Him in the heavenlies (realms having authority upon the heavens, or the realm of spirit) – Eph. 2:6 – and we should seek out and try to find the "**upward things**," or the things being above, as opposed to the things below. Our focus and attentions should be on Christ and His position of reigning at God's right "hand." We are participating in the reign, or kingdom, of the heavens.

Lightfoot gives an insightful paraphrase here: "If this be so; if ye were raised with Christ, if ye were translated into heaven, what follows?" (ibid, p. 206). The "**therefore**" of this verse begins a transition, in the first four verses of this chapter, to the hortatory expositions which follow, on through 4:6.

2. **Be constantly minding** (thinking about; setting your disposition and sentiments toward; paying regard to) **the upward things** (or: the things above), **not the things upon the earth,**
3. **for you folks died, and your life has been hidden so that it is now concealed together with the Christ, within the midst of God** (or: in union with God).

Vs. 2 is a restatement of the admonition in vs. 1, expanding it, then vs. 3 restates the fact of the Christ event given in vs. 1, from the perspective of the past event of our dying "**together with the Christ**," as well as referring back to 2:12 – "**buried together in Him** (jointly entombed with Him)," and 2:20, "**you folks died together**." Then he explains that our life has now been hidden – concealed – together with the Christ. So Christ is also concealed. Where? Within His body, His house, which is at the same time both within the heavenlies and upon the earth. And all of this is "**within the midst of God**, and in union with God!" And so Paul tells those at Athens "**within the midst of and in union with Him we continuously live**..." (Acts. 17:28). Lightfoot reads, "All your thoughts must abide in heaven.... you *died* once for all to the world: you are living another life," and further on says, "You must not only *seek* heaven; you must also *think* heaven" (ibid, p. 206-7). Note the perfect tense of the verb in the second clause of vs. 3. It is a completed work.

The "**upward things** (or: the things above)" refer first to the realm "**in the Christ**" into which we were "**raised**" (vs. 1), but then to our life in "**the Jerusalem above**" (Gal. 4:26), which is a figure of the covenant community, and the "**invitation to an above place** (or: an upward call)" that Paul refers to in Phil. 3:14. The "atmosphere, or heaven," is what is above, and this is a metaphor for the realm of God and the realm of spirit, as contrasted to the earth, which is a figure to living in the natural realm: either realm can be lived in within this physical body, here on literal earth. Our "**expectation** (or: hope)" – ch. 1:5 – comes from living in and by these "**upward things**." This is equivalent to 2 Cor. 3:18, "**continuously observing the Lord's glory**" so that we are "**progressively transformed into the very same image**" of Christ. It calls to mind Paul's words in Rom. 12:1, where we are called "**to stand [our] bodies alongside [the] Well-pleasing, Set-apart, Living Sacrifice by God**." Our identification with Christ in His death is our "**sacred service**." As Lohse says, "What was once, no longer applies. The old life has been put aside forever through the death which they died together with Christ" (ibid., p. 133). Now consider that this all happened before they had even heard of Christ.

4. **Whenever the Christ, our life** [other MSS: your life], **may be brought to light** (or: should be manifested), **you folks also will be brought to light** (will be manifested), **together with Him, within the midst of glory** (or: in union with a manifestation which calls forth praise; or: in a good reputation; or: = in His manifest presence)
> (or: When Christ, the Anointing, can be manifested, then your life – even you yourself, together with Him – will be manifested in His manifest presence).

So the entire Christ (Jesus and His body) have been hidden and concealed, but vs. 4 speaks of both Him and us being brought to light, manifested together. This manifestation comes within the midst of glory – i.e., in union with a manifestation which calls forth praise and establishes a good reputation. Note that Paul says, "**Whenever**..." This can be interpreted as saying, "At any time where Christ may be brought to light, we **also will be brought to light together with Him**." This happens during the proclamation of the good news. The light is a figure of knowledge, of understanding. He is the Light of the ordered system (John 8:12); we are the light of the ordered system (Matt. 5:14) – we are now light in the Lord (Eph. 5:8), being "**living epistles**." His glory is manifested when He is manifested, for His presence is the glory. When we manifest Him, bring Him to light, we bring Him glory and manifest His glory, or, His good reputation.

This transition has reminded the Colossians of what was then (and is now) the new reality of the new creation, while beginning the admonitions of where their thinking should be. The covenant community is a manifestation (the bringing to light) of Christ, and brings glory to the Father.

5. **Make dead** (Put into a state of deadness; Deaden; = Kill), **therefore, the** [other MSS: your] **members** (body parts; = aspects of your life) **upon the earth** (= that pertain to this earthly existence)**: prostitution** (fornication; sexual immorality), **uncleanness, [unbridled] passion** ([uncontrolled] feeling or [excessive] emotion), **worthless over-desire** (rushing upon bad things; obsessive evil cravings), **and the desire to have more and gain advantage over another** (or: selfish, greedy, grasping thoughts and behavior) **– which is idolatry** (the worship of forms, shapes, images or figures; or: service to pagan concepts)

Here Paul turns to his imperatives, which are based upon the indicative statements of vs. 1, 3 and 4 and which make the imperative possible: their having died and been hidden with Christ in God, then awakened and raised with Christ, and that they themselves will be brought to light whenever He is brought to light. So it follow that they should act accordingly: deaden, or kill their own body parts that pertain to this earthly existence! This echoes Rom. 6:11 where we are admonished to make it a habit to consider ourselves as dead people in regard to all devious behavior. Then, in Rom. 6:13,
> **And stop constantly placing your members** (or: body parts) **alongside** (providing and presenting them) **[as] tools** (or: instruments) **of injustice** (disregard for what is right; activities discordant to the Way pointed out); **but rather, you folks at once place yourselves alongside for disposal to God** (or: stand yourselves with God, at [His] side; by and in God, present yourselves; set yourselves alongside [each other], for God) **as if being folks continually alive, forth from out of the midst of dead ones, and your members [as] tools** (instruments) **of fair and equitable dealing in the Way pointed**

out in and by God (of justice and solidarity, for God; of being turned in the right direction, to God; of rightwised relationships with God).

But before we jump to conclusions, he gives a list of what he was talking about, some of which we would not necessarily think of as being members of our body, but perhaps "aspects" of our lives!? E.g., prostitution – yes, we should let that go, along with our sexual immorality and uncleanness. He calls these "**works of the flesh**" in Gal. 5:19. Today we would not normally think of these as part of the average Christian life. But here he is writing a corrective letter to an established called-out community that has been given deep spiritual truths.

So it seems obvious to me that when he first preached the message of goodness, it was not a moralistic religion that he was presenting. It is here, in this letter, that he is fine-tuning their lives, as if to say, "Considering all of the above, you should probably clean up your lives: no more [unbridled] passion, [uncontrolled] feelings or [excessive] emotions." Note my interpretation by adding bracketed words to qualify the things that are not of themselves bad things. Then there are the worthless over-desires (or: obsessive evil cravings and rushing upon bad things): now that will get you in trouble with the men's accountability group! And next is greedy, grasping thoughts and behavior in your desire to have more and gain advantage. Here we are getting closer to what may be frowned on today, but wouldn't get you excommunicated. Lightfoot puts it this way, "Carry out this principle of *death* to the world... and kill everything that is mundane and carnal in your being" (ibid, p. 209). *Cf* 1 Thes. 4:3-8.

We should take another look at the last in this list: "**the desire to have more and gain advantage over another** (or: greedy, grasping thoughts and behavior)" which he equates to **idolatry** (he does the same in Eph. 5:5). Selfishness, or self-centeredness, are forms of self-worship, of putting one's self at the top of the list – and this is simply idolatry. In Paul's day idolatry often involved the first on the list, prostitution – in the pagan temples – and this was placing one's sexual desires above reverence for family and community, as well as the women who were caught in that system. The word "idolatry" also means the worship of forms, shapes and images. We do have a lot of that: at the check-out counter, at the movies, in the fashion industry, etc. – most of which is also very common in the churches and everyday society, so we should not too quickly check this off as not a concern for us. But an insidious aspect of idolatry which has been directly imported into Christianity is the service to pagan concepts – like worshiping a concept of a god that would eternally torment his enemies: not quite like what Jesus said about loving our enemies, which the true God does (recall John 3:16 from your Sunday school class!). The threat of an eternal hell was a way of controlling kings, as well as the masses. Many used this for selfish gain.

Having secret knowledge (such as with Gnosticism, or with Greek and Egyptian mystery religions) was a desire for self-advancement and personal advantage. The mystery religions offered this, along with their temple prostitutes (sexual intercourse was considered one avenue for enlightenment). But the enticement for personal spiritual advancement and for knowledge of God can also be deceptively perverted into a desire to advance the "self."

Witherington points to the rhetorical symmetry of five vices in this verse contrasted with five virtues presented in vs. 12 (ibid., p. 175-6). This list is but a sample, compared to Rom. 1:24-26, 29-31. *Cf* also Eph. 4:31; 5:3-5 (and here, 1 Cor. 6:9-10).

6. **– because of which things God's inherent fervor** (natural impulse and propensity; internal swelling and teeming passion of desire; or: anger; wrath) **is repeatedly** (or: continuously; progressively) **coming** [other MSS add: upon the sons of The Disobedience (or: those having the condition of being unpersuaded; or: the stubbornness); note: "the disobedience" could refer to Adam and Eve eating from the tree, and thus, the "sons of the disobedience" could refer to all of mankind] –

This verse is parenthetical, so I marked it off with dashes. Here Paul is letting them know what God thinks about the behaviors listed in vs. 5. This word is usually translated "anger" or "wrath," which it can mean, but that is on one extreme of its semantic range of meanings. The other extreme is "natural impulse" or "propensity" (both of which sound rather harmless). "Internal swelling and teeming passion of desire" would probably be in the middle of the range. Eddie Browne arrived at the term "**inherent fervor**" as probably the best phrase to cover all the bases of this broadly used word, *orge*, from which we get our English "orgy." So with all this information, what do you think Paul means in this verse – about what God causes to repeatedly come in response to the activities of vs. 5? The answer lies in your view of Who God is, and What He is like.

This word obviously can have sexual connotations, and "internal swelling or teeming passion of desire" can describe the arousal of a lover. So is God just angry (as Christianity has usually painted Him), or do these behaviors arouse His natural impulse and propensity against them? Does He so love the world, and even the church, that His love arouses Him to intervene with corrective measures? The answer lies in your heart.

Steve Dohse responded, "What does God do in response to these natural, earthly desires? Perhaps 'giving them over to it' is His pouring it out thicker until they come to the end of it, realizing sooner or later it does not fulfill; His *orge* could be a double portion . Sort of like, 'You want quail, I'll give you quail!'" [note: a reference to Num. 11; Ps. 78:18-40; 106:14, 15]

Rebecca Mitchell comments, "It seems to me that, in addition to the usual things a Kingdom-living believer would consider applicable, would be the personal things His spirit reveals to us about ourselves, e.g., our individual weak areas, that lead to actual unbelief in practice and a bad report within our lives instead of affirmation of the Good News and Love Himself.

"It could be pride in attainment spiritually, avarice or envy in this area, displays of feelings of not measuring up or of not getting recognition where we think we ought among the brothers and sisters, what some might call a 'stinking attitude' that brings discord in the assembly; worshiping of persons and dearly held beliefs that stumble others and inhibit the free flow of the Word of Truth; stubbornness and lack of teachability when corrections come, whether from the Spirit directly, from one in the body trying to assist us in our growth, or from a word from the pulpit... There could be a myriad of such personal areas that 'clothesline doctrine' would not normally identify but that Father sees as dark blemishes and will work to correct in our hearts, till we are 'whiter than snow.'" (end quote)

Note that the verb "**coming**" is in the present indicative: it is repeatedly, continuously or progressively coming. This is not an eschatological pronouncement by Paul about some future judgment. God's fervent decisions are habitually and continuously coming upon humanity.

7. **within which things you folks also at one time** (once; formerly) **walked about** (= lived your lives), **when you were living within these things.**

So here Paul gives them the benefit of the doubt, assuming that they have made some progress, from the life of Love within them, but just in case not, he continues in vs. 8:
8. **But now, you folks as well, at once put all these things away from [you, as of clothes put off and laid away]** (or: set off; = renounce or get rid of)**: inherent fervor**
       (or: So at this time you yourselves in one stroke set away and get rid of all the [following]:
          even natural impulse, propensity, internal swelling and teeming desire; or: Yet now, you
          people at once lay aside all intense anger, rage and wrath), **strong passion** (rushing of emotions; outbursts of rage), **worthlessness** (poorness of quality; influence of the bad; hateful intentions), **[and] from out of your mouth: blasphemy** (abusive and injurious talk; slander) **[and] foul-mouthed abuse** (obscenity; ugly words; deformed and shameful language).

Comments on Colossians

There is a practical aspect of life in the Kingdom: showing good form; demonstrating Spirit-ordered behavior; living out the Love of God that is within. 2 Cor. 12:20 and Tit. 3:2 give similar instructions. Consider the parenthetical alternatives that express the semantic range of **inherent fervor** (*orge*). These include even our "natural impulse, propensity, internal swelling and teeming desire" – of themselves not necessarily bad things, but aspects of our humanness that can be in conflict with the unity of the Spirit in the community. Vs. 9 continues his admonitions:

9. **Do not keep on** (or: Stop) **lying unto one another! [Be] folks at once stripping off from yourselves** (undressing yourselves from; or: go out and away from) **the old humanity** (the old human; = the old Adam), **together with its practices,**

Abusive or slanderous speech, ugly words and lying are all things that are done with the mouth. "Life and death are in the power of the tongue" – we can either wound or heal with our words.

The last clause, here, is a positive admonition which really says it all. It is an echo of Eph. 4:22, and it seems that he assumes that they will know what he means. In Rom. 6:6 he told them that **"our old, former humanity is crucified together with [Him]."** He is obviously speaking metaphorically here, but he does not give them a list of actual things to do. I suspect that this is on purpose, as he is not trying to get them back into works, or into religious practices. In Rom. 12:2 he gives a more concrete example:
> "**And stop constantly conforming yourself to** (or, as passive: And quit being repeatedly fashioned or patterned together by) **this age** [or, with other MSS: and not to be continuously configured to this age; and to not constantly remodel yourself for this age], **but on the contrary, be continuously transformed** (transfigured; changed in shape, form and semblance) **by the renewing** (or: in the renewal; for the making-back-up-new again) **of your mind into the [situation and condition for] you to be habitually examining in order to be testing and, after scrutiny, approving what [is] God's will** (design; purpose; resolve; intent): the good and well-pleasing, even perfect (finished and complete)! (or: the thing [that is] virtuous, satisfying and able to succeed.)"

So it seems to be a thing of the mind and attitude; perhaps where we put our focus: on ourselves, our want, our needs, or on Christ – both in ourselves and in others. Eph. 6:11 he says,
> "**you folks must enter within** (or: clothe yourselves with) **the full suit of armor and implements of wa**r (panoply; the complete equipment for men-at-arms) **which is God** (or: which comes from and belongs to God), **in order for you to be continuously able and powerful to stand** (or: to make a stand) **facing toward the crafty methods** (stratagems) **of the adversary**
>> (or: that which throws folks into dualism with divided thinking and perceptions; or: the person that throws something through the midst and casts division; the one who thrusts things through folks; the slanderer who accuses and deceives; or, commonly called: the 'devil'),"

So just "enter within... God." And then do however He so leads you.

10. **and then [be] suddenly clothing yourselves with** (or: entering within) **the new one** (the fresh one which existed only recently), **the one being continuously** (or: repeatedly; habitually; progressively) **renewed** (made back up new again, in kind and character) **into full, accurate, added, intimate and experiential knowledge and insight which is down from and corresponds to the image** (an exactly formed visible likeness) **of its Creator** (of the One framing and founding it from a state of wildness and disorder),

Sounds like Eph. 6:11, where the same verb is use of clothing ourselves with the complete armor which is God. The "**new one**" is the new humanity of the new creation – being a part of the Second Human (1 Cor. 15:47).
> "**But rather, you folks must clothe yourselves with** (or: enter within and put on) **the Lord, Jesus Christ, and stop** (or: do not continue) **making forethought** (constructing

provision; planning ahead; performing provident care) **into excessive desires of the flesh** (= into rushing upon emotions which pertain to the inner self or the estranged humanity; = into the setting of feelings and longings upon something of the human nature that is oriented to the System)" – Rom. 13:14. Put on, as your apparel – that which covers you, protects you and presents you to society – the character and qualities of Christ (basically, love, and all which that entails). This puts you in right relationship with others and points your life in the right direction: toward the goal of maturity in Christ. It is also a contrast of living in the spirit (our new life in Christ) as opposed to living in the flesh (our former natural life).

The term "**Creator**" can refer back either to ch. 1:16 (Christ), to 2 Cor. 5:17 (Christ and the new creation in Christ), or to Gen. 1:27.

Lohse points out that "the indicative sentences refer back to the passing from death to life... the imperatival admonitions point ahead, into the actualization of the new life..." (ibid., p. 145).

In the last clause, consider that being a true image-bearer of our Creator corresponds to "**full, intimate and experiential knowledge and insight**" and this recalls the prime goal given in Gen. 1:26. But here it is the full, accurate and added knowledge (*epi-gnosis*), rather than the knowledge, or knowing, (*ginoskein*) of Gen. 2:17.

Note that this is not a static condition: it is the New Being that is being continuously and progressively renewed (present, passive participle – indicating God's ongoing action: *cf* 2 Cor. 4:16), and which leads you into "**full, intimate and experiential knowledge and insight**" – all of which has its source in **and corresponds to the image of** our Creator, which of course is the image of Christ.

11. **wherein** (or: in which place) **there is no Greek** [figure of the multitudes who are non-Jews, and of those who are cultured and civilized] **and Jew** [figure of a covenant people of God], **circumcision and uncircumcision** [figure for religious in-groups and out-groups; there is no longer a covenant people versus non-covenant people], **barbarian** [foreigner who speaks a different language], **Scythian** [figure or example of wild, uncivilized groups], **slave, freeman, but to the contrary, Christ [is] all, and within all**
> (or: Christ [is] all humanity, and within all mankind; or: Christ [is] everything or all things, and within everything and all things; [note: the Greek is plural, and is either masculine, signifying "mankind," or neuter, signifying all creation, in these phrases]).

Ah, the beauty of the New Creation: the sphere and realm of Christ. Paul again inserts an indicative here, among his imperatives. There are no more divisive distinctions; no more religious separations; no more elite people or groups; no more "us and them;" no more class levels (*cf* Gal. 3:28). These are words describing the unification within which Christ created the called-out community. Witherington points out that there are no longer "boundary markers and rituals that divide the community" (ibid. p. 174). This is a picture of the corporate Christ, the reality of God's reign, pictured as the New Jerusalem, "which is above" (Gal. 4:26). It is "**the image of its Creator**" (vs. 10) where the New Humanity is One. Most ethnic groups developed the idea that they were "the people" and everyone else comprised "the others." But here we see no boundary or identity markers. The coming of the Messiah and the new age that ensued put an end to all this in the economy of God. Lightfoot cites Max Muller as having said that the word "barbarian" was eliminated from "the dictionary of mankind" as was "replaced" by the word "brother" (ibid, p. 216). See a similar picture in Gal. 3:28 which includes the absence of the male/female categories. Gal. 6:15 identifies this socio-religious situation as "**a new creation**." 1 Cor. 7:22 turns these categories on their heads, in the covenant community:
> **In fact, the person within the Lord** [= Christ or Yahweh] – **being one that was called [when being] a slave – is [the] Lord's freed-person** (or: exists being [Christ's or Yahweh's] emancipated slave). **Likewise, the person being one that was called [when being] free, or a freedman, is Christ's slave.**

Wherever we do not see this situation wherein there are separating distinctions we are not observing Christ or His kingdom. This is why you often do not see the Truth or the new Reality in the institutional churches; you simply see a hierarchical religion and a code of morality that separate "us from the them." This is why the Spirit still says, "**Come out of her, My people**..."

In the parenthetical alternate rendering of the last phrase of this verse, you will note how I present the Greek *panta* and *pasin* as masculine: "Christ [is] all humanity, and within all mankind." This reflects what Paul called "**the Second Humanity**" in 1 Cor. 15:47 (or: "the Last Adam" in vs. 45). Too often we have simply read over the words "all in all" without thinking of their far-reaching and all-inclusive implications. This is a startling statement! Think what this means! Let it sink into your spirit; digest it; absorb it; let it become you! Lightfoot here says, "Christ occupies the whole sphere of human life and permeates all its developments" (ibid, p. 217). This present reality is the firstfruit of the plan of the ages, as Paul describes its completeness in 1 Cor. 15:28,

> **Now whenever the whole** (or: all things) **may be completely supportively-aligned in Him** (or: subjected/appended to Him; subordinately sheltered and arranged for Him), **then the Son Himself will also be supportively aligned to, fully subjoined for and humbly attached under as an arranged shelter in, the One subjecting, appending and sheltering the whole in Him** (or: attaching all things to Him), **to the end that God can be all things within the midst of and in union with all humanity** (or: may be everything in all things; or: should exist being All in all; or: would exist being everything, within the midst of everyone).

12. **Therefore, as God's chosen, set-apart and beloved ones** (or: God's sacred, loved and chosen people; or: as elect... ones from God), **clothe yourselves with** (or: enter within) **bowels** (internal organs; = the tender parts; seat of deep feelings) **of compassion, kindness** (adaptable usefulness), **humility** (the minding and disposition of things of lowness or of low station), **gentleness** (meekness; mildness), **waiting long before rushing with emotions** (even-temperedness; long-suffering; = putting up with people and situations for a long time),

The phrase "**as God's chosen, set-apart and beloved ones**" refers to the entire community, and is a technical term for God's people that was used of Israel (*cf* Deut. 4:37; 7:7; Ps. 33:12). This description is code for covenant inclusion. Also *cf* Qumran literature (e.g., 1QpHabX,13 and others) for a continuation of this same historic concept among the Jews. 1 Pet. 2:9 expresses the same idea, as does Rom. 8:33, "God's chosen/elect." See also Eph. 1:4f.

Recall what he had just said in vs. 10: clothe yourself with the new humanity. So this is what our new reality, our new being, looks like: our inner life and core of being is compassion, kindness/adaptable usefulness, humility/being disposed to the lower levels of life and tending to them, waiting long before rushing with emotions/being even-tempered and patient with people and our living environment. This is not a list of things to do! It is a picture of our new inner reality! Not only that, vs. 10 told us that this is a picture of God Himself! Now think about that! You will become just like that which, or He Who, is your God. These virtues are not God-ward, but are about how we should deal with people.   Vs. 13 continues His description for us:

13. **being folks continuously holding up [things or situations] pertaining to one another** (or: habitually holding yourselves up, belonging to one another; constantly putting up with one another) **and incessantly giving grace to or doing a favor for** (dealing graciously with and among) **yourselves, if ever anyone may continue having** (or: holding) **a complaint toward someone. Just as the Lord** [= Christ or Yahweh; some MSS: Christ; Aleph* & some Vulgate MSS read: God] **also gave** (or: gives) **grace to and favor for you** (deals graciously in, with and among you folks), **thus also you folks [do the same].**

You see, HE is continuously holding us and our situation up and is constantly putting up with us. If we are joined to Him, we will be doing the same – just doing it naturally, out of our new nature, the New Being in Christ. Incessantly giving grace – is this not what He does? Yes, that is what

Paul goes on to say. We are called to reproduce Him, to reproduce God and be the channel of His increase. Note the corporate plural of the last sentence: covenant living is the setting.

14. **Now upon** (= on top of) **all these things [put on; superimpose] the Love, which continues being** (or: is) **a joining link and uniting band of perfection**
>   (a tie which binds together and pertains to the goal of maturity, being the result of fruitfulness; [the] fastening connection of the finished product; [the] bond producing perfection; a binding conjunction which brings union, which is the goal).

This is the summation, that which God actually is: Love. One root meaning of *agape* is "acceptance without restriction; the whole being's drive and movement toward reunion with another, to overcome existential separation" – Paul Tillich. It is to bind all of our situations and all parts/experiences of our being, as well as the entire community, together into a unified whole, which is love, which is God. This is what Paul meant when he said that the person that is joined unto the Lord is one spirit, or attitude; one Being (1 Cor. 6:17 – where the metaphor is sexual union; but consider that this is the situation spoken of in Gen. 2:24, where God spoke of those thus joined being one flesh – now it is being one Spirit). Again, the context is the corporate community in an accepting relationship with one another. Witherington suggests love being "a supreme virtue binding the other virtues together into a proper ethic" (ibid., p. 180).

15. **Furthermore, let the peace** [= *shalom*] **of the Christ** (belonging to and originating in the [Messiah]; the harmony which is the Anointing [other MSS: God]) **continuously umpire** (act as a judge in the games) **within your hearts** (= in union with the core of your being) – **into which [peace] you folks are called** (were called; were invited), **within one body. And progressively come to be thankful people** (or: continue becoming folks expressing gratitude for the goodness, ease and well-being that comes in grace; be habitually graceful folks).

If we follow Paul's admonition in this first clause, not only will we be guided by His peace, but we will become people of Peace, for this is a call to a continuous way of being. *Cf* John 14:27; Eph. 2:14; 2 Thes. 3:16. Furthermore, this is the goal of our calling, and it is another characteristic of that which binds us together "**within one body.**" None of us were called into war, hostility, violence or any use of force. Those should not be aspects of our character. The path of God's reign is the cross: laying down our lives for our friends. "**God's kind and gentle usefulness** (benevolence with a sweet disposition) **is continuously leading [people] into a change of mind and purpose** (= repentance with a change of heart and a return to God)" – Rom. 2:4.

In all things, peace and harmony (= *shalom*: the well-being, wholeness and prosperity of life) are to rule within the life of the community.

16. **Let Christ's Word** (or: the Logos, which is the Christ; the Idea which is the Anointing; or: the message of and from the Christ [other MSS: of God; of {the} Lord]) **be continuously making its home within you folks** (or: progressively indwelling – centered in and in union with you) **richly, within the midst of and in union with all wisdom, habitually teaching [it] and placing [it] in the minds of yourselves by psalms, in hymns, by spiritual songs and odes, within grace and amidst favor constantly singing within your hearts to God**
>   (or: habitually singing to God [other MSS: to {the} Lord], in union with the grace resident within your hearts {= the core of your being}).

That Word can come from reading Scripture, but I think a better understanding of what Paul meant is the allowing of the "Thought and Idea" (Logos), which comes via His message, or what He "lays out in arranged order" (a logos) in your heart, to be constantly living in your heart, mind and spirit – along with His wisdom – in an abundant, wealthy manner. Note the plural "**you folks**" – this should be a quality of the group. From this your life, your words and your actions will be teaching folks and placing His Word, His Peace, His Wisdom and His Spirit into the minds of one another. A spirit of creativity will bring forth psalms, hymns, poems and spiritual songs within the grace that He has given – and there will be a song in your heart which continuously sings to Him. This is not a religious activity, but a way of being, and it should characterize the entire community.

Witherington points out that the psalms (mainly from the OT) and singing are avenues of instruction (ibid., p. 181). We feed ourselves and others (**placing [wisdom] in the minds**) through this. They are sung to God, but the Spirit edifies us through the experience.
17. **And everything – whatsoever you may be habitually doing, in word or in action** (within a thought or message, or within a work or deed) **– [do] everything** (all; all things) **within and in union with [the] Name of [the] Lord, Jesus** [other MSS: of Jesus Christ; others: of {the} Lord, Jesus Christ], **constantly giving thanks** (expressing gratitude) **to Father God** (or: in union with God, [the] Father) **through Him.**

Neither is this a religious practice, but a life of identity with our Lord Jesus, a life lived that shows forth and represents Him, a life that is produced from out of the midst of His Being (His authority: *ex-ousia*) – all of which is meant by doing everything in union with His Name. Furthermore, we should be constantly giving thanks to the Father, expressing gratitude as you live in God, and this "**through Him.**" He is the means and the environment through which all this can be.

The so-called "Household Codes" that follow, from vs. 18-4:1, flow from what Paul has just been saying, above. God's peace (15), the wisdom from Christ's Word (16) along with the ability and character inherent in His Name (17) are to be lived out practically within the relationships of the households of the covenant community. The life of Christ is to be infused into every part of family living. What Paul admonishes is a stride forward, socially, from the household codes extant at that time. Living in union with His Name gave new motivation for expressing Love in all areas of the community.

Witherington suggests that Paul is injecting "social engineering" with a view to limiting "abuse of power by the head of the household" (ibid., p. 184). Injecting the effects of Christ's life into the core social structure bears fruit in the entire community. It is God's peace and harmony that will now rule within all areas of the corporate life of the called-out.

18. **Wives, be habitually aligned to humbly support** (or, as a middle: place and arrange yourselves in order, under) **[your] husbands** (or: Women, continue subjecting yourselves to the adult males [note: this was culturally appropriate at that time]), **in the same way as there has progressively come again to be a connection in [the] Lord** (or: since there has been an arrival back in union with [our] Master and Owner).

In this group of verses from 18-22 it would at first glance seem that he had forgotten what he had just said in vs. 11. He seems to reintroduce the traditional categories of their society. Here I suggest that like vs. 5-9a, he is drawing his readers back to their daily lives in practical admonitions regarding their outward station in life as he addresses their existing situation. As in our day as well, these divided perceptions and roles still continued, even though there was a new creation, a new heavens and a new earth (symbols for the world of culture and religion that was their environment). Similar "household rules" are found in Eph. 5:22-6:9; 1 Tim. 2:8-15; 6:1-2; Tit. 2:1-10; 1 Pet. 2:13-3:7. Witherington says that Paul is "swimming upstream" as his message of goodness confronts "the cultural assumptions" of the day (ibid., p. 185). The old was passing away in the new creation of the body of Christ.

But note the last part of vs. 18, for he points out the change that had come in relation to the existing status of a wife. He says "**in the same way as there has progressively come again to be a connection in [the] Lord**, an arrival back in union with the Master." In the Ephesian letter, 5:21, he says,

> "**while continually setting and arranging yourselves under** (placing yourselves in humble alignment; subordinating yourselves; being submissive) **so as to support one another, in respect for Christ**

(or: in union with the reverence which is Christ; within Christ's fear; in reverence pertaining to, and the source of which is [the] Anointed One [other MSS: God])." This says the same thing, but it is addressed "**to**... **one another, in respect for Christ**." Keep in mind the situations which he addressed in vs. 5-9a, which began with prostitution and obsessive evil cravings. He is addressing a rough-cut audience with a long history of male dominance. But a change is happening; things are not like they used to be. A wife can view her relationship with her husband in a new way, and her understanding of "submission" is to be transformed, in view of her new place "in Christ." This advice is loving, and practical for the existing situation. "They presuppose the current social structures and viewpoints," says Hans Conzelmann (quoted in Lohse, ibid., p. 156). This admonition, and the following ones, are not new household rules for the covenant community, but show that the called-out folks are to adapt to the prevalent social order, whatever the custom or tradition, yet with the new virtues that come in the Holy Spirit. Witherington point out that "The subordinate member of a given relationship is addressed first (wives, children, slaves), but always in tandem with the head of the household... [who] gets three sets of exhortations..." And "... all the members of the family are addressed as morally responsible individuals capable of hearing and heeding the exhortation..." (Witherington, p. 187-8). Again, the "new" is being expressed.

Note the present, middle form of *hupotasso* in the parenthetical rendering. Here power is given to the wife in this exhortation, to "arrange herself under her husband," and the husband is not told to subordinate the wife. Rather:

19. **Husbands, habitually love [your] wives** (or: Adult males, be constantly showing loving acceptance to the women), **and do not become repeatedly sharp toward them** (or: stop being rough, bitter or insensitive to them).

For the men, this is a new reality, a new world – even though the outward social order continues. The males had been raised to view the females as property, on the level of children and slaves, in most cultures. Things are changing, and the position of women is being elevated in the called-out community, as the reign of God begins to bring change to culture as well as to religion. Was this a seamless, steady advance in the years that followed? No, the kingdom is spreading as yeast through the dough, but in times and areas we see that there were set-backs, just as legalism regained its hold on the message of goodness. But this admonition remains, and is a light in the darkness. Witherington states, "The verb *agapao* is not used in Hellenistic discussions of the household duties of the husband..." (ibid., p. 191).

20. **Children, continue submissively hearing** (or: paying attention), **being constantly obedient to the parents in regard to all things** (corresponding to every situation), **for this continues being well-pleasing, within the Lord.**
21. **Fathers, do not constantly excite** (or: continuously incite or stimulate; repeatedly irritate, vex or provoke) **your children, so that they would not become habitually without strong passion** (discouraged and timid; without motivation; dispirited, listless, moody or sullen).

This advice, concerning children and their Fathers' relationship to them and manner of raising them up, is as good today as it ever was. Note that in vs. 20 he points out that paying attention and obedience "**continues**" well-pleasing to the Lord. This was not a change. But vs. 21 was a change for many fathers, it seems. Some men apparently did not realize that they could break the spirits of their children, and this was not a good thing. And especially, such behavior was not love – did not properly represent "**our Father who is in heaven**." Scholars have found secular writings of this period where the plural *pateres* was understood to mean "parents," not just "fathers." Nyland, in Eph. 6:4, notes that even the singular was found to be used of individual women in two examples in papyri (The Source NT, Smith and Stirling Publishing, 2004, p. 374).

Witherington see "a deliberate modification of the existing patriarchal household structure" in this list of admonitions (ibid., p. 193).

22. Slaves, in regard to all things continue submissively hearing, paying attention and being constantly obedient to those [being] owners (masters; lords) **on the level and the sphere of flesh** (= human, or "earthly," masters) **– not within eye-slavery** (bondage to eyes; = slavery to doing in order to be seen, or working only when someone is watching), **as desiring to please people** (or: wanting to be pleasing to people so as to win their favor; human-pleasers), **but rather within simplicity** (or: singleness) **of heart** (or: single-hearted sincerity), **constantly being folks reverenced by the fear of** (or, as a middle: being ones habitually engendering reverence because of respectful fear toward) **the Lord** [= Yahweh or Christ; p46 & other MSS: God].

The coming of the kingdom of God was not an outwardly observable event (Lu. 17:20), it was a creation of the Spirit. Neither the Lord, nor the sent-forth folks, made an outward attempt to change culture and society at that time. Slavery remained. Like His Law had been in the past, it was "here a little, there a little, line upon line..." Paul took upon himself the concept of slavery and ownership, regarding himself as a slave to Christ (e.g., Rom. 1:1).

Nevertheless, he plants seeds of the kingdom into this system, admonishing them to be people of character that exhibit reverence toward and by the Lord. The witness of Christ was especially to come from the lower levels of society, just as Jesus came primarily to serve the outcasts. His reign was to begin from the bottom (planted in the earth) and grow up – completely inverted as compared to a natural kingdom that came via conquest and violence.

23. Everything – whatever you folks may be habitually doing – be constantly working (doing business; practicing a trade; earning a living) **from out of soul** (from the whole being: intellect, emotions, will), **as to** (for; in) **the Lord** [= Yahweh or Christ] **and not for people** (to mankind),
24. having seen, and thus, knowing that you folks will receive back from the Lord [Yahweh or Christ] **and take away the corresponding compensation of, from and which consists in the enjoyment of the allotted inheritance. Be constantly slaving for Christ, the Owner** (Lord; Master) [or, with other MSS, and as an indicative: For you are constantly performing as a slave in (or: by; with) the Lord, in {the} Anointed One].

Vs. 23 is a marvelous statement of the reality of the New Being. It is a restatement of vs. 17. There was no longer a separation between the sacred and the profane: all activity was to involve the whole being, and was to be done as to, for and IN the Lord – not just for people. The new earth had come; all had changed. They were now servants of God, while they served others (*cf* Matt. 25:40). And vs. 24 assures them that it is from the Lord that they will receive corresponding compensation – even from the "**enjoyment**" an allotted inheritance (Matt. 5:3). We enjoy this right now. Lightfoot points out that the double compound *antapodoma* "involves the idea of 'exact requital'" (ibid, p. 227). Therefore, they were to see the Lord in their masters, and slave for Him. The alternate reading of other MSS is also good: they were in fact constantly performing as slaves for the Lord.

Lightfoot also notes a paradox involved in the word "inheritance": "elsewhere *doulos* [slave] and *kleronomos* are contrasted (Matt. 21:35-38; Rom. 8:15-17; Gal. 4:1, 7)" (ibid, p. 227).

25. Certainly, the person habitually doing wrong (constantly acting unjustly or inequitably; repeatedly being unfair and walking contrary to the Way pointed out) **will receive in himself what he wrongly does** (or: will take for his own dealing what inequity and unfairness he did) **– and there is no partiality** (favoritism; consideration because of personal appearance or of the face presented; receiving of a facade; taking of personage into account).

His rule is just and fair; His judging will be in accord to our works – he has no favorites. This was welcome news then, and it is now. In Him we find our equity, as well as the corrections we may need. He is faithful.

Chapter 4

1. **Owners** (Masters; Lords), **continuously hold at your side and present the right** (the just; the fair; the equitable) **and the equal** (what is the same as something else) **to and for [your] slaves – [from] having seen, and thus knowing, that you folks also continuously have an Owner** (Master; Lord) **within heaven** (or: [the] atmosphere; [other MSS: {the} heavens {or: atmospheres}]).

Paul here concludes his imperatives to the societal categories that he began in 3:18. He stresses fairness and equity and even a sense of solidarity, showing that there was a continuum of relationship from slave, to owner, to Owner. He also points out the reality of the rule-reign-kingdom of God's atmosphere, or heaven – His kingdom was indeed present then and there. The present tense of the verb, rendered "**continuously have**," makes it clear that this was not some reference to a future relationship, but an ongoing one. Paul is simply reminding them of the fact that then existed. His words about justice, fairness and equity by owners towards slaves expresses a marked advance within that time and culture, and shows the trajectory of the kingdom: it is an "upward call" (Phil. 3:14).

2. **Be habitually occupied diligently in prayer** (or: Be constantly stout toward thinking with a view to having well-being; Be continuing persistent and persevering by speaking toward having goodness [in situations]) **within an expression of gratitude** (or: thanksgiving), **continuously watching and remaining awake and alert in it,**
3. **at the same time also progressively praying** (speaking to having ease and goodness) **about us, to the end that God may open a door of the Word for us to speak the secret of the Christ** (or: may open a door pertaining to the message, for us to speak the mystery which has its origin in the Christ – the secret which is the Christ), **because of which** [B G F read: Whom], **also, I have been bound** (or: tied; = imprisoned),
4. **so that I may set it [i.e., the secret] in clear light** (can bring it to light; would manifest it), **as it is continuously binding me** (making it necessary for me) **to speak.**

In vs. 2-4, Paul has returned to general admonitions to the entire community, but they still apply for us all. The word "**prayer**" is literally "toward having it well." To be habitually or constantly occupied diligently (or, in a strong way) means to be continually thinking, speaking and acting with a view to goodness, ease and well-being. Again, this means doing this as a way of life. It means by the Spirit setting even our sub-conscious directed toward that goal. The environment of such is an expression of gratitude, and in a spirit of thanksgiving. He adds to this the need to be continuously watching, remaining awake and being alert. Why? Well, being awake and alert are the opposite of being drowsy and sleeping. This was a common admonition that began with Jesus. They were expecting things to happen on the political and religious scene, and Paul is also repeating what he had said in ch. 2:8, but here he is speaking of their general stance. They should be paying attention to what is happening both their community and outside of it.

But further, it is always easy to become self-centered or preoccupied with family or job concerns, and to forget that we are a part of His reign and are integral to the growth of His kingdom in the earth, which operates from out of a corporate entity, the covenant community. The Jews, and at times the Romans, were their outward adversaries; the law of sin (Rom. 7) was the inward one. Being awake to our lives is necessary to live in His overcoming of the System. Paul elsewhere compared this to running a race in the stadium games. It requires focus.

Paul's request for prayer, "**to the end that God may open a door**" recalls what had happened for them in 1 Cor. 16:9 and 2 Cor. 2:12, which spoke of opportunities, as well as Acts 14:27, which spoke of a "**door of and from faith and trust, to, for and among the ethnic multitudes.**" Note the first translation, "**a door of the Word for us to speak the secret of the Christ**," as well as parenthetical alternate rendering: "may open a door pertaining to the message, for us to speak the mystery which has its origin in the Christ – the secret which is the Christ." In the first one, the Word is the subjective genitive: the Word makes the door, and the "secret" is the message of the

Christ. In the second one, the door is an "opening" for the message to be spoken, and the mystery-secret both comes from Christ, and in fact is Christ Himself – so that when the message is spoken, Christ comes in that message. It was a Secret (Christ coming to all via the Spirit) that was hidden during the age of the old covenant.

5. **Be habitually walking about within wisdom** (= living your lives in union with Wisdom)**: toward those outside** (or: to outsiders; = those not a part of the called-out community), **being ones constantly buying for yourselves – as from out of the market place – the fitting situation** (or: redeeming the season within yourselves; purchasing the fertile moment for yourselves; or: = making the best use of the opportunity in the public concourse),

Here is more admonition to living with wisdom and being aware of good situations (as we would of good buys at the store, taking advantage of sales, etc.). We should be aware of fertile moments both with ourselves, and with others, for implanting life. We should seize the moment, as the Spirit reveals it to us, to let the rivers of living water flow forth to the thirsty. We should scatter His Seed in fitting situations and appropriate seasons.

Since wisdom can in the context of the message be Christ (Wisdom), this may be more that just practical advice for wise conduct. Paul can be speaking to behavior that flows from the Anointing, toward the world at large. (*cf* 1:9-10; 2:6-7)

6. **[with] your word** (your conversation; your message) **– at all times within grace** (or: = always favorable) **– being one having been prepared and fitted by salt** (or: seasoned in salt; or: = one being interesting and not insipid), **[and for you] to have seen, and thus be aware, how it continues binding for you folks to be habitually answering each person with discernment** (or: making a decided reply to or separating [issues] away in order to respond with a decision for each individual).

Our thoughts, words, ideas, conversations and our message should always be favorable, and should be in the sphere of grace, not law. Our lives and interactions with others should not be insipid or boring. We should be full of life (like a meal that is seasoned) and have a habit of responding to folks with discernment – for we are filled with the Spirit – and be willing to make decided and judicious replies for the hope and life that is within us, and within which we live (1 Pet. 3:15). *Cf* Mk. 9:50 and Mt. 5:13; also Job 6:6.

Paul now addresses personal issues, as with regard to the soon coming of Tychicus (vs. 7-8) and Onesimus (vs. 9) and Aristarchus (vs. 10), etc. Paul was concerned about people and relationships, not just teachings and doctrines.

7. **Tychicus, the beloved brother and faithful** (or: loyal; trustworthy) **attending servant – even fellow slave – within [the] Lord** [= Christ or Yahweh], **will personally make known all the things with reference to me,**
8. **whom I send toward you folks unto this very thing, so that you might intimately become acquainted with the things about** (or: concerning) **us** [with other MSS: so that he may come to intimately experience and know the things about and concerning you], **and that he may call your hearts to his side for comfort, relief, aid and encouragement** (or: so he can be a paraclete for you folks).
9. **Together with Onesimus, the faithful and beloved brother – who is from among you folks – they will personally and intimately acquaint you with** (make known to you) **all the things here.**

10. **Aristarchus, my fellow captive** (the one taken at spear-point, together with me), **continues embracing and greeting you folks, as does Mark, cousin of Barnabas, concerning whom you received goal-oriented directions [that] if he should ever come to you, receive** (accept and hospitably welcome) **him,**

11. **and Jesus, the one habitually being designated** (or: termed) **Justus – these being the only folks from among** (or: out forth from) **the Circumcision** (= Jews of the Jewish religion) **[who are] fellow workers [laboring] into God's reign and kingdom – which folks came to be a soothing emollient** (a consoling exhortation; a solace) **to me** (for me; in me).

Vs. 11 contains a revealing comment: there were a few Jews who were laboring with Paul, sowing into God's present reign and kingdom. It is obvious that Paul's work was involved with the kingdom, contrary to what some folks teach.

12. **Epaphras – the one from among you folks; a slave of Christ Jesus – continues embracing and greeting you folks, at all times** (or: always) **in constant struggle as in a contest over [the circumstances of] you folks, within prayers** (speaking to having goodness and well-being), **to the end that you can stand** [other MSS: would at once be set and placed] **[as] mature folks** (or: complete people; finished ones; those having reached the purposed goal and destiny; perfect ones) **and people having been brought to fullness** (or: carried to the full measure) **within, and in union with, all God's will, intent, design and purpose.**
13. **You see, I am presently bearing witness for him that he constantly has** (or: continuously holds) **toil-caused pain** (misery; travail; anguish) **over you folks and those within Laodicea, and the people within Hierapolis.**

The witness of vs. 12-13 expresses the intense solidarity within the body of Christ in Paul's day and circumstances. There was actual response from the situation at Colosse, that came from the intercession by Epaphras as he struggled together with them (as did Paul, ch. 2:1), in his spirit, to the point of pain concerning either their ordeals, or perhaps their growth – Paul does not say, but is perhaps the same subject as discussed in ch. 2:2. His thoughts and words projecting goodness and well-being into them (his prayers), that they would stand – or be set and placed – as mature folks with fullness within all God's will and intent (design and purpose), was to the point of personal pain. He was one with them. May we also have this vision of solidarity and union.

14. **Luke, the beloved healer** (or: physician) **continues embracing and greeting you folks – also Demas.**
15. **Embrace and greet the brothers within Laodicea, also Nympha and the called-out gathering** (or: community) **that corresponds to her** [other MSS: from their] **house.**

The same phrase describing a "house-church" is used in Rom. 16:5 and 1 Cor. 16:19 about the community centered in, and likely meeting at, the home of Prisca and Aquila.

16. **And whenever the letter** (or: epistle) **may be read** (caused to be known again) **beside you** (= in your presence and to you), **you folks make an arrangement to the end that it may also be read within the set-apart community of the Laodiceans; and so that you folks may also read the one from out of Laodicea.**

17. **And say to Archippus,**
> **"Be constantly observing and seeing to the attending service which you received and took to your side, within [the] Lord** [= Christ or Yahweh], **to the end that you may make it full** (or: fulfill it).**"**

18. **The embrace and greeting [is] by my hand – Paul's. Call to mind** (Remember; Be mindful of) **my bonds** (= chains; = imprisonment).
> **Grace and favor [are]** (or: [The] act producing happiness, which is granted as a favor [is]; – Jim Coram) **with you folks! It is so** (Count on it; Amen).

And so ends this beautiful letter. May these truths be absorbed into our hearts. May we remember those that are in any way bound – especially those being so for the sake of the message of Goodness. The following article is presented with the permission of the author:

Comments on Colossians

Colossians, Community & The Church's Meal Table

By Dr. David Byrd

When we consider Paul's letter to the Colossians, we do not attempt to press the issue farther than the evidence warrants, but simply make note of the fact that Paul, who we must presume intends or expects his letter to be read at a communal gathering (most likely a meal), makes it a point to use meal-related terms in his communications concerning the Gospel of Jesus and the church's manner of representing the kingdom of God on earth.

In the second chapter, words such as "Therefore do not let anyone judge you with respect to food or drink, or in the matter of a feast, new moon, or Sabbath days" (2:16) cannot pass by without mention, or without taking them into consideration in light of ancient meal practice, both inside and outside of the church. Also, this very brief listing of feast, new moon, and Sabbath is language that is evocative of the covenant markers of Judaism (works of the law), which we know was a constant source of tension and division in the churches of the day. Paul's insistence that these things are "shadows of the things to come" (2:17a), whereas the "reality is Christ!" (2:17b), reminds us, in the same breath, that the new covenant marker that will identify the people of God and which will be in evidence in their meal practice, is the confession that Jesus is Lord. The new covenant marker serves the same purpose as the old covenant marker, which ultimately was to affirm that the Creator God---the God of Israel---is the sovereign ruler of all. Because Jesus, as Messiah, was understood to be the physical embodiment of Israel's God, the symmetry is quite obvious.

In addition to the language of meals and of the Lordship of Jesus (the Gospel), Paul employs terms that are reminders of that which can be found in both Romans and the first Corinthian letter (as well as Ephesians), with their focus on the unity of the body. Because it is a near impossibility for us to separate "unity language" from the meal table (with confidence that this letter would have been read at a meal table), we are able to discern traces of a reference to the practice of the symposium (the second of the two parts of the Hellenistic banquet, in which songs and poems were shared, ideas were discussed, attendees engaged in sexual relations with slaves and others in attendance, and honor was at stake) when Paul writes "Let no one who delights in humility and the worship of angels pass judgment on you. That person goes on at great lengths about what he has supposedly seen, but he is puffed up with empty notions by his fleshly mind" (2:18). Without getting in to the issues to which Paul makes reference here, the allusion to the boasting that is a common feature of the world's meal tables, to which Paul makes semi-regular reference (thus bolstering our position that these letters from Paul are designed to be read in the context of a communal meal), is difficult to avoid. Clearly, Paul is taking issue with the person that is trying to vault themselves to a more honored seat at the table and a more prominent place within the church community, as that person is still enamored with or attracted by the honor and shame system of the wider world.

With this underscored, we are unsurprised to read "He has not held fast to the head from whom the whole body," as we notice the emphasis on unity, "supported and knit together through its ligaments and sinews, grows with a growth that is from God" (2:19). If we read "the body" appropriately, bearing in mind Paul's use of "the body" to make reference to the unified church (signaled clearly in 1 Corinthians 11 and the need to eat and drink with careful regard for the body), then much sense is made of what comes next in Paul. He writes that "Even though they have the appearance of wisdom" (2:23a), as the "they" are those that vaunt themselves above their brothers and sisters, we more fully understand the point that Paul is making, and its relation to the church and its ability to function in its role as a shining light to the world, as we go on to hear "with their self-imposed worship and false humility achieved by an unsparing treatment of the body---a wisdom with no true value---they in reality result in fleshly indulgence" (2:23b). The "unsparing treatment of the body" is then rightly applied to the church body, thus escaping any unwarranted and unauthorized personal or individual applications, as Paul inherently warns the person that is engaging in such behavior, while they are reducing the message of the Gospel and the mission of the church to "Do not handle! Do not taste! Do not touch!" (2:21), that they are most certainly missing the mark.

Moving forward with this mindset to the third chapter, Paul's description of Christ as being "seated at the right hand of God" (3:1b) is related to the meal table, the protoklisian (the host seat), and the seat of honor that would have been to the right of the protoklisian, thus keeping our focus (along with the original hearers) at the meal table. That meal table, which is so incredibly important in the early church that was to carry out the message of Jesus' Lordship in word and deed, and which is to be representative of the messianic banquet and the rule of God, remains the setting, as Paul once again evokes the practices of the symposium when he writes "So put to death whatever in your nature belongs to the earth: sexual immorality, impurity, shameful passion, evil desire, and greed which is idolatry… You also lived your lives in this way at one time, when you used to live among them. But now, put off all such things as anger, rage, malice, slander, abusive language from your mouth. Do not lie to one another since you have put off the old man with his practices and have been clothed with the new man that is being renewed according to the image of the one who created it" (3:5,7-10).

Obviously, all of these things will cause division at the table, damage to the church body, and the diminishment of the church's witness to the kingdom of God that was inaugurated with Christ's Resurrection and the church's hope for the resurrection to come, which was the preface to this portion of his discourse, as Paul wrote, "Therefore, if you have been raised with Christ" (3:1a). It is with this said that Paul reminds this church of its covenant responsibilities in their representation of the rule of God through their meal practice (as so much would flow from proper meal practice), by telling them that "Here there is neither Greek nor Jew, circumcised or uncircumcised, barbarian, Scythian, slave or free, but Christ is all and in all" (3:11). The mark of the church was the confession of Jesus as Lord of all---all peoples and all nations, and this would be primarily made visible to a watching world by their kingdom-oriented table fellowship.

(from *Pisteos International Daily*, a blog by Dr. David Byrd; posted 1/3/2012 academiachurch.org)

This is considered by many scholars to be Paul's first letter, written from Corinth circa AD 50 (Robinson, ibid.). Thessalonica (named after the half-sister of Alexander the Great) had an estimated population of 200,000 and was the capital of the Roman province of Macedonia. There the called-out community was predominantly Gentile (1:9), but also included Jews (Acts 17:1-4). William Barclay suggest that the coming of Paul to this area was the beginning of the gospel coming into Europe (*The Daily Study Bible Series... Thessalonians*, p. 179).

This letter discusses the previous visit of Paul, Silvanus and Timothy, the result of their proclamation of the Word and their relationship to the Thessalonicans (ch. 1 and 2). Then Paul gives encouragement in regard to trials (3:3-5) and admonitions regarding living in the covenant community (4:1-12), but scholars consider its dominant theme to be eschatology (teaching about last days or the time of the end). The word *parousia* (being present, at the side; often wrongly rendered "coming") appears in 2:19; 3:13; 4:15 and 5:23. But in regard to using this term for a coming of Jesus as the Son of Man, Helmut Koester states that "there is no evidence in pre-Christian apocalyptic literature for such technical usage" (*Paul & His World, Interpreting the NT in Its Context*, Fortress Press, 2007, p. 59). Rather, he suggests that Paul's apocalyptic material in this letter speaks of a **realized** eschatology and on building the **existing** community upon the **presence** of faith, hope and love (ibid., p. 69) – the characteristics of the existing new age inaugurated by the death and resurrection of Jesus, the Messiah. Various preterist scholars consider the references to the *parousia* as predictions of Christ's return in judgment on Jerusalem, via the Romans in AD 70. The first verse tells us that God IS the very environment and atmosphere within which these folks lived. In fact they were *experiencing* union with Him at that very moment.

Chapter 1

1. **Paul, Silvanus** (or: = Silas; D reads: Silbanos), **and Timothy, to the called-out community of the Thessalonians within, and in union with, God our Father, even** (or: and) **[the] Lord Jesus Christ: grace and peace** (or: joyous favor and harmony with the absence of conflict; = shalom [peace and prosperity]) **to you** [other MSS add: from God, our Father and Lord, Jesus Christ (or: God our Father, and {the} Owner, Jesus {the} Anointed)].

Paul begins by expressing solidarity with those with him, and that the ensuing message comes from all of them. As elsewhere, I have here rendered the phrases in which he refers to God and Jesus by giving two possible renderings of the Greek conjunction, *kai*, which join them : "and" or "**even**." Was Paul regarding them as a unity, or as separate? When Jesus "ascended to the Father" (John 20:17), did He assume an identity and solidarity with Him as He said that He had with His brothers in Matt. 25:40? Did He take on the relationship with His People that Yahweh had with Israel?

As Yahweh styled Himself as the Husband of Israel, so does Christ have His People as His Bride. Is the anthropomorphic metaphor of "**father**" here, more one of functional relationship, as with husband/wife, rather than ontological relationship? If this were an ontological statement, does Paul mean that the Thessalonians were within, or in union with, only the Two of Them, and not with the Holy Spirit? Here, of course, I jest in making reference to Trinitarian theology. Recall that Paul said that he "**travailed in birth again**" for those of Galatia (Gal. 4:19). I suggest that we keep an open mind when reading such phrases as these in vs. 1. The Jews referred to Abraham as their father. Was Paul's Jewish background coming through here in showing high regard for Jesus by applying the term "**Father**" to Him?

2. **We are continuously experiencing the well-being of grace in God, and are mindful of the favor of goodness and ease with God, always, which encircles and surrounds all of you**

(or: are constantly always expressing gratitude and feeling thankful to and for God concerning you all), **continuously making mention of you folks upon our thinking and speaking towards having things be well** (or: remembering and being mindful of you people at [times of] our prayers) **in regard to**

I have presented two possible renderings of the Greek verb *eu-charis-toumen*, in the first clause of vs. 2: the first as "**experiencing the well-being of grace**," and then expanded as "**mindful of the favor of goodness and ease**," from the meaning of the elements of the word. The second, "**expressing gratitude and feeling thankful**," from the common lexicons. Whether they "experienced" it, or whether they "gave" it, depends upon how we read this verb. Next, the word "God" is in the dative case, without an expressed preposition, so I give you the possible functions of the dative: in God; with God; to God; for God. I prefer the rendering "**which encircles and surrounds**" for the Greek *peri*, to the secondary meaning of "concerning," but now you may choose, as the Spirit speaks to you.

In the last clause you are also given the literal meaning of the Greek noun *pros-eu-che* (**thinking and speaking towards having things be well**) first, and the common rendering as "prayers" in the parenthetical expansion.

3. **your incessantly remembering** (or: being mindful, without leaving-off throughout,) **of our Lord Jesus Christ's act of faith** (process of trust; work from loyalty), **wearisome smiting and toil of love, and persistent patient endurance from expectation, in front of our God and Father**

> (or: ...upon our prayers, unceasingly mentioning, in the presence of our God and Father, the process of your faith {or: the work which is conviction and trust} and love's exhausting toil {or: the hard labor which is love}, and [your] steadfast remaining under for support of our Lord Jesus Christ's expectation {or: the expectant hope which are our Lord Jesus, [the] Anointed}).

Vs. 3 contains a long string of prepositional phrases. The question arises from the syntax, Whose activities are being referred to: Christ's, as I first suggest, or the called-out group's, as given in the second rendering? The incessant remembering and being mindful was definitely the mental activity of the Thessalonians, but I believe that it was the work of Christ – His act of faith, the wearisome smiting and toil of love, and the persistent endurance from HIS expectation (i.e., the enduring of the cross for the joy set before Him – Heb. 12:2), in the presence of God, our Father – was what they were keeping before their thoughts and memories. The second option draws in the phrase from the previous verse and ties "of your" to the following phrases. Either accords with the syntax, but I think that my first rendering fits the Greek the best.

4. **Brothers** (= Fellow believers; = [My] family), **folks having been and still being loved by God, knowing and perceiving your election** (your being picked out; your being chosen, arranged, gathered or spoken out of the midst),

What a wonderful thing to know and perceive about ourselves, that we are in fact a product of His love, and that He still loves us and has picked us out for His purpose in our lives. We have been elected to serve humanity, to lay down our lives for them, and to inform them that they, too, have been loved by God (for God thus loves the world – John 3:16) and that He has a chosen purpose for them, as well.

5. **how that the message of the goodness of our God** (or: our God's good news; the message of ease and well-being, which is God) **was not birthed into you within word or thought only, but rather also within power and ability, even within a set-apart Breath-effect** (or: in union with [the] Holy Spirit; in the midst of [the] Sacred Breath), **as well as in much assurance having been brought to full measure, according as you have seen and perceived** (or: by extensive absolute-certainty and with much bearing and wearing to the full, just as you know and are

aware). **Of such sort we were birthed** (produced; brought to be) **to, for and among you for your sakes** (because of you folks),

Note that the message CAME via a word (which was the Logos) which presented a thought, an idea, and a Person: Christ. Christ, the Word and message, IS the goodness of our God. But here Paul reminds them that this Word brought power and ability and came within a set-apart Breath-effect – the result of Its work – in union with the Holy Spirit. All of this brought an abundance of "**assurance having been brought to full measure**" and satisfied certainty "by extensive absolute-certainty and with much bearing and wearing to the full," just as they had seen with perception. Paul and his associates had been "**birthed**" upon the scene and into their lives – and this was for THEIR sakes, to announce the message of goodness to them. With this birthing, a new relationship developed between them.

6. **and within much pressure** (or: squeezing; oppression) **you yourselves were birthed** (produced, made to be) **imitators of us and of the Lord, receiving** (taking in hand) **the Word** (or: idea; thought; message) **with [the] joy of [the] set-apart Breath-effect** (or: from [the] Holy Spirit; or: the Sacred Breath's joy; or: accompanied by gracious joy which is a sacred attitude),
7. **so then to produce and birth you as patterns for** (models to) **all those constantly trusting and progressively believing – while being loyal – within Macedonia and within Achaia.**

Paul recalls that this came about in an environment of much pressure, but it produced them to be imitators of both Paul (and his associates) AND the Lord, as they received the message (the implanted Word) that was accompanied by the Holy Spirit's joy. The Thessalonians were now patterns and models – they were imprinted by Christ – for the trusting folks in Macedonia and Achaia. Those could look at them and see Christ!

We should notice that the Person, character and qualities of Christ is the pattern, the spiritual DNA, which is passed on from person to person, from generation to generation – as a grain of wheat that falls into the ground and dies, and then produces a lot more grains of wheat, all in the same likeness and with the same DNA.

8. **You see, from you the Word of the Lord** (or: [Yahweh's or Christ's] message) **has been loudly sounded forth not only in Macedonia and Achaia, but even within every place your faith toward God has gone forth** (or: out), **so that we have no need to be speaking anything!**

The spreading of the reign of God is through the "**sound**ing **forth**" of the Word – the message, which is the Christ – and they had done this, and thus was the seed and pattern spread to other areas who had heard of their life of faith. Thus, they had taken over for Paul and the others: a perfect example of the good news spreading through reproduction.

9. **For they themselves are continuously reporting concerning us of what sort an entrance** (or: introduction) **we had toward you, and how you turned about toward God from the idols** (forms; images seen; external appearances; pagan concepts and world views) **to continuously be a slave to, for and with the living and true** (or: real) **God,**

The work of the sent-forth folks has come full circle and is now being reported back to them that which involved they themselves and their work in Thessalonica. It is a report of changed lives that have by the Spirit been devoted to become slaves to, for and with the real God. Since Jesus had taken on the form of a slave (Phil. 2:7), and had performed as such to the disciples (John 13:4-5), I included the associative function of the dative case, thus, "**with the living and** real **God.**" Jesus is the same today as He was then, still serving humanity although being Lord of all. And thus does Paul describe us as being "**God's fellow-workers**" (1 Cor. 3:9).

10. **even to constantly dwell and remain** (or: abide and lodge) **back up again [with] His Son – [living] from out of the heavens!** (or: His Son, whose origin is from the midst of the atmospheres) – **Whom He raised from out of the midst of dead folks, Jesus, the One**

constantly rescuing (or: repeatedly and progressively dragging) **us to Himself from out of the midst of** (other MSS: away from) **the repeatedly** (or: periodically; continuously; progressively) **coming violent emotions** (inherent fervor; mental disposition of teeming desire; passionate impulse; or: anger; internal teeming & agitation; outburst of rage; wrath).

These folks now lived in the heavens (the atmosphere), having returned to their source, Christ, Who continuously inhabits our atmosphere. Their physical existence had not moved, but their spirits and attitudes had. They were now citizens of the Jerusalem which is above, who is their mother (Gal. 4:26).

Note that Paul identifies God's Son, the Christ, as Jesus. He is the One that is continuously and progressively drawing and dragging us to Himself from out of the midst of the situations of violent emotion, inherent fervor, etc., that is repeatedly and periodically coming. It was then presently coming to them, coming progressively closer with the passing days. But it is something that habitually comes, to test, try and bring improvements to people – just as it did with Job. This is no "once at the end of the world" thing, as history has shown us. It constantly comes and goes (the Greek *erchomai* means both "to come" and "to go").

Chapter 2

1. **For you yourselves have seen and perceived** (thus: know; are aware), **brothers** (= fellow members of the Body), **that our entrance** (or: way into; introduction) **toward you has not been produced, birthed or come to be empty** (without contents; = useless or without results),
2. **but rather, after previously experiencing ill treatment and being outraged** (subjected to insolent, riotous, or insulting behavior) **in Philippi, according as you are aware, we spoke freely and boldly – publicly, as is the right of citizens – within, and in union with, our God, [proceeding at once] to utter God's message of goodness** (or: the good news from God; the message of ease and well-being, which is God) **toward you in the midst of much striving** (conflict; arguing; or: within a large stadium or racecourse; or: in much agony of struggle).

Their original work had been productive, as is now evidenced by the state of faith and trust among the Thessalonians, but that work was done amidst conflict and arguing, including agony (probably of spirit) and struggle. But Paul reminds them that his group had acted with the privilege of citizens who could boldly speak what they had to say, and as always it was the message of God's goodness. This was probably new to those who only knew the pagan gods, or even to Jews who may have been taught (like most Christians) that God is full of wrath.

3. **You see, our calling alongside to assist** (our admonition and encouragement; our work as paracletes) **[is] not out of wandering** (being led astray; deception), **neither out of uncleanness, nor yet within a bait for entrapping or with guile or craftiness,**

The promise of the coming of the Holy Spirit had been termed by Jesus as the coming of another Comforter. The Greek word for this is *parakletos*, or in English, "paraclete." Paul uses this word often, showing that upon receiving the "Paraclete" he and others like him became the same, doing the work of giving assistance, encouragement, etc.

They had operated with good form as upstanding representatives of Christ, without any ulterior motives. They were not what is today called "a cult." They were not trying to get them under their control by entrapment or "mind games" or "guilt trips" of a moralistic religion. Paul never preached anything about a "hell" or "endless torment" to use the guile of fear. His message was GOOD news.

4. **but rather, to the degree that and according as we have been approved by testing under God to be entrusted [with] the message of goodness, ease and well-being, thus we are**

continuously speaking: not as constantly pleasing to people, but rather [as] to the God [Who is] repeatedly testing our hearts!

Vs. 4 makes an interesting point: testing under God in order to be approved to be entrusted with God's message. Now elsewhere, Paul does not say that he had been tested by a committee of people. No group or denomination "gave them papers" to be able to do what they were doing, but they affirm that God had tested and approved them. The fruit of their ministry is their proof.

Not having to please people (those who "sent people out," as it is today, to whom they have to conform, in order for them to get financial support), but rather, even as they did the work God was repeatedly testing their hearts – so that they themselves could be sure of pure motives, no doubt.

5. **For neither did we at any time come to be flattering in word, according as you saw and are aware, neither within a pretense which comes from greed: God is witness!**

They did not speak dishonestly to try to win them or to become their friends. Neither did they try to get offerings, nor were they selling something. Apparently this type of thing happened then, as well as today – thus this disclaimer.

6. **Neither [are we] continuously seeking glory** (or: a reputation) **from among people** (humans) **– neither from you, nor from others – all the while being able [to be] burdensome** (or: as constantly having power in weighty [matters]), **as representatives of Christ** (or: emissaries of [the] Anointed One; sent-off folks from [the Messiah]).

They were not trying to build their kingdom or ministries. They were not trying to become famous. They could have become a financial burden to them, expecting the Thessalonians to support them – but they did not. They could have demonstrated their capacity to impress the people with their knowledge of the Scriptures or of philosophy – but they didn't. As His emissaries, they simply presented Christ to them.

7. **But rather, we were birthed babes** (or: became infants; [other MSS: we were made to become gentle and kind ones]) **within the midst of you folks, as whenever a nursing mother would constantly or repeatedly cuddle to impart warmth to her own children.**

Here they are expressing the humility and the total, tender dependency upon God and the corporate body (the nursing mother – Gal. 4:26) with which they behaved when among them.

8. **Thus, continuously being your affectionately "attached-ones"** (ones having a like-flow [of nourishment from our Nursing Mother]), **we were habitually delighted** (thinking it good; well-pleased) **to share or impart to you not only God's message of goodness and well-being** [other MSS: the good news which is Christ], **but rather even our own souls** (= inner beings and lives; or: = selves), **because you have been birthed** (or: come to be) **beloved ones to us** (or: folks loved by us; or: = very dear to us, accepted by us and appreciated by us).

Paul and his associates saw themselves as one with the community, in total solidarity. Here they continue the metaphor of vs. 7, suggesting that they were "**attached**" to the same breast, and now would (as a mother to them) "**share or impart**" good nourishment to them. They became family to Paul, and he was happy to share all of his inner being, his whole self, with them. This is just the opposite of the titled speakers who keep a distance from the audience. This was an organic relationship.

9. **For you are remembering, brothers** (= fellow believers), **our exhausting labor** (or: = the trouble to which we went; toil; hardship; or: beating) **and hard work, continuously working night and day towards not being burdensome** (or: a weight) **upon any of you, [and] after the manner of a herald we proclaimed God's message of goodness** (the good news from God; or: the message of ease and well-being which is God) **into the midst of** (or: unto) **you folks.**

10. **You and God [are] witnesses of how appropriately and loyally** (or: benignly; in accord with universal law), **justly** (or: fairly; rightwisedly), **and blamelessly we were caused to be to you** (or: for you folks), **the ones continuously trusting and believing with loyal conviction.**
11. **With reference to which you have seen and are aware of how [we treated] each one of you folks, continually calling you alongside to give assistance and relief, exhort or encourage** (perform as a paraclete), **as well as speaking gentle influence and comfort at your side, as a father [to] his own children,**
12. **even continuously giving evidence** (witnessing; confirming by testimony) **unto you folks to be continuously walking about worthily of the God** (= living your lives in a manner equal in value with regard to the God) **[Who is] continuously calling** (or: repeatedly inviting) **you people into His own kingdom** (or: reign; sovereign influence and activity) **and glory** (or: a manifestation which calls forth praise; or: reputation; or: opinion and imagination; or: = manifest presence).

Vs. 9-12 need little comment. He stresses their former deportment among them, and how they performed actual work to earn their own sustenance – as well as heralding the message of well-being, which message is God Himself, coming to them. This parenthetical expansion demonstrates the genitive of apposition. God comes in His Word. Or, taken as an ablative, it can be simply "the good news from God."

He calls them to witness, along with God, their appropriate, loyal, fair and blameless behavior to these believers, and how they ministered aid and performed as paracletes to them – now acting like being their fathers. They were all things to them. Then he reminds them of how he and the others had repeatedly given evidence to them, so that they would lives their lives in the way that corresponded to how they valued God, reminding them that God was continuously and progressively calling them to be a part of His sovereign influence and activities, and so reflect His glorious reputation among other folks. Since the Greek *doxa* can mean "opinion" and "imagination," as well as "**glory**," it would seem that they and we are also invited to participate in His imagination, and share in His opinions.

13. **And so, on account of this, we ourselves also continuously give thanks to God** (or: affirm the goodness of the grace and favor in God) **by an unvarying practice** (or: incessantly; unintermittingly), **because in receiving** (or: taking to [your] side; accepting) **God's word and message, from a hearing from us at our side, you welcomingly accepted not a word of or from people** (or: a human message), **but rather, according as it really and truly is, a word of God** (God's message; an idea from God; a thought which is God), **Which** (or: Who) **also** (or: even) **is continuously in-working** (being active; operating; energizing) **within you folks – those continuously trusting and progressively believing with loyalty.**

Note here Paul's reference to an "**unvarying practice**," or, "unintermittingly" giving thanks and affirming God's goodness and favor. This was a way of life for him, a way of being. It calls to mind the LXX (Septuagint) version of Ps. 150:6,
        "Let every breath praise the Lord [= Yahweh]."
Next he goes on to affirm that the word and message that they brought was in fact from God – and that these folks "**welcomingly accepted**" it as such. Their hearts had been opened by God, and they accepted the evidence spoken of in vs. 12. They did not question it, as the Pharisees had questioned the word of Jesus.

Now Paul affirms that this very Logos (Christ, His thought and idea) is continuously in-working, being active, operating and energizing within them. Can we grab hold of this concept? That Christ, the Logos is continuously working within us? That His thought and His idea are active and operating within us? This is what the new heavens and the new earth (the new creation) is like. We are joined to God who lives within us!

14. **For you, brothers** (= fellow believers), **were birthed** (or: were made to be) **imitators of God's called-out folks** (or: summoned forth communities) **– the ones within Christ being** (or: existing) **in Judea – because you also at one point experienced** (or: suffered) **the very same**

119

things by (or: under) **your own fellow-tribesmen, just as they also [did] by** (or: under) **the Jews** (= the religious leaders of Judaism),

Here is an interesting characteristic and attribute of being an imitator of God's called-out folks: suffering and experiencing mal-treatment from the local religious folks. Today, it is mostly in the form of social ostracism in America, but in other countries it is the same today as it was back then. So if we would imitate God's called-out folks, we should expect opposition.

15. **even from those killing-off the Lord Jesus, as well as the prophets; even from those driving us out and continuously displeasing God, and from folks contrary to** (or: in opposition against) **all humans** (or: people),
16. **while continuously forbidding us** (cutting us off; preventing us) **to speak to the nations** (the ethnic groups; the non-Israelite multitudes; the Gentiles) **– to the end that they may be delivered** (saved; rescued; healed and made whole) **– always [proceeding] unto that which fills up their own failures** (errors; deviations; sins)! **But inherent fervor** (or: swelling passion; teeming desire; or: anger; wrath; agitation of soul) **advanced upon them unto a purpose** (or: on into [the] final act; or: in the end; on into the midst of a destined goal).

Such persecution involved things that were "**contrary to all humanity**." We do hear of this today. The Jewish leaders had tried to silence Christ's body and messengers. They wanted to stamp out what they considered to be "this new religion." They were not concerned about "**the nations**... [being] **delivered**," unless they became proselytes. They were concerned with their own traditions and their own culture. But Paul called this persecution "**that which fills up their own failures**, deviations and sins," and Jesus prophesied their end in Matt. 24 and Lu. 21, along with many of His parables that were directed against the scribes and the Pharisees. Here Paul prophesies of what was to come: God's inherent fervor and teeming desire for His beloved people and Jerusalem. They would be destroyed, but for a purpose, with a goal in view, their ultimate end being grafted back into their own olive tree (Rom. 11:24).

17. **Now we, brothers, being deprived** (or: orphaned; bereaved; torn-away) **from you for a fitting situation of an hour** (or: for an hour's season; = for a short spell, during a specific situation) **– by face** (= in presence), **not by or in heart – we more exceedingly made diligent haste to see your face, in much full desire!**
18. **On that account we intended** (purposed, willed) **to come toward you – indeed I, Paul, once, even twice – and the adversary** (or: "the accuser;" = the enemy or opposer; satan; [note: perhaps a code name for the hostile Jews, as in Rev. 2:9 and 3:9]) **struck within us** (cut in on us; = cut across our path; or: travailed and wearily toiled among us).

Opposition constantly dogged Paul's heels, as the Jews followed him and tried to block his progress. As Jesus spoke to Peter with the term "**adversary** (satan)," so I suggest the figurative use of the word here, or the actual use, if we see that the Greek *satan* was a transliteration of the Hebrew word that meant "adversary, opponent or accuser." All this fits what the Jews were doing to Paul.

19. **For who** (or: what) **is our expectation** (or: expectant hope) **or joy, or shall be a crown** (victor's wreath; encirclement) **of boasting and glorying in front of our Lord Jesus, in His presence** (or: in the place facing toward our Master, Jesus, within the midst of His being present alongside [us]), **if not even you folks?**
20. **For you see, you yourselves are our glory** (or: our reputation; our manifestation which calls forth praise) **and joy!**

He changes the theme away from himself and his troubles, and like the joy set before Jesus (Heb. 12:2), he expresses the same to them: they are his reward and reason for boasting and glorying "**in His presence**" – and he was at that time doing so "in His presence." The fruit of our labors in the Lord is our glory. Folks often seek to have His glory to come upon them, but the Thessalonians were Paul's and his associates' glory and joy – as they were God's glory. Recall the solidarity of Jesus with His brothers (family) in Matt. 25:40. These folks were Christ's glory – His manifestation of Himself in them, which called forth praise. They brought a reputation to God, and even the towns around them heard it.

In Phil. 3:10 Paul seeks,

> "**to intimately and experientially know Him, and the ability – even the power – of His resurrection**,"

which speaks of being in union with the power and ability of the new creation, which was inaugurated by His resurrection. And when four verses later he speaks of

> "**continuously pursuing down toward** [the; or: an] **object in view** (a mark on which the eye is fixed)**: into the prize of God's** (or: the award which is God's) **invitation to an above place** (or: an upward calling having the source from, with qualities and characteristics of, God) **within the midst of and in union with Christ Jesus**,"

I suggest that he is speaking of the same "**victor's wreath** (crown)" to which he is referring here in vss. 19-20, above: the people and communities to which he, as an attending servant, was dispensing God's life and Word, the local expressions of the new creation, the new heaven and the new earth.

Chapter 3

1. **Wherefore** (or: For this reason), **no longer keeping a lid on [our desires]** (or: bearing it no longer), **we thought it a good idea to be left down alone in Athens,**

2. **and then sent Timothy, our brother and God's fellow-worker in Christ's message of ease and goodness, to perhaps set you firmly** (make you stable) **and possibly call you alongside** (to aid, encourage, exhort, console and give relief) **over the [situation] of your trust and faith** (or: conviction and loyalty),

3. **that no one be continuously wagged as a tail** (= shaken or agitated) **within these pressures** (contractions, constrictions; oppressions), **for you yourselves have seen and are aware that we are continually laid into** (= repeatedly destined and set for) **this!**

Consider in vs. 1 that they seem to have been led by what came to them as a good idea. Nothing "hyper-spiritual," it just seemed to be a good idea to stay in Athens, and to send Timothy to Thessalonica. They could see the practical need of these folks being made stable and firmly set in this message of ease and goodness. Recall that Jesus said that His yoke was easy and His burden light (by comparison to what the Jewish religion put on people). The human tendency is to try to make oneself good or right before God. The message of grace can seem too good to be true, so they wanted Timothy to be a paraclete to them, over the situation of their faith, trust and loyalty – i.e., their life in God.

They did not want others to come and "wag them **as a tail**" with Judaism or any "works religion." They did not want them turning to the Law from pressures from the Jews. They did not want them to establish any religion, not even a moralistic one, but to live in spirit and in truth – which conforms to the ease and rest of God. So Paul reminds them, in vs. 3, that he and his partners are committed to their support, in fact "**laid into this**."

4. **You see, even when we were with you we were predicting** (laying it out and telling beforehand) **to you that, "we are about to be continuously pressed** (or: squeezed; oppressed)**," just as it was even birthed** (or: also came to be), **and you have seen and know.**

A squeezing pressure seems to be the constant environment of a follower of Christ.

5. **On account of this I also, no longer keeping a lid on [my desires]** (= when I could bear it no longer), **sent to find out about your faith, trust and loyalty, lest** (or: in case) **somehow the One continuously putting [folks] to the proof** (or: the trier; [note: this could refer to God, or to one of His instruments, as with Job]) **put you to the proof** (tried or tested you), **and our**

exhausting labor (or: = the trouble to which we went; toil; hardship; or: beating) **may be birthed into a void** (or: come to be [entered] into an empty place; or: exist in vain; = be to no purpose).

Paul expresses their concern for these folks and wants to know how they are doing under the pressure which has come to test and purify them (*cf* Mal. 3:2-3). He does not want them to be overcome, be discouraged or to quit, and without support this can happen. They were still young in Christ, but the testing and proving begins early, in childhood, so that His character will be formed in each one. Consider Heb. 12:4-11, where the writer quotes Prov. 3:11-12,

> "**My son, do not be neglecting** (giving little care to) **the Lord's discipline** (education; child-training), **neither be exhausted** (dissolved; = fall apart) **while being continually scrutinized or convicted** (exposed and put to the test; or: reproved) **by** (or: under) **Him, for whom the Lord** [= Yahweh] **is loving, He is continuously and progressively educating** (or: disciplining; child-training), **and He is periodically scourging every son whom He is taking alongside with His hands** (accepting; receiving)."

6. **Yet at the present moment, Timothy, upon coming to us from you and announcing the good news** (message of ease and well-being) **to us of your faith and love, [said] that you always continuously hold** (or: have) **a good remembrance of us, continuously having strong desire to see us – even as we also you!**
7. **On account of this, brothers** (= folks who are as family), **on [the occasions of] all our choking necessity and pressure, by means of the ministry of a paraclete** (or: the Paraclete) **we were comforted and encouraged through your faith, trust and loyalty,**
8. **so that now we can be** (or: are) **living, since** (or: if ever) **you continue standing firm in** (and: in union with) **[the] Lord.**
9. **For now, what gratitude** (or: expression of the goodness of grace and favor) **we continue able to give back to God in return – concerning you folks, upon [the occasion of] all the joy for which** (or: in which) **we are continually rejoicing because of you – before** (or: in front of; in the place facing toward and in the presence of) **our God,**
10. **while night and day, over-excessively repeatedly begging regarding our need to see your face** (= to see you face to face), **and then to freshly adjust to correspondence** (or: thoroughly equip, fit, knit together, mend and bring into agreement) **the things lacking** (the shortcomings or deficiencies) **of your faith and with regard to your loyal trust!**
11. **But our God and Father Himself, even our Lord Jesus, might suddenly make** [note: verb is 3rd person singular; = He might guide] **our road** (path; way) **straight toward** (or: to) **you folks.**

Vs. 6-11 are expressions of their emotional involvement with those at Thessalonica. Timothy had brought back good news of their faith, love and desire to see Paul and company. This brought comfort and encouragement, to the point that Paul says, "**so that now we can be** (or: are) **living**" since he hears that they "**continue standing firm in the Lord.**" Obviously Paul and his friends had put heart and soul into these folks. This brings a response of gratitude to God, in joy expressing His goodness and grace to them all, which then leads to a request that they might see their faces through a personal visit.

Vs. 7 makes an affirmation that shows the solidarity that Paul and his company had with those in Thessalonica. It was through the faith, trust and loyalty of these latter that the former were comforted, encouraged and received the ministry of a, or the, Paraclete. Paul and his fellows were organically joined, in spirit, to these folks.

As I noted in the text, the subject of vs. 11 (God the Father ... Lord Jesus) is singular, as shown by the verb. Whatever the nature of Paul's theology, he saw Them as One.

12. **Now the Lord** [=Yahweh or Christ] **might at some point make you increase** (or: be more than enough; be augmented; [note: in quality and/or quantity]), **even to be abundantly surrounded and furnished** (to super-abound) **by love** (or: to love; for love; in love; with love) **unto each other and into everyone** (or: all mankind), **even as we also into you,**

13. **to establish** (firmly fix; set fast) **your hearts blameless and without defect** (or: to make stable your unblamable hearts) **in separateness** (or: holiness; sacredness) **in front of our God and Father, within the presence of our Lord Jesus with all His set-apart folks** (holy peoples; sacred ones).

You will note in my translation that I frequently insert "[= Yahweh or Christ]" after the word "**Lord**." This is because the LXX, which is frequently quoted in the NT, uses the word "Lord" in place of the Hebrew *Yahweh*. So when "**Lord**" is used by itself, the writer could be referring either to Jesus Christ, or to Yahweh. They did not suddenly divorce themselves from Yahweh when Christ came on the scene. It was Yahweh Elohim Who was considered to be the Father of Jesus.

In vs. 12-13 Paul speaks into their lives that the "**Lord**" might at some point make them increase and even abundantly be furnished "**by love**." "Love" is in the dative case, so it could also read that they would super-abound "in love, to love, for love or with love." Love can be the instrument of their increase; love can attend their increase; love can be that within which they increase; love can be the goal for which they would increase. All of these aspects of their prophesied increase may be the reason why Paul did not specify a preposition before the word "**love**."

And note the interweaving of this love, in solidarity: "**into each other and into everyone**" (or, seeing the broader vision of the goal of this increase in, with, by, for love: "into all mankind"), and then, "**even as we also INTO you**." This is an organic network, an intertwining Vine of love, as their "branches run over the wall" (Gen. 49:22).

This increase in, with, by and for love is intended "**to establish**, firmly fix and set fast [their] **hearts** [the source of love] **blameless and without defect**," in an environment of separateness and sacredness "**in front of God our Father**," which is also to say, "**within the presence of our Lord Jesus**."

But note what he goes on to say, "... **with all His set-apart folks** (holy peoples; sacred ones)." Aside from the inclusiveness of this statement, where is he indicating that the place or environment exists where these Thessalonians are in front of the Father, in the presence of our Lord Jesus, and with all His set-apart folks?
Is he indicating that their growth and love is demonstrated before all the other called-out congregations which hear about it? Is he meaning that Jesus is present with all these congregations and communities? Is he saying that the Father and Jesus, being in heaven, are seeing this that is occurring on the earth?
Does he mean that love is a matter of the spirit, and that they, like what Paul said in Eph. 2:6, are seated together in the heavenly realms in Christ Jesus? Is this a reference to Heb. 12:1, and that the saints referred to here are the "**cloud of witnesses**"? I'm just asking. May the Spirit speak to you about this.

Chapter 4

1. **The remainder** (What is left; or: Finally), **then, brothers** (= fellow believers), **we are continuously asking and calling you alongside to encourage, exhort and comfort you folks in the Lord Jesus, according as you took to your side** (or: received and accepted) **from us how** (or: in what manner) **it is binding [for; upon] you to normally walk about** (= live your lives) **and to be continuously pleasing to God – just as you are even now continuously walking about – to the end that you would progressively superabound to a greater extent** (or: can rather habitually excel and surround [yourselves] by more than enough).
2. **For you have seen and are aware what instructions** (messages alongside) **we gave to you through the Lord Jesus.**

It is evident that the message of God's goodness and ease came with some practical instructions about their daily living, and that Paul repeatedly refers to "**calling** [them] **alongside to**

encourage, exhort and comfort" them in this way of life. Jesus gave many instructions on kingdom living, as for example, in Matt. 5-7. Vs. 1 here says that "**it is binding** for, or upon, [them] to normally live" this way so as to be "**continuously pleasing to God**." The verses that follow speak to some general categories that are qualities of "rightwised living," or, "living in accord to the Way (Christ) pointed out."

Yet this is not another "law" that they are to live by, but rather, he is just giving examples of living by what in Rom. 8:2 he called "the law of Life's spirit, etc.,"

> **For the principle and law of, and which is, the spirit and attitude of 'The Life within Christ Jesus'**
>> (or: For you see, the Law of Life's spirit, joined with [the] Anointing of Jesus; or: For the Spirit's law of life within Christ Jesus; or: the Law from the Breath-effect, which is Life in union with [the] Anointed Jesus)
>
> **frees you away from the Law of the Sin** (or: the principle of failure and the missing of the target; the code of behavior that produces error; the principle of deviation from the goal) **and the Death** (or: immediately set you [other MSS: me] at liberty from the law that deals with and has the character of sin and death).

3. **You see, this is the will** (intent, purpose) **of God: your state of being set apart from the common use or condition** (or: holiness; sacredness; = covenant living) **– you are to continuously hold yourself from** (be distant from; abstain from) **all of the prostitution** [note: figuratively, the worship of idols or false religions, and a break from covenant].

Here is a clear statement of God's will, intent, and purpose for us: our state of being set apart from the common use or condition. This clause gives the literal meaning of what has become a religious term, "holiness." The term "sacredness," although also a religious term, has in recent decades been used in a more general way to express the value of life and creation as special beyond mere utility.

Thus, we should hold ourselves away from prostitution, in any of its forms, which makes our lives common and utilitarian, stripping it of its sacredness – as well as breaking covenant with our mates, in the realm of marriage. But this was a term that the OT writers used of Israel (Isa. 1:21; Hosea 1, 2, etc.) when they turned away from following Yahweh, broke covenant and participated in pagan religions, worshiping idols. So Paul is also referring to remaining faithful to the true God through Jesus Christ.

4. **Each one of you [is] to have seen and thus learned how, know and be aware of his own equipment** (gear; utensils; instruments; vessel; = means of making a living), **to progressively acquire** (procure for one's self) **in set-apartness** (or: holiness) **and honor** (value, worth),
5. **not in a feeling of excessive desire** (or: in union with an experience of full-rushing passion), **just as also the nations** (ethnic multitudes; non-Israelites) **[do] who, having not perceived, do not know** (aren't aware of; aren't acquainted with) **God.**

Note here that Paul contrasts the excessive desire of the ethnic multitudes (or, "nations," the term being a figure that is contrasted to a people who have perceived God's way to live) to making a living and procuring goods "**in set-apartness**, or holiness." To do the latter is to do so without excessive desire. Doing so in "**honor**" means to live honestly, valuing the customer, one's society and the environment. Paul's theology is very "this-worldly."

6. **Thus, no one is to be continuously overstepping and have more** (hold advantage) **in his brother's affair** (result of doing; transaction-effect; development from a matter; = cheat his fellow believers in business dealings), **because [the] Lord** [= Yahweh or Christ] **[is] a maintainer of right** (an executor of justice and equity from the Way pointed out) **concerning all these people and things, just as we also told you before and certified with solemn witness throughout.**

The phrase "**a maintainer of right** (an executor of justice and equity from the Way pointed out)" is from the same word family from which we get "righteousness," or as I translate this, "being pointed in the right direction; or: the Way pointed out, which is fairness and equity in rightwised relationships." Paul is saying that the Lord cares about how we do business, and about our relationship with other people. Thus does He judge us according to our works and actions. Life in His reign is much more than just believing that Jesus is the Christ, it involves living as the Christ – which is done by reckoning ourselves dead with Christ and raised up with Him, the life we live being His life living within us: Christ in us, living His life as us. The resurrection of Jesus inaugurated the new creation and the new arrangement (or: covenant) which brought His reign (sovereign influence and activities; kingdom) to earth in a new way, making all things new (Rev. 21:5). "Jesus Christ is Lord" is our proclamation; we look to Him to maintain right and equity.

7. **For God did not call us on the basis of uncleanness** (or: does not invite us [to be] on [a path lived in] a soiled condition or a dirty environment), **but rather within the sphere of set-apartness** (or: holiness; sacredness; in a manner commensurate with covenant living).

I think that it is noteworthy that Paul uses the word "**uncleanness**" in the context of how we live our lives in relation to other folks' business and personal affairs, and specifically in having an advantage over others. It is in the aspects of daily living in solidarity with humanity and our interactions with them that we are called to be set-apart from the System's perspectives, attitudes and way of doing business. These areas are areas for the expression of love, and the Way that He has pointed out to us.

8. **Consequently, then, the person continuously setting aside** (or: displacing) **is not setting aside** (or: displacing; or: = disregarding) **a human** (or: person), **but God, even the One continuously giving His Sacred Breath into us** (or: repeatedly imparting His Spirit, the Holy One, unto us; constantly gifting His set-apart Breath-effect [to flow] into us).

Thus we see a strong affirmation of God's solidarity with humanity: how you treat others is how you are in this same act treating God. The last clause of this verse is similar to what Paul said in Acts 17:25,
> "... **He Himself being the One constantly giving to all people** (or: all things) **life and breath and all things** (or: everything; the whole [universe])**!**"

This verse is a summation of vss. 3-7. Living in covenant is really about living in honor and sacredness with others, treating them in a way that is right and is in love.

9. **But now concerning loving one like a brother** (or: brotherly love; = fondness for fellow believers), **we have no need to continually write to you, for you yourselves are folks continuously taught by God** (God-taught ones) **to continuously love each other,**
10. **for you are even continuously doing this unto all of those brothers within the whole of Macedonia. But we are constantly calling you alongside** (to encourage, urge, exhort and comfort you), **brothers, to progressively superabound to a greater extent** (or: rather to habitually excel and surround [yourselves] by more than enough [brotherly affection]).
11. **and then to habitually be fond of honor and value [and] to be repeatedly quiet** (or: to be progressively ambitious to live in settled peace), **and by habit to be engaged** (or: involved) **in your own affairs** (or: matters), **and then to constantly work with your own hands** (idiom: = work at it actively), **according as we commanded to you,**
12. **to the intent that you may continuously walk about in good form** (= live your life respectably) **toward those without** (with a view to outsiders; = face to face with those that are not a part of your community), **and then you would continually have need of nothing.**

Vs. 9-12 are an admonition to the virtues of love, honor, value and living in good form. He acknowledges that they presently do this, but that there can be a progression in these "**to a greater extent**." He also points out in vs. 9 that God has taught them to do this, and other things not mentioned, for they are "God-taught ones." Thus we see that God does not only teach us through Scripture, or through teaching and preaching. There is also his encouragement that they would progressively have an ambition to live in settled peace and that they would work actively at being "**engaged in** [their] **own affairs**." The view is to live a life in God's kingdom, right hear on earth. This is considered to be in good form, and will result in their having need of nothing.

But to what extent should we just focus on our own affairs? The answer to this question can have political and international implication. As in all things, the answer lies in love and the leading of God's Spirit. It also lies in our capabilities, as the Lord supplies. But I think that Paul's main thrust in these words is that we not be meddlers, and leave Another's servant to stand before Him.

The next section of this letter turns from practical advice of daily living to concerns about the dead, and their relationship to the eschatological expectations that those in Thessalonica were entertaining.

13. **Now then, we are not wanting** (or: willing, intending) **you to continue ignorant, brothers, concerning the folks who are from time to time falling asleep** [other MSS: those having been put to sleep (= passed away; died), and continuing made to be sleeping], **to the intent that you may not continuously be made to be sad or sorrowful according as even** (or: just like also) **the rest** (the ones remaining or left), **the folks continuously having no expectation** (or: hope).

So first of all, there should be no sadness or sorrow about folks who are from time to time dying. Their attitude and world-view should not be that of either the Jewish world or that of the pagans – those who were without an expectation about those who died. Things have changed; Christ has been raised from the dead (1 Cor. 15); we have been placed into Christ and are a part of the second humanity (1 Cor. 15:45-47); there is a new creation.

14. **For you see, since** (or: if) **we habitually believe that Jesus died and then arose** (or: stood up again), **thus** (in this manner) **also, through Jesus, God will be leading together with Him the folks being made to sleep**.

Note Paul's emphasis on the resurrection of Jesus as the basis of our faith. He stood up again. And we see that when Jesus is on the move (the purpose of standing up again), in this same manner these dead folks are lead together with Him, by God. So the question is: when, where and how does this happen? Paul addresses this in the following verses. But let us also consider what he said in 2 Cor. 1:9b, "**the God Who is continually** (habitually; periodically; repeatedly; or: presently) **awakening and raising up the dead ones!**" The Greek verb in this clause is in the present tense of continual or repeated action, as seen in this translation.

15. **For this we are continuously saying to you in a word of the Lord** (or: in the Lord's Word; in a message which is [the] Lord; or: in union with an idea from [our] Owner), **that we, the presently living** (or: the ones continuing to live) – **the folks presently continuing to be left around unto the presence of the Lord** (or: into the midst of the Lord's [= Christ's or Yahweh's] presence) – **can by no means advance before** (precede; have advantage over; outstrip) **the folks being made to sleep,**

Thus, they can be assured about these dead folks, that those then presently living, who "**in a word from the Lord**," were to be continuing to be left around unto "**the presence of the Lord**" would by no means precede or have advantage over those that were presently dead. The question is then, what is meant by "the presence of the Lord"? Vs. 16 gives an indication:

16. **because the Lord** [= Yahweh or Christ] **Himself will descend from [the] atmosphere** (or: heaven) **within the midst of** (or: in union with) **a shout of command, within the midst of [the] Chief Agent's** (or: an original messenger's; or: a chief and ruling agent's; or: [the] beginning messenger's) **voice, and within the midst of** (or: in union with) **God's trumpet** [note: figure of a

message or a directive for action], **and the dead people within Christ** (or: in union with [the] Anointed One) **will raise themselves up** (or: will stand up again) **first** (or: in first place).

"**The presence** (Greek: *par-ousia* – 'being alongside') **of the Lord**" in this context means an eschatological event which Paul describes in apocalyptic images. First of all we need to consider the word "heaven" which also means "the **atmosphere** of the earth." Recall that we are presently seated in heavenly places, or atmospheric spheres (Eph. 2:6). If we take the meaning of *ouranos* as "atmosphere," the implication is that this realm and sphere is right here, and even touches the earth. Consider that vs. 17 refers to this place as being in "**the midst of air**," the realm of "clouds." I suggest that the idea of "descending" is a relative term that signifies God's specific intervention and involvement in the life of the "earth realm," as compared to the life in the spirit.

His descending is within the midst of, and in union with, "**a shout of command, within the midst of [the] Chief, or a Ruling Agent's, voice.**" This Ruling Agent would either be Christ Himself, or it would be someone, or a composite group, that is at this time speaking for Him, is His Name and authority, and He descends to us within that voice. He goes on to describe this as God's "**trumpet,**" which is a figure of a message. So His message comes, and Christ is encountered within that message. The result is the dead folks raise themselves up (the voice of the verb is "middle"), or, will stand up again, and this speaks of resurrection.

Here we enter another much debated topic. Jesus said, "**I am the resurrection and the life**" (John 11:25). Paul made other significant statements:

> "**Thus you folks, also, be constantly accounting** (logically considering; reckoning) **yourselves to exist being dead ones, indeed, by the failure to hit the target** (or: in the Sin; to the deviation), **yet ones continuously living by God** (in God; for God; to God; with God), **within Christ Jesus, our Owner**" (Rom. 6:11).

So we are to logically consider ourselves to exist being dead, which would put us in the category of those in vs. 16, above, who were then "sleeping," and yet at the same time continuously living by and in God (having been joined to Christ in His death and resurrection – Rom. 6:4-5)?

> "**even us, being continuously dead ones by** (or: in; to; for) **the stumblings aside** (wrong steps; offences) **He made alive together by** (or: joins us in common life with and in; [*p*46, B: within; in union with]) **the Christ – by Grace and joyous favor you continually exist, being folks having been delivered** (rescued and saved, so that you are now safe; made whole)! **– and He jointly roused and raised** (or: suddenly awakens and raises) **[us] up, and caused [us] to sit** (or: seats [us]) **together within the things situated upon** [thus, above] **the heavens** (or: in union with the full, perfected heavenlies; or, although neuter: among those comprising the complete and perfected heavenlies; among the ones [residing] upon the atmospheres; in union with the celestials) **within and in union with Christ Jesus,**" (Eph. 2:5-6).

We should also keep in mind that in Christ, the bearer of the New Being, there is a new creation,

> "**Consequently, since someone [is] within Christ** (or: if anyone [is] in union with [the] Anointed One), **[there is] a new creation** (or: [it is] a framing and founding of a different kind; [he or she is] an act of creation having a fresh character and a new quality)**: the original things** (the beginning [situations]; the archaic and primitive [arrangements]) **passed by** (or: went to the side). **Consider! New things have come into existence** (have been birthed; or: It has become new things; or: He has been birthed and now exists being ones of a different kind, character and quality)." (2 Cor. 5:17)

17. **Thereupon** (or: After that; As a next step) **we, the presently living folks, the ones presently continuing to be left around, will – at the same time, together with them – be seized and snatched away within clouds** (or: carried off by force, in union with clouds,) **into the midst of [the] air** (the air that we breathe in; the mist; the haze; the atmosphere around us; [note: this would be in the earth's lower atmosphere, the place where there is air]) **– into the Lord's meeting** ([Christ's or Yahweh's] encounter). **And thus** (in this way and such a manner) **shall we always be** (or: exist at all times) **together with [the] Lord** [= Christ or Yahweh].

Paul here is speaking of an event that those then living, "**we**," would experience: being "**seized and snatched away within clouds into the midst of [the] air**." Much of Christianity believes this to be a future event, and some have considered Paul to have been misguided to have expected it to happen in the then near future. But others, among them those of the preterist paradigm, believe that this happened when the Lord returned to Jerusalem in judgment, both through the agency of the Romans and in a literal "snatching away" and resurrection during the period of AD 66-70.

It should be noted that Paul did not say that the Lord would take everyone off to heaven, but that they would be with Him "in [the] air." Thus would they be in our atmosphere – close enough to touch. That, of course, is putting a literal spin on the interpretation of his words. A figurative interpretation – since he spoke in apocalyptic terms of a shout, the blowing of a trumpet, and descending – would speak of the joining of the heavens and the earth in the realm of spirit, and thus catching folks up into realm of spirit, similar to the descending of the New Jerusalem as symbolically pictured in Rev. 21:2, and its existence upon earth in ch. 22. This, of course, was a figurative description of the Lamb's wife (21:9), the bride of Christ, God's tabernacle (= His temple, His body) dwelling with humanity (21:3).

I should also point out that this same word "**seized and snatched away**" is used in Matt. 11:12 in the context of the reign of the heavens, where I render it as "grasping it and drawing it up,"
> "**Now from the days of John the Immerser until right now, the reign of the heavens** (or: sovereign rule of the kingdom of the atmospheres) **is itself continuously pressing** (or: is progressively pressing and forcing itself) **forward with urgency, and those urging and pressing forward [toward the goal] are constantly grasping it and drawing it up [to themselves].**"

18. **So that** (or: Consequently) **you must constantly call each other alongside to give relief, encouragement and comfort, as a paraclete, within these words** (or: thoughts; reasons).

This would have been a real comfort to them, and so it can be to us, since He is repeatedly coming to us and walking among us (pictured as lampstands, among which He constantly walks: Rev. 1:20 and 2:1). Note that the One who constantly, or repeatedly, walks among us speaks with "**a great voice** (or: = a loud sound), **as of a trumpet...**" (Rev. 1:10).

Chapter 5

1. **But concerning the times and the fitting situations** (or: specific seasons or occasions; fertile periods; mature moments), **brothers** (= fellow believers), **you have no need [for it] to be continually written to you,**
2. **for you yourselves are accurately aware** (know exactly from having seen) **that a day of the Lord** [= Yahweh] **thus continually comes** (is habitually and repeatedly coming and going; is presently coming) **as a thief in a night** (or: within [the] night).

Now the day of Yahweh was a term that figured a time of judging and of hard times, in the Old Testament; e.g., see Joel 1:15 and 2:1-2; Jer. 30:7; Amos 5:18; Zeph. 1:14-18. Here Paul continues using the figures of "**a day of the Lord**," and "**a thief at night**." It would be a time of dark days – trouble. This letter being written about AD 50, he might have been speaking prophetically of what was to begin in about 15 years. This phrase indicates a special visitation from God where He intervenes in the affairs of humanity. Note that this occurrence periodically or continually comes: it is not a one time, "end of the world" event. Paul had just described it as the Lord's "presence" (Greek: *par-ousia*, i.e., "being alongside") in ch. 4:15, and referred to it as an "encounter" or a "meeting." Having this now connected with the OT term "day of the Lord" would seem to indicate that it is a time of decision and change (or: judging, as in OT times) along with a time of higher experience (air/clouds, which figure "spirit") and a forceful snatching away (*harpazo*, ch. 4:17), in union with clouds, for His people. As pointed out, above, this is associated

128

with the coming of His kingdom, which began with the ministry of Jesus. Vs. 1, here, tells us that Paul must have already described the situations or occasions that would signal this period, for they were aware of this.

3. **So whenever they may be repeatedly saying, "Peace and security from falling** (or: safety; stability),**" then** (at that time) **sudden and unexpected ruin** (or: a surprise of destruction) **is presently standing upon them, just as the birth-pang for the pregnant woman** (or: to the one having [a child] in the womb), **and they may by no means flee out or make an escape.**

Here he points to political and social upheaval, and possibly war. They would be aware of its gathering, just as a woman who is long pregnant usually knows the season of when to expect birth-pangs. And Paul's use of this metaphor may also point to an expectation of a new situation being "birthed." Once it begins, there is no escaping its coming. N. T. Wright (*Surprised by Hope – Rethinking Heaven, the Resurrection and the Mission of the Church*, Harper One, 2008) says that the term "birth-pangs" was a common "Jewish metaphor for the emergence of God's new age" and that it signified "birth of [a] new creation from the womb of the old" (p. 103, 104).

4. **Yet you yourselves, brothers** (= believers), **are not continuously in darkness** (dimness from being in a shadow; obscurity of gloom; absence of daylight), **to the end that the day may** (or: would) **suddenly take you down** (grasp or seize you in a corresponding manner) **as a thief,**

So here Paul assures them that they have the light of this knowledge and won't be surprised. Furthermore, they are not living in the realm of darkness (figured by the conditions and deeds spoken of in Rev. 22:15) which exists outside their called-out community, for the New Jerusalem (a figure of God's people in the new reality and kingdom – see Gal. 4:26) has light (Rev. 22:5) and is a light for the ethnic multitudes and nations that are not yet a part of the City (Rev. 21:23-26). The Thessalonians are the light of the dominating System (or: world – Matt. 5:14) in their area.

5. **for you see, you all are** (or: exist being) **sons of** (= associated with and having the qualities of) **Light and sons of** (= associated with and having qualities of) **Day! We are not** (or: do not exist) **of night, nor of darkness** (or: we do not belong to or have the characteristics of night, nor to or of dim obscurity from shadows and gloom).

This shows that a change has come – old things had passed away. The darkness can refer both to ignorance, and to the old religious systems of Judaism or the pagan religions. But it also refers to the coming dark clouds of judgment, that would soon approach them, as well as the Jerusalem which was of the earth and in slavery to Mount Sinai – the Law (Gal 4:25), putting out the light of the old Jewish religion. The light is a metaphor for Christ and His body. The day referred both to the day of judging, and to the new day of the new age – and the new creation/covenant.

6. **Consequently, then, we may not continuously fall asleep [into death? in awareness?] even as the rest** (= as other folks), **but rather, we can and should continuously be aroused and stirred up from sleep** [comment: thus, awake to be alertly watchful; also a figure for being alive] **and sober** (or: clear-headed).

Paul was very clear here: that to which he was referring was not some far-off event. It was soon to come, and they must "**continuously be aroused and stirred up from sleep and** clear-headed!" They would live to see this happen! The contrasts of falling asleep/being aroused from sleep are metaphorical in regard to their attitudes: they should be sober and clear-headed, as "**sons of Light and sons of Day**."

7. **You see, the folks continuously falling asleep** (or: drowsing) **are sleeping at** (or: from [the]) **night, and the ones continuously being made drunk are becoming drunk at** (or: from [the]) **night.**

Day and night existed at the same time in Paul's metaphor – the difference was whether you were dwelling in darkness, or in the Light. It was the night for the old creation, but at the same time it was the New Day of the new age/creation. It was a conjunction of the ages (Heb. 9:26) – the end of one; the beginning of the next. The Jews were asleep to the coming of the Messiah; they were drunk on the old wine. Again, "**sleeping**... **drunk**" are here used metaphorically.

8. **We, on the other hand, being of Day** (belonging to and having characteristics of [the] Day; having [the] Day as our source), **can and should continuously be sober** (clear-headed), **putting on** (or: clothing ourselves with; enveloping ourselves in; entering within) **a breastplate** (or: thorax) **of faith and love** (or: which is and is composed of faith and love; = have trust & love as body armor) **and, as a helmet, an expectation** (or: expectant hope) **of deliverance** (health and wholeness; rescue and salvation; restoration to our original state and condition),

This was a time to be clear about the message of God's goodness, and put Him on, as a warrior puts on the protection of a helmet and breastplate, as Paul also said in Eph. 6:11,

> "**you folks must enter within** (or: clothe yourselves with) **the full suit of armor and implements of war** (panoply; the complete equipment for men-at-arms) **which is God** (or: which comes from and belongs to God), **in order for you to be continuously able and powerful to stand** (or: to make a stand) **facing toward the crafty methods** (stratagems) **of the adversary**
>> (or: that which throws folks into dualism with divided thinking and perceptions; or: the person that throws something through the midst and casts division; the one who thrusts things through folks; the slanderer who accuses and deceives; or, commonly called: the "devil")."

Once again, Paul's word was for their then-present situation. Nonetheless, it is a practical admonition for everyone of any time or situation. But note that these metaphors are of attitudes and of a life in union with the Christ, who is the Day; the Light. These "weapons" are for our protection, not for offensive action.

9. **because God Himself did not** (or: does not) **place or set us into anger** (inherent fervor; violent emotion; wrath; or: teeming, passionate desire), **but rather, into an encompassing of deliverance** (or: unto establishing a perimeter of safety; into making health and wholeness encircle [us]; into the forming of an encompassing salvation around [us]) **through our Lord, Jesus Christ –**

The Thessalonians, and the rest of the body of Christ elsewhere, were not going to be a part of the oncoming judging that was to come through His "instrument of destruction" (Isa. 54:16), the Romans. He was going to be their "encompassing of deliverance." The word that I have rendered, "**encompassing**," or, "establishing a perimeter," or, "making... encircle," or, "forming of an encompassing" is a participle formed from the verb *poieo* prefixed by the preposition *peri*. It is often translated "acquiring," from the sense of surrounding one's self with material goods. But the verb "**place / set**," which is the antecedent action of our phrase, shows that this is an action by God, so I have rendered it from the elements of the Greek word, and LXX usage (e.g., 2 Chron. 14:13; Isa. 31:5; Hag. 2:10), which speaks to God's protection of His people amidst present danger. The safety and deliverance of the final phrases describe the present state and possession of the community, and refer back to the faith, love and expectation mentioned in vs. 8.

So, more than just an eschatological view of a situation of judgment that was soon to come, it was a present reality that encompassed them.

10. **the One dying concerning and on behalf of us** (or: = while encompassing our [situation]; [other MSS: over our {situation}]), **to the end that whether we can or would exist being continuously awake** (attentively watching) **or continuously falling asleep** [note: a metaphor for "being alive or being dead"], **we can at the same time be alive** (or: live) **together with Him** (= share His life).

Here Paul returns to those presently living and those having died: both categories were alive together with Him. This was the result of His dying over our previous situation: the new creation, and resurrection from our state of having been dead. Recall the words of Jesus, in John 11:26,

> "**And further, everyone** (or: all mankind) **presently** (or: continuing in) **living and trusting** (or: progressively believing; regularly exercising faith) **into Me can by no means** (or: may under no circumstances) **die-off** (or: die-away) **on into the Age. Are you presently believing, trusting and having convinced faith of this?**"

The new age and the new creation, which issued from His resurrection, has changed everything – even death.

Helmut Koester (ibid., p. 65) suggests that Paul is here making the distinction irrelevant between being awake and sleeping, since they could at that present time "**be alive**, or live, **together with Him** and share His life." He points to the verb here being the aorist subjunctive, and that it should be read as a present reality which was not determined by their being watchful (i.e., being awake to this life) but by the then present state of the community. He sees the awake/asleep contrast as metaphorical, just as it was in vss. 6-8, above.

11. **Wherefore, keep on calling each other to [your] side** (to encourage, aid, urge, comfort or exhort), **and by habit let one person build up** (or: edify) **the [other] person** (comment: a one-on-one endeavor), **just as you are even continuously doing.**
12. **Now we are continuously asking you, brothers** (= fellow-believers), **to have seen** (or: observed) **and thus know and perceive those normally toiling wearily among you folks and continuously making themselves to stand before you** (placing or setting themselves before you; or: presiding over you) **and then continuously putting [their] mind in you** (or: putting you in mind; or: admonishing you) **in [the] Lord,**
13. **and to continuously lead them above, from out of an abundance in love** (or: lead the mind through a reasoning process to the conclusion to consider them exceedingly distinguished, in union with love) **because of their work. Keep on being at peace** (or: cultivate harmony [= shalom]) **among yourselves.**

In vs. 11 he exhorts them to continue in encouraging and edifying each other, then in 12 and 13 he admonishes them to have observed so as to know those who toil among them and who take a stand before them, endeavor to put their mind (= their particular thoughts about things) into them, in regards to the things of the Lord, and the life in Christ. This is cautionary advice: don't let just anyone come and feed you their own ideas.

But for those whom they trusted, in accord with their service to the body, to let their estimation of them be loving respect, giving abundant loving distinction and honor to them, for the covenant community is a culture of honor. In all of this, let Peace reign among them, as in their own hearts (Col. 3:15).

We see in *oikodomeo* (build up; edify), vs. 11, the same thought that Paul expressed in 1 Cor. 3:9-17, where an intensified form of this same verb is used. Koester sees in Paul's use of this verb a realized eschatology that "obliterates the distinction between being watchful and being asleep, between life and death..." (ibid., p. 65).

14. **But we are continually calling you to [our] side** (to encourage, entreat and admonish), **brothers: continually admonish and warn** (put a mind into; or: put in mind) **the disorderly ones** (the unarranged; those out of line; those not in battle position or deserters); **continually address** (speak alongside persuasively to and cheer up) **the little-souled folks** (the small of soul; = the faint-hearted); **continually hold yourselves directly opposite** (or: hold against one's self; or: = stand your ground as a shield in front of) **the folks without strength** (the weak ones); **continually be longsuffering and tolerant** (patient; long-passioned; long before breathing violently) **toward everyone** (or: all mankind).
15. **Make it a habit to see** (or: observe) **[that] no one may** (or: would) **give back** (render, discharge, repay) **evil in place of evil** (or: something ugly as opposition to something ugly;

131

worthlessness in exchange for worthlessness; what not ought to be in return for what not ought to be; poor quality for poor quality; wrongdoing with wrongdoing; injury in the face of injury) **to anyone, but to the contrary, continue to always pursue** (follow rapidly; run swiftly to acquire; chase after) **the good** (the excellent; the virtuous) **unto [the benefit of] each other as well as unto all people.**

The letter now moves to admonitions. Vs. 14-15 need little comment, but to point out that the longsuffering and tolerance was to be toward everyone, not just the called-out community. Likewise, "no one may repay ugliness with ugliness," etc. And the good, the excellent or the virtuous were also to be for all people, not just their own group. This is a way of proclaiming that Jesus is Lord by the very lives of those of the called-out community. This is God's reign in action, of seeing Christ in His brothers (Matt. 25:35-36).

16. **Be continuously rejoicing – always** (or: = Find joy in every [situation]; Always express constant joy)**!**
17. **Continuously think, speak and act with a view toward having well-being and goodness – unceasingly** (or: By habit be praying unintermittingly).
18. **Within the midst of everything, be continuously giving thanks** (or: In union with all people, be habitually expressing the goodness of grace and the well-being from favor), **for this is God's intent** (will, purpose) **unto you in Christ Jesus** (or: [proceeding] into the midst of you folks, in union with [the] Anointed Jesus).

Vs. 16-18 are positive admonitions that speak for themselves. They are words of life and success, and describe God's intent and purpose for our lives. They are keys to kingdom living. Note that in vs. 17 I have given a literal rendering of *pros-eu-chomai* (normally rendered "pray"). Note also that this verb is not limited to thoughts or speaking, but also can include action.

I also gave a parenthetical rendering of the Greek elements of *eu-charis-te̲o*, in vs. 18. Here we see that both words, in 17 & 18, contain the particle *eu*: goodness, ease and well-being. And this latter verb is centered around *charis*: grace and favor. We should give pause to consider the qualities of the life that Paul is here admonishing – these are not just "religious" imperatives, but a call to expressing the life of Christ, which is the new creation within us, in our daily living.

19. **Do not continually extinguish** (put out; quench) **the Breath-effect** (or: Spirit; spirit).
20. **Do not continually make nothing out of** (set at naught, despise or scorn) **prophecies** (expressions of light ahead of time),

Here we have two negative injunctions. I suggest that vs. 19 refers to the effect of the Spirit within an individual, or within the community, for no one can extinguish the Consuming Fire (Heb. 12:29). In my rendering "**Breath-effect,**" I have expressed the literal meaning of the Greek elements of *pneuma*. The *–ma* ending means "effect, or result." This word could also refer to someone's human spirit, or attitude. We should not put out a smoking wick, or crush a bruised reed.

We should also value and consider prophecies and expression of light ahead of time (this latter being the literal meaning of the Greek *pro-ph̲e-tes* – the stem *ph̲e*, which, according to Strong, comes from the base *phain̲o*, – "to give light" – which in this case means to give light by what one speaks).

21. **but be continuously examining and putting all things to the proof** (or: yet habitually test every person) – **[then] constantly hold tightly to the beautiful, the ideal, the fine!**
22. **Habitually hold yourself away** (or: abstain) **from every form** (external appearance; shape; figure) **of what is useless and unprofitable, or brings wearisome labor, or is mischievous, malicious, harmful or disadvantageous** (or: from evil's every form).

Comments on 1 Thessalonians

Vs. 21 and 22 give contrasts that also speak for themselves. Note that 21 speaks of either things and situations, or of people: be discerning. Our focus should be toward beauty and the ideal. Expressions of what is base should be avoided, as well as of what is useless – for these waste our time and distract us from our mission. Many religious endeavors, although well-meaning, can also be filled with wearisome labor. As you can see, the Greek *poneros* (normally only rendered "evil") has a broad range of applications. Also *eidos* (form; shape; external appearance) is the root from which *eidolon* (idol) arose, so you can see the depth of Paul's association of these words. Our current culture is overwhelmed with emphasis on external appearance and figure. Our religious ceremonies and practices can even be disadvantageous, if they do not accurately reflect the character of the resurrected life in Christ, the new creation. We should not bring in the forms from the old covenant or the old creation – they are harmful.

23. **Now may the God of peace Himself** (or: Yet the very God who is peace and harmony [= shalom] can) **set you folks apart [being] completely whole** (or: wholly perfect; entirely mature; wholly finished and at the goal), **and may your whole allotment** (= every part) **– the spirit, the soul and the body – be kept** (guarded; watched over) **blameless** (without fault) **within, and in union with, the presence of our Lord** (Master; Owner), **Jesus Christ.**

Here Paul speaks goodness into the full complement (spirit/soul/body) of their lives, describing God as Peace personified, and that they would be guarded and kept "without fault." Note that his final impartations speak to their present environment: the "**presence**" of Jesus Christ, with which they are "**in union.**" Or, he is speaking of the coming "presence" as I discussed it in vs. 1.

24. **The One continuously calling you is faithful** (trustworthy; loyal; full of faith and trust), **Who will also perform** (do, make, form, construct, create, produce)!

He reminds them that God/Christ is full of faith, and thus is loyal to them, and can be trusted. He affirms that God will perform in their lives, create in their lives, do things in and among them, form [Christ] within them, make [goodness to abound], produce [the Spirit's fruit]. It's all God!

25. **Brothers** (= Fellow believers; = Family), **you must also continuously pray concerning us** (think and speak with a view to having goodness, ease and well-being around us).
26. **Draw to yourselves and enfold in your arms all the brothers** (= fellow believers) **in a set-apart expression of affection** (or: a holy kiss).

He wants reciprocity in regard to speaking goodness, well-being and ease; he wants full receptivity of fellow believers, in expressions of affection.

27. **I adjure** (lay the duty on) **you folks [in; by] the Lord [that] this letter** (or: epistle) **be read to** (be made known again for; be recognized by) **all the set-apart brothers** (the sanctified [fellow believers]).

These words and thoughts are for everyone who follows Christ Jesus.

28. **The grace of and from our Lord** (or: the favor which is our Lord), **Jesus Christ, [is] with you. Amen** (Count on it; It is so)!

I have given three function of the genitive in the first phrase. What more do we need? His grace and His favor are the good news in which He Himself comes to us and abides with us.

Robinson (ibid.) sets the date for this second letter at circa AD 50-51. It is similar to the first letter, addressing day-to-day problems. But here Paul is seeking to help balance their perspective with regard to the expected judgment which Jesus had predicted, and which they were expecting Him soon to bring upon Jerusalem. In 2:3-12 he points out what must come first, before the revolt (the standing away, or, departure). The continued political unrest of this period is the scene of this context, but I suggest that Paul also has in mind an interior application for his apocalyptic statements. This would have been most helpful for the immediate situation of the Christian movement in "standing away" from its Jewish forms as it lived within the new arrangement.

Chapter 1

1. **Paul, Silvanus** (or: Silas), **and Timothy, to the called-out community of [the] Thessalonians within God our Father, even** (or: and) **[the] Lord** (or: in union with God, our Father and Lord), **Jesus Christ:**
2. **Grace and peace** (or: Favor and harmony) **to you from God, our Father and Lord** (or: our Father, and [the] Lord), **Jesus Christ** ([the] Anointed)**!**

Note both the corporate solidarity expressed by Paul saying that this letter is coming from the three of them. He is not taking a stand on his own authority as a "sent-forth emissary," nor on this message being just from him. They also are speaking on behalf of, and in solidarity with, God – our Father and Lord. Here I have given some alternatives: in the rendering of *kai*, "**even**" or "and," as well as in the punctuation (there being no punctuation in the early MSS). In vs. 1 this could lead to understanding Jesus the Messiah as either being "God our Father," with "even" meaning "that is to say" – indicating identification and identity, or it could be pointing out that both our **Father** and "**[the] Lord Jesus Christ**" are the spiritual dwelling place of the community, as well as being the Ones within Whom they are in union.

In vs. 2 we see again the potential alternative via punctuation, and we see that these three men who are writing the letter have the ability to extend "**grace and peace from God**" to the congregation. Were this merely a salutation, there would be no need to include the source. But this shows the solidarity that Paul, Silvanus and Timothy share with God.

3. **We continue being indebted to be constantly expressing gratitude to God** (or: We are continually owing [it] to be habitually acknowledging the goodness of grace and the well-being from the favor in God) **– always – concerning you, brothers** (= fellow believers; = Family members), **according as it is continually valuable** (pushes the scales down; is worthy), **because your faith** (or: trust; conviction; loyalty) **is constantly flourishing** (growing above; over-growing; exceedingly increasing) **and the love of each one of you all continuously abounds** (exists in abundance) **unto and into the midst of each other,**

Vs. 3 begins with a verb which says that Paul, Silvanus and Timothy are continuously indebted because the faith, trust, conviction and loyalty of the believers is constantly flourishing, and that their love continuously interpenetrates. The debt that they owe is to be constantly expressing gratitude to God for this. The infinitive for expressing gratitude is composed of the word *charis* (grace; favor) prefixed by *eu*, which means goodness, ease and well-being.

So we see solidarity expressed here: the flourishing of some members of the body brings a debt upon the rest of the body to live a life that expresses gratitude to God and also acknowledges the goodness of the favor and grace that are resident in Him. Thus, in his letter, Paul "enters His courts with praise, and passes through His gates with thanksgiving." What a beautiful way to begin our days, as well as our engagements with others.

4. so that we ourselves boast in you folks among God's summoned-forth ones (among those called-out of God; or: in union with God's called-out communities) **over your steadfast remaining under to give support** (or: persistent patient endurance) **and faith** (or: loyalty; trust) **within all your pursuits** (or: chasings; or: persecutions; harassments) **and the pressures** (squeezings; constrictions; contractions; tribulations; oppressions; ordeals) **which you habitually have again** (or: sustain; hold up).

In vs. 4 he notes their persistent patient endurance in giving support as they "remain under" whatever situations they encounter, which he describes as their being pursued and persecuted, as well as being ordeals which "squeeze" them. The negative environment has brought forth abundant growth and increase, which manifests in a network of love. Paul notes that they habitually have this environment. As the word "have" also means "hold," we can also read this as their being able to constantly sustain it, and hold up under it.

5. [This is] a display-effect (result of pointing-out; demonstration) **of God's fair and equitable** (just; in accord with the Way pointed out) **deciding** (separating for an evaluation or a judging), **[leading] unto your being accounted worthy** (deemed of equal value) **of God's kingdom** (or: the sovereign reign which is God), **over** (or: on behalf of) **which you are also constantly having sensible experiences** (or: normally feeling emotions; or: repeatedly suffering),

I added a copulative, "[This is]," since vs. 5 begins with a defining clause of what Paul has just been talking about: their persecutions and pressures, as he notes in the end of vs. 5.

These constant sense-experiences (normal emotional situations; repeated sufferings) are a demonstration – a display – of God's fair and equitable decision! They lead unto the believers being accounted worthy of God's kingdom! They point out that separations, evaluations and judging are expressions of God's Way, which He has pointed out to us, but also that they engender justice and right relationships (the interpenetrating love and loyalty), and display the value of being a part of God's sovereign reign within the harassments of things that constantly pursue us – and they enable us to sustain them, and support one another within them.

6. since in regard to a person who observes the way pointed out – a rightwised person – [it is right] in the presence of God (or: if [it is], after all, the right thing with and beside God [= on God's part]), **to repay pressure** (or: squeezing and oppression; ordeal; trouble) **to those continuously pressuring** (squeezing; oppressing; troubling) **you folks,**

He continues the subject of the pressures and tribulations which they are enduring in vs. 6-9, here focusing on repayment to everyone who has been involved: relief, ease and a relaxing of the situation of constriction to the believers (vs. 7 – and note that Paul includes himself, Silas and Tim in this, with them, in the phrase "together with us," below: solidarity, once more); and squeezing pressure to those that were afflicting them (vs. 6).

Consider this: Paul has just said that the squeezing pressures that the believers were enduring were leading to their being of appropriate value to God's reign; now he says that their persecutors will undergo this same experience! It will have the same effect! This is the fairness of God's Way. This is His work of turning folks in the right direction (rightwising) and of
> **"progressively working all humanity together into that which is advantageous, worthy of admiration, noble and of excellent qualities"** (Rom. 8:28).

7. and to (or: for; in) **you – the folks being continuously pressed – relaxation** (ease; a relaxing of a state of constriction; relief), **together with us, within the midst of the uncovering** (the unveiling; the laying bare; the revelation; the disclosure) **of the Lord Jesus from [the] atmosphere** (or: sky; heaven), **along with agents of His power** (or: with His agents of ability) –

Vs. 7 tells us that this all happens whenever the Lord Jesus is unveiled in our atmosphere (or: laid bare and disclosed from heaven – the realm of spirit). This could be pointing ahead to what was going to be the judgments upon Jerusalem in AD 70, or to a localized laying bare of Jesus within the lives of the called-out community within Thessalonica. The body of Christ in that area was made up of "agents of His power," or, "His agents of ability." Those folks were living in the "new heaven and new earth": the new creation with God living within us, and within our midst.

The atmosphere, or heaven, is the location of the Jerusalem which is "above" (Gal. 4:26; Rev. 21:10) and is a figure for those "raised up" in Christ. The temple/tabernacle had been God's dwelling place among them, and it was a figure of the people when in the new creation God would indwell them by His Spirit. Since God's dwelling place was also perceived as being the atmosphere, or heaven, the covenant community of this new creation was now the heaven where they had been seated together with Christ within and among them (Eph. 2:6). Thus, Paul is using apocalyptic language in describing how the called-out folks now uncover the Lord within them, laying His life bare to the society within which they lived – and so do we, also, in our day.

8. **within a fire, of flame** [with other MSS: in union with a blaze of fire] **continuously giving justice** (or: repeatedly imparting the effects of fair and equitable dealings from out of the way pointed out, and the maintaining of right) **among** (or: for; in; with; to) **those not knowing** (or: perceiving) **God, even among** (or: for; in; with; to) **those not continuously listening to or paying attention and obeying the message of goodness and well-being, which is our Lord, Jesus** (or: which comes from and pertains to our Master and Owner: Jesus).

We read of flames of fire that symbolized the coming of the Spirit of God upon folks (Acts 2). So the flame of fire is the action of God, Who is a Consuming Fire (Heb. 12:29). The justice that His flame brings imparts the fairness and equity that comes "from out of the way pointed out," *ek-dikesis*, which gives us the maintenance of what is right, or of what has been pointed out to us in Christ. The covenant community was to be the light to their world, bringing change to their society by giving justice and imparting the effects of fair and equitable dealings inherent in the Way (or: Path) which is the Christ-life.

But consider that this is not just within the called-out community at Thessalonica, but "among, in, to, with or FOR" those not perceiving or knowing God. The verb is a perfect participle of *oida*, "to see, perceive," and thus, "know." These folks have not seen God and do not understand God, so of course there is no justice or fairness in their lives. Furthermore, these folks are not listening to or paying attention to the message of goodness and well-being, "which is our Lord, Jesus." In this last phrase I have rendered the genitive form as apposition, or definition. But as you can see in the parenthetical expansion, I have also given it as both an ablative (which comes from) and a genitive of association (which... pertains to). But central to the "gospel" (message of goodness and well-being) is that the Word, which becomes the message, is Christ. But these folks were not given ears to hear or eyes to see (*cf* Matt. 13:11-16), and the instrument of their learning is His fire. I suggest that Paul was here speaking of the Jewish leadership. The fire came with the destruction of both Jerusalem and the temple. This fire also was a part of the birth of the new age and the new creation, as the old age and covenant were completely done away, as well as being the baptism of Fire of which John the baptist spoke (Matt. 3:11) and the refining fire spoken of by Malachi (3:1-6).

The justice for the believer is also a relaxation and ease from ordeals (vs. 7); the justice to, for and in the folks not knowing or perceiving God (in us, or in their situations) is a time of ordeals and pressures (vs. 8).

We read of this flame of continuously maintaining what is right in the symbols of the book of Revelation, specifically in the ministry of the two witnesses in ch. 11. There fire comes out of their mouth (a collective singular) – a figure of the words which they speak. Here, in vs. 8, the imparting of the effects and results of fair dealings (which was the work of the cross) are coming to and in those not listening or paying attention to the message of goodness and well-being (the gospel), which is our Lord, Jesus.

9. **These certain folks who will pay the thing that is right** (incur justice, fairness and equity)**: ruin pertaining to the Age [of Messiah]** (or: an unspecified period of ruin or destruction; or: ruin for an age; eonian destruction having the character of the Age) **[coming] from the Lord's face** [= the Christ's or Yahweh's presence], **even from the glory of His strength** (or: spreading from the manifestation which calls forth praise regarding, and having the character of, His strength) –
10. **whenever He may come and go, to be made glorious within** (to be glorified in union with; to have a reputation within) **His set-apart folks** (holy and sacred people), **and to be wondered at** (marveled at; admired) **within all the folks believing in that day, seeing that our testimony** (or: evidence), **[being placed] on you, was believed** (received with faith) **and is trusted.**

Vs. 9 tells us that this is a condition of ruin and destruction for an unspecified period (or: interpreting "eonian" as qualitative rather than quantitative, a ruin which comes from the Age – a figure of the reign of Christ, and the qualities and characteristics of His person and dealings). These folks will "pay the thing that is right" (vs. 9): a necessary destruction and ruin, in the realm of the Age, which comes from the Lord's presence, even from the glory of His strength – the manifestation of His strength which does and will call forth praise: a positive goal.

Vs. 10 tells us that this happens "whenever" He may come to be made glorious within the believers, in union with those whom He has set apart – even within all the folks that are believing in that particular day, each time He comes to us. I conflated meanings of *erchomai*, "to come; to go," since this is the activity that we see described of Him in Rev. 2:1, "**the One continuously walking about within the midst of the seven golden lampstands** (i.e., the called-out communities)." This is His present and continuing activity. His purpose is to be made glorious within us, so that others – among whom we live – can see Him in His beauty: love and grace.

11. **Unto which end we always continuously pray** (think or speak toward having goodness, ease and well-being), **also, concerning you in order that our God would account you worthy of the calling** (or: of equal value to the invitation) **and would fill** (or: make full) **every delight** (pleasure, good thought) **of virtue** (excellence; goodness) **and work of faith in power** (or: and may make every good disposition of excellence and action of trust full, in union with ability),

We constantly pray to this end, continuously thinking, speaking and doing goodness – as well as projecting the same toward all, that all will become worthy of the invitation, and will fill every delight of virtue and work of faith in power, and in union with His ability. This is a description of life in the reign of the Messiah. It calls to mind Paul's words about the kingdom in Rom. 14:17, that it is,

> "**fair and equitable dealing which brings justice and right relationship in the Way pointed out** (being turned in the right direction; rightwisedness), **peace** (and: harmony; [= shalom]) **and joy** (or: rejoicing) **within set-apart Breath-effect** (or: a dedicated spirit and sacred attitude; or: in [the] Holy Spirit)."

This verse in Rom. speaks of "dealings," of "justice," of "peace and harmony" with a "sacred attitude." Vs. 11, above, speaks of good thought and excellence, connecting these with "**work of faith, and in power**/ability." All these things pertain to a life here and now, and upon this earth, as His reign marries the heavens to the earth; the Spirit to our flesh – transforming everything to where God is all and in all.

12. **so that the Name of our Lord, Jesus** [other MSS add: Christ], **may be invested with glory** (glorified; made to be a manifestation and a reputation which calls forth praise) **within you folks, and you within Him, according to** (down from; in line with; on the level of) **the grace and favor of our God and Lord, Jesus Christ** (or: from our God, and [the] Owner, Anointed Jesus).

This is the goal of the plan of the ages: that the Name of our Lord, Jesus, can be made glorious within everyone, and us within Him, in line with and on the level of the grace and favor or our God and Lord, Jesus Christ. "Our," in the last phrase, can also indicate the source of "grace / favor."

137

I want to point out that vs. 12 ends with the phrase "our God and Lord, Jesus Christ." A similar construction begins this chapter in vs. 1-2, where I give two possible renderings: one separating the terms Father from Lord; one joining them – either is a legitimate translation. May the Spirit make clear to you the correct rendering, or, that they are both correct. Note that the definite article is absent in the Greek text of these phrases.

As we look back over this chapter, it seems evident to me that throughout Paul was speaking of their current situation, and then perhaps of immanent judging of the situation, correcting those that had caused the persecution, giving relief to those who had been abused. The context is Thessalonica. Paul's description of the coming deliverance – which included agents of His power (whether in the heavens/atmosphere/spirit, or in people in that situation) – is applicable to any time in which God intervenes in any situation, bringing His fairness and equity, which comes to a repayment for deeds done, whether good or bad.

This is His ongoing "white throne" judging. We see that this happened in AD 70. It happens "whenever He may come to be made glorious..." History is replete with His visitations – often called "the move of God," or an "outpouring of the Holy Spirit." His flame (a figure of He, Himself, as a consuming Fire) gives the maintenance of what is right, and when His judging is in the land, the people learn fairness and equity (Isa. 26:9b) – the Way pointed out, in rightwised relationships.

Chapter 2

1. **Now we are asking you, brothers (**= fellow believers; = family), **over [the subject of]** (or: concerning) **the presence of our Lord** (or: Master), **Jesus Christ, and our being gathered together** (or: being fully led together and assembling) **upon [the presence of] Him**
2. **in regard to this: you are not at any point to be quickly shaken** (tossed, as by the sea, or caused to totter, like a reed) **away from [your] mind** (mental senses of perception; the ability to be aware and reason; wits; intelligent understanding), **nor to be continuously alarmed** (caused to cry aloud from nervousness or excitement), **neither through a spirit** (or: a breath-effect; an attitude), **nor through a word** (or: a thought; a message; a verbal communication), **nor through a letter – as through us – as though the Lord's Day** (the Day of the Lord [= Yahweh or Christ]) **has been set in place** (placed in; made to stand in; has stood within so as to be here).

Now the "Day of Yahweh" was a term that figured a time of judging and hard times, in the Old Testament [e.g., cf Joel 1:15 and 2:1-2; Jer. 30:7; Amos 5:18; Zeph. 1:14-18]. It was obviously considered to be something to be alarmed about, and inwardly shaken. The term "presence" has more than one significance:
a) it can refer to His ongoing presence, via His Spirit (e.g., when two or three, or more, are gathered in His name, Matt. 18:20; it can refer to His solidarity and identity with His body, as Jesus stated in Matt. 25:35-40; it can refer to Him dwelling in His temple, John 14:20;
b) or, it can refer to His presence for a specific work, such as judging His people, or intervening in history to bring deliverance or rescue. He dwells in our atmosphere (heaven; sky) so He is ever present, and He is "continuously walking about within the midst of the seven golden lampstands (i.e., the churches)," and He walks with feet "like white brass (or: bronze; fine copper – a figure of His judging process) as having been set on fire in a furnace" and eyes "as a flame of fire" – Rev. 2:1; 1:14-15. But in 2:5 He says that He may come unto them and remove their lampstand. In Rev. 2:16 He threatens to quickly come to them and fight against them with the sword of His mouth. He threatened to come to Sardis as a thief (3:3).

I therefore suggest that Paul is differentiating between "the presence of our Lord, Jesus Christ, and our being gathered together upon His [presence]" – as being a habitual occurrence of the meeting together of His body in Thessalonica – and a special presence concerning the expected destruction of Jerusalem that Jesus foretold – "the Day of the Lord." This latter event was a time of shaking the heavens and the earth (Heb. 12:26), and it not only affected the Jews, but also the called-out communities of that period, as this letter suggests, and as we see from the letter sent from John to the 7 communities in 1st century Asia, as cited above. This letter was written prior to the Jewish revolt and the coming of the Lord in judgment via Rome.

3. **May no one at any point beguile or seduce you folks from a deception – not even down from one turn** (or: not according to one method; not in the sphere of a manner or disposition) – **because should not the standing away from** (the departure; the setting away; or: the rebellion; the revolt) **come first, and thus the human from the lawlessness – the person of failure** (some MSS: the Man who missed the mark – sinned; the human being with the qualities and character of error and mistake; [other MSS: the person owned by lawlessness or associated with illegal acts]) **be uncovered** (unveiled; revealed; disclosed): **the son of the loss** (= the person having the qualities of, or the character resulting from, the destruction), 4. **the one continuously occupying an opposite position** (or: constantly lying as the opposing counterpart) **and constantly lifting** (or: raising) **himself up over all** (or: upon everything) **being normally called God, or an effect of worship** (or: reverent awe), **so as to cause him to be seated – down into the midst of the temple of God** (or: God's dwelling place) **– continuously displaying himself, that this/it is God** (or: continuously pointing out that he himself is a god)? 5. **Do you not remember that, still being with you, I said these things to you?**

Historically, the revolt referred to in vs. 3 was the war of the Jews against the Romans, which ended in AD 70. Here I refer you to studies from the preterist viewpoint, such as:
The Last Days According to Jesus – RC Sproul
The Days of Vengeance – David Chilton
The Parousia – James Stuart Russell
The Cross and the Parousia of Christ – Max King
The Perfect Ending for the World, and other works – John Noe ... to name just a few.

From the writings of Josephus, "the man of sin" has been identified by some writers as a historical person of that period and situation. But I suggest that it had a broader reference, both for them and for us: the estranged humanity within each of us, the false persona of the dying ego that is in bondage to the law of sin that works in our members (Rom. 7:23). That war indeed revealed this in all those that were involved in that war, on both sides, if you read that history. It was and is the estranged humanity "having the qualities of, or the character resulting from, the destruction" and loss which is due to Adam's sin.

Vs. 4 characterizes every human being, before he or she has been regenerated, existentially resurrected into the life of Christ. Times of pressure, ordeal or conflict reveal our true condition: whether yet dead in trespasses and sins, or alive and laying down our lives for our friends.

In vs. 3, the "standing-away from" can also have another interpretation: the called-out community (aka: church) "departing" from organized religion (whether the Jewish religion, of the time of Paul, or the Christian religion, of the ensuing centuries), and specifically, "departure and standing-away from" the Law. This separating reveals the life of God within His body, as well as the realm of death where the flesh wars against the spirit. Dan Kaplan has pointed out that there is only one other place where this Greek word is used in the NT, and that is in Acts 21:21 which speaks of the rumor that Paul had been teaching the Jews among the nations to stand away (revolt; apostasize) from Moses (i.e., the Law):
"Yet they have been orally instructed concerning you, that you are repeatedly (or: habitually) **teaching all the Jews down through the ethnic multitudes** (or: nations; non-Jews) **an apostasy away from Moses, constantly telling them not to be circumcising [their] children, nor even to be living their lives** (continually walking about) **in** (by; with) **the customs."**

This may in fact have been the actual revolt, or, standing away from, of which Paul was here referring – the necessity to depart from the Law, as Dan Kaplan has suggested. When Paul made his defense to the crowd in Acts 22, he did not deny the rumor of 21:21.

6. **And now, you know** (have seen and are aware of) **the thing continuously holding down in a firm grasp** (detaining, restraining) **unto the [situation for] him to be uncovered** (unveiled; disclosed) **in his own fitting situation** (or: proper occasion; suitable season; fertile moment).

The word "know" is in the perfect tense of the Greek *oida*, which strictly means "have seen." Those of Thessalonica had seen that which Paul now describes as "holding down in a firm grasp (detaining, restraining)." It was so well known that Paul did not have to tell them who or what it was – unfortunately for us! It was a secret to those outside the called-out community, but those within had seen it and knew what he or it was. It was soon to be unveiled – at the right moment. The pronouns are masculine, so we normally translate this as "him/his." But Paul could have been referring to an object or a situation which in Greek was masculine, and thus have used the masculine pronoun. There is no way to be certain. Whether a man, or the inner estranged human, it was at that time soon to be uncovered. The "thing continuously holding down in a firm grasp (constantly restraining and detaining)" could well have been God, or, the body of Christ (the Perfect Man) – as suggested in the next verse.

7. **For the secret** (hidden purpose; mystery) **of the lawlessness** (pertaining to the condition of being without law; which is the unlawfulness; having the character of being violation of the Law; whose source is the contrariness to custom) **is already continuously working within** (operating; energizing), **[yet] only until the one** (or: man; [note: masculine article]) **continuously holding down in a firm grasp** (detaining; restraining) **at the present moment can birth himself** (bring himself to be; = separate himself) **forth from out of the midst.**

Now the context would suggest that it is "the secret and hidden purpose of the lawlessness" to which Paul was referring in vs. 6 as having been veiled and covered – or hidden. The birthing "forth from out of the midst" could refer to the Christians leaving Jerusalem, just prior to its destruction. Or, it can refer to the Christ coming forth from the called-out body and unveiling the secret of that which is unlawful and contrary to custom. John saw this in the symbol of the woman birthing the man-child in Rev. 12. That, too, had multiple meanings:
a) Israel bringing forth Christ, or His body manifesting His life
b) The called-out folks departing the Jewish religion, or escaping from Jerusalem
c) the birthing of God's sons to deliver creation, in every time and place.

For our day, I suggest that the mystery and hidden purpose of "the lawlessness" is that "law of sin" to which Paul referred in Rom. 7. It is the law in our members that is contrary to the "law of the Spirit of life." Vs. 8 describes what happens when it is uncovered and revealed.

8. **And then** (at that time) **the lawless person** (the unlawful one; the one without law; the man who violates the Law; the person being contrary to custom) **will be uncovered** (unveiled; disclosed), **whom the Lord Jesus will take back up again** (or: lift up; reading *anaireo* with Nestle, Tasker & Concordant texts; Griesbach & other MSS read *analisko*: consume, use up, expend) **by the Spirit** (Breath-effect) **of His mouth, and will deactivate** (render inoperative and useless; make inert) **by the manifestation** (the bringing of light upon and setting in full and clear view, causing an appearance) **of his** (or: its; or: His) **presence –**

Again, the application is both historical (Christ coming and judging, in AD 70), and Christ repeatedly coming and judging within His House. He uncovers the false persona, our estranged human nature, and takes it back up again by the Spirit of His mouth, or with the other MSS, consumes and renders pure and restored. The Breath-effect of His mouth (whether breathing upon us, or speaking to us) is the manifestation of His presence. This, as in ch. 1, above, brings righteousness and restores the Way pointed out: justice, fair and equitable dealings, rightwised relationships.

Reading *anaireo*, we see that His Breath/Spirit takes the false and estranged back into Himself: restoration. Reading *analisko*, we see purification and transformation. This manifestation of His presence comes both individually and corporately. The Christ event inaugurated the new creation in which He is habitually, or constantly, coming to us – dwelling in and among us, while we have been snatched up and seated with Him (Eph. 2:6) in the new heavens, the abode of the new human (earth).

9. **whose presence is continuously existing in correspondence to** (or: in line with; in the sphere of; on the level of) **the adversary's** (opponent's; or: satan's) **in-working activity** (or: is constantly in accordance with the operation of the "adversary," or, satan), **in all power** (or: within all ability) **as well as signs and wonders of falsehood** (or: which are a lie),
10. **and within every deception** (delusion; seduction) **of the injustice** (wrong; thing that is not the way pointed out and which is not right) **within the folks continuously or repeatedly being lost** (or: by the folks progressively destroying themselves) **in return for which** (or: in the place of which) **they do** (or: did) **not take unto themselves and welcomingly receive the love of, and from, the truth** (or: Truth's love; the Love which is Truth and Reality; or: an appreciation of and affection for reality), **into the [situation for] them at some point to be suddenly delivered** (restored to health and wholeness; rescued; saved; restored to the original state and condition).

Now the "manifestation" in vs. 8 can also refer to the bringing light upon this "lawless person." Thus, vss. 9-10 can be read in two different ways:
a) following that which I just described above, seeing that it is Christ's manifestation and presence – meeting the inworking activity of the adversary, in its sphere, and on every level of its activity, within its signs and wonders of falsehood, and within each of its deceptions of injustice within the lost who are progressively destroying themselves, etc. Note that in the last clause of vs. 10 His work leads them "into the [situation for] them at some point to be suddenly delivered!"
b) seeing it as a manifestation of "the lawless person," either as an individual, historically, or as estranged humanity, we see that its presence corresponds to the working of the adversary within, which operates with its false power and lying wonders within deceptions of that which is contrary to the path of life. This causes folks not to receive or retain "the Love (God) which is Truth and Reality (Christ); or: an appreciation of and affection for reality." Nonetheless, the result is the same, as the last part of vs. 10 tells us: deliverance, rescue.

11. **And so, because of this, God is continuously sending to** (or: in) **them an in-working** (or: operation) **of wandering** (or: which is the source of being caused to stray; which has the character of error and deception) **into the [situation for] them to believe, and to trust, the lie,**
12. **to the end that all those not believing the Truth** (or: having conviction of or trusting the reality), **but rather approving and delighting in injustice** (inequity; the thing that is not right), **may** (or: can; would) **at some point be sifted, separated and decided about** (or: judged).

Vs. 11-12 tell us of the intermediary judging of folks who are not presently a part of the called-out community. It is an echo of Rom. 1:24, which is a prelude to the period of sifting, separating and deciding by God as described here in vs. 12. This is an ongoing process, as vs. 11 says: He "is continuously sending to and in them an inworking (or: operation) of wandering." Here we see reference to the repayments noted in ch. 1:6, "squeezing and oppression, ordeal and trouble." As such things made the believers worthy of God's reign (1:5), so it will do in the sifting of these. Again, this applied to the situation in 1st century Thessalonica, and to all times and situations ever since. He is the same: yesterday, today, and on into the ages.

13. **However we, ourselves, are presently indebted** (or: continuously owing) **to be constantly expressing gratitude to God** (or: speaking of the goodness of grace and the well-being of the favor in God) **always, concerning you, brothers** (= fellow believers), **folks having been and continuing to be [so] loved** (preferentially valued) **by the Lord** [= Yahweh or Christ] **that God chose you for Himself, from [the] beginning, unto deliverance,** [other MSS: God selected and took you in preference {to be} a firstfruit into a restoration to the original state and condition (or: into the midst of health and wholeness; {leading you} unto rescue and salvation)], **in a setting-apart of spirit and in faith which has the character of truth** (or: by sanctification from [the] Breath-effect and by trust, which is reality; or: in union with the Spirit's holiness and Truth's faith),
14. **on into which, through our message of goodness, ease and well-being, He also called**

you folks [other MSS: us] **into an encompassing** (or: forming an encirclement; establishing a perimeter; creating a surrounding, and thus a procuring) **of the glory** (or: which is the glory; from the manifestation which calls forth praise) **of our Lord, Jesus Christ** (or: [the] Anointed).

Here Paul and the others turn their focus back to their opening in ch. 1:3, re-affirming their indebtedness to express gratitude concerning the brothers having been so loved by the Lord, and that God had chosen them for Himself from the beginning, and that this is why they were experiencing deliverance. This had the character of a set-apart spirit, faith and the truth of reality. The holiness belonged to the Spirit, and the faith came from the Truth. And as other MSS read, they in Thessalonica were selected to be a firstfruit of the restoration.

Note that our calling is into being encompassed by His glory; His glory forms an encirclement and establishes a perimeter of defense around us! See the use of *peri-poiesis* (an encompassing; forming an encirclement; etc.) in 1 Thes. 5:9, Eph. 1:14, Heb. 10:39 and 1 Pet. 2:9. Furthermore, we see that our "calling" comes through the "message of goodness, ease and well-being." This should alert us to the character of both our call and His glory. Let no one lay upon us any heavy burdens from religious systems, or negative messages about God's plan for mankind.

15. **Consequently, then, brothers** (= fellow believers; = family), **you continuously stand firm and stationary** (or, as an imperative: progressively make a stand; habitually stand firm) **and you continuously have** (or, imperative: progressively get) **in your strength – with a masterful grip – the things handed alongside** (transmissions; traditions) **which you were taught, whether through a word** (or: [the] Logos; a thought or an idea; a message) **or through our letter.**

Here Paul either gives admonition to continue standing firm – or to progressively make a stand – and continue to get the message of the good news in their grip, with strength, through the teachings that had been given to them, or – reading the verb *stekete* as an indicative – he affirms that they "continuously stand firm and stationary." The same goes for the next verb, *krateite*, which is either and indicative or an imperative, and thus he is either affirming or admonishing.

16. **Now may our Lord, Jesus Christ Himself, even** (or: and) **our God and Father, the One loving us and giving a calling alongside pertaining to the Age** (or: performance as a Paraclete with age-lasting aid; eonian relief, encouragement, consolation and admonition) **as well as a good expectation** (or: a virtuous and excellent hope) **in grace** (or: in union with favor), 17. **be at once calling your hearts alongside and establishing** (making to stand fast; making stable and firm) **you in every good** (or: excellent) **work and word** (or: thought; idea; message) [with other MSS: in all the Word and in virtuous action].

His next remarks state again the qualities and characteristics of the new creation in Christ: God's performing as a Paraclete and giving us a good expectation which comes in union with favor and in the sphere of grace. Then we see his admonition to be calling each others' hearts to their sides, which will make them stable and firm in every excellent action and virtuous work and word. It is love, solidarity and action with a view to goodness. May we, too, receive this thought.

Note that this "calling alongside" (*paraklesis*) is described as "eonian" (*aionian*) in vs. 16. It is a quality of the Age of the Messiah, which is a phrase that reaches back with continuity to the OT expectation of the coming Messiah, and which equates to Paul's phrase "new creation" (2 Cor. 5:17).

Chapter 3

1. **The remainder** (or: What is left; Finally), **brothers** (= fellow believers), **keep on praying concerning us** (surrounding us with words and thoughts having goodness and well-being), **to the end that the Word of the Lord** (or: the Lord's idea and message) **would continuously run** (move quickly) **and may constantly be made glorious** (or: be characterized by a manifestation which calls forth praise; be of good reputation), **according as [it is and does] also with you,**

The word "praying" is a verb (*pros-eu-chomai*) that means to think, speak or act with a view toward, and that lead to, having goodness; to project well-being; to focus ease and goodness toward the object of our prayer. We that are joined to the Lord are "one spirit," and God dwells in us, His temple (dwelling place). So our thoughts, words and or actions begin from Him and us, joined together in purpose, and they go out from us as spirit (words and thoughts are spirits) directly to the object of our "prayer." So thus does Paul ask them to "surround him, and those with him, with words and thoughts that lead toward having goodness and well-being."
Their prayer would thus assist the Word of the Lord (His idea and message) in progressively running ahead into new territory, or deeper into the hearts of folks. This success would bring a good reputation to the Word, and result in manifestations which call forth praise to God. Paul then affirms that this is the case with the Thessalonicans.

2. **and that we may be rescued** (dragged out) **away from the out-of-place** (or: improper; absurd; abnormal; off-base; weird; outrageous; perverse) **and misery-gushing people** (or: unprofitable, useless, unsound or evil folks), **for you see, not everyone [is] disposed to the faith**
> (or: this trust and loyalty is not associated with all people; not [yet is] the faith a source for all folks; not from all people [do we find] the faith; conviction [is presently] not a possession of all people; this trust [does] not [now] pertain to everyone).

Here he gives another purpose for their prayers: Paul's and his associates' personal safety, and for their work to be free from unprofitable and improper situations, and that it would not prove to be useless among folks that just gush with misery and outrageous behavior.

Now the final clause of this verse has raised questions. Just what does he mean here? I have given six possible ways of rendering the Greek clause. The first one simply states the present condition of the vast majority of people: they are not at this time "disposed to the faith." For many a surface reason is because of what they see in the lives of "Christians." But the real reason is that God has not yet raised them from the dead; He has not yet made their condition to be a fertile moment – the right season to plant the seed of life in their hearts. In 1 Cor. 15:23 Paul spoke of each one having his own class and order within which to be made alive by God. The birth of His children is up to Him. When they are given ears to hear, then they will hear the word, and it will produce faith within them.

3. **But the Lord** [= Yahweh or Christ] **is** (or: exists) **continuously faithful** (loyal; full of faith), **who will establish** (set you to stand fast) **and keep** (guard; protect) **you folks away from the malicious person** (or: the unsound and unprofitable; the painful labor; the malignant situation).

Note that the situation for which Paul asked them to speak into his life he is here speaking into theirs. He is in vs. 3 "*pros-eu-chomai*-ing" that God will set them to stand fast, and will guard and protect them, keeping them away from unsound and unprofitable situations and malicious people. But further, in his stating that the Lord is faithful, loyal and full of faith, WE can be confident (full of faith) that He will eventually impart faith to those who do not yet have it (vs. 2), and deliver the malicious folks from their malignant situation and condition.

4. **Yet we have been persuaded and so place confidence on you, in [the] Lord** [= Christ or Yahweh], **that the things which we are repeatedly passing along as an announcement to you people, you folks both habitually do and will be doing** (or: normally produce and will continue producing).

Here Paul and his associates continue speaking confidence into their lives, affirming that they are both hearing the message and acting on it. Again, they are *pros-eu-chomai*-ing into them. They recognizes that these folks normally produce effects from the announcement of goodness that he and his associates are repeatedly passing along to them, and they are assured that the Thessalonians will continue producing fruit from this message.

5. **So may the Lord** [= Christ or Yahweh] **make fully straight, then guide and direct, your hearts into the midst of God's love** (the love which is God) **and into the relentless patient endurance which is Christ** (or: the persistent remaining under to support, which comes from the Anointed One and the Anointing)**!**

In the first clause, the word normally rendered "direct" or "guide" means literally "straighten down," or, "make fully straight." This very act would lead the heart into God's love, for a "straight heart" loves and experiences God. The second part of this prayer is that their inner core would enter into the relentless, persisting patient endurance, which also is Christ, and that they would abide in the position to continue giving support – the support that comes from the Anointing, which is Christ Himself, living within the believer.

6. **Now we are once again passing along this advice to you, brothers** (= fellow believers; = family), **in the Name of our Lord, Jesus Christ, to continuously place yourselves away from** (or: avoid) **every brother** (= believer) **[who is] continuously walking about disorderly** (without order; or: behaving with irregular conduct), **and not according to the transmission** (thing given over and delivered alongside; the tradition) **which you folks** [other MSS: they] **received** (took to your side) **from us.**
7. **For you yourselves have seen, and thus are aware of, how it continues necessary and binding [for you] to continuously imitate us, because we were not disorderly among you,**
8. **neither did we eat bread as a gift from anyone, but rather [we were] in wearisome toil** (also: beating; cutting off) **and difficult travail** (or: hard labor), **continuously working night and day so as not, at any point, to be a burden upon** (put extra weight on) **any of you.**

In vss. 6-8 they give practical admonitions to them. In vs. 2 they had asked them to speak into their own lives that they would be rescued from such folks as described in vs. 6. Now they simply say to stay away from these disorderly people. How can two walk together (= live their lives in the same path) unless they are in agreement? He is not speaking about ministering to them, but about living their daily lives in the way that these folks do. They are contrary paths.

Paul tells them to imitate himself, and those with him, as to manner of conduct, and sharing in providing for the community – working, so as not to be a burden. Vs. 8 shows us that they worked physically to the point of weariness, with hard labor. His message had a practical love at its core, and they had been concerned as to how their being with the Thessalonians would affect their everyday lives. Thus they pitched in and helped in the daily work involved with making a living, so as not to have a negative effect on their lives.

9. **[It was] not because we continue having no right** (or: holding no authority from being), **but rather to the end that we ourselves may give to you folks a pattern** (or: offer ourselves as a model and example for you) **unto the [purpose for you] to be continuously imitating us!**
10. **You see, even when we were face to face with you we were repeatedly passing on this advice to you, that if a certain person is not continuously willing** (or: does not normally want, purpose or intend) **to habitually work, let him neither be habitually eating.**
11. **For we continually hear [that] some among you are constantly walking about disorderly** (a military term: out of rank and not taking part in the battle; = living with irregular conduct), **continuously working [at] nothing, but further, are constantly working in the periphery** (or: circumventing work; or: = being "busybodies" and meddling).

Vss. 9-11 flesh out his practical admonitions, giving specific examples. His message had a strong work ethic. He was not hesitant to point out freeloaders and folks that just spent their time at the edge of the work – looking like they were participating and producing, but were in reality circumventing work. He was writing to a "community" of believers. They apparently lived their lives with a certain aspect of communal living. They were a social unit.

12. **But to such people we are now passing along this advice, and calling [them] alongside to encourage, exhort, admonish, bring relief and entreat [them], through** [other MSS: within; in union with] **our Lord, Jesus Christ, to the end that, habitually working with quietness** (or: silence), **they may continuously eat their own bread** (= food which came from their own work).

Here Paul, Timothy and Silas bring a gentle word, yet straight to the point: "habitually work with quietness, and eat from their own production." We can glean another insight from these admonitions: they had a view toward a continued, normal life – in regard to their physical existence. The kingdom of God affected their inner beings and way of living, and thus how they ordered their behavior among other people, but it had a view to a life here on earth, with His will being done here – just as it is "in heaven." This letter does not talk about "church services," rituals, ceremonies or other religious activities. It speaks to a practical living of the Christ life.

13. **Yet you yourselves, brothers** (= fellow believers), **while continually doing well** (performing beautifully; creating the ideal; doing finely), **you should not at any point be in a bad disposition** (or: be or do from out of what is ugly, worthless or of poor quality).

It strikes me how this letter begins with calming and assuring them, and ends with quiet admonitions. He had spoken of pressures and ordeals, and of how God would judge those that were persecuting them. Now, amid all that, he simply says for them to continue doing well, perform what is beautiful and create the ideal. Create the ideal! We are to effect positive change in our environments! There is no thought of desiring to be taken out of our situation, but to be beautifully performing our lives as a witness of Christ's presence in and among us. And amidst being squeezed, don't be in a bad disposition, or react in an ugly manner. Can you just see him smiling as he writes this?

14. **But if a certain person continuously does not obe**y (or: listen under and humbly pay attention to) **our word** (or: message; logos; thought and idea) **through this letter, you folks be regularly noting this person** (setting for yourself a mark regarding this one) **and do not continuously mix yourselves together with him or her, to the end that he or she can** (or: would) **be turned about** (or: be turned back upon himself [= to consider his situation and behavior]).

Now his tone changes, and a firm directive is given: don't continue to socialize with those who make it a habit not to obey. But there is a loving motive for this: "to the end that he or she would be turned about and consider their behavior." The care, love and outreach to even such as these is to be their motivation.

15. **And yet you must not consider [him/her] as an enemy, but rather you must continuously admonish** (or: put [him/her] in mind), **as** (or: as being) **a brother [to him/her].**

Again Paul stresses deeds and attitudes of love for those with whom it is hard to live, with folks that are burrs under you saddle. They are brothers (part of the family). Don't excommunicate them. Don't ask them to leave. Put them in your mind and *pros-eu-chomai* them.

16. **Now may the Lord of the peace** (or: the Lord [= Christ or Yahweh] Who is peace and harmony [= shalom]), **Himself, at once give the peace to you folks through everything** (or: through all humanity; through all [time] and every [situation]), **within every turn** (or: in every way; [other MSS read: within every place]). **The Lord** [Christ or Yahweh] **[is] with all of you.**

He ends his admonitions concerning the disobedient and lazy with a reminder that God is a God who is peace, a Lord of harmony. And these Thessalonians will be given peace through every situation and through everyone – even amidst their being squeezed and persecuted. This will happen at every turn of their lives, and in every way. Why? because the Lord is with them – He is present. The parousia existed at that time, and with them. His parousia (presence) is with us, too.

17. **The greeting** (salutation) **is by my hand – Paul's – which is a sign in every letter; thus, in this way, I normally** (or: from time to time) **write.**
18. **The grace and joyous favor of our Lord, Jesus Christ, [is] with all of you folks! Amen.**

His final word of assurance to them: Christ's grace and favor is with them, and this is because the Lord is with them (vs. 16). Pressures and ordeals may abound; heaven and earth may shake; worlds may collide; but we have His grace, His favor, His presence. It is so.

The letters to Timothy, Titus and Philemon are personal letters and have been called the Pastoral Letters, since advice and instruction is given toward how life in the called-out communities should be lived. Robinson give that date for this first one as circa AD 55, but many scholars think that these were written later, and by a disciple of Paul, because in some of the terms which the writer uses they see a fairly developed ecclesiastical organization. However, I suggest that this is because the traditional translations have not translated these terms, but rather have transliterated them and made them to be titles and offices, instead of functions. They were descriptions of positions in the secular papyrus literature, but that does not mean that Paul did not use them as functions within the communities (e.g., *diakonos*: one who renders attending service to another; ch. 3:8, which became the title "deacon" in the church hierarchy, a position of church government rather than a function of attending service). We do not see organizational instructions from Jesus, in the Gospels, and the 1st century called-out communities appear to have been house "churches."

Furthermore, the false teachings and practices described in these letters portray a picture of Gnosticism which Paul wrote against in his letter to the Colossians. There are also admonitions against Jewish genealogies, myths and legalism, all of which were extant during the time of Paul's other writings. The vocabulary and style of these letters are different from elsewhere in Paul, but the content, context and type of letter also differ from the others so this should not seem unusual. Whichever the case may be as to authorship, the Spirit within the Words gives evidence for them being "God-breathed."

Chapter 1

1. **Paul, one sent away with a commission pertaining to [the] Anointed Jesus** (or: Jesus Christ's representative and envoy), **down from** (or: in line and accord with) **an imposed arrangement from** (an injunction of; a decree and charge set upon [me] pertaining to) **God our Savior, even** (or: and) **from Christ Jesus, our Expectation** (or: expectant Hope),

Instead of following the tradition of transliterating the Greek *apostolos* to read "apostle," I translated the word, giving its meaning in English: one sent away (or: off) with a commission; or: a representative; an envoy. I question the tradition that this word was a title, or that it signified a church "office." It seems logical that it describes a function (*cf* Phil. 2:25).

Paul makes it clear that God has given him the authority to speak His word concerning "an imposed arrangement" which pertains to Him as our Savior. He goes on to identify this one as Christ Jesus, and points out that He is our Expectation. In Rom. 8:24 he tells us that we are saved by, in, to, for and with expectation, and here he identifies this expectation as Christ Jesus, Himself. It is significant that our salvation, which brings a present change in us and in our situation, with our relation to God and to humanity, also points us to a future that has an expectation, one that is filled with Christ. But we can tend to read the "our" in an individual, personal way, where throughout Paul's writings he normally speaks corporately, such as in Col. 1:27, where it is "... **Christ within you folks, the expectation of the glory**." Our expectation can also be Christ, our Savior, within the ethnic multitudes (the nations being included in and participating in the covenant), as one-by-one they are added to the called-out communities.

2. **to Timothy, a genuine child** (a legitimate born-one) **within the midst of faith** (or: in union with trust)**: Grace and favor, mercy and compassion [together with] peace and harmony** [= shalom], **from God, our Father, even** (and) **Christ Jesus, our Lord** (Owner; Master).

In describing Timothy as a "genuine child; a legitimate born-one," I suggest that he is making reference to John 1:13, that Timothy is one that has been "born from out of the midst of God," as it is stated there, as opposed to one that was "born" into Christianity by human persuasion, or a child by natural or racial lineage. His birth came by and was within the midst of faith, or, in union with trust. Here Paul uses the "birth metaphor" for covenant inclusion "in Christ."

Paul clearly states his central message right at the start: grace and favor, mercy and compassion, together with peace and harmony, which all come from God. He again goes on to identify the God of Whom he speaks: our Father. Here we see that this is the One Who gave birth to Timothy. Paul proceeds with the identification of this God: "even Christ Jesus, our Lord, Master and Owner." Now as in vs. 1, I have given the other main meaning of the Greek conjunction, *kai*, rendering it also "and." May the Holy Spirit (not mentioned by these words in this verse) illumine you as to which reading is correct, or if both are, as we consider this divine mystery.

3. **Just as I called you alongside – while traveling into Macedonia – to encourage you to remain focused in Ephesus, to the end that you should pass on an announcement** (should notify; would bring along a message) **to certain folks** (or: for some) **not to continue teaching different things,**
4. **nor yet to constantly hold toward myths** (or: stories; fictions) **and unbounded** (= endless) **genealogies, which things habitually hold investigations and inquiries alongside which involve speculations and disputes, rather than God's house-administration** (management; stewardship) **– the one within trust and in union with faith.**

Paul is recalling a previously given admonition to Timothy. He reminds him to keep his focus on the community in Ephesus, and to tell them not to continue with the teaching of different things which were outside the message of the good news in Christ. Whether it be Jewish myths, or stories from pagan religions, or fictitious ideas, none of these were to be held on to or embraced or mixed into the Word of Truth. Our humanity always wants to add thoughts to what God has revealed. The study of genealogies is also to be abandoned; we know no one after the flesh any longer (2 Cor. 5:16) – there is a new creation.

These "**different things**" which Paul identifies in vs. 4 are a distraction, and they waste time with investigations and inquiries which result only in speculations and disputes. Their focus should be on the house-administration and stewardship of God's house – His people within the called-out community, and their needs. He then qualifies the characteristics of this house and this administering: "**the one within trust, and in union with faith.**"

5. **Yet the purpose and goal of the notification** (the message and announcement which is brought alongside and passed on) **continues being love**
      (the whole being's drive and movement toward reunion with another, to overcome existential separation; acceptance of the object of love without restriction, in spite of the estranged, profanized and demonized state of the object – Paul Tillich) **forth from out of the midst of a clean heart and a good conscience** (virtuous knowing-together; profitable impression of reality) **and of unhypocritical faith** (or: unfeigned trust; or: loyalty that is not overly critical; or: belief that lacks the qualities of being overly concerned with small details or hyper-evaluations),

Here he gives the central focus of the message of goodness which has been passed on to them: **love**. This is the goal for which Christ came: the Love which is God. Consider well the parenthetical definitions of *agape* by Paul Tillich. This is much more than an emotion. Then he sets a clear view of the type of love and the environment from which it is to flow: a heart (core of our being) that has been cleansed by the blood of Jesus Christ (1 John 1:7), and a conscience that has been transformed by the renewing of the mind (Rom. 12:2), along with "unhypocritical faith."

On this last phrase, I have given a broader semantic range of meaning. Dr. Ann Nyland, in her *The Source New Testament* (Smith and Stirling Publishing, 2004) has pointed out that the normal understanding of the transliterated word "hypocrite," and its cognates, did not come to have this meaning until much later than when the New Testament letters were written. Wilckens, in an article in the *Theological Dictionary of the NT* (Vol. VIII, Wm. B. Eerdmans Publishing Co., 1972, pp 559-571), supports this, saying that not until the Byzantine period did this word group come to have the direct negative sense now associated with it. However, it was used throughout most of the literature of Dispersion Judaism (Second Temple literature) to describe wrongdoing, or the "evildoer," so suggesting that this was "acting" or "pretending" does not fit the contexts. Thus, along with the more widely accepted meaning of this word, I have given meanings based upon the elements of the Greek word which is composed of *krisis* (separation and evaluation so as to make a decision) and the prefix *hupo* (as an intensifier: hyper-; overly-; or: under – whether from a low position, or, to take under close examination).

6. **of which things some** (or: certain folks), **being without a mark or target** (or: deviating and swerving from the goal), **were turned aside from out of [them] into vain** (fruitless; profitless) **talking and idle disputation,**
7. **wanting to be teachers of Law and custom, [yet] by habit not mentally apprehending either what things they are saying or about what things they are constantly insisting** (thoroughly asserting and maintaining).

Paul now points out that certain people lacked this goal of love, and so were "**turned aside from out of**" the clean heart, the good conscience and now their faith was tainted by being hyper-critical, etc. Now all they have is fruitless talking, and idle disputes. They consider themselves to be teachers, since they have nit-picked the fine points of the letter; but not understanding the spirit of grace, they return to legalism, and preach principles from the old covenant Law, bringing death as they go. They simply parrot what others say because they don't really understand the issues, or simply speak from personal prejudice. They don't know what they are talking about, but to make their point they speak loudly, bullying the conversation.

8. **Now we have seen and thus know that the Law** [= Torah] **is beautiful** (ideal and of good quality; useful; fine), **if ever anyone could be continuously making use in it** (employing and behaving with it, by it and to it) **lawfully,**

But the fact is, no one could then, nor can now. In Rom. 3 Paul makes the argument that all mankind is "**under [the direction, power and control, or result, of] failure** (the missing of the target by falling short or shooting astray through lack of skill and ability or by distraction; or: error; a mistake; sin)" – vs. 9b. An then, in vs. 23 says, "**You see, all at one point veered off the mark** (or: all folks deviated; or: everyone fails; everyone sins), **and they are continually posterior to, falling short of, inferior to and wanting of, God's glory** (of a manifestation of God which calls forth praise; of a reputation which comes from and has the character of God; of God's opinion and imagination; of [having] an appearance of God)." Thus there came to be distortion, and we have seen the response from Jesus, especially to the Pharisees. For those then under the Law He told them to do what they say, but not what they do. They nit-picked and emphasized minor points – being hyper-critical about folks who did on a sabbath what they thought ought not to be done then – while neglecting justice and mercy (Matt. 23:23).

9. **having seen and knowing this, that a law is not continually being laid down for one in accord with the Way pointed out** (a just one; one who lives in right relationship with fair and equitable dealings; = one in new covenant standing, i.e., in Christ), **but for lawless people and for insubordinate** (non-self-subjecting; out of rank) **folks; for irreverent ones** (folks devoid of awe) **and for failures** (folks shooting off-line and missing the target; people making mistakes); **for those without regard for divine or natural laws** (impious, maligning, disloyal ones lacking loving-kindness) **and for profane folks** (people without connection to the set-apart and holy, who live in what is accessible to all); **for those who strike** (or: thrash) **fathers and for people who strike** (or: thrash) **mothers; for those murdering men;**
10. **for men who use prostitutes** (or: who are male prostitutes; fornicators; or: = those who "worship" in pagan temples); **for men who lie with males** (sodomites); **for kidnappers** (those catching men by the foot; = slave dealers); **for liars; for ones who violate their oaths**

(perjurers); **and whatever different thing which is continually occupying an opposite position** (lying in opposition or in replacement) **to the sound and healthful teaching,**

I think that Paul's list speaks for itself, and needs no specific comments. A law is codified because of the estranged, alienated and distorted human nature. It addresses the demonic within our being, the snake in our garden. This all applies to the old age, the old order of the "earthly and fleshly" realm within which people live their lives, until they enter God's reign through being born from above, through the Jerusalem which is above (Gal. 4).

The central contrast to those who exhibit negative or deviant behavior, is those who are living in covenant relationship as part of the called-out community. These others, listed in vs. 9-10, are those who have not yet been made alive in Christ (1 Cor. 15:22, 23). The new reality has not yet been birthed into them.

Sadly, we observe many who carry the title "Christian" but who "**occupy an opposite position to the sound and healthful teaching**" which corresponds to the message of goodness.

11. **[which is] in accord with** (or: down from; in line with and on the level of) **the good news of** (or: the message of goodness and ease pertaining to) **the glory and reputation of The Happy God, which I, myself, was persuaded to believe** (or: upon Whom I am made to trust).

Paul's message brought glory to God, and a good reputation about Him being "**The Happy God.**" Something persuaded Paul and caused him to believe – made him trust this message of the goodness of God. That "something" was Jesus Himself, who confronted Paul on the road to Damascus. It was the Spirit of God that transformed Paul, and transferred him from the authority and jurisdiction of the darkness (Judaism, the old covenant, the old creation), into the reign of God's Son (Col. 1:13; John 3:19). So if someone's message does not present God as "the Happy God," it is not in accord with Paul's gospel. It should also have the characteristic of God's glory and good reputation.

12. **I continue holding** (or: having) **grace and favor by and in the One enabling me** (putting ability within me; empowering me)**: Christ Jesus, our Lord, because He considers me full of faith** (or: deems me loyal and faithful), **Himself placing [me] into a position of giving attending service,**

Paul was persuaded, and now he continues possessing grace and favor, in and by Christ Jesus who is enabling him and empowering him. It is Jesus, the true Lord of God's Empire, that by His Spirit is "**enabling**" the "**empowering**" Paul. The "**in and by**" render the locative and instrumental functions of "**the One**" in the dative case. Christ has transformed Paul and now deems him to be loyal and faithful, even full of faith. Now the Lord had placed him into a position of giving attending service to the called-out communities. All is done by Christ.

13. **– one being formerly a blasphemer** (a vilifier and slanderer; one using abusive speech and hindering the Light while bringing injury) **and a persecutor and a violent, insolent aggressor** (an overbearing, insolent, riotous and outrageous person), **but to the contrary, I was mercied** (or: given mercy), **because, being continuously ignorant** (without intimate, experiential knowledge or personal insight), **I acted** (or: did it) **within unbelief** (or: in distrust).

Paul was mercied and received grace. He had acted in distrust of this new message, and was ignorant of its reality – he had not yet experienced the Lord, to receive insight. He does not spare himself in sharing the kind of person that he formerly was.

14. **Yet our Lord's grace and favor overwhelms** (is above more than enough; is overabounding) **with faith and trust, as well as love, which are resident within Christ Jesus.**

This is a powerful statement. What we need but don't have is all resident with Christ Jesus, and in His appointed time His grace, favor, faith, trust and love simply overwhelm us. They are more than enough for us and are overabounding to us and drag us to Him. Picture in your mind a tsunami wave. This is what Paul is saying here, and he speaks from personal experience (the Damascus road event). God overwhelms us and draws us to Himself.

15. **The Word [is] full of faith, and [is] deserving of every welcome reception of equal value, because** (or: Faithful and trustworthy, even worthy of all and complete acceptance, [is] the message and saying that) **Christ Jesus came into the ordered System** (the world of secular culture, religion, government and economy; or: the cosmos) **to rescue failures** (to deliver those missing the target; to save and make sinners healthy and whole; to restore outcasts to their rightful position), **of whom I myself exist being first** (or: am foremost).

The conjunction that joins the first clause to the second can be rendered either "**because**," or "**that**." So I translated the clauses to accommodate each of these renderings of the conjunction. Each way makes sense, but has a different emphasis. I really liked "**The Word [is] full of faith**," because this makes a strong statement about the source of our faith: it comes to us during the proclaiming of the Word. But the third clause "**Christ Jesus came into the ordered System to rescue failures**" is also a "**faithful and trustworthy**" message.

Consider the applications of the verb *sozo* (rescue; deliver; save; make healthy and whole; restore to former condition or position), and the substantive *hamartolous* (failures; those missing the target; sinners; outcasts [or a group or society]). Putting these meanings in the various combinations, above, gives us a broader understanding of what it means to be "saved." This word has its primary application to situations and conditions in this life. Christ came to bring salvation here to us in the here and now.

Again, Paul does not spare himself. He takes first place among those who miss the target – at least that is how he views himself. We can take comfort in this, for look at what God made of the foremost failure.

16. **But nonetheless, through this I was mercied** (or: I am given mercy), **to the end that within me first** (= as the foremost case) **Jesus Christ may point out so as to publicly display every emotion which is long in arriving** (all long-suffering patience) **with a view to being an underline** (toward [being] a subtype; as facing a sketch or outline; for a pattern) **of those about to be habitually believing** (or: progressively trusting; one-after-another placing faith) **upon Him, [leading] into the midst of eonian life** (into Life which pertains to and has the qualities and characteristics of the Age [of Messiah]; into life of, and which lasts through, the ages).

The verb tense of "mercy" is aorist passive, so it can read as a simple past, or of a present reality – both are true, for this is the tense of simple fact. Paul was in his day "**the foremost case**" of receiving mercy. God used him as a canvas upon which to paint His own "**long-suffering patience**," or literally, His "**every emotion which is long in arriving**." God does not mind waiting, but He always has a purpose in mind. Here Paul was going to be a subtype, a pattern that would "**underline**" a display of God's mercy, and publicly show others that were in his day (and now, our day) about to **one-after-another make it a habit to trust, believe and place faith upon** Christ. This, of course, leads directly into the midst of eonian life.

This leads us to the last phrase of the verse. The expressed preposition *eis* indicates motion from outside something, leading on to piercing it and entering into the midst of it. Thus have I supplied the verb **[leading]**. I could have said [piercing]. God's faith, trust and belief – which He implants into us – have power and lead into life. The term "**eonian life**" is only one possible rendering, as I indicate in my parenthetical expansion. Eonian is the adjective form of the noun eon, our English word for an age – an unspecified but usually long period of time. I chose this word "eonian" because it seemed a better alternative than Rotherham's and other's "agelasting," or Young's "age-during."

But the critical issue is that there is no certainty as to what is meant by the term "age" when used in its adjective form. Those who choose the term "eternal" simply break the rules of language. An adjective cannot have greater force than the noun to which it is related. The Jews had a concept of two ages: the present, and the coming Age of Messiah. Now this brings in the aspect of quality, rather than quantity. The term age was historically used of the lifetime of an individual. Ages have beginnings and endings. There are a plurality of ages in Scripture. The terms "eternal" or "everlasting" have no place here.

Heb. 9:26 speaks of the middle of the 1st century as being "**a conjunction of the ages**." The old covenant Jewish age was coming to an end, and the "beginning end" (as of one end of a rope) of the next age was being birthed in God. Those were "eonian times." But mostly, they were times where God's presence impacted history with an age-lasting effect. We are not told how long this present age will last, but Paul speaks of "**the ages to come**" in Eph. 2:7.

Finally, I give you another option of the adjectival phrase, "**Life which pertains to and has the qualities and characteristics of the Age [of Messiah]**." This, again, speaks of quality – the quality of life in God through union with Christ. Time is not under consideration here – it is a type of life: Christ's life, and speaks of membership and participation in the new covenant.

17. **So, to [the] King of The Ages** (or: eons; indefinite time periods), **to [the] incorruptible** (undecayable; unspoilable), **invisible** (unseen; not-able-to be seen) **One, to [the] only God** [some MSS add: wise; so: only wise God], **[be] honor** (value; worth) **and glory** (reputation which calls forth praise), **on into the ages** (or: indefinite time periods) **of the ages. It is so** (Amen)!
>   (or: Now in and by the King to Whom belongs the ages – in and by the imperishable, invisible [and] only One – in and by God [is] honor and glory, [leading] into the [most important] eons of the eons. So it is!)

So my above discussion leads to this verse. He is the King of all the ages, for they were created through His Son (Heb. 1:2), and to Him belongs honor and glory – "**on into the ages** (or: indefinite time periods) **of the ages**." Note the alternative translation which gives different functions of the noun cases, for your consideration. Here we see that honor and glory have their source and residence in God. The last phrase expresses a Hebrew idiom of using a noun (either singular or plural) followed by a prepositional phrase using the plural of the same noun, e.g., like "the holy of holies." May I just say this: there is a lot of time out ahead of us, in the future of mankind and all of creation. There are ages yet to come.

The phrase "**King of The Ages**" can be seen as a title of Christ, and is equivalent to saying "Jesus is Lord." Note the additions of the verbs, in brackets. The first rendering, with the supplied copula **[be]**, is a doxology. The alternative, with [is], is a statement of fact.

18. **I am presently placing this passed-on message** (notification; announcement) **to your side, child Timothy, down from the preceding prophecies upon you** (or: in accord with the prophecies habitually leading forth upon you), **to the end that you may constantly perform military service** (or: do battle; perform warfare) **within them** (or: in union with them) – **the beautiful** (fine; ideal) **military service** (or: battle; warfare),
19. **while constantly holding** (or: having) **faith** (and: trust) **and a good conscience** (a profitable knowing-together) – **which some** (or: certain ones), **thrusting away** (or: pushing and driving away), **experienced shipwreck about the faith** (or: concerning [their] trust, confidence and loyalty):
20. **of whom are Hymenaeus and Alexander, whom I gave** (or: hand) **over to the adversary** (or: satan) **to the end that they would be child-trained, educated and disciplined with a view toward maturity, [so as] not to constantly blaspheme** (speak abusively or slanderously; vilify; malign; defame; give a false image or misrepresent in a way that hinders the Light).

Comments on 1 Timothy

Vs. 18 tells us that this message (letter) which he is writing is so that Timothy can constantly perform "**beautiful military service**." I suggest that this phrase is but a metaphor, not a reference to the so-called "spiritual warfare" (which phrase is non-existent in Scripture). In Eph. 6 he uses the metaphor of a soldier's equipment, but all these things are qualities and characteristics of God: faith, fairness and equity (or: the rightwised life in the Way pointed out), truth, deliverance or health and wholeness, His Word. Paul is telling Timothy to have the discipline and commitment like a Roman soldier has, but here it is the realm of beauty, the fine, the ideal, all of which is Christ. Live Christ's life as He lives in you.

In vs. 19 he makes this clear by saying, "**while constantly holding faith and trust, as well as a good conscience**." Some folks thrust these things away, and find their life in the kingdom like a boat that is "**shipwrecked**." But these are necessities of covenant living.

Vs. 20 gives us an example: **Hymenaeus and Alexander**. Now note what he next says, "**whom I gave** (or: hand) **over to the adversary** (or: satan)." Why? "**to the end that they would be child-trained, educated and disciplined with a view toward maturity, [so as] not to constantly blaspheme** (speak abusively or slanderously; vilify; malign; defame; give a false image or misrepresent in a way that hinders the Light)." Paul is using satan to child-train (Greek: *paideuo*) and educate these men! God used satan to test Job. God gave Paul an agent of the adversary (satan) to strike him in the face, so that he would not be exalted above measure (2 Cor. 12:7). Does this sound like satan has a kingdom that is opposed to God? No, that sounds like satan is God's tool, His "waster" that He created as "an instrument for His work," whose purpose is "to destroy" (Isa. 54:16) that which is contrary to God. But this instrument has its end in our lives, just as Paul said to the called-out folks in Rome, "**Now the God Who is The Peace** (the God of harmony Who is the source of *shalom*) **will rub together, trample and crush the adversary** (the opponent; the satan) **under your feet swiftly!**" (Rom. 16:20). Paul also uses the adversary (satan) in 1 Cor. 5:5,

> "**[you are] to hand over such a man, with the adversarial [spirit]** (or: in the adversary; by the opponent; or: to satan), **into a loss of the flesh** (or: an undoing and destruction of this [estranged human nature]; a loss of [his "dominated existence" – Walter Wink]) **– to the end that the spirit may be saved** (rescued; delivered; restored to health, wholeness and its original state and condition)**: within the midst of and in union with the Day of the Lord** [= Christ or Yahweh; other MSS add: Jesus; others read: our Lord, Jesus Christ]."

In Lu. 9:1, even before He had gone to the cross, Jesus "**after calling the twelve together unto Himself, He gave to them power and ability, as well as authority, upon all the demons** (Hellenistic concept and term: = animistic influences) **and thus to be habitually giving care for, treating or curing sicknesses and diseases**." This does not sound like satan was in command of hordes of demons, or is even ontologically in opposition to God. We should keep in mind the world view of those living in 1st century Palestine: they had assimilated many concepts of the pagan cultures that had dominated them for centuries. There is no theology or cosmology about demons in the canonical OT. We only find this appearing in Second Temple literature. See my discussion of 1 Pet. 5:8 in this volume, in the chapter "Comments On 1 Peter," where what is traditionally translated "the devil" is shown to be OUR adversary, or adversarial situation, not God's adversary. Also, consider the discussion on Jacob 4:7, in the chapter "Comments On Jacob (James)."

The present tense of the verb "**blaspheme**" indicates that these two men had a habit of constantly doing this, thus the need for corrective discipline and education through an adversarial circumstance, situation or experience (here Paul was not specific).

Chapter 2

1. Consequently I am habitually calling you alongside to encourage, counsel and exhort you to first of all be constantly making petitions for needs, prayers (speaking, thinking and doing toward things being well), **encounters** (or: intercessions; meetings within situations to converse or hit and obtain the objective), **[and] expressions of gratitude** (or: of the goodness of grace and favor) **over** (or: on behalf of; for) **all mankind** (humanity) –

Paul is completely inclusive in his exhortation. We should take on the concerns of all humanity, make requests regarding them, project goodness and well being to them, intercede on their behalf by doing something or having encounter with them, and express gratitude over their very existence, as well as expressing the goodness of God's grace over their situations.

2. over (or: for) **kings and all those being folks within a position of holding control over** (or: above) **[others]** (or: being in superiority or high station), **to the end that we may continuously lead** (or: carry through) **a course of life that is still – at rest** (free from all agitation or disturbance with tranquility arising from without), **and also quiet – peaceable** (gentle, exciting no disturbance in others, with tranquility arising from within) **in all reverence** (pious and devout relations with everything) **and majestic seriousness** (dignity and gravity which inspire awe).

Political prayers are encouraged, so that we may continuously lead a course of life that is still – with no upheavals or turmoiles – as well as prayers that our lives would also be at rest, quiet, and peaceable: "with tranquility arising from within." Now this sounds nice. This is a good goal to have, especially considering his letters to those that are in the midst of persecutions. Reverence and "majestic seriousness" sounds a little stuffy, but in reality if you create in your mind a beautiful quiet scene out in nature, I think we can see what he means. Reverence towards life and seriousness about our environment are good things.

3. This [is] beautiful (fine; ideal) **and welcomingly received from the presence of, and in the sight of, God, our Deliverer** (our Savior; the One Who heals us and makes us whole, restoring us to our original state and condition),

So vs. 2 describes the "beautiful life." And there is no mention of material goods. This fine and ideal situation comes about from having God's presence with us, and having His "eye" turned on us (speaking metaphorically). We receive this from Him, the One Who heals us, make us whole and restores us.

4. Who is constantly willing (continuously intending and purposing) **all mankind** (all humanity) **to be saved** (delivered; rescued; made healthy and whole), **and** (or: even) **to come into a full, accurate, experiential and intimate knowledge and insight of Truth** (or: into a realization of reality),

What an intent and purpose – and He wills it to be so, so it will come to pass, for He always does according to the counsel of His will (Eph. 1:11, where we find the noun for of this same word here, in its verbal form). This is a beautiful and ideal plan that He has for humanity. Can we imagine all humanity with a " **full, accurate, experiential and intimate knowledge and insight of Truth [and] a realization of reality**"? That will be "heaven," my friends, and will make the earth a wonderful place to be. All mankind delivered and made whole! It indeed takes faith in this word from Paul, to really believe it, but this is the final goal of all humanity. Jesus said, "**you will come to know the Truth** (or: Reality; that which is unsealed, open and without concealment) **by intimate experience, and the Truth** (Reality) **will liberate and make** (or: set) **you free!**" (John 8:32). This was spoken to Jews who had believed, and thus we can see that God has an intent that all will at some point believe and enter into participation of covenant life.

5. for God [is] One, and One [is the] Mediator of God and mankind, a Man, Christ Jesus (or: for [there is] one God, and one medium between God and humans, [the] human, Anointed Jesus),

We know from John 3:16 that God loves the whole world, and vs. 4 above confirms this. So when we think of a mediator, we must think of humans that are the hostile ones, while God is full of love and conciliation (2 Cor. 5:19). So our Brother, the Man Christ Jesus, mediates this love and conciliation to humanity. And according to my second rendering, the Anointed Jesus is the only medium through which this goodness can come. "**For neither is there a different name under the [dome of the] sky** (or: heaven) **that has been given, and now exists as a gift, among mankind** (or: in the midst of humanity) **within which it continues binding and necessary for us to be saved** (restored to health and wholeness; delivered and kept safe; returned to our original state and condition)!" (Acts 4:12). The Christ/Messiah event was/is the turning point of all of human history. (*cf* the short study on "A Mediator" added at the end of the comments on this letter)

6. the One giving Himself a correspondent ransom (a ransom in the place of and directed toward the situation) **over [the situation of and] on behalf of** (or: for) **all** (everyone; all humanity and all things) **– the witness** [note: "the witness" is omitted by A; other MSS: the evidence of which] **[will come] in its own fitting situations** (or: the Witness for their own seasons; the Testimony to and for His own particular occasions; the evidence [appears] in its own fertile moments) –

Here we see inclusiveness again. The ransom fully faced and corresponded to the situation of all humanity, and of the whole creation. The word "correspondent ransom" is the Greek *lutron* (a price paid for release from slavery or captivity) with the prefix *anti-* (in an opposite position, facing toward in order to assist in a manner equivalent to the need). He gave Himself as a payment to redeem mankind, placing Himself "**over**" our situation – a picture of Love covering the multitude of sins and mistakes (1 Pet. 4:8).

The evidence of this will be witnessed in its own fitting situations or fertile moments. This is equivalent to what he said in 1 Cor. 15:23, "**each person within his or her own class or division** (or: ordered rank; place or appointed position [in line]; arranged [time] or order of succession)."

7. into the midst of which I, a preacher (or: herald) **and one sent with a mission** (an envoy and representative), **was placed** (or: am set) **– I am speaking truth, I am not lying – a teacher of multitudes** (nations; the multiplied ethnic groups; non-Jews), **within faith and Truth** (or: in union with trust and reality).

Paul was placed into this "**correspondent ransom**" and was sent by Jesus to be a teacher of multitudes (Greek: *ethnos*; used of a swarm of bees, thus, a multitude of ethnic groups; often used to refer to the pagan societies that are non-Jewish). He was also "**placed**" into the environment of God's reign, which is "**faith and Truth; trust and Reality**." I capitalized Truth and Reality to indicate that this is really referring to Christ, into Whom we have been placed, in covenant relationships – within both His death and His resurrection life, and now within His body which is the called-out community.

8. I am wanting and intending, then, the men (adult males) **within every place to habitually pray** (constantly think, speak and act toward having ease, goodness and well-being), **continually lifting up loyal and dutiful hands that are pure from all crime, apart from impulse of intrinsic fervor** (or: passion and swelling desire; or: anger, indignation or wrath) **and reasonings** (debates; divisions in thinking; dialogues; computations).

He is speaking to the adult men of that time and culture, and he was referring to a way of life: constant or habitual prayer (which literally means: think, speak and act toward having ease, goodness and well-being). This corresponds to 1 Thes. 5:17, "**Continuously think, speak and act with a view toward well-being and goodness – unceasingly** (or: By habit be praying unintermittingly)." He is not just talking about in an assembly of the community, but within all of life.

Lifting up "**loyal and dutiful hands**" is a metaphor from the religious practice of that day and culture, but the hand is a figure of what a person does – his work or activities. Just as he is to "continuously pray," Paul is here speaking to his way of life and his activities: he is to constantly lift up (= offer to God) a loyal and dutiful life that is pure from all crime, and apart form impulsive fervor or negative expressions of such, and apart from divisions in thinking, debates and reasoned dialogues that have a negative flavor.

9. **Likewise, women to habitually adorn and arrange themselves in an ordered and arranged system of proper behavior and descent clothing: with modesty, so as to be unseen** (or: as having downcast eyes), **and soundness of mind** (sanity and sensibility), **not in braids** (or: inter-weavings) **and in golden ornaments, or in pearls or expensive garments,**

In using the word "**likewise**," we should see that he is speaking to the same level: on the sphere of the spiritual that also is lived out in the practical. The women are to do the same as the men, but instead of using the metaphor of lifting hands, he says "**in an ordered and arranged system of proper behavior and clothing: with modesty and soundness of mind** (sanity and sensibility)." Here is another cultural metaphor, speaking of an attitude and way of life. As with the men, here he follows with a negative metaphor, this time regarding ostentatious living or personal vanity. In each case the metaphors can also be followed, if the Spirit so leads the individual, but these are not the point, and should not become a religious law.

10. **but rather – what is suitable** (proper; fitting; becoming) **in** (or: for; to) **women giving instruction on reverence for God** [note: refers to women who taught "God-fearers" in synagogues, to prepare these folks for conversion] **– through good works and virtuous actions.**

Here is the general category to which he is leading: good works and virtuous action. This is like what Jacob (or: James) said, that for faith to have life it must be joined to works and thus bear the fruit of love. It is interesting that he parenthetically refers to a specific situation: women giving instruction on reverence for God. The subject concerned a way of life that was being taught – reverence for God. So like the other cultural examples, he is referring to our inner lives which bear fruit in our outer lives.

11. **A woman** (or: wife) **must be habitually learning – within calm quietness** (without making a fuss; in peaceableness and gentleness, exciting no disturbance in others, and with tranquility arising from within) **– in union with every humble alignment while giving support** (or: within every subordinate arrangement).

Once again, we need to be aware of the cultural environment. What he is saying is contrary to how he was raised in Judaism: a woman was not to be taught Torah. But we are now in the new creation – all has changed, and these folks needed to know that culture, class and gender prohibitions no longer applied. But it was not a revolution, for what he says here regarding women and wives also applied equally to men: humble alignment to Christ, while giving support to one another (*cf* Eph. 5:21 and Rom. 12:10).

12. **Now I am not turning upon a woman, so as to direct her to be habitually teaching** (or: Yet I do not habitually turn on a wife, to regularly teach [her]) **– neither to continually act in self-authority to use arms for murdering an adult male**

> (or: = habitually to be a self-appointed master to domineer over a man [note: this may have been an exhortation against Gnosticism, and a possible rendering could be: And I am not permitting a woman to teach that she is the originator of a man]) **– but rather to**

exist (or: be) **within quietness** (gentleness, exciting no disturbance, with tranquility arising from within) –

Paul is not now putting a burden upon women to do things that they don't feel ready to do – he is not "**turning upon**" them. And he is not promoting a gender revolution to symbolically "murder a man." He is instead calling them to the same thing to which he called all, in vs. 2, above: a quiet, tranquil life of gentleness.

13. **for you see, Adam was molded and formed first, thereafter** (or: next), **Eve.**
14. **Also, Adam was not seduced and deceived, but the woman being completely cheated out by seduction** (or: thoroughly deluded) **has come to be and exists within deviation** (transgression; a stepping by the side),
15. **yet she will be delivered** (rescued; saved; made whole and restored to her original state and condition) **through the Birth** (or: birthing) **of the Child – should they dwell** (abide) **within faith** (and: trust) **and love and the results of being set-apart** (holiness), **with soundness of mind** (sanity; sensibility).
The Word [is] full of faith! (or: Trustworthy [is] this message.)

As above, I suggest that Paul is speaking with metaphors in 13-15. He is speaking to the human condition. The female aspect of the nature of every human is the deceived, estranged soul which listened to the carnal wisdom within us (figured by the serpent in the Garden, which Garden was a figure for our internal life). To be carnally minded is death (Rom. 8:6), just as to partake of the tree of knowledge of good and evil (to have a legalistic mindset; to live from the Law which tells us what is right and what is wrong, and that we must do works to be right) within us brings death.

Adam is a figure of Christ (Rom. 5:14), and Eve a figure of His body. We all, His body, were "**cheated out by seduction**" and had come to "**exist within deviation**" (we side-stepped away from the Way pointed out, the tree of Life, the Christ). But Christ, like Adam, took on our transgressions, and we are delivered when the man-child (Rev. 12:5) was given birth within us. That birth comes from living with Christ, dwelling in the faith which He is, and in the love which He is, and the state of being set-apart, which He is, with the "**soundness of mind**" which He gives, which is the mind of Christ. His Word is crammed full of His faith. And this is a trustworthy message!

Chapter 3

1. **If anyone is habitually stretching himself in reaching out toward a distant object upon which the eye is fixed, he is by habit craving a beautiful deed**
> (or: If anyone continues reaching after visitation for inspection and tender guardianship, he fully desires a virtuous action; If anyone stretches out in reaching for the duties of looking around upon things {duties of one who watches upon, or oversees}, he completely desires ideal work).

Of the three renderings which I have given here, I chose for my first option the most literal as it would have the widest application. It is beautiful to stretch oneself toward something that is not close at hand. It is ideal to fix ones eyes upon a distant object. This can take us beyond our present environment and circumstances, and give us hope. It can set a goal for us. It can challenge us into action. Taking action which stretches us toward a goal is a fine thing.

As for the second option, this is a practical outworking of love for others. It qualifies us as His sheep, rather than His kids (immature goats) – Matt. 25:34-40, and is a vital function within any community.

The third option describes the function of a supervisor or overseer – and this, too is an ideal work in which to be involved, in any area of life, but especially in the life of the community.

2. **It is therefore binding upon** (necessary for) **the person fixing his eye upon a distant object** (or: the one doing visitation for inspection and tender guardianship; the one watching upon or overseeing) **to be someone not to be laid hold of** (thus: one in whom is no just cause for blame), **a husband of one wife** (or: an adult male in relationship to one woman), **sober** (unintoxicated; clear-headed; moderate in habits), **sound in mind** (sensible), **have his world ordered and arranged** (or: systematic, proper, descent and decorous), **be fond of strangers** (or: hospitable), **skillful and qualified to teach,**

3. **not addicted to wine** (or: one who keeps wine at his side), **not quarrelsome and apt to strike another, but rather, yielding** (lenient; gently equitable; reasonable; considerate), **not disposed to fight nor belligerent, not fond of silver** (= money),

4. **habitually putting himself at the head of** (= lead, provide for and protect) **his own household so as to beautifully** (ideally; finely) **stand before and lead them, having children in the midst of humble alignment for support** (or: within subjection) **with all majestic seriousness** (dignity and gravity which inspire awe) –

Verses 2-4 are normally considered to be "qualifications" for the third rendering of vs. 1, above. But these characteristics apply to all three. If any of the things on this list are not present in the individual, it would be a deterrent to performance of any of the three renderings. They are qualities that are advantageous for everyone and for any function – not just for a position of "leadership."

5. **now if anyone does not know** (has not seen and is not aware) **to put himself/herself at the head of** (= lead, provide for and protect) **her/his own household so as to stand before and lead them, how will s/he be thoughtful of, take an interest in, and take care of, God's called-out community?** –

6. **not a novice** (neophyte; a newly placed member of the body), **lest, being inflated with the fumes of conceit, s/he may fall into an effect of the adversary's judgment**
> (the result of sifting, separation and decision made in regard to someone who thrusts or throws something through another; or: a judgment-effect from the adversary).

Here Paul speaks to the situation of a family and the function of a parent, and relates this to similar functioning in the called-out community. There are often orphans that need parenting; children in dysfunctional or abusive homes that need a paraclete to guide them; young folks away from home who need pro-tem oversight and admonition; economic or natural disasters where organizational or triage skills are greatly needed. Furthermore, the same skills that are needed in raising and leading a family are also needed in teaching the spiritually young who may still need the "milk" of the Word.

In none of these situations should a novice or a young person with no experience take on these functions.

7. **Yet it is also necessary and binding to continuously hold** (or: have) **a beautiful witness and testimony** (= a fine reputation) **from those outside, so that s/he would not fall into reproach** (lest s/he may fall into a censorious report regarding character) **and [into] a trick** (snare; gin; device; stratagem) **belonging to or devised by the adversary** (or: whose source is the one who, or [that spirit and attitude] which, thrusts things through folks and causes injury or division; or: which is the adversary).

The witness and testimony from folks outside the community of faith will come from their observation of the fruit in our lives. If they see the fruit of the Spirit, or the life of Christ, then it will be a beautiful testimony that they give on behalf of the called-out folks. Lack of this will mean that the fruit is not there, only leaves (our works), and if our functioning is without the Spirit of Christ, we will fall into the snares that our own carnal/estranged nature sets for us (see Jacob {James} 1:14-15), or, into the stratagems of divisive or adversarial people.

8. **Attending servants, similarly, [should be] serious** (dignified with gravity) **– not double-talking** (or: speaking with double meanings; or: divided in thought or reason), **neither [being] folks having a propensity toward much wine, nor people eager for dishonorable** (deformed or ugly; = dishonest) **gain –**

9. **continuously holding** (or: having) **the secret** (or: mystery) **of the faith** (trust; loyalty) **within** (or: in union with) **a clean conscience.**

This advice would apply to households, or to functions in the community at large. Those who serve are the backbone on the community, and their having a living and honest relationship with Christ is essential for the growth and health of the entire community.

10. **And so, let these folks also be first put through a process of examination, testing and proving. Thereafter, let them be regularly giving supporting service [to the community], being folks that have not been called up before a judge** (or: free from accusation; unimpeachable).

Here Paul gives wise guidance concerning choosing those who will have the honor of providing service to the community. It is the same wisdom that a person would use in choosing employees for one's business.

11. **Women** (or: Wives) **[of the community], similarly, [should be] serious** (dignified with majestic gravity, inspiring awe), **not devils** (or: adversaries; women who thrust things through folks), **sober** (unintoxicated; clear-headed; moderate in habits), **full of faith and trust** (or: faithful; trustworthy; loyal) **in all things.**

We should remember that Paul is instructing Timothy concerning the makeup of what were then newly birthed communities of called-out folks – groups within the secular towns. These are expressions of the new creation: people living under the new covenant with Christ as their head. This was a new concept, a new world for these folks, so cultural and social characteristics – as well as the spiritual aspects of their lives – were in need of being addressed. As we all have experienced, being birthed into His reign begins a journey of transformation. So Paul is giving a description of how the wives and women of this new community should seek to become. This was a new way of life for everyone.

Notice that I first rendered *diabolos* in traditional way, "devils," to call attention to the fact that this word is used of people. Next I parenthetically inserted its literal and proper meaning.

12. **Let those giving supporting service be adult males having a relationship with one woman** (or: husbands of one wife), **habitually placing themselves in front of their children, as well as their own households, to beautifully** (or: finely; ideally) **lead, protect and provide [for them].**

Again, recall the cultural aspect of those to whom Timothy would take these instructions. Today we would not use the term "adult males," but would more likely say, "Let them be ladies and gentlemen having a relationship with one spouse, in accord with our custom..."

Note that a core quality of the lives of these communities was "beauty," or, "what is fine and ideal." This is a call to excellence, which comes with the life of Christ.

13. **You see, those giving supporting service in a beautiful and ideal manner continue in** (or: by; for; among) **themselves building around themselves a beautiful** (fine; excellent; ideal) **circular staircase** (that which enables folks to step up to a higher place) **and much freedom of speech** (confident outspokenness and boldness which is the right of citizens) **resident within faith, trust and loyalty – that which is resident within, and in union with, Christ Jesus.**

Here Paul uses a picturesque metaphor of a carpenter, mason or builder to describe those folks who provide supporting service to the called-out community – or to the community at large – and do it in a beautiful and ideal manner. He says that "**they progressively build a fine and beautiful circular staircase**" around themselves (both within and without) which enables both themselves and others to figuratively ascend in God. The word picture comes from *peri-poiew* (to build around, or to construct an encirclement), and the word *bathmos* (a step or staircase). This would recall the ladder in the story of Jacob' dream, Gen. 28:12, and then an aspect of God's house as Jacob mentioned in vs. 17, as well as the metaphor which Jesus gave to Nathaniel in John 1:51.

Such service to the body also comes with outspoken freedom of speech, which is the right of citizens of God's kingdom, members of the Jerusalem which is above (Gal. 4:26), participants of the covenant. This freedom and boldness is resident with the faith which He gives us because of our union with Him. Within Him is also trust and confidence, and through our supporting service we can pass this on to others.

14. **I am writing these things to you, expecting to come toward you swiftly** (in quickness; or: = soon),
15. **but if ever I should be slow** (or: delay), **[I am writing this] to the end that you may see and thus know how it is necessary and binding to be twisted and turned back up again within God's household** (or: to be treated, conducted or caused to behave in God's house), **which is** (or: exists being) **a called-out community of [the] Living God** (or: whose source is a living God; which has the qualities and character of [the] living God; or: which is a living god), **a pillar and foundational seat of The Truth** (or: a base from and an effect of a settling of reality),

I have given the literal rendering "**twisted and turned back up again**" to give a graphic picture of what must happen in our lives when we become a part of God's household. The Spirit of God seizes us, twists us around to face back up again. Note that the voice of the verb is passive – God acts upon us. Most versions treat this as though it were a middle voice, as though this is something we must do, rendering this expressive verb something like "conduct yourself" or, "behave," but these fall short of the meaning. Paul is speaking of being apprehended, or grasped, by God. He had experienced this (Phil. 3:12-13). Our prior behavior was to the most part the opposite of what he has been instructing in this chapter. We have needed to be twisted back up (rightwised, turned in the right direction and placed in the covenant) to be a part of His house, a called-out community of the Living God.

You might wonder about the last parenthetical option, "which is a living god." This rendering is giving the genitive case the function of apposition. Note that I did not capitalize "god," for it is referring to the community, in this construction. Recall that Yahweh said to Moses, "I have made you a god to Pharaoh..." (Ex. 7:1). We are the temple of God, and as Moses presented God to Pharaoh, so we present God to the world.

The last phrase, which also refers to the called-out community, makes another astounding statement – that we are "**a pillar and foundational seat of The Truth** (or: a base from and an effect of a settling of reality)." The term "pillar" calls to mind what the Lord called an overcomer in Rev. 3:12, "**a pillar in the temple**." That we are also a "foundational seat" shows that The Truth (Christ: the new Reality) dwells and is stationed within this community of believers. We are "**a base from and an effect of a settling of reality**." What a concept. We are the new creation – which is the new reality.

16. **and so confessedly** (admittedly; with common consent and sameness of speech) **great is the secret** (or: mystery) **of the reverence** (the standing in awe of goodness, with adoration; the healthful devotion and virtuous conduct of ease, in true relation to God)**:**
> **which is made visible** (manifested) **within flesh** (= a physical body),
> **is rightwised** (set in equity and right relationship in the Way pointed out; also = is placed in covenant) **in spirit** (in union with Breath-effect),

> **is seen by agents** (or: messengers),
> **is heralded** (preached) **within multitudes** (among nations and ethnic groups),
> **is trusted and believed within [the] world** (an ordered system; secular culture),
> **is received back in good opinion and reputation.**
> (or:
> Who [some MSS read: God; others: He] was brought to clear light within flesh (= the natural realm); was shown righteous and just (= set in covenant) within spirit and attitude;
> was seen by agents; was proclaimed among Gentiles {non-Jews};
> was believed within [the] world of society, religion, and government;
> was taken back up again, within glory – a manifestation which calls forth praise!)

Taking the first rendering, we see that the secret of the true reverence was made visible within flesh (i.e., a physical body). This, of course, refers to Jesus Christ. But it also can refer to His corporate body. The verbs are all in the aorist tense, thus I give the two renderings, first "is," second "was," as this is a fact tense, independent of time or type of action.

Rendering the verb "is" points to Christ within His called-out community. Rendering it "was" points to Jesus in particular, in His historical 1st century life.

Now consider the parenthetical rendering. Here the Greek particle "hos" is translated "Who" instead of "which" – either is correct. Note also the variant readings of other MSS. Jesus is clearly the subject of all that follows, in this rendering.

Looking at the following clauses, in each option, above, we see that if it is speaking of His corporate body, then this community was one that was "**rightwised** (turned in the right direction) **in spirit**." But if it is speaking of Him, then He was "shown [to be] righteous and just in spirit and attitude."

It is interesting to note that **agents** (messengers) both saw Him and see us. Christ is heralded within and among the ethnic multitudes – but so is His present manifestation on earth, His body of believers. This latter was a new phenomenon – "Christ in us." And both are believed and trusted (the true called-out are) within the ordered System, called the world.

The final verb means either to be received or taken. In the first rendering, it is speaking of the sent-off folks (missionaries) being received back into the community attended by good opinions and a positive reputation (two meanings of the Greek *doxa*). In the parenthetical translation it refers to Jesus being taken back up into the atmosphere (or: heaven) again, "within glory – a manifestation which calls forth praise!" (two other meanings of *doxa*). This verb is prefixed with the Greek particle *ana*, which can simply mean "back," in a reflexive sense, or "back up again," in all its possible meanings.

Don Luther writes:
"The whole of Paul's Epistle to Timothy has to do with the House of God, and how you behave in it. It's true that the meaning here in vs. 16 is concerning the Christ, but how much more relevant to see it as the corporate Christ! ....
[T]he 'and' of verse 16 seems to connect it more with the preceding verse. It would seem that if there were punctuation marks in Greek, that following the end of verse 15 there should be a colon or comma. Verse 16 seems to be an appositive to verse 15, or maybe an expansion of "the Church of the living God." Amazing what a different light can come from just the appreciation of the aorist tense.

"Also, put this together with:
Eph 5:32. 'This is a great mystery: but I speak concerning Christ and the church.'
The great mystery is not just Jesus (according to Paul) but Christ AND the church.
Cf. Eph 3:3 'how that by revelation was made known unto me the mystery, as I wrote before in few words,

3:4 whereby, when ye read, ye can perceive my understanding in the mystery of Christ;
3:5 which in other generations was not made known unto the sons of men, as it hath now been revealed unto his holy apostles and prophets in the Spirit;
3:6 to wit, that the Gentiles are fellow-heirs, and fellow-members of the body, and fellow-partakers of the promise in Christ Jesus through the gospel,'
And in later vss.,
3:10 'to the intent that now unto the principalities and the powers in the heavenly places might be made known through the church the manifold wisdom of God,
3:11 according to the eternal purpose which he purposed in Christ Jesus our Lord:'

"This manifestation of Christ by the Church is the answer to Jesus' prayer in Jn 17, ergo that the world would not only see, but also BELIEVE!"

Chapter 4

1. **Now the Spirit** (or: Breath-effect) **is explicitly saying that within subsequent seasons** (in fitting situations and on appropriate occasions which will be afterwards) **some of the faith** (or: certain folks belonging to this trust) **will stand off and away [from the Path, or from the Community]** (or: some people will withdraw from this conviction and loyalty), **habitually holding toward** (having a propensity to) **wandering and deceptive spirits** (or: straying and seducing breath-effects and attitudes) **and to teachings of demons**
    (to teachings about and pertaining to, or which are, demons [note: a Hellenistic concept and term: = animistic influences]; or: to instructions and training which come from animistic influences [= pagan religions]),
    [comment: this prophesied about the future institutionalization of the called-out community, and the introduction of pagan teachings, all of which later came to be called "orthodox"]

Paul was not talking about far-off times, but to the night and darkness that was soon to follow the day and light of the 1st century called-out groups. There would come a departing from the Path which is Christ, and from the sense of being an organic community, to a structured and stratified organization that mirrored the old covenant, with grace being replaced by ritual and institutionalized religious works, with freedom (Gal. 5:1) being replaced by control, with joy being replaced by fear – and for a period of time, the Judaizers would win. Even today, following the light shed by the Reformation, we see a recurrence of the same, even to bringing back the celebration of the feast of the old covenant, in some circles, with as much emphasis upon what the believer must do to be saved, as upon the work of Christ.

Such things are the result of deceptive spirits that come from a religious mind-set. They come from a fear of loss of control. They come from our alienated desires to be famous and to even be worshiped. They are the demons which are created by the thinking of estranged humanity, and this distorted, self-worshiping paradigm creates the teachings which both create and support Jezebel among us (Rev. 2:20-23).

Instead of recognizing the demonic in our fallen nature, a whole system of spirit beings – based upon ancient Greek, Roman, Persian and Egyptian mythology – has been created to where much of Christianity sees the realm of spirit from a dualistic viewpoint: God versus the devil. They have forgotten that there is only One God. So they teach about demons and imaginary spiritual principalities, making satan a king of his own kingdom, when all the time Scripture has pointed out that satan dwells in and among the churches (Rev. 2:9, 13, 24; 3:9) and power over satan has been given to the called-out (e.g. Lu. 10:17-19; Rom. 16:20; Mat. 28:18).

2. **within perverse scholarship of false words**
    (or: in association with overly critical hairsplitting of false messages; in the midst of gradually separated interpretations of false expressions; or: in union with deceptive

decisions by speakers of lies), **from folks having their own consciences cauterized** (seared; branded) **as with a hot iron,**

Note that the "**teaching of demons**" comes within "**perverse scholarship of false words**," as well as what is given in the parenthetical expansion. Consider also that these "**wandering spirits**" and teachings about demons also come from people with defective consciences – not from some exterior spirit world.

3. **coming from people habitually forbidding** (preventing; hindering) **[folks] to be marrying [and to be] constantly abstaining from [certain] foods – which things God creates** (or: created; reduced from a state of wildness and disorder) **into something to be shared and partaken of with thanksgiving by those full of faith** (by the faithful and loyal folks) **and by those having experienced full, intimate knowledge and realization of the Truth** (or: of Reality)**!**

Here Paul again asserts that these things come from people with distorted mind-sets and alienated ideas that are usually religious in nature. Note that marrying and eating are simply natural things that are meant to be enjoyed, shared and partaken of with gratitude – and that our "**faith**" applies to these things, too. The Reality in Christ has set us free from superstition and religion, and has brought us into practical, rightwised covenant relationships, right here!

4. **Because all God's creation** (or: every creature of God) **[is] beautiful** (fine; ideal), **and not one thing is to be thrown away – being habitually received with thanksgiving –**
5. **for it is continuously** (or: progressively) **being set-apart** (made holy; rendered sacred) **through God's Word** (or: by means of a word which is God; through a message and an idea from God) **and an encounter** (or: a meeting and falling in with someone; or: conversation; or: hitting on target within a matter to assist; thus: intercession).

Wow! Can you hear it? All God's creation is beautiful and sacred and to be habitually received with a grateful heart. God's Word continually sets all creation apart and makes it holy. God's Word has encountered the earth realm; He has fallen in with us, hitting the target for us, and is in fact our intercession. It is no longer just the temple that is the holy place. He split the curtain and has brought His holiness into all of life – if we can perceive this, and see Him in all things. There is no longer any law concerning diet or marriage, except the law of, and which is, **the spirit of The Life within Christ Jesus** (Rom. 8:2). We are simply to live our lives in His sacredness and freedom – in love,

> "**since [you are] full of power** (if capable; if or since able) **regarding that which has its source in you folks** (or: as to that which proceeds from yourselves corporately), **[live] being folks continuously at peace with all mankind** (in the midst of all people)," – Rom. 12:18.

6. **Placing these things under as a base or foundation, to give advice or make suggestions to and for the brothers** (= fellow believers), **you will be a beautiful** (fine; ideal; excellent) **supportive servant of Christ Jesus, habitually being inwardly nourished by the words of the faith** (or: in the arranged expressions, utterances and messages of trust; or: with ideas of loyalty; or: for thoughts from trust), **and of the beautiful** (fine; ideal; excellent; good quality) **teaching in which you follow alongside closely** (or: to which you nearly accompany and attend).

The "these things" of the first clause refers to what Paul has just been saying. So Timothy is to found new believers upon this base, and in so doing he will be an ideal, fine and beautiful supportive servant of Christ. At the same time, he himself will be "**inwardly nourished**" by this same message of faith, and ideas of loyalty and trust, that he shares to and for God's family.

Paul characterizes the teaching which he shares with Timothy as being BEAUTIFUL. This should be a measuring rod for critiquing what is coming from the "Christian community."

7. **Now you must constantly refuse and avoid** (excuse yourself from) **profane and old-womanish myths, yet habitually be training and exercising yourself, as in gymnastic discipline, toward reverence** (standing in awe of wellness, with adoration; healthful devotion and virtuous conduct of ease, in true relation to God),
8. **for gymnastic discipline for bodily exercise is beneficial toward a few things and with a view to a few people** (or: for a little while), **yet reverence** (devoutness; standing well in awe; virtuous conduct from ease with God) **is beneficial toward all things and with a view to all people, continuously holding** (having) **a promise of life – of the one now** (at the present time), **and of the impending one** (the one being about to be).

Stay away from profane myths and folk traditions. What would this have been in Paul's day? Could it be an admonition to read Second Temple literature with a critical and discerning eye?

Make it a disciplined way of life to be reverent toward all life, for all life comes from God. Gymnastic discipline is good for body and soul, but reverence "**is beneficial toward all things and is with a view to all people**" – or, as Peter said, "**Value, prize and honor all people**" (1 Pet. 2:17). At the same time, be continuously holding (for yourself, and for others) a promise of life – both of the present one, and of the impending one. Eonian life is both in this age, and the next; both in this present life, and in the next. It is the life of Christ. These words of Paul are "concepts which are engaged in a process of movement, and which call forth practical movement and change" (Jurgen Moltmann, *Theology of Hope*, p 36, Fortress Press Edition, 1993).

It is not clear to which Paul was referring here, when he used the phrase "**the impending one**." Perhaps, being in the midst of the close of one age and the beginning of the next (the conjunction of two ages: Matt. 13:39-49; 24:3; 28:20; Heb. 9:26), he meant the what was to follow the destruction of the Temple, which Jesus had prophesied. Perhaps he left it unspecified so that we could all apply it to our own lives, in our own "theology of hope" which always sees a future in the economy of God. Moltmann cited E. Block as saying that God has "future as his essential nature" (ibid., p 16).

9. **The Word [is] full of faith** (or: Faithful and Trustworthy [is] this message) **and worthy of all welcomed reception,**

My first rendering speaks of the Logos being full of faith – trust is its DNA. My alternate rendering connects the first phrase with vs. 10, below. The definite article was sometimes used to mean "this."

10. **for into this [end] are we constantly working hard unto weariness, and are continuously struggling in the contest** (contending for the prize; other MSS: being reproached), **because we have placed our expectation** (or: set our hope) **and thus rely upon a living God** (or: upon [the] living God), **Who is** (exists being) **[the] Savior** (Deliverer; Rescuer; Restorer to health and wholeness) **of all human beings** (all mankind) **– especially of believers** (of folks full of faith and trust; of faithful ones)**!**

Likewise, he is either saying that they are working hard to have folks accept the Word, because it is loaded with faith, or he is saying that because it is a trustworthy message, and thus worthy of acceptance, that they are constantly working unto weariness and struggling against opposition. Either way, it is because they have placed their expectation upon and thus rely upon a, or [the], living God.

But here is the punch line: **[He] exists being [the] Savior of all human beings!** Now THAT is a faithful and trustworthy message, and everyone should receive this message, but sadly, most in the institutional Christian religion do not, at this time. However, this is also true because the Word, Christ, is full of faith – and it is His faith that saved every human being, e.g., Gal. 2:16,

> "**having seen and thus knowing that humanity** (or: mankind; or: a person) **is not normally being put in right relationship** (made fair and equitable; made free from guilt and set into the Way pointed out; rightwised and made to be a just one; = being presently brought into covenant) **from out of works of Law** (or: forth from a law's deeds or actions from custom), **but instead through Jesus Christ's faith** (or: faith that belongs to and originates in Christ Jesus)."

And in Gal. 2:20 Paul tells us,

> "**I am constantly living within faith, trust and confidence – in and by that [faith] which is the Son of God** (or: in union with the trust and confidence that is from God's Son [with other MSS: in the confidence belonging to God and Christ])."

Now it should be noted that this does NOT say that He is "a potential" Savior, for if He does not save everyone, then He is NOT the Savior of all human beings. This, of course, especially includes believers, for these have already been made alive in Christ and have been grafted into the olive tree (Rom. 11:17), and thus made to be members of the covenant. The rest will be made alive in their own groups (1 Cor. 15:22-23).

11. **Be constantly announcing these things to those at your side, passing them along from one to another, and keep on teaching them!**

Please note that he did not say that this is for "the back rooms" or for only the "elite" to know. This is the message that is to be passed along from one to another, and they are to keep on teaching them. Those in the secular culture will love this news, just as the outcasts of Jesus' day loved Him. Those within religions will also love it, when Father gives them eyes to see and ears to hear.

12. **Let no one be despising** (thinking down on; having a negative opinion of) **your youth. On the contrary, continue coming to be a model** (pattern; example) **of** (or: pertaining to) **those full of faith** (of the faithful ones; for believers): **in word, in conduct** (behavior), **in love, in faith** (or: trust), **in purity** (or: propriety).

Here is wise and practical counsel. Timothy is to BE the message, as well as to proclaim and teach it. Chronological age is now insignificant, for it is the Spirit of Christ that empowers him and speaks through him. Truth, faith and teaching are no longer the possession of the "elders," but of the Anointing. It is a new creation.

13. **While I am coming, continue holding toward a propensity for the reading** (in the means of knowing again), **for the calling alongside to give relief, aid, exhortation, comfort and encouragement** (in the work of a paraclete), **for the teaching** (to the instruction and in the training).

These three things are central: reading the Scriptures; performing as a paraclete; and teaching the message, instructing folks in the Scriptures so that they will have a firm foundation, and training them in the things of the kingdom life and covenantal relationships.

14. **Do not make it a habit to neglect the care of or disregard this result of grace** (or: the effect of favor) **residing within you, which was given to you through a prophecy** (a coming or manifestation of light ahead of time), **accompanied by a laying on of the hands of the body of elder folks.**

Taking the definite article as demonstrative (which is considered to be its first use), I have rendered the phrase above (Greek: *tou charis-matos*) as "**this result of grace**," or using a simple definite article, "the effect of favor." Rather than seeing this as a specific "gift" that was imparted to Timothy by a prophecy and with a laying on of hands, I see Paul referring to "this result of grace" which is the message of goodness and well-being, and the work of the cross of Christ. It resides with all of us, and has been given to us through a spoken word of Light that comes to us ahead of time, imparting life to us through the called-out community – in this case, a body of the older folks. The laying on of their hands was an expression of love and solidarity. It may have been a symbol of the prayers that they were projecting into him, but the gift was the life within the Word that was spoken into him, and now resided within him as the Living Word, the Christ. It is this Christ-life that we are called to give care to, and watch over – as in 1 John 5:21, where he says,

> "**Little children** (born ones) **keep yourselves in custody** (or: guarded)! – **away from the idols** (the external appearances; the forms; or: = false concepts)!"

15. **Continually meditate on, give attention to and cultivate these things; be absorbed in them** (exist centered within them), **to the end that your cutting a passage forward** (your progress and advancement) **may be visibly apparent to all** (for everyone).

Here he refers back to all that he has been saying. It is like the need to sharpen a saw if your cutting will be effective: meditate on the good news of the Christ, give attention to the messages that have been given, and be absorbed in Him and in His brothers (all humanity). In this way a person's life will cut a clean and clear passage forward that will be apparent to all. The character of covenantal, kingdom living is: life, which constantly tends toward the new, the future, and the expectation of the glory of God. This forward advancement brings peace and joy as His government increases (Isa. 9:6-7).

16. **Habitually have a hold upon yourself and the teaching** (or: Constantly attend to yourself and to the instruction and training). **Continue abiding on and remaining** (or: Constantly dwell on, while staying; Be progressively and fully persisting) **in them, for, continuously doing this, you will rescue** (deliver; save; restore to health and wholeness) **both yourself and those regularly hearing you.**

It is like the old advice given by the airline attendant: if you need oxygen, put the mask on yourself first, then you can be breathing so as to help others. Care of our own garden, the sharpening of our saw, giving attention to our own condition and to "**the teaching**," and then "**abiding on and remaining in them**" – these are the things that keep us going for the long run, and give us the ability and resources to rescue other, and sometimes deliver ourselves.

Chapter 5

1. **You should not inflict blows upon** (or: = verbally attack; severely criticize; give reproofs to) **an older man. To the contrary, habitually call [him] alongside, as a father, to aid, give relief and assist, to encourage and exhort** (= be a paraclete to him). **[Treat] younger men as brothers,**
2. **older women as mothers, younger women as sisters, within all purity and propriety.**

Again, as Peter said, "Honor and value all people" (! Pet. 2:17). Paul is here pointing out the practical living out of the life of Christ. He is not making laws, but pointing out the Way of Life. He is portraying solidarity and showing us that we are all family. He is saying, "Love."

3. **Be constantly honoring** (valuing; thus: = assisting and supporting) **widows – those actually being widows.**
4. **But if any widow currently has children or grandchildren** (descendants), **let these keep on learning to first show reverence with ease and virtuous devotion to goodness with pious care, for and in their own household, and to keep paying a due compensation to their parents and grandparents** (progenitors), **for this is welcomely received in God's sight.**
5. **Now the one actually being a widow, and having been left alone** (= without a dowry and destitute), **has placed expectation upon, and now relies on God, and constantly remains**

focused in requests regarding needs, and in prayers (thoughts, words and deeds aimed toward goodness and well-being) **during night and during day,**
6. **yet the woman continuously indulging herself in riotous luxury** (excessive comfort; sensual gratification), **continuing being alive** (or: [though] living), **she is dead** (or: she has died).

Paul addresses an important aspect of living as a community, as did the called-out group in Jerusalem, reported in Acts ch. 6. Apparently in the culture to which Timothy was sent, older folks and widows were either neglected or abused. In vs. 3, I suggest a practical meaning of honor and value be "assisting and supporting" – actually doing something for them. As with the teaching of Jesus in the parable of the sheep and the kids (Matt. 25), having actions and works as a fruit of our faith was central to the message of the kingdom and new covenant living. At the same time, he is recognizing that within these communities there will still be manifestations of the estranged human nature, so vs. 4-6 speak to some potential situations which could negatively affect themselves or others. He speaks wisdom into such cases. Vs. 4 tells us that these communities still lived with the core of there being households, and pious care is admonished. The widow (vs. 5) that "**has placed expectation upon, and now relies on God, and constantly remains focused in requests regarding needs, and in prayers** (thoughts, words and deeds aimed toward goodness and well-being)" obviously has an important function to play – both night and day. We see in vs. 6 the common metaphorical use of the word "dead" (as with the prodigal son of Lu. 15). A person that behaved in a manner such as he described would be of little functional use to the life of the community, so would be considered as one dead.

7. **So keep on announcing these things along the way** (telling them to the one at your side), **to the end that they may be folks not to be laid hold of for being reprehensible** (thus: people in whom is no just cause for blame).

The living out of the reign of God within the community is a practical, sensible life, and the Spirit-led discipline of the members is a useful fruit to be enjoyed by all. Lack of this can bring negative reactions and cause problems.

8. **Now if anyone is not habitually having forethought or perceiving beforehand in order to provide for those who are his or her own** (= relatives), **and especially ones of the household** (family or domestics) **s/he has disowned** (turned her or his back on; denied; renounced; refused) **the Faith-loyalty and is worse than an unbeliever** (or: has disregarded and declined their trust and exists being worse than one without faith).

Paul makes a direct correlation between living with ethical behavior – taking on one's responsibilities – and "**the Faith-loyalty,**" or living in trust. If one does not live in accord with the Way pointed out (loyal fairness, equity, rightwised covenantal relationships), this person's situation and life is worse than that of the folks yet outside the called-out community. A person with faith in Christ, yet denying Him in his way of life, is worse than someone in the secular world that has no faith in Christ. This is a strong statement by Paul. It undergirds the idea that to be "saved" is not just "accepting Christ as one's Savior," but is an organic, existential change in one's being that has an expectation of growth and the bearing of fruit (John 15:1-6) – of being alive in Christ and being a living member of His body that receives His life and produces His life.

9. **Let a widow be put on the list, and continue enrolled, who has become no younger than sixty years old, a wife of one man** (= not married a second time?),
10. **having a continuing reputation founded in beautiful acts** (ideal works; fine deeds): **if she nourishes children** (or: reared a family), **if she is** (or: was) **hospitable to strangers and foreigners, if she washes** (or: bathed) **the feet of the set-apart folks** (the holy ones; the saints), **if she successfully wards off distress for those being constantly pressured** (or: relieves those consistently being in tribulation and affliction), **if she follows up on every good work** (attends to every virtuous deed).

This is more practical advice for communal living. It is evident that special care was to be given to widows of 60 years or more, but it was still expected that they would continue offering support to the community by being productive in a variety of ways. She would in this way provide needed services in return for her daily sustenance.

She would be like a flower in a garden, performing beautiful acts which adorn the community. Hospitality to strangers, doing what Jesus did for His disciples, warding off distress, doing follow-up on community good works! What an asset to the community – as well as ending one's life being the greatest within the community (Matt. 23:11).

11. On the other hand, turn aside requests of (or: refuse) **younger widows [from being on the list], for you see, whenever they may develop headstrong pride** (live strenuously or rudely) **against Christ** (or: may come down to the level of sexual impulse, be in the sphere of sensual desire, feel licentious or become wanton in relation to or in regard to the Anointed [body]) **they are continually wanting to be marrying** [note: it was a Gnostic belief that a person could gain knowledge (gnosis) by having sex with someone],
12. habitually holding an effect of a decision: that they set-aside the first faith-loyalty (or: continuing to possess the result of a judgment, because they displace their first trust).
13. Yet at the same time, they also are constantly learning inactiveness (idleness; unemployment), **wandering around the houses** (= going from home to home), **and not only [are they] inactive** (ineffective; unemployed; idle), **but further [they are] also gossips** (babblers; ones bubbling over with prattle) **and meddlers** (or: gaining knowledge by supernatural means or practicing magic), **women constantly saying unnecessary things** (or: continuously speaking the things they should not speak).

For Paul to go into such detail in vs. 11-13 there must have been numerous situations like what he describes. His concern is for a healthy community, and here he gives examples of unloving behavior, unproductiveness and worthless communications. I suggest that his reference to "**wanting to be marrying**" may refer to casual sexual encounters (the basic meaning of marriage is sexual union, e.g. Mk 10:7-8, not the ceremony of the custom of later generations, and some Gnostic sects encouraged having sex to gain spiritual insight). Note the alternate parenthetical rendering "may come down to the level of sexual impulse... in regard to the Anointed [body]..." I do not think that he would have been opposed to young widows entering into a respectable marriage, for unless they did they would in that culture have had no means of honest support. Many who were widowed, or their husbands had divorced them and sent them away, found it necessary to resort to prostitution to survive. Jesus spoke against the practice in the Jewish culture of His day where a man could divorce his wife "for any reason." See notes in Matt. 5:32 and 19:9-10 in my translation.

The "**headstrong pride against Christ**" may refer to an attitude held in regard to the called-out community, which is the body of Christ.

Vs. 12 seems to indicate that Paul is referring to a person who has in some way broken faith with the community, or "set-aside" the faith from Christ, as vs. 15 suggests, and is experiencing the result of a judgment upon her. Some have suggested that he is referring to one who had made a pledge to dedicate her life in service to the community (the body of Christ), and as it were be married to Christ, but now had displaced this trust. The intent of this verse is uncertain.

The secondary meaning of *periergoi* (gaining knowledge by supernatural means or practicing magic) may refer to Gnostic practices, or to employing "spiritual" methods to gain insights into the supernatural realm via trances, or through imagined or internally projected visions or visitations in which the person tries to "work around" (the literal meaning of the word) the normal and sanctioned means of attaining knowledge: communion with the Father and study of His Word.

14. I am wanting and intending, therefore, younger women to be marrying: to be bearing children; to continuously rule and manage a household; to be by habit giving not even one

starting point (base of operation; opportunity; incentive; inducement) **favoring verbal abuse** (slander; reviling) **to the person occupying an opposing position** (or: in the one lying in opposition; for the opposer or the opposing counterpart),

So we see that Paul did in fact want younger women to marry and continue in the norms of the community, so as not to give folks outside the community a reason for slandering the community. The Jews, especially, of that day were still actively opposing the called-out communities with verbal abuse. In the culture and economic situation of that time and place, being married, having children and managing a household was the best position and way of life for a woman. But I do not think that Paul was establishing a spiritual law that would apply for all time. He was writing into specific situations of his day.

15. **for you see, already some** (or: certain folks) **were turned out [of the path]** (or: were turned aside [from the goal]), **behind the adversary** (= to follow after satan; or: = some were by their opponents turned out of the midst of the community to the adversarial counterpart [religion] which lay behind them).

My last suggested interpretive paraphrase, above, states what I see as the point of his subject matter in the previous verses. Some of these folks may have been offended by the behavior that they were seeing within the community, so they were leaving the Path of Christ and returning to the more regulated life of the Jewish religion, which was the active adversary to the called-out folks. Others may have followed the adversarial spirit within themselves, and turned to the Hellenistic or Roman cultures, becoming completely secular in their way of life.

16. **If any woman of faith** (or: faithful, trusting and believing woman) **continues having widows [in her circle of influence or in her family], let her continue warding off [disaster] for them** (or: relieving and being sufficient for them [= by paying their expenses]), **and then the called-out community [will] not be continuously burdened** (weighed down), **to the end that it may continually ward off [disaster]** (or: bring relief and be sufficient [by paying expenses]) **for those actually being widows.**

I think that his point is clear here – if an individual has the means to help a widow in her sphere of influence, then this will relieve the community as a whole, in the area of welfare. Again, Paul's foremost concern is the soundness of the community, for this is the representative of Christ in the area.

17. **Let the older men – ones having beautifully** (ideally; finely) **placed [themselves] at the head so as to stand before, to lead and to provide – be considered worthy of double value, worth and honor, especially those being continually wearied and spent with labor in [the] Word** (or: in the midst of the message) **and by teaching** (or: instruction and training),
18. **for the Scripture is saying, "You shall not muzzle a bull** (or: ox) **when it is threshing out grain,"** [Deut. 25:4] **and, "The worker [is] worthy** (of equal value) **of his wages."** [Luke 10:7]

And again, the context is the community and its relationship to those older men who are providing leadership through "labor" in the message. They are to be valued, honored and provided for, since they are providing spiritual food for the community, supporting its life and health through teaching and training. That he specifies "older men," we might surmise that these are those who have the wisdom of years and also are beyond the age of physical productivity. Laboring in the Word and instructing would not seem to be the recommended position for younger men, who had households for which to provide, and children to raise – they did not have the types of jobs and the conveniences which we have in our day that would allow the time for such things.

19. **Do not normally accept** (or: receive; entertain) **[from the] outside** (= from outside the community) **an accusation down on** (or: charge against) **an older man, except "upon two or three witnesses,"** [Deut. 17:6]

20. **yet habitually put to the proof, test or expose** (or: lay bare and reprove) **the [older men] habitually missing the target or constantly being in error** (or: the [older men] repeatedly sinning; those continuously failing) **before all onlookers** (or: in the sight of all), **to the end that the rest, also, may continue holding reverence** (or: having respectful fear).

There was to be a maintaining of "the Way pointed out" and rightwised behavior, but they were not to judge these older men who were serving them by the standards of the Jewish, or the secular, communities. If it applied to their personal behavior, the fairness of "two or three witnesses" would be needed, for the equity that is in Christ called for this.

Likewise, the community was to be evaluating the older people who were found to be habitually missing the goal or constantly being in error, and bring this to the light in the sight of all. Such folks were expected to be the leaders and examples, so like the judging of prophecy within the body (1 Cor. 14:29) it would be necessary to have checks and balances. The health of the community required this.

21. **I continue bearing complete and thorough witness** (or: I habitually give evidence and testimony throughout) **in the sight of God and of Christ Jesus and of the selected, picked out and chosen agents** (or: messengers; folks with the message), **to the end that you may keep watch on so as to guard these things apart from effects of fore-decisions** (prejudgment; prejudice), **continually doing nothing** (constructing not one thing) **down from** (in accord with; on the level of) **inclination** (or: a leaning toward [something]) **or bias.**

Paul is calling for fairness and lack of prejudice concerning the things which he has just been advising. He is reminding them that God – even Jesus Christ – and those of the body of Christ at large, and in other communities (His chosen agents: the folks with the message), were present and had the communities in view, observing their behavior, so that they should keep watch and guard what he has told them. Personal inclinations, desire or bias should not influence their decisions, but there was a need of oversight – as parents over children.

22. **In practice, place** (or: lay) **your hands quickly upon no one, neither be habitually partnering with, participating in or sharing in common in the failures** (errors; sins; misses of the target; deviations from the goal) **belonging to other folks. Constantly keep yourself pure** (or: Make it a habit to watch over and guard so as to preserve yourself with propriety).

The call, here, is to purity and not participating in the failures of other folks. So I suggest that "**place your hands**" is a metaphor of a symbolic act of making such folks a partner or common participant in community endeavors, and this is not something that should be done "quickly," i.e., before knowing the person, lest inadvertently the community then would be joined to his deviations from the goal.

23. **No longer continue being a water-drinker, but rather, habitually make use of a little wine because of your throat** (or: orifice of the stomach; neck of the bladder) **and your thick** (or: close together, firm, solid) **or frequent weaknesses** (deficiencies in strength; infirmities; sicknesses [note: this may have been a bladder ailment cause by the local water, causing frequent urination]).

This is no doubt a specific admonition for Timothy's specific case and situation, but it also makes clear that Paul was not opposed to drinking a little wine.

24. **The failures** (shortfalls; errors; mistakes; deviations; sins) **of some people are obvious** (portrayed before the public), **continually proceeding into a separation and then a decision which leads into judging, yet also, for certain** (or: with some) **folks, they are normally following upon** (or: after; = they have not yet caught up with them; or: they habitually accompanying [them]).

25. **Similarly, the beautiful acts** (the excellent deeds; the fine and ideal works) **are obvious** (portrayed before the public), **and yet the ones habitually holding otherwise** (having [acts or deeds] in a different way) **are not able to be continuously hidden.**

Here Paul makes some general statements both about folks who make mistakes and about folks who perform beautiful acts and excellent deeds. In both cases, their works and actions are at some point seen and observed. The former normally come into eventual corrective judgment, and I think that he is implying that the latter come into praise and recognition. When you sow seeds, in time the crop comes into view.

Chapter 6

1. **Let as many as are** (or: exist being) **slaves, joined under a yoke, constantly regard** (consider; esteem) **their own masters** (or: owners) **worthy of all honor, to the end that God's Name and the teaching may not be repeatedly blasphemed** (defamed with a false image; vilified; misrepresented in a way that hinders the Light; spoken of injuriously; slandered).

It was not yet time for slavery to be ended, but the slaves were set free from the bondage to the will, the slavery to their alienated humanity and their estranged condition with regard to their Father in the atmosphere – and liberated into a spiritual relationship to others who have been made alive in Him, and into union with God in Christ Jesus. So now they can truly honor and value their masters in the physical realm – and this will bring a good reputation to the called-out community.

2. **Further, let not those having believing masters** (or: trusting and loyal owners who are full of faith) **be in the habit of despising** (having a condescending attitude about; be thinking down upon) **[them], because they are brothers** (= fellow believers). **But rather, let them consistently perform as slaves to a greater extent, because those being continual recipients of their good service** (receiving the well-doing in return; those being supported by the benefits) **are believers and beloved** (or: are folks full of faith and love).
Keep on teaching these things, and keep on encouraging by calling others alongside to aid and exhort them (or: continually perform as a paraclete).

It is a new reality in a new creation – Christ brings excellence and the ability to love the boss, valuing him or her all the more because they are now family. As we are slaves to Jesus Christ (Rom. 1:1), we can also serve others. And we, like Timothy, are to be paracletes to others.

3. **If anyone continues teaching something different, and is not approaching by sound words** (or: in healthful messages; with sound thoughts or ideas) **– in or by those of our Lord, Jesus Christ – even in the teaching which accords with reverence** (or: by instruction which is down from a standing in awe of wellness, with adoration, and with training that is in line with a healthful devotion to virtuous conduct for goodness, that is in true relation to God),

Paul gives four criteria for teaching the message of the Christ: 1) it must be the same message that he taught, not something different; 2) it must come by sound words, in a healthful expression and with sound thoughts and ideas; 3) it must come in and by our Lord, the Anointed Jesus; 4) it must come in teaching which accords with reverence, etc.

Something different would be adding elements of the Law into the message of grace, or saying something that contradicts the teachings of Paul. Lacking any of these four would be to build without a foundation, or to the side of the Path. Unsound words would be bringing in new concepts from Greek philosophy or pagan religions. The teaching and message must be freighted with the Lord; it must come in His Spirit and by Him giving the thoughts, ideas and message to the teacher. It must be in line with a true relation to God, and correspond to reverence and respectful awe.

If these criteria are not met by the teacher or the teaching, then it would be wise to shun them.

4. **he has smoldered and has been puffed up with the fumes of conceit, continues versed in nothing** (capable of nothing; unskilled and able to fix upon nothing; understanding nothing of how to know), **but rather, continues being sick with a morbid craving concerning investigations** (or: seekings; questionings; inquiries) **and debates** (word fights; disputes; controversies), **forth from out of which things continually come to be** (or: are birthed) **envy, strife** (discord; contention), **blasphemies** (slanderous or abusive speeches which vilify, give a false image, defame, aver harm or hinder the Light), **bad** (labor-inducing; unprofitable; malicious; misery-gushed) **suspicions and intrigues,**
5. **altercations and mutual irritations from throughout rubbing against** (= friction with) **people being folks having been utterly spoiled, ruined, corrupted or perished in the mind** (= lost their wits), **and having been deprived from the Truth** (or: defrauded of reality), **folks continually prescribing it a customary law, inferring providing** (or: procuring; acquiring; furnishing and supplying to one's self; capital; financial gain) **to be the Reverence** (the standing in awe of wellness, with adoration; the healthful devotion in true relation to God; or: devoutness).

Vs. 4 describes such a teacher, and points out his self-centered character, lack of qualifications and the resulting bad fruit from his or her instruction: morbid cravings about investigations and questionings; debates that bring strife, envy, abusive talk, along with bad suspicions and intrigues. Not very good results.

Vs. 5 continues the list: altercations and irritations from mixing with people who have been spoiled, ruined and corrupted in their mind – or who have lost their wits. The reason for their condition is that they have been deprived from the Truth (Christ), or they have been defrauded of reality. They are not living in the New Reality (Christ), yet they claim that what they have and preach is the real teaching, the true "Reverence" toward God, and "present truth."

6. **Now the Reverence** (or: devoutness and standing in awe of the ease and well-being associated with God; virtuous conduct for goodness, that is in true relation to God) **is a great providing of supply** (or: means of acquiring; furnishing and supplying to one's self; or: capital) **along with a contented self-sufficiency from independent means,**
    (or: Yet is great financial gain accompanied with independent means this Reverence?)

The term "the Reverence," or, "this Reverence" is a code word for living a godly life, being in right relationship with God and humanity: covenantal community in the new creation. In vs. 6 Paul is either making a statement about true Reverence – that it is a great providing of supply for our needs, making us contented and self-sufficient from independent means – or, he is questioning that the kind of "Reverence" referred to in vs. 5 – which is "**inferring providing** (or: procuring; acquiring; furnishing and supplying to one's self; capital; financial gain)" – is the true Reverence.

I suggest that true Reverence does bring a great supply and provision – in the realm of our spirits and God's reign, and in the advantages of a community in covenant with God and with one another. Material financial gain and capital is incidental, with no direct correlation. See Heb. 11:36-38. But acquiring great financial gain and independent means is not the true "**devoutness and standing in awe of the ease and well-being associated with God,**" as we see suggested in vs. 7 as Paul continues his thought.

7. **for we carried** (or: You see we brought) **nothing into the world** (the ordered system; secular society) **[and] it is evident that neither are we able to carry anything out.**

You don't get to take it with you, so material gain is most short-termed.

8. **So, continuously holding** (or: having) **nourishments** (foods; sustenance) **and effects of coverings** (clothing or shelter) **we will be defended, made a match for, and warded off by these things** (or: we shall be contentedly satisfied with and suffced in these things).

Here is the path of true peace. Having the basic necessities for living, we will be defended by God and be made to be a match for our situations. This is ease and goodness. The parenthetical rendering of the last clause makes a statement about the attitude of the follower of Jesus Christ.

9. **Yet those wanting and determining to be rich are continually falling in – into a trial and a trap and many senseless and hurtful strong passions** (many over-desires void of understanding and bringing weakness; disadvantageous wants and needs), **which things habitually swamp those people, sinking them to the bottom, into ruinous corruption** (or: destruction) **and loss,**

This paints a woeful picture for folks who are determined to be rich. Jesus said that it is with difficulty that such people will enter into the kingdom of God. The last clause is quite a picture – who would want to go this route?

10. **for a root of all the bad things** (the worthless qualities; the injurious situations; the poor craftsmanship; the ugly personalities; the malicious desires) **is the fondness of silver** (= love of money; = covetousness) **of which some, habitually extending and stretching themselves out to reach, are caused to wander off** (or: were led astray) **away from the faith and they pierce themselves through with a rod and put themselves on a spit** (or: they run themselves through, stabbing themselves all around) **for** (or: in; to; with; by) **many pains.**

The problem is our over-desires: our determination to be rich; our love for money. Not only does it sink our boat, it leads us astray and ends up putting us on a slow roast over some fire (the corrective dealings of God, through our circumstances or through other people). Who really wants this pain?

11. **However you, O human from God** (or: O person whose source and origin is God), **be constantly fleeing** (taking flight from) **these things. But continuously pursue** (or: rapidly follow, press forward and chase) **fair and equitable dealings in right relationships in the Way pointed out** (rightwisedness; justice; = loyal covenantal living), **faith** (trust; trustworthiness; loyalty), **love, persistent remaining under in patient yet relentless endurance to give support, meek and gentle sensitivity** (mildness of temper).

Yes, Timothy, turn and run from the desire for wealth, and take a stand against the spirit of covetousness that dwells in our estranged humanity. Instead, focus on the goal (Christ), and pursue the Way pointed out, etc., as well as faith/trust, love, giving persistent support (in patience) with meek and gentle sensitivity. In other words, abide in the Vine and let Him produce His fruit which promotes and enhances the new covenant, and is a boon to all.

12. **Constantly contend** (as in the public games in the stadium or on the racecourse) **the beautiful** (ideal; fine) **struggling contest of the faith** (or: whose source and character are trust, conviction and loyalty). **Take hold of** (or: Get a firm grip upon) **the eonian life** (the Life that has the quality and characteristic of the Age, and pertains to the eons, continuing on into the ages) **into which you were called – even [when] you agreed with** (or: confessed; said the same thing with another person) **the beautiful** (fine; ideal) **like-message of agreement in the sight and presence of many witnesses.**

As elsewhere, Paul uses the stadium games, the racecourse, as an example of disciplined, purposeful living with a goal and expectant future – which is indeed a struggle at times, yet is also beautiful. As you would take hold of the person you are wrestling, take a firm grip on the life of Christ – the life that has the character of this Age of the Messiah, this life in the Spirit of God. We have all been called into this Life of the new covenant. Paul reminds Timothy that he had agreed with and confessed this beautiful "**like-message**" of agreement in the midst of the called-out community – and before society at large. There were the light of their world.

13. **In the sight and presence of God – the One continuously bringing forth all things as living creatures** (the One habitually or repeatedly generating all things alive, keeping The Whole alive) **– and of Christ Jesus, the One who was testifying the beautiful like-message** (or: fine confession; making the ideal and excellent public declaration) **on [the occasion with] Pontius Pilate, I am announcing to you** (bringing this message to your side) **and passing on this notification,**

Paul states his position: in the sight and presence of God. He is standing before the One that is continuously bringing forth all things as living creatures. In other words, he is being as honest and truthful in speaking to Timothy as he is in speaking to God.

There are a couple things to note here: 1) Paul recognizes that he lives in God's presence, and that God is viewing His behavior. We should live with this same awareness; 2) God is habitually or repeatedly generating all things alive, and is keeping the whole universe alive. What an insight that he, by the Spirit, reveals this fact to us. This is another reason to have reverence toward all of creation: God's life is within it all. (*cf* Rev. 21:5 in my translation)

Paul also lives in the presence of Jesus Christ and reminds Timothy that, as he had done, so also did Jesus before Pilate, "**testifying the beautiful like-message** (or: fine confession; making the ideal and excellent public declaration)." Jesus gave witness to the truth, as had Timothy, and now so is Paul in making this announcement and passing on this notification to him.

14. **[that] you yourself keep watch on, so as to guard and preserve, the spotless, not-to-be-laid-hold-of-for-blame implanted goal** (impartation of the finished product within; inward directive; or: irreprehensible commandment), **until the shining upon from** (or: the display in clear light of) **our Lord, Jesus Christ** (or: the manifestation pertaining to, and which is, our Owner, Jesus [the] Anointed [= Messiah]),

Paul, and the other writers of the NT, frequently advise people to keep watch on their lives, so as to guard what has been given to them – in this case the implanted goal, the impartation of the finished product within, which, by the way, is a spotless one which can have no accusation of blame. There is no fault in this covenant (Heb. 8:7). This is the Christ life which has come to him, and to us, by the implanted Word of Life. As one would tend a garden, or a special plant that he has planted, so are we to watch over and guard this life and the directive which is in fact the interior goal itself. It is Christ within us. This can be a tender plant until it is displayed in clear light.

This "**shining upon from our Lord**" is both like the sun shining upon the plant, giving it its life, and also the manifestation which is our Lord, Jesus Christ, and calls to mind 2 Cor. 4:6,
> "**the God suddenly saying** (or: the God Who once was saying), **"Light will shine forth** (give light as from a torch; gleam) **from out of the midst of darkness," [is] the One who shines forth within the midst of our hearts, with a view to illumination of the intimate and experiential knowledge of God's glory – in a face of Christ**
>> (or: [is] He Who gives light in union with our hearts, [while] facing toward an effulgence and a shining forth which is an intimate knowing of the praise-inducing manifestation whose source and origin is God, and which is God, [while] in union with face to face presence of Christ)."

I have given the construction of the Greek in this final phrase of verse 14 first as an ablative, which shows the source of the "shining upon," and then with two functions as a genitive: that of association and reference, and then of apposition.

So this shining upon and manifestation comes from our Lord, pertains to our Lord, and in fact IS our Lord shining both upon us and out from within our hearts. I suggest that this is not an eschatological event at the end of the age, but an occurrence which can happen from time to time in our lives, as He manifests Himself through us and to us.

15. **which, in its own fitting situations** (appropriate seasons; appointed occasions; fertile moments), **will exhibit and point out The Happy and Only Able One** (only Powerful One; alone Potent One)**: The King of those reigning as kings, and Lord** (Master; Owner) **of those ruling as lords,**

Note the plural, "**situations**." This is not a one-time event, but happens periodically in accord with His plans. When God sees that it is a fertile moment for us, or an appropriate situation, He will exhibit and point out "**The HAPPY and Only Powerful One**" to us and to others. He is the King of those reigning as kings, and the Lord, Owner and Master of every one who is ruling as an owner or a lord. The situation in Rev. 11:15 & 17 has happened! He is in charge of all.

16. **the Only One continuously holding and having possession of immortality** (absence or privation of death; deathlessness), **the One continuously making inaccessible** (or: unapproachable) **light His home** (or: dwelling), **Whom not one of mankind sees, saw or perceived, nor is able or has power to see or perceive, in Whom [is] honor** (value; worth), **and eonian strength** (might having the qualities and characteristics of the Age; strength enduring through and pertaining to the eons). **It is so** (Amen)**!**

What a glorious proclamation! The first statement has been the basis of much theological talk, as this is taken as an ontological statement of inference about humanity. Since God alone has immortality, or, the absence of death, therefore humanity does not. That people have died, and do die, makes this claim obvious. The Scripture clearly states, "The soul that sins shall die" (Ezk. 18:4). This use of the Heb. *nephesh* means "a person." So from this perspective, people are not immortal, there is no absence of death in them. Now in Matt. 16:25 Jesus says,
> **"You see, whoever may intend** (or: should purpose; might set his will; happens to want) **to keep his soul-life safe** (to rescue himself; to preserve the interior life that he is living) **will loose-it-away and destroy it. Yet whoever can loose-away and even destroy his soul-life** (the interior self) **on My account, he will be finding it!"**

This seems to be a different use of the word "soul," which here I have rendered "soul-life," even though it (Greek *psuche*) corresponds to the Heb. *nephesh*.

So in both senses, the soul is not immortal. This second use may be from the introduction of Greek thought into the Hellenized Jewish culture, but we find our Lord here using it in this way, and so we need to accept this use. Now as to whether or not we are "a spirit that has a soul" is a topic for another discussion. *Cf* Gen. 3:19 and Heb. 9:27.

It is interesting that He makes "**inaccessible ligh**t" His home, yet we are called His temple, which means we are His dwelling place, from whence He shines forth, as in 2 Cor. 4:6, above. Furthermore, no human has or can see Him, yet Jesus said to Philip, "**The one having seen Me has seen, and now perceives, the Father!**" (John 14:9), so Jesus and Paul are using the word "see" in two different ways. Paul then says that honor/value/worth and eonian strength exists within Him: He is our source for these things.

17. **Pass along the notice** (or: be announcing) **to those rich** (or: wealthy) **within the present age** (the current eon) **to not be habitually high-minded** (proud; arrogant; or: to ponder high things), **neither to have put expectation upon, and thus rely on, the uncertainty** (insecurity; non-evidence) **of riches** (or: wealth), **but rather, upon God, the One continuously holding all things alongside for us** (or: the One constantly offering and providing all thing to us) **richly, unto [our] enjoyment** (or: into beneficial participation; unto the obtaining of a portion to enjoy; [leading] into pleasure),

Here is more practical instruction: rely upon God for your sustenance, enjoyment and pleasure. Material wealth has a way of disappearing, but God "**continuously hold[s] all things alongside for us**." What a promise!

18. **to be habitually energizing goodness and working at virtue** (or: working profitably), **to continue being rich in beautiful deeds** (to continue wealthy in ideal actions and in union with fine works), **to be liberal contributors** (folks good with giving) **– folks having the qualities of community** (people who partner and are ready to share; folks who are fellow participants),
19. **constantly securing and laying away in store for themselves** (or: in themselves) **a beautiful** (fine; ideal) **foundation, into the thing being about to be** (or: unto [that which is] impending; = for the future), **to the end that they can from Being** (or: pertaining to essential existence) **receive upon themselves things pertaining to the Life** (or: so that in themselves they could lay hold upon the existing life; or: in order to lay claim to a way of being that is really life).

This list of admonitions in vs. 18-19 are to be experienced and done from out of Him as the source, provision and ability (vs. 17) to do these things. It is He who energizes us; He who works virtue through us and is rich in beautiful deeds through us, etc. His love causes us to contribute liberally and makes us to be people who have "**the qualities of community**," etc. This kind of life secures a beautiful foundation for our future. The goal is to be receiving upon ourselves the things pertaining to the Life – from Being (or, God). The alternate renderings present two other understandings of what Paul was saying in the last clause of vs. 19: 1) to be able to lay hold of the life that is within us; 2) to lay claim to a way of being that is really life. All three of these readings are a good end and aim in life.

20. **O Timothy, guard and protect that which is placed beside [you]** (or: = the deposit laid up in trust), **constantly turning yourself out of the profane, empty voices** (vacuous sounds; fruitless discussions) **and oppositions** (or: standings against in an opposing position; disputes; antitheses; opposing technical or theoretical arguments) **of the falsely named "knowledge" or "insight"** (or: even contradictions of the lie termed "Gnosis"),

Again we see the admonition to "**guard and protect**" what has been given us. I.e., do not let some other care of this world or some philosophy lead us off the Path. There are profane, empty voices, along with oppositions which come across as knowledge, understanding, insight or new revelations, but they are false. Note his reference to Gnosticism in my parenthetical expansion, in which I transliterated the Greek *gnosis* (knowledge; insight).

21. **which some are continuously professing and making announcements upon. They miss the mark** (or: are without a mark), **swerving** (deviating) **around The Faith and trust.**

Here Paul expands what he said in vs. 20: they either miss the goal, or they have no goal; they deviate from the Path, and miss out on having the Faith of God, and the trust that He gives. But pray for them, their time will come, because:

Grace [is] with you folks! (or: The unearned Favor [is] together with you!)

This is a fact. Be aware of it, enjoy it, drink from it – it is your source and your life.

A MEDIATOR

"**Wherefore, He was indebted** (or: obliged) **to be assimilated by** (or: made like or similar to) **the brothers in accord with all things** (or: concerning everything; = in every respect; or: in correlation to all people), **so that He might become a merciful and a faithful** (or: loyal) **Chief Priest** (Leading, Ruling or Beginning Priest) **[in regard to] the things toward God, into the [situation] to be repeatedly and continuously overshadowing the failures** (mistakes; errors; misses of the target; sins) **of the People with a gentle, propitiatory covering and shelter.**" (Heb. 2:17)

"**... and to come into a full, accurate, experiential and intimate knowledge of Truth, for God [is] One, and One [is the] Mediator of God and mankind, a Man, Christ Jesus** (or: for [there is] one God, and one medium between God and men, [the] human, Christ Jesus)." (I Tim. 2:4,5)

In view of the contexts of these verses, I would suggest that the reason of His being called a "**Mediator**" here has to do with His sacrifice on the cross (or, stake), and not with the ensuing relationship between us and God, which resulted from this act. Note what is said in I Tim. 2:6, which follows His designation as the "*One mediator of God and mankind*,"
> "**The One giving Himself, a correspondent Ransom on behalf of everyone -- the testimony [to come] in their own seasons** (or, fitting situations)."

This could also read, from vs. 5,
> "**... a Man, Christ Jesus -- the One giving Himself an in-place-of price of release over** (for; on behalf of) **all men** [reading *panton* as a pl. masc.], **in their own personal seasons** [reading with the Alexandrian MS, which omits "the testimony"]

The word for "ransom," or "price of release," is *lutron*. In vs. 6, this word has a prefix, *anti-*, which gives the sense of "in-place-of" or "correspondent," which suggests its adequacy of payment for all mankind.

But, to our subject, for the above reason, I do not think that His mediatory function applies to His praying to the Father on our behalf, but rather to our salvation and being ransomed, which He already accomplished.

In Eph. 2:18, I think that the "through Him" refers to His work as the Christ, not to Him as a "go-between." Note the context, beginning with vs. 13,
> "**But now, within Christ Jesus, you -- the ones once being far off** (at a distance) **-- came to be** (were birthed; are generated; are become) **near, within the blood of the Christ.**
> **For He Himself is our Peace -- the One making the both one, and destroying** (unbinding; loosing; razing), **within His flesh, the middle wall of the fenced enclosure: the enmity** (the characteristics of an enemy; the hostility), **rendering useless the Law.... and may reconcile the BOTH within one body -- by God through the cross -- within Himself killing the enmity.**
> **And coming, He brings, and proclaims as good news, Peace to you, the ones far off, and Peace to those nearby, that through Him we BOTH continuously have** (or: hold) **the procurement of access** (conduct toward the presence; admission; being led), **within one Spirit, to** (toward) **the Father.**"

In John 14:6, where Jesus says, "**No one habitually comes** (or, goes) **to** (or, toward) **the Father, except through Me**," this is an explanation, or further revelation, of what He was saying in the first part of the verse, "**I am the Way, and the Truth, and the Life.**" Then in vs. 7, knowing Him is associated with knowing the Father, He concludes saying,
> "**... and from this time you know Him, and have seen Him.**"
Skipping ahead in His discourse to vs. 19-20,
> "**Yet a little while.... you [i.e., the disciples] shall know that I am in my Father, and you in me, and I in you.**"

This was prior to His going to the Father (vs. 12), before His crucifixion and resurrection and glorification.

So what about vs. 13, "**and whatever you may ask in My name**..."
And vs. 14, "**If you ask anything in My name, this I will do**,"? Is this a formula that we should speak when praying? Note the very next thing He says, in vs. 15,
> "**If you LOVE Me, you will keep My commands, and I will ask the Father, and He will give another One called alongside to help, that He may remain** (dwell;

abide) **with you on into the age**."
What is He saying here? Is it not relationship (love) and companionship which is intimate? The whole tone of this passage is not distance or separation, but union.

A person's name gives his identity. It speaks of his character. It can imply ownership or relationship. It can represent authority. Note how Paul figures our relationship to Christ. He calls us "His body." John symbolically refers to us as the Lamb's bride. My body has the same name as my head. I gave my name to my wife. The overcomer will have God's name written on him; will have God's city, new Jerusalem, written on him, and Christ's new name written on him (Rev. 3:12). In Rev. 14:1 we see those with the Lamb having His Father's name written in their foreheads -- once again a figure of identity, character, ownership, relationship (His body, I suggest). I also think that this is symbolic of having the mind (figured in the forehead) of Christ.

I suggest that the phrase "**in My name**," refers to being in Christ and having His authority. I believe that there are many levels of experiencing this, just as there are levels of growth in Christ, from childhood to maturity. Relationships change as we grow up. Responsibility and authority are given to the mature and responsible. But as we are joined unto the Lord, we are joined unto His Name, and we become "no more I, but Christ" Who dwells within me.

Now we see that the disciples spoke such things as, "**In the Name of Jesus Christ of Nazareth, rise up and walk**." (Acts 3:6). Peter used this same title in Acts 4:10. But in both cases he was speaking to someone, not praying. He was identifying the authority that he was using, in the first case, and in Whose Name there is salvation, in the second case.

Now note how Stephen prayed in Acts. 7:60, a simple communication, written for us to read, "**Lord lay not this sin to their charge**." He did not end it with a formula. He did not even say, "Amen."

Jesus taught His disciples to pray as being in relationship with God, "**Our Father**..." We are "**a house of prayer**." Paul's prayers in Eph. 1:17-23 begins with a request for them, "**That the God of our Lord Jesus Christ, the Father of glory, may give unto you**..." and then in vs. 20 shifts into statements about what He (i.e., God) did in Christ, and for Christ, and ends with a comment about the church.

In Col. 4:2, Paul enjoins them to "**Be habitually occupied diligently in prayer** (or: Be constantly stout toward thinking with a view to having well-being; Be continuing persistent and persevering by speaking toward having goodness [in situations]) **within an expression of gratitude** (or: thanksgiving)"

Returning to the word "**mediator**," it was used of Moses and, like the sacrifice of Christ, it referred to a specific event: in this case the giving of the Law (Gal. 3:19). This ordained the old covenant. Jesus, in His blood (Matt. 26:28), ordained the new covenant, together with the new commandment: love. Once again, Heb. 8:6 speaks of Christ as "**the mediator of a better covenant**," being contrasted to Moses in vs. 5; and in Heb. 9:14-16, "... **the blood of Christ -- Who through a spirit pertaining to the ages offered Himself without blemish to God.... And for this cause He is the mediator of a new covenant.... [there is] a necessity to be brought [the] death of the one arranging** (covenanting)..." And finally, Heb. 12:24, "**and to Jesus, a mediator of a new covenant, and to blood of sprinkling**..." Note the tie-in of His sacrifice to being a mediator, in all these references. It was the historical event of Christ -- His death and resurrection -- which mediated between God and estranged mankind, and brought us all near. He function as a Mediator, continues to be in bringing men, individually and in their own order, into living relationship with their Father who was always in love with them. And He is the "**medium**" of spirit through which folks are placed into Him.

Note my translation in Heb. 9:14, "**a spirit pertaining to the ages**," for aionian spirit. The "spirit of sacrifice" is the redemptive and saving spirit which is seen throughout God's plan of the ages.

John A. T. Robinson (*Redating the New Testament*) suggests the date of this letter by Paul at circa AD 58. Other scholars date it later, but from ch. 4:6-8 it appears that he felt that he had "finished the race" of his life or ministry, at the time of writing this second letter to Timothy. It is another of what scholars have categorized as a "Pastoral Epistle." Although a personal letter, the plural "you folks" in the last verse shows that it was meant to be shared with the communities.

Chapter 1

1. **Paul, one sent off with a commission pertaining to** (or: from) **Christ Jesus through God's will, intent and purpose, down from, in line with and with a view to [the] promise of Life – the one [which is] resident within Christ Jesus** (or: through God's design which corresponds to Life's promise, or the Promise which is life: the one belonging to, pertaining to, and from Jesus – in union with [the] Anointing),

Paul did not make a choice to be a person sent off on a mission; he was sent off through God's will, intent and purpose. This sending came down from a Promise, which is life; he was sent in line with Life's promise, and with a view to [the] promise of Life. Each of these renderings gives a different shade of focus, based upon the possible functions of the Greek preposition *kata*, and the functions of the word "life" in the genitive case.

In the parenthetical translation, I give three possible renderings of the name Jesus in the genitive case, and give a second option of the Greek *en* as "in union with." Note that here I separated "Jesus" from "Christ," which I render "[the] Anointing," because they are in two different cases, this latter being the dative case that corresponds to *en*. Most translators overlook this difference, but I chose to point it out as thus potentially indicating the second meaning of the Greek *Christo*. "Within Christ" stresses sphere, location and position; "in union with [the] Anointing" stresses relationship and union with the substance, quality and character of "Christ."

2. **to Timothy, a beloved child** (or: brought forth one; born one)**:
Grace and favor, mercy, peace and harmony** [= shalom] **– from Father God, even Christ Jesus, our Lord** (or: from God [the] Father, and Christ Jesus, our Owner).

In the first letter Paul called Timothy a "genuine child," while here he uses the term "beloved child." I think that these show how Paul regards Timothy's character in the first, while noting how he feels about him in the second. It also shows that Paul was not locked into a mindset of terms. Then he blesses Timothy, or (as there is no verb in this phrase) makes a statement about the source of grace, mercy and peace: they [are] from Father God. As elsewhere, I give the possible renderings of the conjunction *kai* (even; and) as indicating either identity, in the first, or separation, in the second. Note that "Lord" also means "Owner."

3. **I constantly hold grace in God** (or: I am habitually having gratitude to God; I repeatedly possess favor, by God), **in Whom** (or: to, for, by or with Whom) **I continually render sacred service – [handed down] from [the] ancestors** (or: those born earlier; forefathers) **– within a clean conscience** (or: co-knowledge; a joint-knowing from shared seeing), **as I constantly hold** (or: am presently having) **an unceasing remembrance** (or: a memory which leaves no interval) **about you within my expressions of need** (or: seekings of aid; requests), **by night and by day,**

The first clause gives three possible rendering. The first gives the literal of *charis* as grace, but scholars also emphasize the idea of "gratis" in the word, and so tend to render it "thanks" or "gratitude." These latter I regard as secondary aspects of what Paul is saying. The verb means to have, to hold, to possess. Note the different prepositions before "God," as possible functions of the dative spelling of "God."

The word "Whom" is also dative, so you see the options. I also want to point out that Paul does not use the word "worship," but rather the verb "render sacred service," indicating that he continually or constantly does this. He also indicates that this service comes from "[the] ancestors," so that he is implying continuity from the old covenant, yet he does it in a different way since he is not performing as a priest in the temple. Things have changed; the old has passed away.

I expanded the rendering of "conscience" to show the literal meanings of the Greek elements of the word, which I think is worth pondering. I suggest that the other party of the "co-" or "joint-" is God.

Timothy is ever in his thoughts and memory, as he expresses His needs to God, both day and night. The construction indicates that both are concurrent, and around the clock. The one is not separated from the other.

4. **constantly and fully longing** (or: by habit yearning upon [you]) **to see you – having been reminded and being caused to be remembering your tears – so that I may be filled full of joy,**

Vs. 4 shows the relationship Paul feels toward Timothy, feeling their separation and the attendant emotions which they both have.

5. **taking** [other MSS: continually getting] **a suggestion to my memory of the unhypocritical faith**

> (or: the faith that is not overly critical of matters; the trust that is not deficient in its ability to sift and decide; the reliance which is not hyper-judgmental; a faith that is not scrutinizing and judging from an inferior position, and then becoming gradually separated) **resident within you, which first inhabited** (made its home within) **your grandmother, Lois, and then in your mother, Eunice. Now I have been persuaded and stand convinced that [it is] also within you.**

The first rendering, "unhypocritical" is the common one, but consider the parenthetical options, based upon recent research in Koine Greek, and upon the elements which compose the word: *a* (without) – *hupo* (either "under," and thus "low," or, as an intensifier, "hyper" or "overly") – *kritos* (separating, evaluating, scrutinizing, judging, discriminating). Basically, Paul is saying that Timothy's faith and trust are not distorted or harmful. This quality is resident within him, and was also in both his mother and grandmother. It is interesting that Paul twice affirms that this is in Timothy, the second time associating it with his ancestry – through his mother's line. Faith is something that is implanted in a person by a word or teaching from another person.

6. **For** (or: Because of; With a view to) **which cause I am periodically reminding you to habitually and progressively give life by fire again to** (or: revive the fire of; cause the live coal to blaze up for; rekindle the dormant fire into flames of; to again put a spark to) **God's** [A reads: Christ's] **effect of grace and result of favor, which has being** (is; exists) **within you through the imposition** (or: the placing or laying upon) **of my hands,**

Paul urges Timothy to "cause the live coal to blaze up, etc." to give fresh life to the effect of grace within him. This "effect, or result, of favor and grace" may refer to the life of Christ within Timothy, or it could refer to a specific gift – but if this latter, it is interesting that Paul does not specify what it was.

The fact that this came to exist within Timothy "**through the imposition of** [Paul's] **hands**" may be referring to a symbolic act of doing so, as Paul prayed into him, with a view to goodness and well-being, imparting words from his own being into Timothy. Or, it may mean that the actual "placing or laying [hands] upon" him transferred energy and life into him through this act.

7. **for you see, God does not give to us** (or: did not supply for us) **a spirit of cowardice** (or: a Breath-effect or attitude of timidity in us), **but rather [a spirit and attitude] of ability and of power, as well as of love and of soundness in frame of mind**
> (of wholeness in thinking; of healthiness of attitude; of sanity; of sensibility; of controlled reasonableness; of rational moderation; anatomically: of a saved diaphragm).

From this verse continuing on the thought of vs. 6, I think we should conclude that it is the result of grace which was imparted to Timothy, and here Paul describes it as a spirit and attitude of ability and of power and of love and of soundness in frame of mind. On this last phrase, note the expansion of renderings. I gave the anatomical one to reveal an aspect of Greek thought and perception through their using a part of the body to picture a concept.

8. **Therefore, do not become ashamed of** (or: You should not, then, be embarrassed by) **the testimony of and from our Lord** (or: the witness pertaining to our Master; the evidence which is our Owner), **nor yet, [of; or: by] me, His bound-one** (or: His prisoner). **On the contrary, down from God's ability** (or: in the sphere of power, which is God), **experience things of bad quality** (or: worthless encounters) **together with [me] for the message of ease, goodness and well-being**
> (or: But rather, corresponding to God's power, suffer evil and hardship with the evangel; But further, accept your share in bad treatment – in accord with the ability which comes from God – in [the Way of] the Good News),

Again, we see that Paul's focus is "**the testimony of and from our Lord**; the witness pertaining to our Master; and the evidence, which is our Owner" – not a specific gift that Timothy may or may not have had. It is, in fact, "**the message of ease, goodness and well-being**," and Timothy is admonished to, in the sphere of power which is God, and down from God's ability, "**experience things of bad quality**" along with Paul. The parenthetical alternate renderings of the last clause show the variety of nuances that can be expressed from the Greek.

Paul was no doubt in prison when writing this, but he (like Job) does not recognize the intermediary agency and refers to himself as "**His bound-one**."

9. **pertaining to and from the One delivering and calling us** (or: which is rescuing, healing restoring, saving and calling us) **in a set-apart calling** (or: to a holy invitation; for a separated and consecrated call); **not corresponding to our works** (or: down from our deeds; in accord with and on the level of our works' actions), **but on the contrary, corresponding to** (down from; in accord with; on the level of) **His own prior placing** (or: previously setting-forth; thus: definite aim and purpose which He personally is bent on achieving), **even grace: that [which is] being given to us within Christ Jesus** (or: corresponding to His own predetermined purpose and the favor being given to us, [which is] belonging to and pertaining to Jesus, resident within Christ), **before times having the qualities and characteristics of the ages** (before [the] age-lasting time periods; prior to eonian times; = before [the] time segments of [the] ages [began]),

In the first phrase of this verse I gave three functions of the genitive, "pertaining to," "from," and "which is." The first two would make God the antecedent (in vs. 8), while the last one would make the message the antecedent. Either is viable in the Greek text.

The message, referred to in vs. 8, "pertains to the One delivering and calling us" – in a set-apart calling. Note that this last phrase is in the dative without an expressed preposition, so the functions of "in, to and for" are given, in relation to this "call" or "invitation" – since they all make good sense to the context. Therefore, prayerfully consider each option.

181

The next phrase makes an important negative affirmation: it is NOT in correspondence to our works, NOR coming down from our deeds, NOR in accordance with or on the level of our works' actions. To the contrary, this set-apart calling is from and in line with "**His own prior placing – even grace**!" It accords with the grace and favor which is given to us within Jesus Christ. The parenthetical alternate says the same thing in a different way.

The last phrase of this verse tell us that this placing and predetermined purpose took place before the ages began or were created. I think that the suggested paraphrase says it best: "before [the] time segments of [the] ages [began]." God had everything planned out before He even created time, which happened concurrent with the creation of the universe. We were in His mind in this "**before**." What assurance, confidence and expectation this should give to us.

10. **and now** (at the present moment), **being set in clear light so as to become visible** (or: manifested) **through the bringing to full light** (or: the complete shining upon; the full appearance in light; the complete manifestation by light) **of our Deliverer** (Savior; Rescuer), **Christ Jesus – on the one hand, idling down death** (or: The Death) **so as to make it unproductive and useless, yet on the other hand, illuminating** (giving light to) **life and incorruptibility** (the absence of the ability to decay; un-ruinableness) **through means of the message of goodness, ease and well-being –**

It is both the calling and the grace/favor which are being set in clear light so as to be made visible. And this comes through our Savior, Rescuer and Deliverer – Jesus Christ – also being brought to full light, being completely manifested in a full appearance. His being shined upon and manifested had two effects: 1) it idled down death so as to make it unproductive, and 2) it illuminated (or: gave light to) life and incorruptibility. The agency of this was the message of goodness, ease and well-being. So Paul leads us back to the message again: it is through this that Christ comes to light among the nations.

But let us consider effect #1: if this is referring to "the Death," i.e., the death that entered into all creation through the disobedience in the Garden of Eden, then Christ rendered this existential realm and event both unproductive and useless – meaning in essence that "there is no more death" in the new creation, despite its existence in the natural, or old creation. Remember that death used to reign (Rom. 5:14) "**from Adam as far as and as long as Moses** [= Law]." But Moses is no more. Death has lost its job in the new Reality which is Christ.

At the same time, both life and incorruptibility have been given light and have been illuminated in the Life of Christ. What does this mean? For one, it is a Life that has the quality of the Age of Messiah, and lasts through the ages, so that those continuously living and believing (or: trusting) in fact, in this kind of life, "**can by no means die, on into [this] Age**" (John 11:26). It is the power and quality of His Life that gives incorruptibility. But this is not a thing of the flesh, of the natural realm – as was shown by Jesus Himself, as well as His followers.

11. **into which** (or: into Whom) **I am placed** (or: I was put): **a herald** (a public announcer; a proclaimer; a preacher) **– even a person sent off with a mission** (an envoy; a representative; or: = a messenger) **– and a teacher** [other MSS add: of the ethnic multitudes (nations; Gentiles; Goyim; non-Jews)].

The first phrase of vs. 11 can refer to either the message (into which), or Christ (into Whom). It was really into both that he was placed/put: to be a herald that was sent off with a mission, as well as a teacher/instructor.

12. **For** (Because of; In view of) **which cause I am also continuously experiencing** (also: feeling; being affected by; suffering) **these things. But still, I am not feeling shame** (or: I am not experiencing embarrassment), **for I have seen and thus know by Whom I have believed and now put my trust** (or: in Whom I have relied and continue placing confidence), **and I have been persuaded and am continuing convinced that He is able** (He continues being powerful)

to watch over, guard and protect – on into that Day – the deposit placed alongside of me (or: what is entrusted to my charge).

It is because he was placed into the message and into Christ, and further, because he now functioned as Christ's herald and envoy, as well as a teacher, that he was having the experiences to which he refers. The word "experiences" has a wide semantic range, as indicated by the parenthetical expansion. It was not only suffering that he was experiencing.

In all his experiences he felt no shame or embarrassment, because he had seen, and thus knew, by Whom he had believed and now put his trust. Note that the dative phrase can also read, "in Whom..." Having this experiential knowledge has persuaded him that Christ is able, and continues being powerful, to watch over, guard and protect the deposit entrusted to him. He does not specify what this deposit is, but we can deduce that it would have included the Christ life within him, as well as the message which he was sent to herald. The phrase **"on into that Day"** most likely refers to the "Day of Christ, or Day of the Lord" to which he elsewhere refers. That could have been the day when Christ would come for him personally, at his death by the hand of the Romans, or, he could have been enigmatically referring to the Lord's coming in judgment (the term usually referred to this, in the OT) through the Romans, which happened in AD 70.

13. **Keep on holding a pattern** (that which underlies and delineates the sketch or model) **of words that continue giving health, healing and a cure** (or: Habitually have a model of thoughts, ideas and messages [that] are being progressively sound and healthful) **– ones of which you heard** (or: hear) **from my side – within the midst of faith** (or: in union with trust) **and love: that [which is] resident within Christ Jesus.**
> (or: Continually be possessing the under-type – the one within [the] Anointing of Jesus – of healthful discourses and conversations which you heard from me, in faith and love.)

The syntax of this verse can read in either of the two ways which I have rendered it. In the first, it is referring to a pattern of words; in the second to an underlying type or pattern which is in Christ. Again, in the first, it is referring to words that are giving health, and that have a model of sound thoughts, etc., that are in union with trust and faith, which in fact are resident within Christ; in the second it is referring back to healthful discourses and conversation which Timothy had heard from him, in faith and love. Both readings make good sense, and reveal Truth.

14. **Watch over, guard and protect the beautiful deposit placed alongside [you]** (or: the fine and excellent thing that is entrusted to [your] charge) **through means of the set-apart Breath-effect** (or: Holy Spirit) **[that is] continuously inhabiting us** (or: by a set-apart spirit: the one constantly making its home within us).

Once again Paul refers to guarding the deposit, here calling it **"beautiful."** Following the consistency of the ongoing context, I suggest that this deposit is the life of Christ and the message from Him. Note the means of watching over and protecting: through the set-apart Breath-effect (or: Holy spirit) which continuously inhabits us – makes It's/His home within us! This last phrase confirms that we are His Temple, but the reality of it is almost beyond comprehension. Still, we must accept this as fact, and live knowing that we are thus constantly in His presence, and that His presence is continuously within us!

15. **You have seen, and thus know this, that all those within [the province of] Asia were turned away from me – of whom are Phygelus and Hermogenes.**
16. **May the Lord** [= Yahweh or Christ] **give mercy to the house** (or: household) **of Onesiphorus, because many times** (often; frequently) **he refreshed me** (he breathed back cool on me; he souled me up again), **and he was not ashamed of** (or: embarrassed by) **my chain** (= my imprisonment).
17. **On the contrary, on coming to be in Rome, he urgently** (quickly; diligently) **searched for** (or: seeks) **me, and found** (or: finds) **me.**

18. May the Lord [= Yahweh or Christ] **give to him to find mercy, beside [the] Lord** [= Yahweh or Christ], **within that Day! And how much** (or: how many things) **he gave in attending service within Ephesus, you yourself, by intimate experience, continue knowing better.**

Vs. 15 seems almost incomprehensible – how could all those within the province of Asia have been turned away from him? In that he mentions two men specifically, I think that we can assume that he means either the Christian leadership within this province, or he is merely citing two prominent figures of his opposition who were influencing all the congregations. Most likely he is simply speaking with Asian rhetoric (a more sophisticated form of 1st century Hellenistic Greek), employing hyperbole to stress the emotion of how the rejection of his message was affecting him. I suggest that it was through the Judaizers and their return to the Law and ritual that this turning away came about. And we see today that much of Christianity is still turned back to the Law, and away from the message of grace which Paul heralded. We are so blessed to have the record of God's grace through his writings, else we would have only the traditions of the church which often make God's word of no effect.

We see Paul projecting mercy, in 16-18, to the house of Onesiphorus, for his service and faithfulness. Why should he speak for the Lord to give him mercy? Because Paul knew that the Day was coming – the Day when the Lord's presence would be beside Onesiphorus (and others) in a time of judging Jerusalem and the Jewish leadership. Those times would have ripple effects out into the provinces, as the Christians would flee Jerusalem, and many Jews would be killed. There would also come more times of persecution of Christians from Rome.

But this is another aspect of Asian rhetoric, lifting up the contrast of one who continued in support of him (incidentally, the name Onesiphorus means "profitable"), injecting positive emotion to overcome the negative that he had just expressed. We find similar situations throughout the history of the church.

Chapter 2

1. You, then, my child (or: one born of me), **be habitually enabled** (continuously and progressively empowered; repeatedly made powerful inside) **within the grace, and in union with the favor, [which are] within Christ Jesus** (or: [by being] in union with [the] Anointing of Jesus).

Paul again affirms his spiritual relationship of being a father to Timothy, and encourages him to make it a habit to be enabled and empowered in God's grace and favor. He makes it plain that this ability and power, which reside in the sphere of grace and favor, are available to him through union with "[the] Anointing of Jesus," thus having their source in Christ Jesus, not within Timothy.

2. And whatever you hear (or: heard) **from my side through many witnesses, at once place** (or: set) **these things to the side for people full of faith** (or: deposit and commit these things, in trust for safekeeping, to trustworthy and loyal people; inculcate these things in reliable humans) – **whosoever will be competent** (or: adequately qualified) **to also teach others** (or: different folks).

The tense of the verb "hear" is aorist – which simply states a fact without reference to time or kind of action – and thus can refer to what was heard, or what he may now hear. Paul indicates that the information of which he speaks came from him personally, but through many witnesses, and that Timothy is to pass this along to folks that are full of the faith and trust of Christ. The message or teachings are not to be given over to those that are not yet adequately qualified to be teachers, but rather to those who are competent enough to teach and train other folks. Thus, neophytes should not be teachers. It is those who are "full of faith and trust," and are thus "trustworthy, loyal and reliable," to whom the Word and teaching of God should come. Jesus spent three or more years teaching and training His disciples before having them receive the message which was to be proclaimed. Paul himself spent years being taught of the Lord.

3. **Experience things of bad quality** (or: worthless encounters) **together** (or: Accept your share of bad treatment and evil) **as a beautiful** (ideal; fine) **soldier of Christ Jesus.**

Here he uses the life of a soldier as a metaphor of how Timothy should handle hardship and bad experiences and indicates that these worthless encounters are corporate experiences. The verb means "**to experience** (which can include suffering) **the bad together**," which means this is a shared experience, just as a soldier is part of a "company of soldiers." We are part of a body, not lone individuals. How we handle such things should reflect beauty and that which is fine and ideal – in other words, it should manifest Christ, just as a soldier exhibits the reputation and character of his commanding officer.

4. **No one serving a tour of duty as a soldier** (currently performing military service or being at war) **habitually intertwines or entangles himself in** (or: by) **everyday affairs** (undertakings and activities; business performances) **of the course of life** (or: of making a living), **in order that he may please** (or: be acceptable to) **the one enlisting him in military service** (the one collecting soldiers to gather an army).

The metaphor is continued to advise not becoming distracted away from the message of Christ or one's place of responsibility in God's reign. Christ's followers are to be specialists that have a kingdom job, and are not to become entangled (and thus become ineffective) by the cares of this life. The key words here are "**habitually intertwine[d] and entangle[d].**" He is not saying that one should not have a job or raise a family, for it is these very things that support the called-out community and are a part of kingdom living. But these and other involvements should not hamper us in doing the will of the Father, Whose will is relational in its nature. It is the spirit of the system – be it cultural, economic or religious – that brings the bondage through entanglements.

5. **So also, if anyone may be repeatedly competing in the athletic games, he is not normally being crowned with a winner's wreath if he does not compete lawfully** (according to the rules of the game).

Paul moves to another metaphor: following the rules of the game. For us it is following the principles of the kingdom, which Jesus taught, and living in accord to the "**the principle and law of, and which is, the spirit of 'The Life within Christ Jesus'**" (Rom. 8:2), which Paul teaches.

6. **It is constantly binding** (It is of continual necessity) **for the farmer** (or: field worker) **that is habitually laboring in the field to be repeatedly first in taking a share of the fruits.**

And now another picture: the person doing the work should be the first to reap the benefits of the labor. It is a life of love and giving, but it is foremost a life of fairness and equity, for this is the Way pointed out (rightwised living within God's covenant with mankind).

7. **[So] give constant thought to** (or: Continually put your mind to, so as to perceive and understand) **what I am now saying, for you see, the Lord** [= Yahweh or Christ] **will give comprehension and understanding** (a sending and bringing things together into union) **to you** (for you; in you) **within all things and among all people.**

First, let us note that Paul advises giving constant thought to what he, by the Spirit, is saying. This is consistent with the path of the fathers who meditated on the Words of God. Next we have the promise that the Lord will "**give comprehension and understanding**" to us – within all matters, and among our relationships with all people. And these things and people are impacted by what Paul writes to the called-out communities.

8. **Be habitually keeping in mind** (or: remembering) **Jesus Christ, being the One having been aroused and raised, and now continuing risen, forth from out of the midst of dead folks: from out of David's seed!** (or: [Who was] from out of David's seed.) – **corresponding to and in the sphere of my message of goodness, ease and well-being** (or: in line with the good news that came through me),

Here he points out what should be the center of our thoughts, which is the core of his message: Jesus Christ (not our personal ascension in Him). We should keep in mind His being aroused and now being raised forth from the midst of dead folks. Consider what he here defines as dead folks: David's seed! This could refer to those of Christ's lineage who had physically died, and having gone to them He was three days later raised up from the midst of them. Or, Paul could be speaking metaphorically of the Jews that, although physically living, were dead in and by their trespasses and sins. Both perspectives correspond to Paul's message of goodness, ease and well-being. But the larger picture is the entire story of Israel, David being a catch-word and marker of Israel's salvation history. Jesus entered this history, and their story was consummated in His death, which became the death of Israel as it was. He was aroused and raised up from out of this history as the Messiah no longer just of Israel, but of the entire Adamic race (humanity). In His resurrection mankind was gifted with goodness, ease and well-being (*eu-angelion*: the Gospel).

9. **in which I am continually experiencing bad situations** (suffering evil; experiencing bad treatment and conditions of poor quality) **to the point of bonds** (fetters or imprisonment) **as a worthless worker** (a criminal; one who acts badly; a worker of evil), **but by comparison, the Word of God** (or: God's thought, idea and message) **has not been bound or imprisoned, and thus remains untied!**

Paul continues his reference to his message, which now he says is the source of his constantly experiencing bad treatment and conditions of poor quality – even to the point of imprisonment, as if being a criminal or a worthless worker. Nonetheless, his message, **"the Word of God and God's ideas"** are not bound with him, and so remain untied and free. Here we see that even his bonds did not silence him.

10. **Because of this [fact], I continue remaining under to support all people and to patiently enduring all [situations], on account of** (= for the sake of) **the selected and picked-out folks** (the chosen-out people; the elect group; the choice ones), **to the end that they, also, may hit the target of deliverance** (rescue; health and wholeness; salvation) – **that [which is] within Christ Jesus** (or: the one pertaining to Jesus, resident within Christ: inherent in the Anointing) – **together with glory** (or: an appearance; an opinion; an imagination; a manifestation which calls forth praise) **which has the characteristics and qualities of the Age** (or: eonian glory; an age-lasting reputation).

Here is the joy which is set before Paul: the benefit of those to whom he was sent, who he here characterizes as selected and picked-out folks. On their account, he **"continue[d] remaining under to support all people, and patiently enduring all [situations]."** *Panta* (all – plural) is both masculine and neuter, thus my conflated rendering showing that it includes both people and situations (or: things). He is saying that he is remaining in prison, under those conditions, to give support to the called-out communities. The point to grasp here is not how great Paul was, but that what he did in living in the reign of God and in covenant with the called-out had an effect upon those to whom he had been originally sent and was now ministering life via this letter, and I'm sure through his prayers. He was expressing his solidarity with them, but even while imprisoned, in the spirit He was sending forth goodness into them. His "remaining and enduring" had an end in view: that they also may hit the target of deliverance and wholeness which is within Christ Jesus – together with a manifestation which calls forth praise (or: glory) which has the quality and character of the Age of the Messiah, and lasts for the eon to come.

Consider well what this says to us: we, in whatever place or situation, can have a real effect upon those to whom we direct our spirits via our prayers (our thoughts and words are spirit and they are life), and to whom we give service. While laying down our life for our friends, while taking up our crosses, we can do the works that He did. As out of His body came blood and water, out of our innermost being can come a river of living water, bringing life wherever it flows (Ezk. 47:9). We can radiate His glory into every environment to which He directs us.

11. **The Word** (or: Logos) **[is] full of faith.** (or: Trustworthy [is] this statement and the message:) **For since we died together with [Him]** (or: For if we jointly die), **we will also live together** (or: jointly live; co-live);

Christ, the Logos, is full of faith, and His message is trustworthy. The Greek word *ei* can mean either "since," or "if." We can see the second statement positionally and existentially when rendered "since," and we can also see it as a principle of His reign when rendered "if." But note the union depicted in "live together," "jointly live" and "co-live." We are one, as Jesus prayed that we would be (John 17:21, 23).

12. **since we are continuously remaining under for support** (or: if we continue patiently enduring), **we will also reign** (rule as kings) **together with [Him]; if we shall deny** (disown; not consent; renounce; turn our back on [other MSS: are repeatedly denying]) **[Him], That One also will deny** (disown; not consent to; renounce; turn His back on) **us.**

Here, in our doing what Paul did (vs. 10) we not only co-live with Christ, we also co-reign with Him. Likewise, if we deny Him by denying support to others (Matt. 25:45) – or disown, renounce and turn our back on Him – because we are joined to Him and He is within us, we will crucify Him again (put Him back up on the execution stake again – Heb. 6:6) in ourselves, and then like He disowned the Jewish leadership (Matt. 25:12, figured by the foolish virgins), He will have to do so to us and we will have to go off into a time of pruning and burning (Matt. 25:41, 46; Heb. 6:8; 1 Cor. 3:12-17).

13. **[Yet] if we are habitually faithless** (or: unfaithful; untrustworthy; disloyal; without trust or faith), **That One is constantly remaining faithful**
> (or: [Now] if we are repeatedly disbelieving or distrustful, That One continuously remains full of faith, trust, belief and reliance – That One constantly remains loyal and reliable),
for to deny (disown; renounce; not consent to) **Himself, it continues that He cannot** (He is not able; He has no power)**!**
> (or: = You see, He cannot turn His back on Himself!)

But there is hope and an expectation, for the good news is grace and mercy. Even if we are unfaithful, or even without faith and belief, His faithfulness covers our mistakes and sins – for He cannot deny and disown Himself. He cannot deny what He did for humanity on the cross, and He cannot deny humanity because they are now a part of Him in the New Creation, the Last Adam, the Second Human. To do so would be to turn His back on Himself! This shows God's solidarity with mankind.

14. **[So] keep reminding [them of]** (or: suggesting to [their] memory; causing [them] to think about) **these things, repeatedly bearing thorough witness** (giving full evidence and testimony) **in the sight and presence of God** [other MSS: {the} Lord {= Christ or Yahweh}], **not to be constantly debating** (or: fighting about words; contending over meaning of terms; entering into controversies) **– [progressing] into** [other MSS: upon] **nothing useful or profitable; [leading] on to a downturn** (or: an overturning; an upsetting; a negative turn of events [= the opposite of edifying]) **of, or for, those folks continuing to listen and hear [it].**

Paul returns to an admonition for Timothy to keep on reminding them about what he had just said in vs. 13, and before, and to repeatedly give full evidence about it. Note again, that this is to be done "**in the sight and presence**" of God. God is right here; we live in His presence.

Then comes practical advice: don't be constantly debating or contending over the meaning of terms or repeatedly entering into controversies, because this leads into nothing useful or profitable and even brings a downturn to the lives of those who constantly hear such things.

15. **Make haste, with earnest endeavor and diligence, to place yourself alongside as an approved and qualified workman, in and by God** (or: to hand yourself over to and for God, as a tried and approved workman), **one without cause for shame, consistently cutting a straight and direct [path** {cf Prov. 3:6 and 11:5, LXX} **in, to, or with] the Word of the Truth**
> (or: habitually cutting an upright and erect [line through] the Word of Truth; continually cutting with the message of reality in a straight direction; constantly making a straight cut {or: wound} with the speech of this Reality; also: = dealing straightforwardly with the discourse of Reality; or: repeatedly dividing and marking out straight [boundaries] by the Reason which is Truth).

The two renderings of the first clause are based upon the two meanings of the verb (place; present), and the optional functions of the dative case (in; to) of the word "God." The first speaks to his association with the community, alongside of other workers; the second speaks to his relationship to God. His behavior should not bring shame to the community or to God. His life should cut a straight and direct path (a metaphor of rightwised living in fair relationships of the new covenant) with respect to the message of this new Reality.

The last clause should be understood in the metaphorical context of a "**qualified** (or: approved) **workman**," in the first clause. All the alternate renderings of the last clause should be considered, but they should all be related to the "**workman**." 1 Cor. 3:9b-15 may be a parallel use of this metaphor, and if so, then Paul is again speaking to how a person builds (with straight and upright lines, as opposed to crooked ones) and she or he is working upon God's house, i.e., His people. The Word is the material that this workman uses to build the house. This message of the new reality (new creation; new covenant) must be used in a straight and upright way.

If, as I have suggested in the brackets of the translation above, Paul is switching metaphors and is calling to mind Prov. 3:6 (in the LXX) where this same word *orthotomeo* (to cut straight) is used, then it might refer to one who goes before and "cuts a straight and direct path," as in the Septuagint version of Prov. 3:6 (cf also Prov. 11:5 in the LXX where this word is again used with *hodos* – path; road; way). And here, again, the Path or Way is Christ, the Logos. Timothy is to cut through all obstacles and open up the Word of Life for folks which leads them directly to the Father, through the Spirit of Christ.

16. **Yet continue staying at the periphery, going out around so as to avoid the profane, empty voices** (the speeches or discussions without content which cross the threshold into the sphere of that which is not set-apart). **You see, they will cut a passage forward** (progress; advance) **upon more aspects of irreverence** (things pertaining to impiety or attitudes that lack awe),
17. **and their word** (speech; discussion; or: thoughts and ideas) **will have** (or: hold) **pasture** (or: pasturage) **for gnawing and eating away like gangrene** (or: a spreading ulcer) **– of which sort are Hymenaeus and Philetus,**
18. **the very ones who miss the mark, deviating around the truth** (or: reality), **repeatedly saying a** [other MSS: the] **resurrection has already occurred, and constantly turn back** (or: turn again; overturn) **the faith, trust and loyalty of certain folks** (or: of some).

Vs. 16 brings to view the negative path which Paul advises to avoid. We should keep to the periphery, and skirt the profane, empty voices and discussions without content. These lead straight to increased irreverence, and give food to that which eats away like gangrene (which is the result of a lack of circulation of the life-giving Blood through the body of Christ).

He cites two men who he says miss the mark and deviate around truth and reality of the inclusive covenant in Christ. They do this by repeatedly saying that a (or: the, with other MSS) resurrection has already occurred – which statements are overturning, or turning back (to Judaism?) the faith, trust and loyalty of certain folks. Paul does not discuss this further, so we would surmise that the, or a, resurrection has not yet happened since the resurrection of Jesus. But Paul does not give any hint, here at least, as to when he expects this to happen. He makes reference to one in 1 Thes. 4:13-18 (see my discussion of that passage in my comments on 1 Thes.). Since this is in that letter associated with Christ's coming in the clouds – which is normally a figure of coming in judgment – then Paul may have been looking for this to happen with God coming in judgment on Jerusalem (e.g., following the prophecies of Jesus in Matt. 24) which did happen in AD 70 (see books on Preterism for this viewpoint).

19. **Nevertheless** (or: However), **God's firm and solid deposit which is placed down** (a deposit of money; treasure; or: a foundation; basis) **stands, continuing to hold** (or: have) **this seal:**

> **"[The] Lord** [= Yahweh] **knows** (or: knew) **by intimate experience those being of Him** (or: the ones that belong to Him; those having Him as their source),**"** [Num. 16:5; Nah. 1:7]

and:

> **"Let everyone repeatedly naming the Name of [the] Lord** [= Yahweh or Christ] (or: by habit using the Lord's name) **stand away from** (withdraw from; keep away from) **injustice** (that which is unfair and inequitable, which negates relationship and does not correspond to the Way pointed out).**"** [Num. 16:26]

Note that Paul is using OT Scriptures to be a "seal" of God's firm and solid deposit and foundation. The new covenant is rooted and founded in the old; the new creation is an inward renewal and transformation of the old. Paul is using the Torah to establish what he has been saying, but, although referencing it, he is not mixing it in with his message of grace. The first quote indicates that Paul does not consider those of vs. 17 to be "of Him" at this point. The second quote reminds folks that if they claim to be "of Him" by naming the Lord's Name, that they should live a rightwised life in covenant, which is the Way pointed out.

Paul is quoting the Septuagint (LXX) and so renders the Greek "Lord" where the Hebrew has Yahweh, which I have added in brackets to point this out. There is a continuity of Yahweh's presence, involvement and Person. Yahweh knows us by personal, intimate experience, through His Spirit, and Christ, dwelling within us.

20. **Now within a great house** (= a palace**), there are not only golden and silver containers, equipment and utensils, but also wooden ones and earthenware** (ones made of baked clay). **And on the one hand some which [come] into [use for] honor** (things of value; = to be used on special occasions), **on the other hand some which [come] into [use for] dishonor** (things without value; = for everyday use).

Paul is using the metaphor of household containers and utensils to illustrate different levels of existence in God's "**great house**." They each have their own function within the house, and each serves a good purpose; and even if they are used for "**dishonor**," or, "everyday use," it does not make them not a vital part of the household.

This metaphor could be describing the spiritual and God-breathed level, on the one hand, and the carnal and natural, on the other. Or, it could refer to folks that have been born into Christ, on the one hand, and folks who have not yet been "**born back up again**" (John 3:3). The metaphorical comparison should not be taken too far, so as to indicate a person's ultimate destiny, for the following verse indicates that one's kind of use, within our Father's house, can change.

21. **If, then, anyone should ever clean himself out from these** [aforementioned worthless, dishonorable and common] **things, he will be a container** (or: utensil; piece of equipment) **[placed] into [use for] honor and things of worth, having been set aside** (dedicated and being one made sacred and holy) **for honorable and valuable use by the Owner** (Master of the

house), **one having been made ready and now being prepared, [directed and now proceeding] into every good work** (or: virtuous action).

So Paul gives further explanation here, showing that even if a person is, or was used, in the sphere of the dishonorable, he can still clean himself in the blood of the Lamb or the water of the Word, and he will be transferred into the higher realm of life, ready for the Master's use for virtuous action. But lest we deduce self-work for inclusion in the covenant from Paul's words **"clean himself,"** note the perfect, passive participle **"having been set aside."** This is the work of God in Christ. Once placed into Christ, we are given the power and ability of His Spirit to clean ourselves in His life that dwells within us. This is being immersed (or: baptized) into the Holy Spirit and the Fire which is God (as John the immerser/baptizer foretold).

This admonition is in line with his thought expressed about the workman in vs. 15: another encouragement toward a life of excellence through the power and ability of Christ within us. Again, the focus is on a life lived in community with others, for service to people here, and now.

22. **So repeatedly take flight away from the youthful** (juvenile; adolescent) **over-desires** (or: rushing upon innovative things; or: full passions for revolutionary or modern wants), **yet constantly run after and steadily pursue justice** (fair and equitable dealings, in rightwised relationships corresponding to the Way pointed out; also = covenant participation), **faith** (trust; fidelity), **love [and] peace, together with all those persistently** (repeatedly; habitually) **calling upon the Lord** [= Yahweh or Christ] **from out of a clean heart.**

This verse gives a practical application for what was just advised in vs. 21. He is speaking to Timothy, but also as an example for those in the called-out community, folks already living by the grace of God, having been freed from sin and law. So now they have the power of the Spirit to energize them to take flight from things of immaturity, and to run after the values of the community and the fruit of the Spirit: rightwised relationships and justice; faith and trust; love and peace – and do this in partnership with the rest of the summoned community, "from out of a clean heart" – one that has been sprinkled by Christ's blood (Heb. 10:22).

23. **Yet further, consistently refuse** (avoid; request to be away from) **the stupid** (dull; silly; foolish) **and uneducated** (ignorant; crude; untrained) **questionings** (seekings through discussions or debates; controversies), **having seen and now knowing that they are repeatedly giving birth to** (or: generating) **fights** (battles; conflicts).

Here is more from which we should flee, and which we should refuse: the stupid and uneducated questionings which repeatedly generate conflicts and fights.

24. **Now it is continually binding for** (or: it is a constant necessity to) **a slave of [the] Lord** (= Yahweh's or Christ's slave) **not to be habitually fighting** (or: it is not necessary for the Lord's slave to be battling or contending), **but to the contrary [he/she] is to be gentle** (kind; mild) **toward all, qualified, skillful and able in teaching, one holding up under poor conditions** (or: having an upward focus in bad situations; holding an "up attitude" in regard to evil),

This first rendering of the first clause should guide us in regard to whatever stand we may take in regard to doctrines, politics or other issues in life: we are **"not to be habitually fighting."** We live in a kingdom of peace, Melchisedec is our Priest. Note the inference to Timothy being the Lord's slave, just as he referred to himself as one in Rom. 1:1. We are owned by the Lord, and should consider ourselves to be at His disposal. This life is not about us, or about us fulfilling our dreams. It is about Him, and about Him in other people. As Paul admonished in Rom. 12:1-2, our attitude and outlook should be one of taking a stand beside the Living Sacrifice, and being renewed in our thinking about our life here.

The parenthetical renderings shows us that we need not contend for our point of view, or battle against the views of others. We are called to love, and thus "**be gentle**, kind and mild toward all."

We need to learn how to teach, and learn the subject of what we propose to teach, so that in this we can be qualified and skillful. We are called to be like Paul – to hold up under poor conditions, and maintain an upward focus in bad situations. These admonitions have had constant historical occasion for application.

25. **in accommodating meekness and with consideration constantly educating** (training; disciplining; instructing; correcting) **those habitually setting themselves in complete opposition or who offer resistance. May not God at some time give a change of thinking to them** (or: Would not God grant in them and supply for them a change of mind), **[directing and leading them] into a full and accurate experiential knowledge of Truth and reality?**

Again Paul focuses on the fact that we all should be educating, training, etc., other folks – even those who repeatedly set themselves in complete opposition to us and who constantly offer resistance. Obviously this is what God does to and for such folks. Like Him, we need to do this in "**accommodating meekness**" and "**with consideration.**" What a picture Paul describes here!

Now look closely at the question Paul asks, regarding what he has just admonished us to do. Paul has an expectation for educating, instructing and correcting folks (child-training them): his question suggests that God WILL give a change of thinking to them, granting in them and supplying for them a change of mind.

And then his rationale for our behaving toward them in this way: "**May not God at some time GIVE a CHANGE OF THINKING to them**...?" We read in Phil. 2:13,
> "**for you see, God is the One habitually being inwardly active, constantly working and progressively effecting [results] within you folks – both the willing** (intending; purposing; resolving) **and the [situation] to be continuously effecting the action and inward work – above the thing that pleases** (or: over [the situation of] well-thinking and delight; for the sake of [His] good pleasure)."

26. **And then they can and may sober up** (or: would come back to their proper senses) **from out of the adversary's snare** (or: forth from out of the midst of the trap of the person who thrusts something through folks) **– being folks having been [previously] captured alive under** (or: by) **him, into the will** (intent; design; purpose) **of that one** (or: that person).

So we educate them, God puts a change of mind in them, then they can come back to their proper senses from out the adversary's snare. They have been captured and trapped by someone thrusting something through them (a false perception; treatment or a word that wounded them; a dominating situation that pierced their soul; past corporate divisions; etc.) and bringing them under his will. The world is full of such situations. Religions have done this; ideologies have done this; cultures have done this; twisted mind-sets have done this; bad spirits and controlling attitudes have done this – all the things that are adversarial to the Spirit of God, have done this. But with instruction, God will impart a change of thinking by imparting the Word of life into them. This will sober them up (out of the drunkenness from teachings and doctrines of Mystery Babylon – Rev. 17:2, etc.) and bring them to their proper senses, releasing them into the freedom in Christ.

Chapter 3

1. **Now progressively come to know this and continue realizing it, that within [the] last** (or: final) **days hard seasons** (difficult occasions and situations; irksome, perilous or fierce seasons or situations that are hard to deal with; hard appointed periods) **will set themselves in** (will take a stand within; will put themselves in place),

Paul is giving Timothy an imperative: "**progressively come to know this**..." He needed to know and be warned about the hard seasons and difficult situations (note the plural) that were going to be coming to their world within the last days of that "**present evil age**" (Gal. 1:4). Timothy and those to whom he had been sent (as well as the rest of the Roman Empire) were going to encounter these things in their near future – as we know from our historical perspective of those times.

The phrase "**will set themselves in**" or "put themselves in place" is a poetic way of saying that it would not gradually happen and would not be part of the status quo. Something hard to handle was going to insert itself into their lives.

2. **for the people** (the humans; mankind) **will continue being folks that are fond of themselves** (self-loving; selfish), **fond of silver** (= have affection for money or things of monetary value which makes them stingy), **empty pretenders** (impostors; ostentatious self-assumers), **haughty and arrogant** (superior-appearing), **blasphemers** (abusive slanderers; folks who defame with a false image; or: light-hinderers), **uncompliant and disobedient to parents, ungrateful** (or: unthankful), **undutiful** (disloyal; without regard for divine or natural laws; malign),
3. **without natural affection, unwilling to make a treaty** (implacable; not open to an agreement), **devils** (adversarial slanderers; folks who throw or thrust something through people to hurt or cause divisions), **without strength** (without [self-] control), **uncultivated** (wild; untamed; ferocious; fierce), **without fondness for expressions of good or aspects of goodness** (or: without affection for good people; unfriendly; averse to virtue),
4. **betrayers** (traitors), **rash** (forward-falling; reckless), **folks having been inflated with the fumes of conceit** (or: ones being beclouded in smoke), **pleasure-lovers** (ones fond of [their own] gratification) **rather than friends of God** (ones fond of God),
5. **continuously holding** (having) **a form of reverence** (virtuous conduct; pious awe) **yet being folks having refused** (or: turned their back on) **and now denying its power and ability! And so, be habitually turning your steps in a direction away from these folks and avoid them,**

This is a universal list describing people who live according to their estranged human nature, being alienated from existential life in His called-out community. Every generation, since the one spoken of by Paul here in the 1st century, seems to spawn folks like this – it is the human predicament into which we are called to bring the message of goodness, ease and well-being: Christ being birthed within them. But this condition was also what was bringing the coming judgment upon their world, as Jesus predicted. Vs. 4 calls to mind the rich man (a figure of the Jewish leadership in Jesus' day) of Lu. 16:19. The friends of God would have tended, clothed, house and fed (Matt. 25:35, 36) Lazarus, in this parable in Luke. In the days of Paul and Timothy those seasons (referred to in vs. 1) were soon to set in.

Vs. 5 described the Pharisees and Judaizers, but again, every generation produces this kind of religious behavior. Stay away from their system of religion, but love the people.

6. **for you see, forth from out of the midst of these folks are the people repeatedly slipping-in, into the houses,** (or: worming their way into households) **and habitually leading into captivity little women**
> [note: this is the diminutive of "women," thus, perhaps: women of undeveloped character, ability, or inward stature. While the word for "woman" is feminine, the noun "little women" and the following participles are neuter – or – neutral – so this rare word may be a figure for what was a cultural view for "feminine" aspects of all people, e.g., their feelings and emotions, or general receptive qualities]

– those having been piled on and now being heaped up with failures (errors; misses of the target; deviations from the goal; sins), **being constantly, or from time to time, led by** (or: in; to) **various** (diverse; many-colored) **over-desires** (or: full passions; wants and wishes that are rushed upon) [A adds: and gratifications],
7. **at all times** (or: always) **folks** [note: again a neuter, or neutral, participle] **that are constantly learning, and yet not at any time being able or having consistent power to come into a full, accurate experiential and intimate knowledge of Truth** (or: reality).

Vs. 6 is similar to Judah (or: Jude) 4, 8, 10-13, 16-19 (vs. 18 giving the setting as being "the last time," which is the same situation of which Paul is here speaking). The "houses" refers to the house "churches" of the called-out communities. Unfortunately, we can still see these things in our own day.

Vs. 7 aptly describes the Pharisees. And the religion which became their successor, following AD 70, continues to do the same thing – it is unable to bring them to the experiential knowledge of Jesus Christ. But the application of these two verses are, unfortunately, timeless and universal.

8. **Now, in the manner which** (or: by the turn or method that) **Jannes and Jambres took a stand in opposition to** (or: resisted and opposed) **Moses, thus, also, these are continually taking a stand in opposition to** (opposing and resisting) **the Truth and reality: people** (humans) **being ones having had the mind decayed down** (ruined and spoiled down; corrupted; depraved; put into a sorry state), **folks failing to meet the test** (disqualified ones) **on all sides of** (or: about) **the faith** (or: = ones whose trust does not pass the test, from any angle).

Here again we see a picture of the Pharisees and Judaizers who were continuously adversarial to Paul – the agents of satan who came to strike him down. Now Paul tells us that their minds have become ruined and decayed: they are experiencing God's judgment already (*cf* Rom. 1:28; John 3:36). Their concept of faith, and understanding of trust, fails the test. They remain under the curse of the old covenant Law, and the judgment upon Adam. In opposing Christ, they became like the religions of Egypt that opposed Moses. Paul reaches back to Israel's salvation history to put these opponents in an analogous context – a bit more Asian rhetoric to emphasize his point to Timothy.

9. **But they will make no further progress** (will not cut a passage forward) **upon more [folks]** (or: Nevertheless, they won't get very far), **for their mindlessness** (madness; lack of understanding; folly) **will be quite evident** (very plain; obvious; outstanding and in clear visibility) **to all, even as the [madness] of those [two,** i.e., Jannes and Jambres] **came to be.**

The lack of understanding and mindless religion of Jannes and Jambres became evident when God's power was proved greater than theirs. The power of the risen Christ and the pouring out of His Spirit now was obviously greater than the Jewish religion whose Glory and Power had departed, and whose temple cultus was about to vanish.

10. **Yet you, yourself, follow** (or: followed) **closely beside me: in the teaching, by the instruction and with the training; in the leading, by the guidance for conduct; in the purpose** (or: with the fore-setting or by forth-setting; to and for the proposal; [used of setting-forth of the loaves in the holy place of the Temple: Mat. 12:4; Heb. 9:2]); **in the trust, for the faith, by the conviction and with the faithful loyalty; in and by the long-waiting to be in a heat and breathe violently** (or: with long-suffering patience); **in and with the accepting love; in and by the steadfast remaining-under** (or: with persevering, patient endurance while giving support); 11. **in** (or: by) **the pursuits and with persecutions; in** and by **the effects of the experiences and with results of the sufferings – the sort of things that were birthed in me and happened to me in Antioch, in Iconium, in Lystra; the sort of pursuits and persecutions which I bear up under** (or: carried-on under) **and yet out of the midst of which the Lord [=** Yahweh or Christ] **drags** (or: snatched) **me forth from all of them.**

In vs. 10 he gives a list of practices, virtues and qualities that Timothy is (or has been) following (notice the emphatic *Su*, which I render as "yourself") in association with Paul (here I read Paul as using the associative genitive "me" as the object of the verb, which then corresponds to the verb prefix *para* ("beside") rather than the possessive genitive "my," and thus aligning vss. 10-11 with vs. 12; had he intended to say "**my** teaching," etc., the personal pronoun should have been in the dative – to agree with the following list of substantives). This also better explains his use of *hoia* ("**the sort of things that**") in vs. 11. These are qualities of the Holy Spirit, characteristics of kingdom life and aspects of the covenant living in the Breath-effect. Here I conflated the possible functions of the dative, along with the semantic range of the nouns. Consider the locative function, (indicating sphere of each noun, rendered "in") and the instrumental function (rendered "by'), as well as the associative function (rendered "with"). Note the definite article before each noun. This should alert us to the fact that Paul is not using these nouns as generalities, but is referring to the specific things and qualities that pertain to covenant inclusion in the new creation within the Christ-life. Timothy follows beside Paul (the verb is in the aorist indicative, so this is not an imperative, and it can refer to either present action, or past action) as they are being led and empowered by the Spirit – this is not a "to-do list," but rather, they are shared qualities and aspects of those who are in Christ.

Then in vs. 11 he moves to the aspects of "carrying one's cross" (Matt. 16:24-28 – note that vs. 27-28 speak of the same coming "last days" of which Paul here speaks), and the things which Timothy and should expect to have to "remain under." He continues using the aorist tense, referring to specific things in his past, yet in the last two verbs showing that he both did, and from time to time still does experience. Yet he ends with an expectation: the witness from his own life – the Lord's deliverance and an ongoing faithfulness (the Lord had "snatched" out of those things, but – as a timeless aorist – it is His nature that He "**drags [him] forth from all of them**." Here we see an example of God's covenant righteousness in faithfully "saving" Paul out of difficult situations – right here in this life. It was the Judaizers and the Jews of the old covenant religion who were pursuing and persecuting him.

12. **And indeed** (or: And so) **all those habitually resolving** (intending; willing) **to be continuously living in a reverent, devout and pious manner with virtuous conduct from ease and goodness within Christ Jesus will be pursued, persecuted and harassed.**

Now he makes vs. 11 quite plain: we will all be pursued, persecuted and harassed. He speaks of no exceptions.

13. **Now people of a bad condition and of an harmful disposition** (useless and malicious humans who bring misery and hard labor), **as well as sorcerers** (folks who wail and cast spells; or: impostors and swindlers; those who juggle a situation), **will cut a path forward upon the worse** (or: will advance and make progress from bad to worse), **repeatedly leading [folks] astray** (or: causing [folks] to wander [from the Path]) **and progressively being led astray** (or: caused to wander).

Just as we will be persecuted, those who are "**of a bad condition**" will continue on from bad to worse. Those of false religions, or perhaps here the Judaizers, will repeatedly lead folks astray, while themselves being progressively caused to wander.

Consider the semantic range of meaning for "**sorcerers**." The first parenthetical definition describes being in an ecstatic state of emotion or spirit, while speaking to situations or about people. This can be seen in many religions and in a variety of circumstances. The second and third definitions more describe social and commercial manipulations in order to gain advantage.

People can be led astray by false religious practice (e.g., impostors who pose as prophets, while speaking from their own imaginations) as well as by false and unjust economic schemes. Teachings which give support to controlling the people by a select few have led multitudes astray.

14. **Yet you, yourself, be constantly remaining within what you learned and in those things of which you were persuaded and became convinced** (became assured), **having seen, and so knowing, from whose** (what folks') **side you learned [these things],**
15. **and that from an infant** (babe) **you have seen and thus know [the] sacred Scriptures** (or: Temple writings)**: the ones being constantly able** (those continuously having power) **to give you wisdom – [that leads you] into deliverance** (wholeness, good health, rescue and salvation) **– through Jesus' faith, resident within Christ** (or: through means of the faith and trust that [exists] in Jesus [the] Anointed; by the faith which is Jesus, in union with an Anointing).

Consider well this imperative: "**be constantly remaining within**" what Paul had taught him. Don't go to other religions or philosophies. Vs. 15 advises him to stay with the Scriptures – get wisdom from them, not the mystery religions or even the writings of the rabbis. The Scriptures continue having power and are constantly able to give wisdom and bring deliverance and wholeness. But note how he ends this imperative: all this comes through Jesus' faith, which is resident within Christ, and is accessible through union with the Anointing. It was His faith that accomplished our salvation; this same faith resides with Christ.

The last two phrases have the name Jesus in the genitive, corresponding with "through," and thus my final rendering of apposition "the faith which is Jesus," along with the genitive of possession, "Jesus' faith." The Greek of "resident within Christ" puts "Christ" in the dative because of the preposition *en* (resident within), so I have separated the terms Jesus and Christ. However, many grammarians overlook this and simply render it as in my second option, "in Jesus [the] Anointed." May His Spirit unveil the correct understanding to us, or as often, cause us to see that both are correct.

16. **All Scripture [is] God-breathed, and [is] beneficial to furtherance toward instruction** (or: Every inspired-of-God [temple] writing [is] also profitable {of advantage; [gives] augmentation} with a view to teaching and training), **toward** (with a view to) **testing unto proof** (or, negatively: exposure; laying bare), **toward full restoration to straightness** (or: straightening-up upon; = improvement), **toward child-training** (education; discipline) **of the person within the Way pointed out** (the one in rightwised [covenantal] relationships with fair and equitable dealing), 17. **to the end that God's [corporate] Person** (or: the person belonging to God; the human having his origin in God; humanity in relation to God) **may be exactly fitted** (can exist being precisely prepared; would be entirely suited), **being one having been completely furnished and equipped toward every good work** (with a view to every virtuous and excellent action).

Again Paul directs us to stay with the Scriptures, reminding us that they are "**God-breathed**," and thus beneficial in all the ways that he lists. The Greek *graphe* (writing) is here used to refer to the temple writings, not writing in general. It became a technical religious term for the Jewish, and later the Christian, religions.

The parenthetical rendering of the first clause shows that the Scriptures were beneficial for teaching and training. The phrase "**toward** (with a view to) **testing unto proof** (or, negatively: exposure; laying bare)," has historically been abusively misused, but when done in love and in quest for right understanding can lead "**toward full restoration to straightness** (or: straightening-up upon; = improvement)." The Scriptures are best used in this way through the Holy Spirit applying them to us, personally. Following the Reformation, Christians made use of them to give children a general education, as well as to instruct them in the things of Spirit and life in the kingdom – or, as I have rendered it "**within the Way pointed out**."

Humanity in relation to God needs the Scriptures so that they can be exactly fitted, precisely prepared and entirely suited, being completely furnished and equipped with a view to doing good works and acting in excellence (e.g., social and environmental responsibility; bringing and existential expansion of God's reign with our communities), and to rightly bearing the image of God.

Chapter 4

1. **I am habitually giving thorough witness** (or: constantly testifying and showing evidence in every direction), **in the sight of God – even Christ Jesus: the One now being about to be progressively separating living folks and dead folks** (or: continuously making a decision about or judging living ones and dead ones) **down from** (in accord with; corresponding to; in the sphere of; in respect to; in line with; [other MSS: even]) **His full manifestation and His reign** (or: [with other MSS: and then] His added display as well as His sovereign kingdom activity).

honor all people." This is to be done "**within every emotion which is long in arriving** (in all long-suffering patience)." This admonition would apply to all of the foregoing imperatives. I have added a short study on this word at the end of the comments on this chapter.

Then he says, "**and by teaching** (or: in union with instruction and training) **give aid, relief, comfort and encouragement as you call [others] to your side** (perform as a paraclete)." I give here a transliteration *paraclete* of the Greek word that has been brought into English as "Paraclete" (Comforter) referring to the Holy Spirit, in John 14:16, 26. Just as we are to do the works that Jesus did, we are also to do the works of the Holy Spirit. We do this by teaching and in union with instruction and training.

3. **For you see, there will be an appointed season** (a situation; a fitting period of time) **when they will not hold up to themselves** (or: sustain; hold themselves upright by; hold themselves up in; or: put up with; tolerate) **instruction** (teaching and training) **that is being continuously healthy and sound, but rather, they, habitually having their ear gratified by rubbing, scratching or tickling** (having their hearing titillated; hearing what their ears itch to hear; or, as a middle: constantly procuring pleasurable excitement by indulging an itching) **will pile and heap upon themselves** (accumulate for themselves) **teachers in line with and corresponding to their own rushing emotions** (over-desires; full passions),
4. **and then, on the one hand, they will twist the ear** (or: the hearing) **and turn away from the Truth and reality, yet on the other hand, they will be turned out** (have their [steps] turned out of [the Path] into a direction) **upon the myths** (fictions; legends; speeches; rumors; stories; tales; fables; things delivered by word of mouth).

In vs. 3-4 Paul warns Timothy of a coming season that corresponds to the coming judgment of the Lord. The need for the admonitions in vs. 2 applies to this season that was soon to be upon them all. Paul had already encountered these things through the Judaizers in Galatia, and elsewhere, as well as false sent-forth folks that had come in among the people at Corinth (2 Cor. 11:13). Judah (Jude) also warned of this, and Jesus spoke of the arising of false prophets, and then the love of many growing cold because of the increase of lawlessness (Matt. 24:11, 12).

Here Paul describes another aspect of this season, showing the cause of folks straying from the Path of life: they will not hold up to themselves, or keep themselves in, instruction and teaching that is healthy and sound, but will instead seek teachers that tell them things that gratify their rushing emotions and over-desires. An over-desire is something that you want too much; a rushing emotion is that which compels us beyond the leading of the Holy Spirit, a feeling that is not in line with sound teaching, but pushes us to want to experience good feelings. These lead us to turn our hearing away from Truth and reality, and be led astray into myths, fictions, rumors, stories – things that come to us by word of mouth. This is a condition that has been among the called-out communities even in this age, and to the present moment.

5. **Yet you – you be habitually sober** (not intoxicated [by such things]; clear-headed and steady) **within all things and among all people; experience the bad and the ugly** (or: suffer the evil and the worthless) [A adds: as an ideal (beautiful; fine; excellent) soldier of Christ Jesus]; **perform [the] act** (do [the] deed; produce the action; construct a work) **of one who brings goodness and well-being and announces ease and good news** (or: act [like] a man who has good news to tell); **be fully bent on and bring your attending service to full measure, with complete assurance and absolute certainty!**

So Paul stresses to Timothy not to be intoxicated by such things, but rather to keep a clear head and be steady: sober. He would be within the midst of such things, as we are now, but he was to experience these ugly and worthless things while at the same time producing the action and constructing a work of one who brings goodness and announces the well-being and ease that are in Christ. He is to "**be fully bent on and bring his attending service to full measure**" within such situations and among all people, and do it "**with complete assurance**" that God was working through him. This same word, *plerophoreo*, is used in 1 Thes. 1:5 in its noun form

197

describing how Paul and Timothy had brought the good news to that town. Keep in mind that he was sent to called-out communities of believers. In our day it can mean being sent to "churches" that have turned to myths of pagan traditions (which have over time become "orthodoxy").

6. **You see, I, myself, am already being progressively poured out as a drink offering, and the fitting situation** (the season; the occasion) **of my loosing up** (or: my kairos of loosening again [the tent pegs and ropes, or, the ship moorings]; or: the situation of my dissolution [as in breaking camp]) **has taken its stand upon [its appointed place] and is imminent.**

Paul realizes that his end is near, of which he here speaks metaphorically. He had taken up his cross to follow Christ and had been already pouring out his life on behalf of the called-out, but now the final time approached – as it did for Jerusalem. The parenthetical expansion on "**loosing up**" indicates that it is his time for moving on – one way or another. It could mean that he expects a soon release from imprisonment, and vs. 7 may simply refer to this stage of his ministry.

7. **I have contended the beautiful contest in the racecourse** (or: I have with agony struggled, wrestling in the ideal combat {the fine fight} in the public games); **I have finished the race** (ended the racecourse; reached the goal of my contest; I have fought to the finish); **I have kept** (observed; watched over; guarded; kept in custody) **the faith, trust, confidence and loyalty.**

As he reviews his years since being apprehended by Jesus on the road to Damascus, he knows that he has done this by the Spirit of God, which enabled him to do what he metaphorically calls "**contended the beautiful contest**," etc. He guarded Christ's faith, kept in custody the trust that Jesus had given to him, and had done so with confidence and in the loyalty of Christ. A testimony that gives an example for us all.

8. **For the rest** (or: Finally; Henceforth) **the winner's wreath of the Course having been pointed out** (the athlete's laurel wreath consisting of the rightwised relationship in fair and equitable dealings, and pertaining to the justice of right behavior on the course; or: = the wreath from covenant inclusion and participation) **continues laid away for me** (or: is presently reserved in me), **which the Lord** [= Christ or Yahweh], **the Fair** (Equitable; Just; Rightwising; [Covenant]) **Judge** [of the games], **will pay to** (or: award in) **me within the sphere of that Day – yet not only to me! ... but further, also, to all those** (or: in everyone) **being ones having loved His full appearance in Light** (or: the complete manifestation of Him; His fully bringing things to light; the shining upon things pertaining to Him; His full and accurate manifestation).

The dependent clause that begins this verse ties in the metaphor of running the Course (or: the Way; the Path) with rightwised living – fair and equitable relationships that are just and are turned in the right direction, i.e., toward Christ, in covenant membership and participation. This life in Christ is sometimes called walking. Paul often refers to it as running or being in one of the stadium games. He knows that he has won the wreath that was given to a winner of these games. What he means is that his life has been successful in that to which he had given it. He depicts God as the Judge at these games who awards the wreath to the successful contender. He knows that this is not just for him, but for ALL those "**having loved His full appearance in Light**."

The dative case without an expressed preposition is seen in "**me**" (for; in; to) twice and in "**to all those**/in everyone." Any of these renderings make sense, but the locative "in" speaks of this recognition (the wreath) and the award being within us.

Now he does not make that last phrase clear as to which manifestation he was referring. Jesus came as the Light (John 1). But in using the same term "manifestation, etc." here as he did in vs. 1, perhaps he is – in tying it to the end of the course (his life, and the age) – referring to the upcoming manifestation which accompanied the destruction of Jerusalem in AD 70.

The rendering "His fully bringing things to light" and "the shining upon things pertaining to Him" can apply to any point since He first came, and to the continuum of His presence through His Spirit ever since.

9. **Make haste with earnest endeavor and diligence to come to me quickly,**
10. **for you see, Demas, loving the present age, forsook and abandoned me and went into Thessalonica; Crescens into Galatia; Titus into Dalmatia.**
11. **Only Luke is with me. Picking up Mark, be bringing [him] with you, for he continues being very useful to me, with a view to attending service**
12. **– now I sent off Tychicus with a mission into Ephesus –**
13. **[and] in coming, be bringing the traveling cloak, which I left behind in Toras with Carpus, and the little scrolls – especially the parchment notebooks** (or: vellum [note: which is made from dressed animal skins]).

These verses pertain to personal matters concerning Paul, and his desire to have Timothy soon come to him, etc. They obviously apply to his present time and context.

The Greek φαιλονης/φελονης, here translated "traveling cloak," literally means "bark." The Syriac version renders it "valise; book carrier." Vincent notes that the 5th century lexicographer Hesychius (of Alexandria) explained this word as a "case." He also says Phrynicus (3rd century) describes it as a receptacle for books or other things, and that this word "a wrapper of parchments" was translated figuratively in Latin by *toga* or *paenula* "a cloak." Nevertheless, Vincent and most other scholars stay with the traditional rendering, "cloak."

14. **Alexander the coppersmith** (or: metalworker) **displayed many bad** (worthless; evil) **things [in his behavior] to me – the Lord** [= Yahweh or Christ] **will award to him** (or: give back in him; pay back for him) **corresponding to his works** (down from his deeds and on the level of his actions)
15. **– from whom you, yourself, also be constantly guarding yourself against, for he stands** (or: stood) **in opposition to our words** (or: thoughts, ideas and messages).

Paul acknowledges Alexander's deeds, but leaves it up to the Lord to do as He sees best in giving back in him (or: to him), or perhaps even "pay[ing] back for him" to the level of his deeds, and down from his actions. His decision will be fair and equitable. Yet Paul advises Timothy to guard himself in regard to Alexander.

16. **Within my first verbal defense no one happened to be beside me** (no one came along with me), **but rather, all forsook** (abandoned; other MSS: were forsaking and abandoning) **me – may it not be put to their account** (may it not be counted against them)**!**

Here, again, Paul refers to everyone abandoning him. I don't think that he is saying this to complain, but rather to let folks know that they can expect the same. Good news, when it is in conflict with established religions, comes with a price to the person bringing it.

17. **Yet the Lord** [= Christ or Yahweh] **took a stand beside me** (or: stood alongside in me) **– and He empowered me** (enabled me; gave me inward ability), **to the end that through me the message that is being heralded** (the contents of the public proclamation) **would** (or: may; could) **be fully carried throughout with complete assurance, to full measure, and with absolute certainty, and so [that] all the ethnic multitudes** (nations; Gentiles; Goyim; non-Jews) **would** (could; may) **hear [it] – and I was dragged** (or: drawn) **from out of the mouth of a lion!**

But look at Paul's reward: having the Lord take a stand beside him! We, too, can expect to be empowered (inwardly enabled) by His presence. The Lord is here to "stand alongside us," or "take a stand in us," so that through us the message will be heralded and fully carried throughout, with full assurance. Note that he then says "**and so [that]**" all the ethnic multitudes would hear

[it]. In other words, this same message was presented to the Jews first, but now through the Lord's inward ability in Paul it came to the rest.

The Lord taking a stand beside him was not just for moral support: He dragged Paul out of danger (metaphorically, from the mouth of a lion). His adversaries were about to devour him – Alexander and the Judaizers. Is this the same lion that Peter refers to in 1 Pet. 5:8?

18. **The Lord** [= Yahweh or Christ] **will drag** (or: draw) **me away from every harmful act** (malicious or evil work) **and will deliver me into the midst of the reign and kingdom – the one [having dominion] upon the heavens** (or: into the realm of His activities and way of doing things: the one [exercising authority] upon, and which can be compared to, the atmosphere) – **which is from Him and belongs to Him, in Whom [is] the glory** (or: for Whom [is] the reputation; by Whom [is] the manifestation of that which calls forth praise; to Whom [is] the good opinion), **on into the ages of the ages** (or: into the principle ages which consummate all the ages; into the obscure time periods of the ages). **It is so!** (Amen)

This first clause shows Paul's confidence in what God will do for him, based upon what He had done in the past (vs. 17). Note the descriptive verb that he uses, "drag," and the picture it produces of God working on our behalf. And the change of locations or spheres: away from harmful acts and malicious works, and into the midst of the realm of His activities and way of doing things – into the midst of His atmosphere. This declaration is similar to what he said in Col. 1:13,

> "**He who drags us out of danger** (or: rescued us) **forth from out of the midst of the authority of the Darkness** (Darkness's jurisdiction and right; = the privilege of ignorance), **and changes [our] position** (or: transported [us], thus, giving [us] a change of standing, and transferred [us]) **into the midst of the kingdom and reign of the Son of His love.**"

The next part makes a statement about Him, "in Whom [is]....," etc. Observe that I choose to supply the present tense "**[is]**," rather than the normal doxology form "[be]." There is no verb in the text, and I see Paul continuing in making a declaration, rather than slipping into a religious doxology.

I give a literal rendering of the last phrase first, and then expand it with two parenthetical options, the first of which gives a suggested influence of Hebrew idiom (such as, "the holy of holies"), with the second being another literal rendering which suggests a future time too distant to presently see.

19. **Embrace Prisca and Aquila and the household of Onesiphorus, as you give them my greetings.**
20. **Erastus remains in Corinth, but Trophimus, continuing weak in sickness, I left behind in Miletus.**
21. **– Make haste with earnest endeavor and diligence to come before winter** (the rainy and stormy season)! **– Eubulus, Pudens, Linus, Claudia and all the brothers** (= fellow believers) **each send hugs and good wishes.**

These verses give personal greetings, speak of individual situations, a final instruction to Timothy about his return, and sends greetings from those with Paul.

22. **The Lord** [= Yahweh or Christ; A reads: Jesus; others: Jesus Christ] **[is] with your spirit** ([is] in accompany with your breath)! **Grace and favor [are] with you folks. It is so!** (Amen.)

The first statement is a personal affirmation to Timothy, about the Lord, or Jesus, being with his spirit. The last statement is to the community, affirming that God's grace and favor are with them.

Comments on 2 Timothy

A Short Study on Epitimao

The first definition that Bullinger gives for the word normally translated "rebuke" (*epitimao* -- from *epi*, upon, or, fully [in composition]; and *timao*, to hold in value, honor, respect; to consider precious or ascribe worth) is: "to put further honor upon, estimate higher."

The Analytical Greek Lexicon's first listing for this word is: "to set value upon."

Liddell and Scott give: "1. show honor to; 2. raise in price."

Now there are other meanings and uses of this word which have a negative connotations, such as, (of judges): lay a penalty on (a person), or, estimate value (as in damages to be awarded); censure; chide; admonish strongly; enjoin strictly.

So what determines whether we choose the positive meanings, or the negative? Should both be included in a verse such as II Tim. 4:2? Perhaps there would be appropriate occasions for a negative word to someone, as an admonition, if the Father so spoke to us to do so. And how about where Michael is speaking in Jude 9,

> But Michael (The One Who is like God), the ruling agent (the first,
> chief, or original messenger), when making a distinction (a thorough
> separation; a discernment) to the devil, reasoned (deliberated, spoke
> through) concerning the body of Moses. He did not assume to bring
> a blasphemous judgment upon [him], but rather, He said, "The LORD
> [= Yahweh] might hold you in honor (may set value upon you).

Now notice Jude 10 continues,

> Yet THESE [men who came in unobserved – vs. 4] blaspheme what
> indeed they DO NOT UNDERSTAND...

Note the contrast of these to the behavior of Michael in vs. 9.

Turning to the gospels, Mat. 8:26b uses our word in speaking to the winds. May I suggest a different approach to this verse, as follows,

> Then, being roused, He respectfully gives direction to the winds and
> to the sea, and there comes to be a great calm.

Now consider that in vs. 27 the disciples say "that the winds as well as the sea are obeying Him." He did not "devalue" them as our English "rebuke" often does, He simply gave respectful direction for them to become calm.

Let's move to Mat. 12:15-16. Here this word is translated "charged" by the KJV, and "warned" by the NIV & Concordant versions. Jesus has just cured all those who were following after Him at that time. Then, He "gives respectful direction" (I suggest) "to them to the end that they should not make Him manifest."

In the situation of Mat. 16:21-23, Peter uses this word in what seems to me to be a contradiction of what Jesus has just told them must happen to Him. Do we need to make Peter out to be giving Jesus a "rebuke" (i.e., "sharp, stern disapproval; reprimand")? Peter begins his statement to the Lord using words that are considered to be a Hebraistic formula, "May you be spared this, Lord!" Literally the phrase reads, "Propitious to You," or "Favorableness for You, O Lord!" Then Peter goes on to say that "this will by no means be for You." So, I feel that Peter, tho' speaking a contradictory thought, did so respectfully, even adding honor and worth to his Lord (in his carnal mind). Therefore, I suggest something like the following for vs. 22,

> And Peter, having taken Him to himself, begins to respectfully add
> honor to Him by enjoining Him, saying, "May mercy be shown to You,
> Lord..."

Peter regards Him of much greater value than what he understands Jesus to have indicated would happen to Him in Jerusalem. Peter is thinking of Him as their King, not someone to be abused by the elders and priests!

Now the use of this word in regard to the actions and words spoken concerning the little boys brought to Jesus (Mat. 19:13) would seem to fall into the negative connotation, yet it need not imply that the disciples were disrespectful to those who brought the boys, or to the boys themselves. Jesus, in vs. 14, indicates that their actions and words "hindered" access of the boys to Him, but this could have been done by "strong admonition," or simply by "enjoining" the parents to not bother Jesus. The term "rebuke," in our day, carries a connotation of a "put down." This was not necessarily the case.

In the case of the two blind men crying out to Jesus, in Mat. 20:30-31, the *New World Translation* simply says,

> But the crowd sternly told them to keep quiet.

How about Mark 9:25? Here Jesus speaks to the unclean spirit, and gives it orders to get out of the man's son, and to enter no more into him. Would it not fit the description of the event to say that Jesus "respectfully gave orders to the unclean spirit"? Or, do we need the concept of a "rebuke," considering the broad meaning of this word? In view of the fact that until the advent of Jesus, "God's wrath was continuously abiding" (John 3:36) upon all, and that this was part of His Father's plan, would it not seem reasonable that although He was unloosing the works of the devil, that He might do so with respect toward the evil which His Father had created (Isa. 45:7 or Amos 3:6, in a literal translation)?

Well, my object was not to look at every use of this word, but rather to cause you to consider the context when you see the word "rebuke," in the common translations, and ask Father, "Just what is being meant by *epitimao* here?" Can there be a sense of honor, value and respect – the root concepts of this word – as it is used in this verse?

According to Robinson this was written circa AD 57. Titus was a missionary co-worker, having been a traveling companion (Acts 28), and Paul considers him his son in the faith (1:4). This is the third extant letter by Paul that scholars have classified as "pastoral," and he is sending it to the island of Crete where he had left Titus (1:5) with the newly founded community there.

In chapter 1 Paul addresses the qualities and character traits that the older folks should have if they are to be leaders in the community, God's house-managers, or care-givers and overseers (1:6-9). Next he speaks to the situations of unruly people who have negative qualities (1:10-16).

Chapter 2 first covers admonitions to various categories of community membership, followed by personal instructions to Titus, then advice for slaves, ending with general admonitions all of which are based upon God' saving and redemptive work. Chapter 3 speaks to issues for focus in regard to socio-political aspects of the called-out community, while reminding folks of the existential condition from which Christ delivered them, and again describing the results of the Christ event (vss. 3-7). 3:9-11 returns to personal advice to Titus.

Chapter 1

1. **Paul, God's slave** (a slave of God; one bound to, subjected under and owned by God), **yet one sent away with a commission** (as an emissary, envoy or ambassador) **from, pertaining to and belonging to Jesus Christ** (or: a representative of Jesus [the] Anointed), **with a view to and corresponding to [the] faith of God's chosen folks** (or: in line with a trust and loyalty possessed by and characteristic of God's selected and picked-out ones) **and the full, accurate and precise intimate knowledge and experiential insight of Truth and Reality – the [truth and reality] corresponding to and in accord with reverence** (or: down from goodness which produces virtuous conduct with devoutness, and in line with ease from a true relation to God) –

Paul considers himself to be God's slave: one owned by Another and who does the will of his Lord. He was one sent away on a mission for Jesus Christ, the subject of which mission was the faith of God's chosen folks, and in line with their trust in and loyalty to Jesus Christ. He brought to them the full, accurate and precise intimate knowledge and experiential insight of the Truth of God, and the Reality in Jesus Christ. This truth and reality was the New Being embodied in the risen Messiah, the source of the new creation. It was also the truth and reality that corresponds to reverence toward God and His creation, and which produces "virtuous conduct with devoutness," and comes from goodness which is "in line with ease from a true relation to God." The last phrase of this verse gives an expanded definition of both the preposition *kata* (corresponding to; in accord with; down from; in line with), and of the noun *eusebeia*, whose prefix *eu-* means goodness and ease. This particle qualifies the virtuous conduct and devoutness which exemplify a true relation to God. Any sense of "religion" in this word should be viewed through the lens of the new heavens and earth that Christ has brought into being (Rev. 21:1).

2. **[based; standing] upon an expectation** (or: hope) **of and from eonian life** (life having the quality and characteristics of, and its source in, the Age [of Messiah]; life for and throughout the ages) **which the non-lying God** (the God without falseness) **promised – before eonian times** (prior to the times belonging to the ages).

This reverent knowledge is based upon an expectation of life for and through the ages, and which has the quality and characteristics of the Age of the Messiah, from whom this life comes. The truth-telling God promised this Life (the Christ life) before the ages were created. This is like the Lamb slain from the casting down of the ordered system (Rev. 13:8; 1 Pet. 1:20). This promise came before the creation of the universe, for eonian times began with its creation, but it could only come through the Christ (John 3:15; 17:2), and knowing the Father and Jesus (John 17:3).

3. **Now He manifests** (or: brought into clear light) **His Logos** (His Word; the Thought from Him; the Reason, Idea, communication and expression from Him; the discourse pertaining to Him; and message which is Him) **in Its** (or: His; or: their) **own seasons, fitting situations and fertile moments within** (or: in the midst of) **a proclamation by a herald – which I, myself, was made to trust and believe – down from, in accord with and corresponding to a full arrangement** (or: a setting-upon; a complete disposition; a precise placing in order; an injunction) **of and from God, our Savior** (Deliverer; Rescuer; Restorer to health, wholeness and our original condition).

God manifested His Word in Jesus, and He still does this in Its, or His, own seasons (note the plural), fitting situations and fertile moments. His method is to do this within a proclamation by a herald. So when the Word is proclaimed, the Word and Idea from God, the message which is Him, confronts the hearer.

Note the expanded expressions of the Greek *logos*, and of "Him" in the genitive and ablative cases (the spelling for both is the same), and the final function of apposition of the genitive, which is that of definition ("which is").
Paul was one such herald. He was MADE (passive voice) to trust and believe, as God so arranged it, in accord with a precise placing of events and Paul himself in the right order. God "set upon" Paul, and Paul is an example of how God is our Savior – God does it all. When He does, all we can do is say, "Yes, Lord." It is He Who makes us trust Him and believe Him.

4. **To Titus, a genuine born-one** (legitimate child [one born in wedlock]) **down from and corresponding to a common and partnered** (equally owned, shared and participated-in) **faith, trust and loyalty:**
Grace (or: Favor), **and peace** [= shalom; A, C2 & others: mercy; compassion], **[are; continue coming] from Father God** (or: God [the] Father) **– even Christ Jesus, our Deliverer** (or: and [the] Anointed Jesus, our Savior, Rescuer and Restorer to health, wholeness and our original condition).

Titus was "born again" down from and in accord with their shared faith, trust and loyalty. His legitimacy speaks to the existence of the marriage of Christ, the Lamb, to His wife, the new Jerusalem (Rev. 19:7; 21:1-2). And in Rom. 10:17 Paul tells us,
> "**Consequently, the faith** (or: the trust; confidence) **[comes or arises] from out of the midst of, or from within, hearing, yet the hearing [comes] through a gush-effect of Christ, even through the result of a flow which is Christ** (or: through Christ's utterance; through something spoken concerning Christ; or: by means of a declaration which is anointed, or from Christ; through a word uttered which is Christ; [other MSS: God's speech])."
So it was the flow of Christ from out of Paul that had brought a hearing within Titus, and within that hearing was the faith and trust that gave birth to him.

It is noteworthy that in vs. 3 God is called our Savior and in vs. 4 Jesus Christ is called our Savior. It should also be pointed out that the Greek *sodzo* has a semantic range that means more than "rescue and save," but also means "to restore to health and to the original state or condition." Lawrence Garcia suggests here that this refers to the re-constitution of humanity to its original purpose. This would infer not only our state of being, but also our position, mandate and vocation – given by God in the beginning – to steward creation (Gen. 1:28). The favor and peace, in this context, would reach farther than our individual circumstances and would imply the prosperity of the new creation that comes with the Age of the Messiah (2 Cor. 5:17; Rom. 8:21; Gal. 6:15-16) in conjunction with the second Humanity (1 Cor. 15:42-49) and the new Eden (Rev. 22:1-5).

5. **From the source of, and because of, this grace and favor, I left** [other MSS: was leaving] **you off in Crete, so that you, yourself, could correct and amend – so as to be fully straight throughout the midst – the things habitually lacking, leaving defects or remaining undone, and [so] you, yourself, could thoroughly establish [the] older folks** (or: correspondingly

make [the] elders to stand fast and be firm), **city by city, as I, myself, made thorough arrangements for you.**

Grace and favor are the source and the reason for all that Paul did. Thus should it be with us. He dropped off Titus in Crete so that he could straighten things out there, throughout their midst: things that were lacking, things that left defects and things that remained undone. Titus was to establish the older folks so that they would stand firm in the Lord, as he went from city to city where Paul had made thorough arrangements for him.

6. **[Now] if anyone is normally not one being called up, or arraigned, before a judge** (= habitually exists being one free from reproach); **[is] a husband of one woman** (or: wife), **having trusting and believing children** (or: born-ones that are full of faith); **[is] not one in the midst of a [legal] charge** (or: an accusation; being considered in a category) **of being a person without healthful wholeness** (or: of being unwholesome; being in a desperate case without hope of safety; being prodigal; being wasteful; being on an unsaved course; being incorrigible; being dissolute and debauched) **nor [of] insubordinate [qualities]** (things not put in submission; things not placed under the arrangement; un-subjected and unruly [traits])
7. **– for you see, it continues binding and necessary for the person who sets his eyes upon the distant goal, having a full-scope view, and successfully hits the target** (or: the one who surveys, inspects and watches upon; the scout; the tender guardian who oversees with attentive care) **to continue being one [that is] not normally called up, or arraigned, before a judge** (= to habitually exist being one free from reproach). **As God's house administrator** (house manager; house dispenser and distributor; estate steward), **[he should] not [be] one who pleases himself** (or: gives himself to pleasure): **not impulsive** (prone to passion, irritation or anger; not ruled by his own mental bent, disposition or propensities; not one teeming with internal swelling or motion), **not addicted to wine** (or: beside himself with wine; = not a drunk), **not quarrelsome and apt to strike another, not one eager for dishonorable, deformed or ugly gain.**

I suggest that in vs. 6 Paul begins addressing some of the areas of a person's life that could be defects (vs. 5), or things in which there are lacks, and here he begins speaking about what the "straightened" life should look like.

The first clause of vs. 7 gives the reason for listing such qualities given in vs. 6, for he is speaking about one who lifts his eyes to the upward calling (Phil. 3:14), and who has in mind the goal of winning his race (1 Cor. 9:24). The word describing such a person can also refer to one who surveys a situation, or inspects and watches upon it, or people. It can refer to a scout, or to one who is a tender guardian who oversees folks with attentive care. Such folks often serve the body of Christ in dispensing life and spiritual food to the called-out community. They are people who would be good in administrating the affairs of God's house, and being stewards of the mystery of Christ, as was Paul (1 Cor. 4:1). Pouring forth love to others would be inhibited by the negative characteristics listed in the last part of the verse. Paul proceeds to the positive attributes in the following verses.

8. **But to the contrary, [he should be] fond of strangers** (have affection for foreigners; be hospitable), **[be] fond of the good and have affection for virtue and excellence, [be] whole, healthy and liberated** (sound) **in frame of mind and disposition** ([be] sane), **[be] fair and equitable, and in rightwised relationships within the Way pointed out, [be] loyal, dutiful and pure from all crime, [produce] inner strength** ([be] self-controlled),
9. **habitually holding himself firmly to** (or: clinging face-to-face to) **the full-of-faith Word** (message; thought; idea; Logos; or: the faithful word) **– down from, corresponding to and in line with the Teaching and training – to the end that he can be powerful and able both to be constantly encouraging** (habitually performing as a paraclete; repeatedly exhorting; continually calling folks alongside to give them assistance or relief) **in the teaching that continues being sound and healthy, and to repeatedly put to the proof so as to convince**

by demonstration, or to refute by exposure of the test, the folks habitually speaking in opposition and contradicting.

In vs. 8-9 we see how a mature member of the called-out community should be and behave. These are the good works for which we were created in Christ (Eph. 2:10). The literal rendering, "have affection for foreigners" should speak loudly to us in our day of mixed cultures. Being fond of the good, and having "**affection for virtue and excellence**" holds a high view of the called-out community. Being whole and healthy in our dispositions describes the New Being in Christ. The fairness and equity calls for justice, and a "**rightwised relationship**" is one that is turned toward Christ – Who is the Way pointed out. "**Loyal, dutiful and pure from all crime**" defines the semantic range of the Greek *osios*. Then Titus is called to "**[produce] inner strength ([be] self-controlled)**," the ellipsis being that this is done through union with Christ. All the inserted verbs of vs. 8 are taken from the verb of being in vs. 7, of which vs. 8 is an extension.

Notice the first part of vs. 9: clinging face-to-face to the full-of-faith Word that is in line with the Teaching and which comes from the training. Paul so frequently emphasizes the importance of the message of the Christ and the unveiled Word which had been brought through the sent-forth folks. But don't miss the fact that the reason for this is that a person thus taught and trained can be "**powerful and able**" (*dunatos*) to do the work of a paraclete. It is all about being able to help others: calling folks to our side for encouragement, exhortation, giving aid, comforting and giving assistance. This is the work of the called-out community. This disposition and frame of mind comes through "**sound and healthy**" teaching that affects how we live with and toward others.

He ends vs. 9 by showing that action should be taken in response to folks who habitually contradict or speak in opposition. We should not be remiss in confrontation if it is needed. Examples of such are given from their time and culture. We should be able to extrapolate from these.

10. **You see, many folks, especially those from out of the Circumcision** (= the Jews), **are** (constantly exist being) **insubordinate ones** (not submitted to the arrangement; un-subjected to the order), **empty, vain and profitless talkers, even seducers of the intellect** (deceivers of the mind; people who mislead thinking),
11. **who it continues necessary to repeatedly muzzle** (gag; put something upon their mouth; or: reign them in), **who are habitually turning-back whole households** [i.e., into the Law cultus of Judaism] (or: = constantly upsetting entire families), **repeatedly teaching things which it is binding to not [teach]: a "grace" of ugly** (deformed; disgraceful) **profit, gain or advantage!**

Vs. 10 and 11 give specific examples of those who oppose the message of grace, and we see that this especially came from the Judaizers (those who wanted to mix Law with grace) – or even those who held to the old covenant religion. Paul wanted them silenced – reigned in and gagged! They taught a false grace which promoted using the kingdom of God in a way that gave them advantage over others, which produced ugly profit, and disgraceful gain.

The phrase in vs. 10, "**empty, vain and profitless talkers, even seducers of the intellect**" is saying that the Jews, or Judaizers, were trying to persuade folks to their point of view by use of logic, clever reasoning, or perhaps the teachings of the rabbis. But Paul says that all their words are empty and without profit, compared to the new age of the Messiah that had come, and the new life within the Christ. Both in the history of the church, and likewise in our own day, philosophy, logic, and reasoning from tradition or doctrine can turn-back whole households into legalism or profitless religious practices which destroy the freedom in Christ or distort the message into an "other-worldly" focus that produces selfish escapism and a kind of personal piety that neglects the care for our neighbors and for all of creation.

12. **A certain one of them, their own prophet** (= poet), **said, "Cretans [are] always** (or: ever) **liars, worthless little wild animals** (little beasts of bad quality), **inactive and idle bellies** (= unemployed gluttons)."**

13. **This witness** (or: testimony [of the poet Epimenides]) **is true** (genuine; real). **Because of which case and cause, be repeatedly cross-examining them abruptly while cutting away [at the case] and bringing the question to the proof, so as to test and decide the dispute and expose the matter – to the end that they can be sound and healthy within the Faith and in union with trust and loyalty,**
14. **not habitually holding to** (having [a propensity] toward; heeding and clinging in the direction toward) **Jewish myths** (or: fictions; or, possibly: oral traditions) **and to implanted goals** (impartations of a finished product within; inward directives; commands) **whose source and origin is people** (or: human commandments) **[thus] continually being twisted and turned away from the Truth** (or: reality).

Vs. 12 shows us that prejudice was a part of their deformed grace, and in vs. 13 Paul affirms that Epimenides said this. So because of this situation, Paul admonishes them to repeatedly cross-examine these folks, while cutting away at this case and bringing the question of what they are doing to the proof, testing and deciding the dispute and exposing the matter. The goal is for them to be sound and healthy within the Faith, and in union with the trust from Christ and the loyalty inherent in Him.

Vs. 14 advises them not to heed, cling to or have a propensity toward Jewish myths, which implant the wrong goal within people. Holding to people's (i.e., human) fictions or oral traditions which are not founded upon Scripture will twist and turn people away from the Truth.

15. **To the pure folks, everything [is] pure** (or: All things [are] clean for, with and in the clean ones). **Yet to** (or: for; in; with) **those having been stained and remaining defiled** (corrupted; polluted), **and to** (or: for; in) **faithless people** (those without trust; unbelieving ones), **nothing is pure or clean – but rather, their mind, as well as the conscience, has been – and now remains – stained, defiled and corrupted.**
16. **They are repeatedly adopting the same terms of language, and habitually making confession and avowing to have perceived and now know God, yet they are constantly denying** (repudiating; disowning; refusing) **[this] by the works** (in the actions and things done), **continuing being detestable** (abominable), **incompliant** (stubborn; disobedient; unpersuasive) **and disqualified** (disapproved; rejected after trial) **with a view toward every good work** (excellent and virtuous activity).

Keep in mind that the first statement in vs. 15 is not a Pharisaic maxim which leads to pietism, which we observe that developed in later strains of Christianity. It is a promise of freedom to those who have been made clean through the Word which Jesus brought (John 15:3), and in Lu. 11:41 He said that all is clean to us (*cf* Acts 10:15, and Jesus' words to Peter). It is also a statement affirming a disassociation with the purity laws which were identity markers of Judaism. At the same time, for folks who have not yet come into this reality (who are without faith and remain unbelieving) – and existentially remain stained and defiled – this is not the case, and to them nothing is pure or clean because of the condition of their minds and their ways of thinking about things. Purity comes only through the work of the blood of the Messiah, and as 1 John 1:7 says,

> "**the blood of Jesus, His Son, keeps continually and repeatedly cleansing us** (or: is progressively rendering us pure) **from every sin** (or: from all error, failure, deviation, mistake, and from every [successive] shot that is off target [when it occurs])."

Vs. 16 shows that these folks have a religion, for they profess to know God, yet their lives prove otherwise. And religious folks are often the most self-righteous and condemning of others, having an exclusive world view that their group is the only right group, with the result being that they themselves are detestable, incompliant and disqualified with regard to virtuous actions. And such folks often invade the called-out communities, as we see in Judah (or: Jude) 4,

> "**For you see, some people came in unobserved, from the side – those of old** (or: folks from long ago), **folks previously written into this judgment** (or: the effects and result of this decision)**: [to exist being] impious ones, people continuously changing**

the grace and favor of God into licentiousness, as well as repeatedly denying and disowning our only Sovereign and Lord (or: Supreme Ruler and Owner), **Jesus Christ** [= Messiah]."

Chapter 2

1. **You yourself, however, keep on speaking what things continue being fitting for, suitable in and proper to sound and healthy teaching.**

We should all really hear this. Speak what brings soundness of spirit, soul and body, and which is based upon the Rock, Jesus Christ. Speak things that are fitting and suitable for folks to hear, that are based upon something which they have in common with us: the Word, not our experiences. Teaching should not be based upon experiences. Speak of things from the new covenant, the new creation, the New Being – not things from the in-part and the shadow of reality. Speak from an informed familiarity with your subject, basing it upon the historical context, life situation and world view of the people to whom your topic was originally written. Speak only things that edify, building God's house (temple/people) with "gold, silver and precious stones."

2. **Old** (or: Aged; Older) **men are to habitually be moderate and sober in the use of wine, serious** (grave; solemn; dignified; worthy of respect and honor), **sound of mind with a rational** (or: sane; sensible) **and wholesome way of thinking and attitude, being continuously sound and healthy in the Faith** (or: by trust; with loyalty; for confidence), **in** (or: by; with) **the Love, in** (or: by; with) **the Remaining-under in support** (or: the persistent, patient endurance).

They are to be respected members of the called-out community and be continuously sound and healthy: in faith, by trust, with loyalty and for confidence. Next Paul highlights the central theme of the message of goodness: Love, and then includes one of the main ingredients of love: remaining under – a situation; people – in support of something or someone. This also involves patient personal endurance throughout all of life.

3. **Old** (or: Aged; Older) **women, similarly** (or: likewise), **[are to be] women in a state and resultant condition proper and fitting for being engaged in the sacred** (suitable in demeanor for serving the temple; or: = living a life appropriate [for] a person [being] a temple), **not folks who thrust-through or hurl [a weapon, or something hurtful] through [someone]** (or: not devils nor slanderous adversaries which bring division and hurt), **nor women having been enslaved by** (or: to) **much wine.**

"**Proper and fitting for being engaged in the sacred**." What a picture; what an example to follow. Each of us will have his/her own interpretation of these words, but should not make our understanding a law for others. The paraphrase, which follows the = sign in the parenthetical expansion, is of *hiero-prepēs*: that which is proper and fitting for a temple, or for sacred rites. We should remember that we are His temple.

The phrase "**folks who thrust-through or hurl... through**" is a literal rendering of the elements of the Greek word *dia-bolos*. This word is normally translated "devil." Modern translations render it "adversaries; slanderers" in this verse, as I did in the parenthetical expansion. This should give us a clear picture of 1st century use of this Greek word. It is here in the plural. It is talking about people who wound and hurt other people, and often cause divisions by their slanderous or adversarial words and deeds. We may need to adjust our spiritual cosmology, in regard to this word "devil." Too many of us have had a religious paradigm, a word of rebuke, or a controlling edict, etc., thrust through us.

The reference to "**much wine**" can be literal, or figurative of "too much 'spiritual ritual,' 'doctrines about religious laws,' or 'spiritual activities or experiences.'"

[They are to be] teachers of beauty and of what is fine, excellent and ideal,
4. to the end that they can (or: may; would) **habitually bring the young women to their senses** (or: cause new [wives] to be sound-minded and with a healthy attitude) **to habitually be affectionate, friendly, loving and fond of passionately kissing their husbands [and] children,**

Teachers of beauty and of what is fine, excellent and ideal. Ah, how we all need such instruction. Consider how different a paradigm the young would have, as compared to the fare they receive in our culture – and sometimes in our religions.

The goal of this is to bring young women to their senses (in this example – keep in mind the century when this was written, and their culture; but it would be a fine thing for the older women among the called-out to do this for young women of marriageable age, or young wives). It seems to me that the advice of the last part of this verse would help to promote healthy families and sound marital relationships. The effects upon the whole called-out community would be very positive.

5. ones sound of mind with a rational (or: sane; sensible; clear headed) **and wholesome way of thinking and attitude, untouched so as to be undefiled and pure** (chaste), **workers at home** (domestic; = mistress of the house), **good** (virtuous; with qualities of excellence), **being women that are by habit supportively aligned to** (or: continue being humbly arranged for) **their own husbands, to the end that God's thought and idea** (God's Logos; God's Word; God's message) **can not be constantly blasphemed** (abusively defamed; misrepresented).

The first couple admonitions are universal and for the ages. Being "**workers at home**" speaks to that culture and time – and to many others – but is not universal, as it certainly does not fit the modern culture of an industrialized society – there being some exceptions, of course. But the idea behind these specifics is to be industrious, productive and supportive of those with whom they are in relationships. Anything less is not love, and would thus bring criticism from those outside the community of Christ.

The phrase "**untouched so as to be undefiled and pure** (chaste)" speaks figuratively to the entire community, as being the wife of Christ: untouched by false ideas about God, Christ or the work of the cross; undefiled by the culture or religions that do not come from the New Being – Christ.

6. Similarly (or: Likewise), **be repeatedly and habitually doing the work of a paraclete: calling the younger men alongside to give them relief or support, and to encourage them to be continuously sound in mind** (sane; sensible) **and to be keeping a wholesome attitude and way of thinking about everything –**

The work of a paraclete is coming to a person's side to give aid, comfort, relief, support and encouragement – whatever they need. This is what the Holy Spirit does for us. God is our divine Paraclete (Comforter). Being sound in mind (sensible) and keeping a wholesome attitude toward life is good advice for all. Note again the practical admonitions for a life lived here on earth – not off in the psychic or supposedly "spiritual" realms of glory or the heavens. We are to serve God by serving humanity. We need to be sane and sensible. The supernatural (God) has come to dwell with humans (Rev. 21:3).

7. [while] constantly holding yourself at [their] side, offering (tendering; presenting; exhibiting) **yourself [as] a model** (example; pattern; an impression) **of beautiful actions** (fine deeds and ideal works), **[exhibiting] incorruptness** (absence of spoil or ruin; incapability of decay) **[and] seriousness** (gravity; dignity) [*p*32 & other MSS add: freedom from envy; willingness] **within the teaching:**

We are to stand beside folks and live our trust and understanding of the Christ-life. As He lives His life through us, as us, we will produce beautiful actions, for it is our Father who does the works, which of course are fine and ideal, as well. In so doing, incorruptness and seriousness of life will automatically issue from our new being, and we will be like a tree bringing forth fruit in season. Note Paul's continued references to "**the teaching**." We do not need new things to be taught, for the Scriptures (the teachings of Jesus and His sent-forth folks) have life enough for any situation.

8. **[presenting] a healthful message** (a sound word; a thought or idea full of and promoting health)**: one without down-oriented knowledge and not bringing a downward experience, thus being unworthy of – and not containing any – condemnation** (or: uncensurable), **so that the person in the contrary and opposing position** (or: [acting] out of contrariness) **can** (may; would) **be turned back within himself** (or: be put to shame and be made to show reverence and regard), **continuing having nothing slight or mean** (cheap; paltry; ill; sorry; good-for-nothing; thoughtless) **to be saying about us.**

And again he says, "**a healthful message**, a sound word, a thought or idea full of, and promoting, health." We do not need "**down-oriented knowledge**" which brings "**a downward experience**" and leads to "**condemnation**." If we are without these, the person behaving in a contrary way can be turned back within himself so as not to have anything slight or mean to say concerning us.

9. **[Encourage] slaves to habitually place themselves in subjection** (or: to be continually in humble alignment, supportively arranged under) **their own owners** (or: masters) **in all things – to be constantly well-pleasing and satisfying, not repeatedly speaking contrarily or refuting** (or: talking back), **nor embezzling** (secretly putting aside for oneself; pilfering),

The new creation was inward, not on the outside; Christ did not start a revolution in society, but a transformation in the spirit. So Paul tells Titus to encourage the slaves to remain in their station in life with proper behavior and supportive attitudes in all things. Basically they are to love, and to live that love, with excellence and honesty. The inward new creation would produce an outwardly transformed life.

10. **but to the contrary, habitually displaying all good faith** (every virtuous trust, faithfulness, confidence, loyalty and reliability), **so that they can progressively set the teaching, which pertains to, and whose source and origin is, God, our Deliverer** (Savior; Rescuer; Restorer to health, wholeness and our original state of being), **into the System – in all things, within every area and among all people!**

Note the words "**habitually displaying**." Folks were to be able to observe "**all good faith**, every virtuous trust, loyalty and reliability, etc." This admonition has a purpose: to progressively set the teaching and message from God INTO the System – into the very system of slavery, as well as the cultural, political and religious systems – in all things, within every area, and among all people. This same advice holds true for our day as well. Our goal is to infuse the kingdom into our world.

11. **For God's saving grace**
(the salvation-imparting influence and boon of undeserved kindness, favor and goodwill whose source is God and which brings deliverance, rescue, restoration and health) **has been fully set in clear Light** (was fully manifested and made to completely appear) **for all mankind** (or: to all humanity; in all people)
[other MSS: You see, the joyous favor of God: a Savior for (to; in) all mankind, has been fully displayed; or: So you see, the grace, which is God, was made to suddenly appear {as} a Savior for all humans],

This is the reason to be acting in the way that he admonished in vs. 10: God's saving grace is for all mankind, and it has been fully set in clear Light, first within Jesus, and now within His body. We are the light of the world/system.

If we render the dative case function of the word "**all**" as location, then it means that God's saving grace is made to fully appear in all people. The other MSS's readings tell us that God is a Savior in all humans and for all people. This is a completely inclusive statement.

12. **progressively educating and training us so that, being people refusing** (renouncing; denying; disowning; turning our backs on) **the irreverence** (lack of awe or pious fear; disrespect of and absence of duty to God) **and over-desires** (full-rushing passions) **pertaining to the System** (or: whose source is the world), **we can** (may; would) **live sensibly** (with clear-headed soundness of mind and wholesomeness of disposition and attitude) **and equitably** (fairly; justly; rightwisedly; relationally in a way which reflects the Way pointed out) **and reverently** (in devout goodness, awe and virtuous conduct, and with ease and well-being from relationship with God) **within the current age** (or: the present indefinite period of time, or eon),

This grace/favor progressively educates and trains us so that we can live sensibly and equitably within our own current age – this present indefinite period of time. We are able to do this because Christ has transformed us into being people that now have the power, ability and freedom, by His Spirit, to refuse the irreverence and over-desires that come from the System of religion, culture, economy, politics and government. We have become people infused with the Christ-life, which causes us to live with clear-headed soundness of mind and a wholesome disposition. He has placed us in the Way (Christ, Himself) that has been pointed out to us, and He has turned us in the right direction (toward the Father), while making us fair, equitable and in right relationships – with God and with others. His Spirit within us produces the fruit which is devout goodness in awe and virtuous conduct, while being at ease in the well-being of a relationship with God.

13. **being folks continuously receiving with welcoming focus, and granting access and admittance to, the happy expectation – even the full manifestation** (the complete display in clear light) **of the glory of our great God and Deliverer** (or: Savior)**: Jesus Christ,**
14. **Who gave** (or: gives) **Himself over us** (= over our situation; on our behalf), **to the end that He could loose and redeem us from all lawlessness – by payment of a ransom – and would cleanse and make pure in Himself** (for Himself; by Himself; with Himself) **a people being encircled around [Him], laid up as a super-abounding acquisition of property, zealous** (bubbling up; or: boiling hot; = extremely enthusiastic) **with regard to beautiful actions** (or: for ideal works; from fine deeds).

In vs. 13 Paul continues describing who we now are: folks now continuously receiving with welcome focus "**the happy expectation**," which is the full manifestation, and complete display in clear light, of the glory of our great God and Deliverer/Savior: Jesus Christ. Note that Paul here calls Jesus our great God, and that we continuously receive the full manifestation of His glory. That manifestation of His glory is Jesus, Himself. We need look for no other glory than Him. The glory is not a realm, but God Himself, as manifested in Jesus, and Jesus is the One who gave and gives (aorist tense) Himself over our situation, to loose and redeem us from our bondage to lawlessness (our alienated nature), so that He would in, by, for and with Himself cleanse and make pure a people (= humanity, the new creation, the second Humanity) that would encircle Him and be His "**super-abounding acquisition of property**" – a people boiling hot with zeal to do beautiful actions, create ideal works, and perform fine deeds.

The phrase "**continuously receiving with welcoming focus**," in vs. 13, is a literal rendering of the present participle of *pros-dechomai*. *Dechomai* means to welcome by taking into ones hands or arms, and thus to receive, grant access and admittance to something or someone. The preposition *pros*, which is prefixed to this verb, emphasizes the direction or focus of this action: the happy expectation, which is the complete manifestation of the glory, which is our great God:

Jesus, the Messiah. This verb does not contain the idea of "waiting," as it is often translated. In Col. 1:27 Paul tells the folks in Colossae that "the expectation of the glory" is Christ within them. We receive from this expectation, and grant admittance to it, from the lives of the folks of the called-out communities – His body.

15. **Be constantly speaking these things, and habitually performing as a paraclete** (calling folks alongside to support, give relief and encourage them), **even be continuously putting [folks; situations] to the proof so as to convince by demonstration – or to refute by exposure of the test – with every complete disposition and full arrangement** (precise placing in aligned order; or: injunction).
Let no one surround you with his intellect, mind-set, opinion or attitude (= don't let anyone frame your way of thinking).

So Titus is to constantly tell this to people, and to habitually perform as a paraclete (Paul keeps saying this), while at the same time continuing to put folks and situations to the proof in a demonstrable way. Or, he is to refute by exposure to the test of their spirits (1 John 4:1), or of their alignment to the Message. He is to do these things "**with every complete disposition and full arrangement** (or: precise placing in aligned order)." Paul does not give details of this, but it seems that he means to do a complete job of it.

His next warning is about not letting anyone surround him with their intellect, their personal mind-set, their opinion, or, their attitude. This is a good word picture which he has drawn. Folks can try to overpower you with themselves in this way. The verb is *peri-phronew*. *Phronew* means to be in a frame of mind, to focus the intellect, to be of an opinion, to have a mind-set or attitude. The prefixed preposition *peri* means around, as a circle, and thus gives the verb the added meaning of "to **surround**, or to encircle." The idea of "despise or disregard" (as it is often mistranslated here) is found in the verb *kata-phronew*.

Chapter 3

1. **Repeatedly bring folks under recollection, constantly causing them to think again and remember to be habitually placing themselves in subjection to** (or: to be supportively aligned with; be continually arranged under by) **governments** (or: rulers; sovereignties; originating headships) – **to** (or: by) **those having the right of authority – [and] to continuously comply in persuaded obedience, yielding to these authorities; to constantly be ready ones: facing and progressing toward every good work** (or: virtuous action);
2. **to be in the habit of speaking injuriously of** (blaspheming; slandering; defaming) **no one; to be folks who are non-contentious** (not disposed to fighting or quarreling), **gentle, lenient, considerate and suitably reasonable, constantly displaying all kindness and gentle tenderness while behaving agreeably toward everyone** (all mankind; all humanity).

First of all, he is basically saying to be good citizens and be supportive to others. Next, be ready and focused with a view to all sorts of good works and virtuous actions. Then, he tells us to love, to be non-injurious in our speaking, to be non-contentious, but rather to be gentle and reasonable, and to display ALL kindness and gentle tenderness, while behaving agreeably toward everyone. This is a beautiful picture of Christ, and should also be a picture of us, as He manifests Himself through us. Once again, Paul's message is about a life lived here, among other people.

3. **You see, we also were, ourselves, at one time people habitually being foolish, senseless and without understanding** (without perception or proper use of our minds) – **noncompliant and disobedient ones, folks being constantly caused to wander and being led astray** (or, as a middle: repeatedly deceiving ourselves; habitually going astray), **continuously being and performing as slaves to various** (a diversity of many kinds of) **full-rushing passions and pleasures** (enjoyments; gratifications), **habitually carrying ugly**

worthlessness (bad quality or malice) **and envy** (or: jealousy) **throughout** (= leading a bad life)**: detestable ones** (abhorrent folks) **continuously hating one another.**

This is a sad picture of the first Adam, our estranged and alienated human nature, before we were born back up again into the Last Adam with a regenerated human nature of the New Being. Note that he says that we were performing as slaves. We were not free. Until Christ made us free we did not have a free will. So we should not expect those who are still in bondage "**to various full-rushing passions and pleasures,**" etc., to be able to freely choose Christ. God must first impart life and freedom into them, and then transform them. Until He does, His inherent fervor (or: wrath) is continuously dwelling upon them (John 3:36), and we observe these negative behaviors.

4. **Yet, when the beneficial usefulness in meeting needs and the affectionate friendship for mankind** (the fondness for, the liking of, and the love – as shown in kissing – for humanity) **of God** (or: coming from, and which is, God), **our Deliverer** (Savior; Rescuer; Healer; Restorer), **was fully set in clear Light** (was made to completely appear; was fully manifested) –

Oh, what a beautiful picture of God: beneficial usefulness to humanity; meeting the needs of mankind; affectionate friendship for people; fondness for and the liking of humans; love for mankind. This is our heavenly Father; this is God, our Savior! He has manifested Himself in Jesus, and now is doing so in us. What a contrast to the human predicament, as described in vs. 3. This is the solution for all mankind – a God Who is lovingly helpful to all. Note the expanded functions of the genitive case: coming from, and which is, God. When we receive His attributes, via His Spirit, we receive Him. The Old Testament concept of God being our Savior and Deliverer echoes 1:3 and 4, 2:10 and 13, above, and is again connected to Jesus in vs. 6, below.

5. **not from out of works** (actions; deeds) **[which arise from] within religious performance which we ourselves do** [= deeds associated with the temple cultus of the old covenant]
>   (or: not forth from actions in union with an act of righteousness which we, ourselves, did; not in a relationship based upon our own performance; not [done] in a system of justice, equity and fairness which we, ourselves, constructed), **but to the contrary, down from and corresponding to His mercy, He delivered us** (or: He saves, rescues and restores us to the wholeness and health of our original condition) **through a bath of a birth-back-up-again** (or: [the] bathing of a regeneration; note: can = a ritual immersion pool of rebirth) **and a making back-up-new** (of a different kind and quality) **again from a set-apart Breath-effect**
>   (or: of a renewal and renovation whose source is [the] Holy Spirit; or: a set-apart spirit's creating or birthing [us] back-up-new-again; a renewal which is a holy spirit) –

I think that the first clause, along with the parenthetical expansions, speaks for itself. Our deliverance and salvation comes down from His mercy – not from any ritual we may perform or mantra which we may be coerced to speak, but from His mercy. Mercy is something that is given to us; it is an act on our behalf; it is performed for us. It is thus, in this way, that HE delivered US.

The "**bath**" refers to immersion for cleansing, or in this case for rebirth. But note that it denotes a renewal which is holy spirit, and comes from The Holy Spirit, God's Breath-effect. We see this pictured in the symbol of water baptism, but this is but a figure of that which takes place by being immersed into His Spirit, which includes being immersed (baptized) into His death (Rom. 6:3). The birth-back-up-again and the making back-up-new-again happened universally when, after being buried together with Him into His death (Rom. 6:4), we were also raised up with Him so that "**thus also we can walk around** (or: we also should likewise conduct ourselves and order our behavior) **within newness of life** (in union with life characterized by being new in kind and quality, and different from that which was former)" (Rom. 6:4b). Existentially this happens to us one at a time, as in our own group, or order, we are made alive in Him (1 Cor. 15:23). As He is the One Who delivered us, so also He is the One Who gives us birth by raising us up again, into His Life. The whole operation is the action of God, and we are but passive subjects being acted upon by Him. It is just like a natural birth – a baby is born because of the love and union of its parents; the baby has nothing to do with it, but is the result of what the parents did. We are like Adam in the beginning: formed soil into which He breathes life.

6. **which** (or: from which source) **He pours forth** (or: poured from out of) **upon us richly through Jesus Christ, our Deliverer** (Savior; Healer; Rescuer; Restorer),

Note, again, that He "pours forth upon us" His Spirit, His Breath-effect (vs. 5) – giving us life, and this happened "through Jesus Christ, our Rescuer." And all the action is His. We are able do NOTHING, until He gives us life.

7. **to the end that, being rightwised, and set in right relationship in the Way of fairness and equity which has been pointed out** (also: = being placed in covenant membership) – **by and in the grace and favor of That One – we can** (could; may) **come to be** (or: be birthed; be made to exist being) **heirs** (possessors and enjoyers of the allotment), **corresponding to, in line with, and down from [the] expectation** (or: a hope) **that comes from eonian life** (or: of life whose character, origin, source and realm is the Age [of the Messiah]; or: a life of unspecified duration which leads on into the ages; [the] life of and for the ages).

Next, He turns us in the right direction (rightwises us) and sets us in right relationship in the Way of fairness and equity, which has been pointed out in Him Who IS the Way, the Truth and the Life. This is done "**by and in the grace and favor of That One.**" The end in view is that we can and would come to be heirs (possessors and enjoyers of the allotment) of all that which comes down to us from – and in line with – the expectation that itself comes from eonian life. This life of Christ (the life whose character, origin, source and realm is the Age of the Messiah, and is of and for the ages) gives us Him as our inheritance (as Yahweh was the inheritance for the tribe of Levi, in type). This life is pregnant with expectation that comes from a dynamic God in a new creation.

8. **The Idea** (The Logos; The Word; The Message; The Thought) **[is] full of faith** (or: faithful; trustworthy), **and I am continuing in intending** (determining; designing; or: wishing; wanting) **to progressively set you on thoroughly good footing** (to make you continue thoroughly stabilized and confidently insistent) **about** (or: concerning) **these things – to the end that those having put trust in God** (or: the ones having believed God and now having faith in God) **can habitually give careful thought and concern to constantly put themselves in the forefront** (or: to continually promote, maintain and stand themselves for the interests) **of beautiful deeds** (ideal works; fine actions). **These things continue being beautiful** (fine; ideal), **as well as augmenting a furtherance for humanity** (profitable to mankind; beneficial in people).

The Idea (Christ) is all that he has been sharing from vs. 4 through vs. 7 – and this Idea is full of faith, and this is a trustworthy message. Paul is sending this Word with the intent and design to set Titus on thoroughly good footing and to make him continue thoroughly stabilized and confidently insistent about these things. This was also so that the folks having put trust in God can habitually give careful thought and concern to constantly put themselves in the forefront of beautiful deeds, and fine actions. Paul's thrust is always towards living the life of Christ with ideal works – it is not about us going to heaven some day!

Now look at the next statement: "**These things** (i.e., the good works) **continue being** ideal and **beautiful, as well as augmenting a FURTHERANCE for HUMANITY!**" What a vision! This unveils God's purpose for mankind: growth and furtherance via His reign among people.

9. **Yet habitually set yourself at the periphery** (or: step around) **so as to avoid unintelligent** (stupid; foolish) **questionings** (or: seekings; investigations) **and genealogies** (studies into births or descents), **also strife** [other MSS: quarrels] **and fights** (contentions; conflicts; battles) **about Laws** (or: customs; or: = things related to the Torah), **for they are contrary to progress** (without benefit; unprofitable; regressive) **and ineffectual** (futile; vain).

Titus is to stay with the main objective, as stated in vs. 8, and not get involved in stupid questions or unintelligent investigations – which include genealogy studies and strife/quarrels about customs or things related to the Torah. Why? Because they are "**contrary to progress**" (i.e., the progress expressed in vs. 8), "regressive," and are futile!

10. **After one, and then a second, putting-into-the-mind** (= impartation; admonition) **of a person who chooses or promotes a sect or party** (or: of a factious person), **progressively decline yourself** (or: repeatedly excuse yourself),
11. **having seen and thus knowing that such a one has been and remains a person turned from out of the midst** (or: twisted inside-out; perverted) **and continues missing the target** (constantly fails to properly aim toward the goal; habitually errs; repeatedly makes a mistake), **being continually a person having made a decision corresponding to himself** (or: one separating himself down and out of line; or: self-condemned and sifted to his own level).

Now consider the context of this directive to Titus. It is someone who wants to break away from the community and form his own sect. Also, such a person is turned away from the central focus of the group (furtherance of humanity) and thus is constantly failing to properly aim in the right direction – toward the goal of the called-out folks. He or she is concerned about himself, his/her own kingdom (or: project), and their personal spiritual path or experiences – and such folks as this make decisions that correspond to themselves. But the result is condemning themselves to being sifted down to their own level – which is out of line with the body of Christ.

12. **Whenever I shall send Artemas or Tychicus toward you, urgently endeavor to come toward me in Nicopolis, for I have decided to spend the winter there.**
13. **With urgent endeavor and diligence, at once send on ahead Zenas, the expert in the Law** (or: the lawyer), **and Apollos, so that nothing may be lacking for them.**
14. **Now let our people** (our own folks) **be progressively learning how to habitually put themselves in the forefront** (to continually promote, maintain and stand themselves for the interests) **of beautiful actions** (fine deeds; ideal works) **[directed] into the indispensable needs** (or: wants of compressed necessity), **so that they may not exist being unfruitful ones.**

Vs. 12-13 are personal directions for Titus regarding the other folks listed. Vs. 14 restates what he told Titus in the last part of vs. 8, but here specifying the "**indispensable needs**" of the community, so that no one would be unfruitful. Beautiful acts and ideal works both make those doing them fruitful, and also engender growth for ideal deeds (fruit) in those being helped.

15. **All those with me continue embracing and greeting you. Greet and embrace our friends in [the] faith** (or: those who have love and affection for us in trusting allegiance and loyalty). **Grace and favor [are] with all you folks! It is so** (Amen).

Paul here expresses the affection of himself and those with him, and in spirit sends their embrace and solidarity to Titus, and wants him to pass the same on to their "**friends in [the] faith**." Note that this last could also be rendered as I did in the parenthetical expansion. Then he gives them all his usual reminder, that grace and favor are with them all. And yes, "**It is so!**"

Again following Robinson, the date given for Jacob writing this is circa AD 47-48. As with 1 Peter, he makes reference to the older folks of the covenant communities (5:14), and speaks of teachers/instructors in 3:1. These were the leaders within each group. 2:2 speaks of their meeting together as either a "gathering" or a synagogue (Greek: *sunagoge*), and with the Jewish character of the letter it has been suggested that it was at the time and/or situation where the followers of Christ were still predominantly Jewish. One can easily see the continuity from the old covenant to the new. As with other NT writers, Jacob addresses tests and trials in the first part of ch. 1, then from vs. 19 through vs. 27 speaks to how folks should live in covenant life.

There is a discussion in chapter 2 of works, deeds and actions within community life, chiding those who show preference to rich people, while at the same time showing disregard for the poor. Here we also find the "royal law of love," and vs. 12 says, "**Thus keep on speaking and thus keep on doing** (performing)**: as those being continuously about to be separated and decided about** (evaluated; judged; made a distinction between; scrutinized) **through means of a law** (or: custom; [p74: word; message]) **of freedom and liberty**." Vs. 17-26 show that it is faith and trust that include a person in covenant membership of the Way pointed out, using OT examples.

Chapter 3 discusses the control of one's speech (the tongue) and speaks of two kinds of wisdom. Chapters 4 and 5 present various admonitions about negative behavior and social injustice. The letter ends with exhortations to the brotherhood concerning positive aspects of covenant life in the communities.

Chapter 1

1. **Jacob** (or: James) **a slave belonging to God and to [the] Lord, Jesus Christ** (or: a slave pertaining to God, even in fact, really, to [the] Lord and Owner [or, perhaps: = Yahweh], Jesus Christ), **to the twelve tribes** (or: sprouts and branches which sprang forth) **who are to be constantly rejoicing within the scattering** (or: which are within the midst of the dispersion [= the planting], "To constant joy and gladness!").

As elsewhere, I have rendered the conjunction *kai* as both "**and**" and "even," or expanding the thought, "even in fact, really," as it is sometimes used. May His Spirit (curiously not mentioned here) give you His insights on this. As the word "**Lord**" was used for Yahweh in the LXX, I have inserted that possibility here, as well.

Now the question arises, were the twelve tribes still in known existence in the 1st cent. AD, or was Jacob (the correct rendering of the Greek, *Iakobos*) using this phrase to indicate "everyone who is a descendant of Jacob/Israel"? Or, was he perhaps speaking enigmatically, using the term as a figure for those who were in relationship to the true God, or for the body of Christ, as John used the term in Rev. ch. 7, where the list omits the tribe of Dan, and omits the tribe of Ephraim (which in the OT prophets was at times used as representing the ten tribes), listing instead Joseph and Manasseh?

Two other things are to be noted in this 1st verse: he expects them to be rejoicing, so it is likely that he is directing his remarks to those who have the joy of the Lord, the followers of Christ (as further evidence see 2:1, below); it is written to those within the scattering.

On this second point, the question is, to which scattering (dispersion) is he referring? Of those natural Jewish tribes that had been scattered in OT times, who were now Christians? Or, was it in reference to Acts 8:1 or 11:19, to those scattered from Jerusalem in that period? Or was this simply a general letter written to all believers, of what at that time was considered a Christian sect of Judaism? Was Jacob's paradigm that of Christ, the Messiah, being the fulfillment of the Jewish religion, and was he speaking as Paul to those who were Jews of the heart (Rom. 2:28-29)? The views on this vary. It is also noteworthy that Jacob refers to himself as Christ's slave, as did Paul in Rom. 1.

2. **My brothers** (= fellow Israelites, or, fellow believers; = My family), **lead every rejoicing** (or: lead the path of all joy) **whenever you may fall into – so as to be encompassed by – various trials** (or: multi-faceted ordeals; [a tapestry of] tests and provings; or: experiments and attempts of varying hues),

Peter said "**keep on rejoicing and being glad**" about the "**burning within and among [them], which... [had] a view toward [their] being put to the test**..." (1 Pet. 4:13,12). Here Jacob uses a verb meaning "to **fall**," prefixed by a preposition that means around, or a circle, so the colorful picture is of inadvertently stumbling into a situation where there are multi-faceted ordeals on every side that **encompasses** them with provings – but in the Lord, this is a good thing. Paul said that such things lead "**unto your being accounted worthy of God's reign**," (2 Thes. 1:4-5). Pressures, ordeals, tests, trials, persecutions and provings seem to have been a main theme in the life of the 1st century Christians.

3. **habitually knowing by intimate experience and insight that the thing by means of which your faith, trust and confidence is proved** (tested and accepted) **is continually producing** (or: is progressively working down-in the results of) **persistent patient endurance**
> (a steadfast remaining and dwelling under some ordeal or situation; or: a holding up under sustained attacks; or: a relentless giving of sustaining support).

Jacob's list here corresponds to what Paul said, above, of "**being accounted worthy**" of involvement in God's sovereign activities. Testings and provings have positive results. He expected them to know this by their own intimate experiences, through which they would have gained insight. I have here expanded the meaning of the Greek present participle of *ginosko*. They knew this by their way of life in Christ, and he is saying that it is important to have their faith, trust and confidence tested and proved in order to be accepted. It does not say that this acceptance is needed by anyone else, but rather, since this proving is constantly and progressively producing persistent, patient endurance, it would seem that the acceptance is needed by those undergoing the ordeals. It would go without saying that such productive proving would be acceptable to God.

4. **But patient endurance** (remaining under and/or sustained support) **must habitually be having a work brought to completion** (a complete action; a perfect work; a mature production which reaches its goal) **to the intent that you may be** (or: can exist as) **perfect ones** (complete, matured and finished folks who have attained the goal), **even ones having an entire allotment** (or: whole folks having every part), **being left behind in nothing** (or: lacking not one thing).

Like young saplings that endure the storm winds, we too grow stronger as He brings on the maturity and fruitfulness in our lives. Here he points out that with such ordeals being brought to completion we have "**an entire allotment**, having every part" that we need, so that we may attain our goal that He has set for us. It is noteworthy that maturity and completeness requires patient endurance – a remaining under hard situations, as well as giving sustained support to others within these experiences. Do we wonder why we all have the trials and provings that are the foundation of the process of growth that brings us to our destined goals?

5. **So, if any one of you is continually left behind** (or: lacking) **in regard to wisdom, he must keep on asking** (requesting) **from the side** (= immediate presence) **of the God [Who is] continuously giving to everyone singly** (one at a time; or: simply; or: = generously) **and is not constantly reproaching or demeaning, and it will be given to him.**

Comments on Jacob (James)

You might say that God has good form, all we need to do is ask for the wisdom that we need – He won't be upset about it or put you down, but will personally attend to it. The Greek word translated "**singly**" is often given an idiomatic rendering of "generously," and this is a beautiful picture of God, but I also like the literal rendering of "one at a time" and "singly" – which shows a personal touch. We should also note that Jacob here admonished us to "**keep on asking**" in regard to what we might lack. This is a way of life.

6. **Yet he must keep on asking in faith and conviction** (or: continue making [his] request in union with trust), **making not one hesitation from habitually distinguishing and constantly evaluating differences** (undecidedly separating throughout; discerning between uncertain points; judging dividedly to produce doubt) **within himself, for the person repeatedly making undecided distinctions** (making a separation and judging dividedly unto doubt) **within himself is like a surge of the sea, being constantly raised and tossed by the wind.**

All He asks of us is a little trust and faith (which He Himself imparts to us), and that we ask with the conviction that He hears and will respond. He desires us to be stable, with good footing (which He also effects for us – Rom. 16:25; 1 Thes. 3:13, etc.) – yet then to be moving on without hesitation or imbalance. We are in relationship with God, after all, and "**making undecided distinctions**" or having divided judgment leads us to doubting Him. This is not the way a rightwised person lives. A person living in the Way pointed out (in right relationship with God) lives with confidence in God, and will not be overthrown by chaos of estranged humanity (the sea), nor will he be thrown off balance or directed by the surges from society.

7. **For that man must not habitually suppose** (or: normally assume) **that he will receive** (or: take in hand; seize; get) **anything from beside** (= from being in the presence of) **the Lord** [= Yahweh, or, Christ].

A person that is not in a trusting relationship with God will not be able to receive anything from Him. We are saved by grace, through faith and trust. It only follows that without this gift from God, we will not be able to receive His answer to our request. This is a simple fact, not a put-down. If religion or society tosses us about, it is because we are not abiding in the Vine (John 15). Our stability comes from Him, so we are encouraged to focus on Him (Heb. 12:2) and abide in Him (which pictures a living relationship).

8. **A two-souled** (or: = divided-willed; or: = emotionally split) **adult male [is] unstable** (unfixed; inconstant; turbulent) **in all his ways.**

This is a restatement of the last part of vs. 6. It is another observable fact about humanity. Jacob is not making accusation here, but rather affirming the reality of what he has just been saying.

9. **Now let the low** (humble; not rising far from the ground) **brother** (or: fellow member/believer) **continually boast** (or: be habitually loud-mouthed) **in his height** (or: exaltation),
10. **but the rich, in his lowness** (or: humiliation; depression), **because he will pass by as a flower of grass** (or: = a wildflower).

Here we have a truth about the realm of God's kingdom presented in an apparent paradox. Jesus taught that the way to being exalted in the kingdom was by taking the lower position (Lu. 14:10), and Mary holds out promise for the humble person (Lu. 1:52). He said in Matt. 5:3,
> **"The destitute folks [are] happy in spirit because the reign of the heavens continually belongs to them**
>> (or: Blessed [are] those dependent for support on the Spirit, for the kingdom from the sky and the atmosphere is continuing to pertain to them; The people who need to beg for sustenance [are made] happy by the Breath-effect because the effect of the sovereignty of the heavens is being a source in and for them)**!"**

218

And for the rich it is good to be brought low lest he have difficulty in entering into God's reign (Matt. 19:24). Then 1 Tim. 6 points out further concerns:

9. **Yet those wanting and determining to be rich are continually falling in – into a trial and a trap and many senseless and hurtful strong passions** (many over-desires void of understanding and bringing weakness; disadvantageous wants and needs), **which things habitually swamp those people, sinking them to the bottom, into ruinous corruption** (or: destruction) **and loss,**

10. **for a root of all the bad things** (the worthless qualities; the injurious situations; the poor craftsmanship; the ugly personalities; the malicious desires) **is the fondness of silver** (= love of money; = covetousness) **of which some, habitually extending and stretching themselves out to reach, are caused to wander off** (or: were led astray) **away from the faith and they pierce themselves through with a rod and put themselves on a spit** (or: they run themselves through, stabbing themselves all around) **for** (or: in; to; with; by) **many pains.**

So lowness, humiliation and depression of situation are things to be desired! Our being transitory is a condition for which we should boast, realizing that in His reign this is height and exaltation, and a financial loss that brings us low is in His sight a place that positions us for being lifted up.

11. **For the sun rises with scorching heat and withers the grass, and its flower falls off, and the beauty of its face** (= loveliness of its appearance) **loses itself** (finds destruction in itself). **Thus also, the rich one will be extinguished** (faded; withered) **in his goings** (journeys; business; ventures; way of life).

Jacob points out that we are in a realm where our natural life deteriorates and we grow old. Eventually we fade and our life is extinguished, our involvements end. So the rich should remember that at any time his soul may be "requested," as in the story which Jesus told of the farmer who decided to build a bigger barn (Lu. 12:16-21).

12. **Happy and blessed is the adult male** [A and other MSS: person] **who is continuously remaining under a proving** (a putting to the proof; or: a trial; an ordeal), **because upon being birthed approved** (or: growing and becoming proved and accepted) **he will lay hold of the circle of the life** (or: life's crown; life's encirclement; the encirclement from this living existence; or: the wreath which is the Life) **which He** [some MSS: the Lord (= Yahweh or Christ)] **Himself promised to those continuously loving Him.**

As to this pertaining to "**the adult male**," we should keep in mind the historical context of a male-dominated society. Perhaps the enlightenment in Christ motivated the scribes of A and other MSS to use the word "person," but we have no way of knowing which word the original used. If the former, perhaps Jacob was trying to emphasize the maturity of the individual who would remain under a proving, and not run away.

The reward he points to is a wreath, which was given to a winner in the stadium games, such as the person who won the race. This is an echo of Paul in Phil. 3:12-15 where he says,

"**I am continuously pursuing down toward** [the; or: an] **object in view** (a mark on which the eye is fixed)**: into the prize** (or: award) **of God's invitation to an above place** (or: an upward calling having the source from, with qualities and characteristics of, God) **within the midst of and in union with Christ Jesus.**"

But the literal meaning of the phrase is "**the circle**, or the encirclement, **of the life** (or: = the [Christ] Life)." It is "**the Life**," which is associated with the Way and the Truth. Having this encircle us is indeed a prize worth running for, a reward for which it is worth remaining under the ordeal. John used this exact same phrase in Rev. 2:10, in the context of being faithful on until death, within the pressures that the called-out in Smyrna would undergo. Interestingly, John in the next vs. goes on to say this death, which he symbolically calls "the second death," would not hurt or injure them – for you see this is a dealing of and in God, and is later defined as "the lake of fire" in Rev. 20:14.

But the best part of this vs. is that the qualifying for this circle of life (= a life which envelops us) is simply that we continuously love Him. And we love because He first loved us (1 John 4:19) – it was He Who implanted His love into us.

13. Let no one, while being continuously probed and put to the proof, be saying "I am constantly being probed and put to the proof (tested; tried) **in an ordeal from God," for God is One Who is not put through an ordeal, not probed, put to the proof or tried, and is [thus] without experience from not having made an attempt, in regard to things of bad quality** (or: you see, God exists un-testable, and lacks experience, from worthless situations or evil things or mean people), **and so He Himself is repeatedly probing no one, nor constantly putting even one person in a test, to the proof or through an ordeal.**
14. Yet each person is repeatedly probed and put to the proof (tested and tried in an ordeal), **being continuously dragged** (or: drawn) **out and entrapped under his own over-covering passion** (by his own longing, craving or lust; by what he sets his desires upon).

I have expanded the renderings of the verb "probe, prove, test, try, attempt, become experienced through trying, or put through an ordeal," as well as the noun, in these two verses to give the semantic range of the word. The idea of "tempt" should not be imported into this word, even if it seems to make the interpretation of the text easier. The above English words all fit into a single idea (a composite of those words) which is the meaning of this word. It was widely used in secular literature and in the LXX (Septuagint). The *Concordant Version* and Dr. Ann Nyland's *The Source NT* concur, as do the majority of the examples given in Kittel's *TDNT*, and it is the primary meaning in Liddell & Scott.

Here is an important concept to understand. First of all, God is incapable of being probed or tested or tried in regard to worthless situations. Nothing puts Him to the proof from conditions of bad quality, evil things or mean people. He is without experience in these things from not having made an attempt to do or be any of these things.

We, on the other hand, are born into an environment which is full of things that are contrary to our estranged nature, the flesh. And that very estranged nature, the "false persona," is characterized by "**over-covering passion**, craving, lust and longing" which continually drag and entrap us under our own dead selves. God is behind the trials, tests and ordeals, for He created our environments, but here Jacob reveals to us that the real proving comes from us, ourselves, and thus he assures us that **[God] is REPEATEDLY probing no one, nor CONSTANTLY putting even one person in a test, to the proof or through an ordeal.** And note carefully that the verb is in the Greek present tense, which signifies repeated, habitual, constant, continuous or progressive action: so it does not say that God NEVER probes someone, or tests them with an ordeal. But He does not do this constantly, or even repeatedly. "Bread-corn must be crushed, yet would He not be evermore threshing it... [with] the wheel of His cart..." (Isa. 28:28, Rotherham).

God is ultimately responsible for tests and ordeals, for we have only one Creator, one God, and our adversary reports to Him and is controlled by Him (as did satan report to God in Job 1:7; 2:2, and was given limits in what it could do). Yet it is foolish to try to put Him on trial for all the pain, injustice and death that colors all of history. However, He Himself, does not bring the continued ordeals or the repeated tests, but rather it is the worthlessness within folks which brings the constant tests and trials to us.

Recall also that in Lu. 22 Jesus said to Peter,
>   **31. "Simon, O Simon! Look, and consider. The adversary** (or: opponent; satan) **makes** (or: made) **A REQUEST concerning you men: to winnow [you folks] as grain!**
>   **32. "But I Myself urgently asked concerning you, [Simon], to the end that your trust and faith would not leave from out of [you]** (or: = give out). **And so at some**

point, you yourself, upon turning around, make your brothers immovable (or: stabilize and establish your fellow members).**"**

15. **Thereafter, with the over-covering passion conceiving** (seizing together so as to become pregnant), **it continuously gives birth to failure** (or: repeatedly brings forth an offspring of missing the target; progressively bears sin). **Now the failure** (error; sin; missing of the target), **being brought to full term** (being finished off; being fully formed with all its parts; being brought to its goal) **continues producing** (keeps generating; from pregnancy progressively bears forth) **death.**

.

So here we have an overview of the process. It starts from within, and our own missing of the target conceives and then gives birth to death. This is a commentary on the Genesis account of Eve and Adam. The pattern continues in the inner estranged humanity, and is worked out in our daily lives until Christ delivers us from this cycle of death.

16. **Do not be repeatedly caused to wander** (or: Be not continuously deceived), **my beloved brothers** (= family members; = fellow believers)!

Ideas and concepts can cause us to wander or be deceived. We should guard our minds, or as Prov. 4:23 says, "[More] than any guarding, preserve your heart (= core of your being), for from it [spring the] outflowings of life" (CVOT). Rotherham's footnote says: "Sources (origin and direction)" of life. But we should also take up the shield that comes from faith, to quench the assaults from our adversaries (Eph. 6:14-18). Jacob continues with specific reasons for this admonition.

17. **Every good leaving of a legacy, profitable contributing or excellent dosing, as well as all virtuous giving, and** (or: All giving [is] beneficial, and yet), **every perfect gift** (finished, complete or mature result of giving) **is from above, descending from the Father of the lights, beside Whom there is no otherness at [His] side** (or: in the presence of Whom is no parallel otherness; [other MSS: along with Whom {is} not one interchange, variation, shifting or mutation]), **nor a shadow cast by turning** [other MSS: an effect caused by the passing of shadows].

The Greek substantive *dosis* in the first phrase properly means "giving," but it has also been used for specific giving as in "a legacy, a contribution or a dose (of medicine)," in Greek literature. It seems profitable to our understanding of this broad statement by Jacob, to include these uses here. The syntax of the Greek also allows for the parenthetical rendering, which makes an even broader statement. If this latter is taken, then the conjunction *kai*, translated "**and**" in the first rendering, can be used as a contrasting connector, and translated "and yet," to signify that "all giving is good," but the "perfect, mature and complete" gifts come from above, descend from the Father..."

The phrase "**Father of the lights**" may have been a code word of either the Jewish or the Christian communities, but Jacob does not explain it. The "lights" could refer to the lampstand in the temple, and this in turn is a figure of a called-out congregation (Rev. 1:20). Jesus said that His followers were "the light of the world" (Matt. 5:14). Paul said in Eph. 5:8, "**for you folks were once existing being darkness, yet** (or: but) **now [you are] light, within and in union with [the] Lord.**" And in Phil. 2:15 he said, "... **you folks are continuously shining** (giving light; or: appearing; made visible by light) **as illuminators** (causes of light; or: luminaries) **within [the] ordered System** (world of secular culture, religion, economics and government)." So I think that we can conclude that Jacob was here referring to our Father.

Then, speaking of the Father, he says that there is "**no otherness at [His] side.**" When someone is at His side, He is the same as the Father – there is in that place no "wholly other" that the theologians attribute to God. This is astounding. It is similar to what John said in 1 John 3:2,
   "... if it (or: He) **should be** (or: whenever it {or: He} may be) **made visible, apparent and manifested, [then] folks like to Him** (like-ones to Him; ones like Him; people

resembling Him) **we will be, because we will see and perceive Him just as** (according and exactly as; in the manner that) **He constantly exists** (or: He is)."

Considering the other MS readings, "along with Whom {is} not one interchange, variation, shifting or mutation," we can see that in His presence there is no changing of position or alternation (no interchange), but rather there is sameness and continuity (no variation), stability (no shifting) and pureness of being (no mutation). There is only the fullness of having reached the goal.

In the final phrase, we see that there are no shadows in His presence, for the shadows from the Law have been cast out (Heb. 8:5; 10:1; Gal. 4:22-31). There is no turning, for He is the goal, and if He should turn there will always be Light.

18. **Being purposed** (intended; willed), **from pregnancy He brought us forth by a Word** (collected thought; message) **of Truth and Reality – [placed] into us – to be** (or: to continuously exist being) **a specific firstfruit of His created beings** (or: of the effects of His act of creating; or: from the results of the creation which is Himself).

Our coming into being within Christ was a purposed event. It is the result of His will. The Jerusalem above was our mother (Gal. 4:26), and it was by participation in and with her that she became pregnant and then He brought us forth (we were born again, born from above – the realm of spirit where the New Jerusalem dwells) by a message of Truth, a Word of Reality being placed into us. His goal was that we would be a specific firstfruit of His created beings, or (treating the next to the last phrase as an ablative and the last one in apposition): from the results of the creation which is Himself. In creating all that there is, He took from out of Himself, and formed Himself into a new expression of Himself, and we are a part of that expression, or Logos.

19. **You folks have seen and are aware, so understand, perceive and know [this], my beloved brothers. So every person must continuously be quick** (swift) **into the [position or place] to listen and hear, slow into the [readiness] to make vocal utterance,** [and] **slow into intrinsic fervor** (internal swelling of passion; teeming desire; or: agitation; anger; or: a particular mental bent).

The first statement refers back to vs. 18. The verb of this sentence is both an indicative and an imperative, in form, so I have rendered it both ways in a conflation. The second sentence is an outflow from the first, because they know who they are and perceive their position in Christ and with God. The admonition needs no comment.

20. **For you see, an adult male's intrinsic fervor** (or: mental bent; temperament; disposition; or: swelling desire and passionate longing; or: anger and indignation) **is not working out** (producing; bringing into effect) **God's fair and equitable dealing** (rightwised situation which accords to the Way pointed out, in right relationship; the quality of the thing which is right and just; also: = the covenant life from God).

If we consider the semantic range of the noun which I first rendered "**intrinsic fervor**" (Greek: *orge*), we can see that none of these meanings produce God's fair and equitable dealing, or relationships which are turned and pointed in the right direction. If a person follows his own mental bent, he will likely be selfish and have no consideration for others. The same applies to his disposition. Swelling desire and passionate longing get us out of balance, and can get us into trouble. Anger or indignation do not bring peace, and often overlook what is right and just.

21. **For this reason, putting away from yourselves all filthiness and encompassing superabundance of bad quality** (ugliness; baseness; malice; evil; qualities that ought not to be), **you folks must receive** (take with your hands) **in gentleness** (meekness) **the implanted** (ingenerated) **Word** (collected thought; idea; message), **the One being continuously able** (or: the one which is constantly powerful) **to deliver** (rescue; keep safe; heal and make whole) **your souls** (your inner self and being).

This first clause shows the results of following one's "**intrinsic fervor**." It leads to all filthiness (impure aspects that result from our estranged existence), which are the result of our false persona, of the law of sin in our members (Rom. 7:23) and of our surrounding environment. The word of admonition from Jacob, here, has in it the power to accomplish the "**putting away**" of these, for this Word is Christ. It also gives us the ability to receive it in gentleness – being implanted into our being – and It (or: He) has the power and ability to deliver, to rescue, to keep safe and to heal and make whole our inner being, giving us our true persona and eliminating the estrangement.

22. **Now you must continuously come to be** (or: be progressively birthed) **performers of [the] Word** (or: makers of collected thought; framers of an idea; authors of a message; producers of reason; [the] Word's doers), **and not only hearing ones** (listeners; those hearing in an auditorium), **continuously deceiving** (reckoning aside; miscalculating) **yourselves.**
> (another combination of these options yields: So you folks must be progressively birthed to be authors of a message, and not only those in an auditorium, continuously miscalculating yourselves.)

Jesus said to His followers in John 15:
> 14. **"You folks are** (exist continuously being) **My friends! So if you can – or would – [simply] keep on doing** (or: be habitually producing) **whatever I, Myself, am constantly imparting as the goal in you** (or: repeatedly giving as inner direction to you; progressively implanting as the end for you)**!..."**

I have given the semantic ranges of both the verb "perform... do" and the noun "**Word**... thought... idea... message... reason." Consider the possible ways that this clause can be translated. They all make sense, but give us different understandings of what Jacob may have meant here – and possibly he meant all of them. It is an outstanding admonition, especially when you tie it to what Jesus said in John, above.

This reading gives a different admonition:
> **"So you folks must be progressively birthed to be authors of a message, and not only those in an auditorium, continuously miscalculating yourselves."**

Now this is because of the Word He has implanted in us, as stated by Jacob in vs. 21.
I think it also quite significant that to be only a hearer is to "reckon aside and miscalculate yourself." So all who simply "go to church and listen" or "sit at home and watch," and yet do not perform the message or author an idea, are deceiving themselves. This is a life that must be lived, and we are co-laborers with the Creator.

23. **Because if someone is a hearer of [the] Word** (a listener to a thought, idea or message) **and not a doer** (performer; producer), **this one is like** (resembles) **an adult male contemplating** (considering; attentively pondering) **in a mirror the face of his birth** (genesis; origin; existence; generation; lineage; or: = the face with which he was born)**:**
24. **for he contemplated himself and has departed, and immediately forgot of what sort** (quality; manner) **he was.**

The point is that just like we easily forget what we had for lunch last Thursday, if we don't make the message, the Word, the idea of Christ, to be our daily life, we immediately forget what the message was, and go our way thinking that we are living the Way pointed out, following the Path which is Christ. If we are only a listener, we can soon forget our true identity in Christ.

25. **But the one stooping down beside in order to attentively view into** (giving a penetrating look into) **the perfect** (finished and realized; matured; completed; full-grown and fully developed; purposed and destined) **law – the one which is freedom** (or: the one whose source is, and which has the qualities of, freedom and liberty) **– and then remaining** (abiding; dwelling) **beside [it] – not being birthed** (or: coming to be) **a hearer of forgetfulness** (or: a forgetful listener), **but**

rather a performer of work (a producer of action) **– this person will be happy and blessed within his performing and in union with his producing.**

In Rom. 8:2 Paul called this law **"the principle and law of, and which is, the spirit of 'The Life within Christ Jesus'."** In Gal. 5:1 he said **"For the [aforementioned] freedom, Christ immediately set us free."** Jacob here says that, having taken time to stoop down and attentively view into this new perfect law – which is FREEDOM, which is Christ in us – we should be remaining in this place, with this freedom at our side, being a person who actually lives this life. And this will result in our being happy and blessed in this performing and producing. What a thought, what an idea, what a simple message! It is not a message of "works," but a message of the FREEDOM of living it, apart from the bondage of rules, and of do's and don't's, and attending "services," and of "you must be a part of our group."

Next he repeats the admonition: not to be a hearers who forgets, but rather to be a performer and a producer – one who brings increase to God's reign. And the blessing is in the performing and is united with and in the center of the producing.

26. **Now if someone habitually supposes [himself]** (or: thinks [himself]; presumes; or: constantly appears or seems) **to be religious** (occupied with rituals and ceremonies), **while not habitually guiding his tongue with a bridle, but rather is repeatedly deceiving his heart, the religion** (ritual; observance of a religious system) **of this person is useless** (futile; empty).
27. **Pure** (clean) **and unstained** (undefiled) **religion, by the side of** (= in the presence of) **God, even the Father, is this: to habitually visit so as to continuously look upon with the eyes in order to help** (or: oversee) **orphans and widows within the midst of their pressure** (squeezing; distress; ordeal; tribulation); **to habitually keep oneself unspotted from the controlling ordered System** (or: the world of secular culture, religion, economy and government).

And yet the "church" is full of gossip, back-biting, put-downs, maligning the character of folks, criticism, complaints, murmurings, expressions of dissatisfaction with everything from the weather to the government. You don't see much use of a bridle. And it makes all the ritual and attending of meetings to be futile, empty and useless! Out of the heart flow the issues of a person's life. And many folks show that they have an empty life – they are deceived, thinking they are in union with Christ, yet remaining estranged to His Life. Instead of there being a community of love, there is a disassociation of hard feelings.

Vs. 27 is in the first part an echo of Matt. 25:35-36. And we should see that these orphans and widows are Him (Matt. 25:40).

But how does the "**controlling ordered System**" get spots on us, pollute us? It is from the spirits in those systems. The spirit of "the secular paradigm" in our culture, where nothing is sacred. The spirit of control and empty ritual in our religions. The spirit of greed in our economy. The "dominating spirit" in our government. We are in these systems, but we do not need to be a part of the spirits that control them or are embodied by them. We can confront these spirits with the Spirit of Christ, the Spirit of Love and Acceptance, the Spirit of forgiveness and of laying down our lives for them, the Spirit of the kingdom and sovereign activity of God.

Chapter 2

1. **My brothers** (= fellow believers, or, fellow Israelites, or, Family), **stop, or do not have the habit of, holding the faith of Jesus Christ, our Lord** (Master; Owner), **Who is the glory** (the manifestation Who calls forth praise), **in respect of persons**
> (or: do not persist in holding our Lord's [= Yahweh's or Christ's] trust in partiality or favoritism, or in the receiving of faces or personalities, thus affecting the reputation of Jesus Christ).

Here I will mention that the use of the word "**brother**" had a wider semantic range than just referring to the men in the organization, as my expansions indicate, above. The parenthetical alternate rendering explains the thrust of the verse. However, in the first rendering, the phrase "**Who is the glory**" – giving the genitive as apposition – brings out an important statement about Jesus, our [Messiah]. He is the glory of God. He is the Head of the body, the Second Man and the last, or *eschatos*, Adam (1 Cor. 15:45-47), "God's image and glory" (1 Cor. 11:7).

2. **For if a gold-ringed adult male, in a shining or radiant robe, may enter into your gathering** (or: synagogue), **but then a poor person** (one reduced to beggary; an indigent) **in a dirty or filthy robe** (or: shabby clothing) **may also enter,**
3. **and you should look upon** (or: gaze upon and regard) **the one wearing the shining robe** (= expensive, new clothes), **and you may say, "You sit here in a fine and beautiful [manner or position]** (= in a place of honor)," **and to the poor one you may say, "You stand there," or, "You sit under my footstool** (= on the floor near my feet; = a place beneath my position),"
4. **are you not thoroughly separated and disconnected within yourselves** (or: discriminating and making a distinction among yourselves) **and have birthed yourselves to become** (or: caused yourselves to be) **judges having the qualities of evil reasonings** (or: decision makers whose motives are wicked designs and harmful logistics)**?**

Since this is a general letter, I don't think that vs. 2-4 are referring to a specific situation, but rather is an example of showing preferential treatment. Apparently the called-out communities had some problems in adjusting their cultural norms to the New Reality in Christ. Vs. 4 explains that such behavior displays a loss of solidarity that results in their being separated and disconnected within their own minds, and among each other. They are judging others on outward appearances, rather than seeing Christ in each other and honoring Him equally in all. The last phrase shows that such behavior is also the result of evil reasonings and wicked designs, rather than having the mind and attitude of Christ. In John 7:24 Jesus told folks to stop judging by appearances.

There is also the element of people being focused on financial prosperity or social position that is being addressed. In contrast to what Jacob is here pointing out, Jesus went to the outcasts and told the poor that God's reign and sovereign activities belonged to and pertained to them. So already His message had become forgotten or discarded. Folks had resumed the attitudes of the Pharisees, giving preferential treatment to those in the higher levels of their societies.

5. **Listen and hear, my beloved brothers! Did not God at one point choose** (call and speak out; pick out; select) **for Himself the poor folks in the System**
   (or: Does not God Himself lay out and collect the beggars and those who slink and cower with wretchedness in the world of society, culture, religion and government) **– rich folks in faith, trust, loyalty and conviction, and also heirs** (those who possess by distribution of an allotment) **of the reign and kingdom which He promised to and assured for those continually loving Him?**

The System can refer to the ruling society, their local culture, their economic stratification, or their religious system. In any or all of these, God chose those of low rank. But these became rich in the characteristics of God's reign – to the point that they are heirs (= sons of the King). Note again the qualifying characteristic: those who constantly live their lives with love for God. Continually loving God implies relationship, not just religious behavior. Many whom Christianity would reject as non-religious, profane or morally outcast, may well be loving God, even if they reject Pharisaical Christianity.

6. **But you folks dishonor and devalue the poor. Are not the rich people continuously exploiting you people, repeatedly exercising [their] power and abilities against you? Are they not continually dragging you into courts of law for judicial hearings?**

7. **Are they not constantly defaming** (slandering; speaking abusively of; vilifying; or: hindering the light of) **the beautiful** (fine; excellent; honorable; ideal) **Name – the one being called upon** (= put upon), **and conferred on, you folks?**

Here Jacob is having in mind those finely-dressed folks to whom the called-out communities are showing a fawning deference. To the very folks who take unfair advantage of them, as well as speaking abusively of "**the beautiful Name**" (we can presume that he is referring to the Name, Jesus, the one being "conferred on" them). The word "**defaming**" (etc.), in vs. 7, is the verb often rendered "blaspheming." If these rich people were Jews (and note in vs. 2, above, that this gathering may be in a synagogue), they would certainly not having been blaspheming God with their words. So how were they "slandering the beautiful Name"? In Rom. 2:23-24 Paul points out that the behavior of God's people caused God's Name to be blasphemed among the ethnic multitudes (non-Jews; Gentiles). It is the behavior of these rich folks among their congregation that is vilifying God's Name and "hindering the Light" of the good news, while the rest of the called-out community devalues and dishonors the poor. In today's Christian world the poor are sometimes considered less spiritual or without faith. It is presumed by some that if this were not the case that they would otherwise be prospering.

8. **Since, however** (or: If, really), **you are continuously bringing to its goal** (finishing; bringing to fruition; perfecting; ending; bringing to a close; fulfilling) **the royal law** (or: kingly custom; sovereign distribution; rule fit to guide a king), **you are performing beautifully** (doing ideally; producing excellently), **down from and in accord with the Scripture,**
> **"You will love your neighbor** (the one near you; your associate) **as yourself."**
> [Lev. 19:18]

The Greek word *'ei* can mean either "since," or "if." I chose to put a positive spin with my first rendering, but included the second meaning. You may choose which you think he was doing, speaking the positive into their lives, or questioning the fact of their fulfilling "**the royal law**" and "rule fit to guide a king." Since he earlier referred to this law as "**the perfect law of liberty** and rule of freedom," in 1:25, I suggest that we should ask, Did their above behavior of favoritism lead to freedom, or maintain bondage? Another possibility is that he was being somewhat sarcastic.

His reference to Lev. 19:18 echoes what Jesus answered about the greatest commandments in Mark 12:31. In vs. 34 He responds, to the scribe's reply in agreement with Jesus, that he is not far from the reign/kingdom of God. Jesus, John and Paul come readily to mind in their emphasis on love and acceptance of those around us. This Christ-love is that which fulfills the Scriptures.

9. **Yet if you habitually show favoritism** (accept faces; behave with partiality), **you are continuously working error** (a miss of the target; a failure; sin) **being ones by proof of guilt repeatedly convicted as transgressors** (folks stepping aside or across [the line]), **under the Law** (or: exposed as deviators by the custom).

Favoritism leads to elitism, and we will want to get into that elite group. God makes choice and "elects" a group or a person for a specific job, but He does not show favoritism. Paul admonishes Timothy to "**continually doing nothing** (constructing not one thing) **down from** (in accord with; on the level of) **inclination** (or: a leaning toward [something]) **or bias**" (1 Tim. 5:21). And in Matt. 5:45-46, Jesus says,
> **"because He is repeatedly making His sun to rise back up again upon bad** (evil; wicked) **folks as well as [upon] good** (virtuous) **folks, and He is habitually sending rain upon fair and equitable people** (those in right relationship; those within the Way pointed out; just ones; rightwised ones) **as well as [upon] unfair and inequitable people** (those not in right relationship; those not in the Way pointed out; unjust ones). **You see, if you should happen to love the ones constantly loving you folks, what wage or reward do you continue holding** (or: having)**?"**

In Acts 10:34 Peter tells us that "**God is neither partial nor takes folks at face value** (does not receive faces or appearances)."

Jacob's mentioning the Law (or: custom) may have been a reference to Deut. 1:17 or 16:19. All of Christ's emissaries used the Torah or the Prophets to substantiate their points. Paul does this frequently. What is meant here, is that even under the old covenant such behavior as favoritism was condemned. He continues in his comparison in the following verses.

10. **For you see, whoever perhaps kept** (or: may have guarded and observed) **the whole Law, yet possibly at some point stumbled in one thing, had become held** (or: caught) **within all [its aspects]** (or: = is liable for and susceptible to everything).

11. **You see, the One saying, "You should** (or: may) **not commit adultery," also said, "You should** (or: may) **not murder."** [Ex. 20:13] **Now if you are not committing adultery, yet you are now being a murderer, you have come to be** (you have been birthed) **a transgressor of** (a deviator from; [p74 and A read: one who stands away from]) **law** (or: custom).

In vs. 10 the verb "**kept**" is in the aorist subjunctive. I have rendered this here as a simple past tense, which would indicate that Jacob regarded such things as a thing of the past, since the new covenant had come with Christ (see the book of Hebrews, which compares the old with the new, and shows that Jesus is now the Great High Priest of the living temple, His body). But it could also be rendered as a simple present, for at the time of the writing of this letter the physical temple was yet standing and the Jews were still keeping the Law.

These verses are ominous. If we choose to keep one or more of the old covenant laws, we are held within the old covenant, and come into bondage to all of it. The mixing of any of the Law (Torah – including the "ten commandments") into the administration of grace is a deadly mistake. Paul said that when the commandment came into his life, he died (Rom. 7:9-10). He also gave solemn warnings against such in Gal. 3-5.

12. **Thus keep on speaking and thus keep on doing** (performing)**: as those being continuously about to be separated and decided about** (evaluated; judged; made a distinction between; scrutinized) **through means of a law** (or: custom; [p74: word; message]) **of freedom and liberty.**

Jacob's argument and warning against living under the Law is brought to its logical conclusion: live as folks that are about to be continuously, from time to time, evaluated by a law of freedom and liberty (Gal. 5:1). It is no longer the Law of Moses that will judge them, but the law of the new covenant – for Christ is the end of the Law for those who have become believers (Rom. 10:4).

13. **For you see, the separating and deciding** (or: scrutinizing and judging) **is merciless to the one not performing mercy. Mercy is consistently speaking loudly and boasting down against separating** (making decisions; scrutinizing; judging)**!**

It is important to see that vs. 13 flows directly from vs. 12. We live under the constant judging (evaluating; making decisions about) of the Lord – and this is a good thing, for it is both correctional and can be promotional. So here in vs. 13 he points us toward a life of "**performing mercy**." We are called to this (to be "**containers of mercy** {or: instruments of mercy} – Rom. 9:23), to be dispensers of God's mercy to others. It is the balancing ingredient in His judging, for His judging comes from His mercy seat, and we receive favor from this "**throne of grace**" (Heb. 4:16). Furthermore, recall Paul's words in Rom. 11:32,

> "**For you see, God encloses, shuts up and locks all mankind** (everyone; the entire lot of folks) **into incompliance** (disobedience; stubbornness; lack of being convinced)**, to the end that He could** (or: would; should) **mercy all mankind** (may make everyone, the all, recipients of mercy)**!**"

14. **What is the advantage** (the furtherance; the increase)**, my brothers** (= fellow believers; = family) **if a certain person may keep on claiming to continuously have faith** (or: may be now

saying [that he is] habitually having trust, loyalty and conviction), **yet he may not normally have works** (or: keep on possessing actions and deeds)**? Is the faith** (trust; loyalty; conviction) **not continuing able** (constantly having power) **to deliver** (rescue; save; make whole and heal; restore) **him?**

I made the second sentence in vs. 14 a question, rather than a statement (recall that there was no punctuation in the earliest MSS). The answer to this rhetorical question is "Yes." Even the faith as a grain of mustard seed can move mountains. When the man asked Jesus to help him with his unbelief, Jesus did so and granted the requested healing. Now the answer to the first question would be "No increase, no furtherance along the path, and thus no advantageous benefit." Actions and deeds are needed in order to produce life and gain an increase. A man can say that he has faith to have children, but if he does not have intimate action with his wife, there will not likely be an increase in their family – unless, of course, other actions are taken. But still, whatever faith and trust he does have is God's faith within him, and THAT still has power and ability to restore him, heal him, and make him whole so that with the body coming alongside to encourage him he can let the faith grow into action.

15. **Now if a brother or a sister may continuously subsist** (or: should begin now in a position under [circumstances]) **as naked ones** (= without sufficient clothing), **and may constantly be deserted** (or: wanting) **of daily food,**
16. **yet a certain person out from among you folks may be saying to them, "Be now humbly departing in peace** (or: Continue leading [your life] under [these circumstances] in union with harmony), **be continuously warming yourselves and be habitually fed and fully satisfy yourselves," but you would not give to them the body's necessities – what is the advantage or resulting benefit?**

Here we have a practical example that parallels what Jesus said to the "**sheep and the kids** (immature goats)" in Matt. 25. Life in the kingdom is not just in words or prayers, but also in deeds. We also have a witness from John that "**Little children** (little born-ones), **we should NOT be habitually loving in word** (by a word or thought), **nor even in** (or: by) **the tongue, but rather within action** (deed; work) **and truth** (or: REALITY)" (1 John 3:18).

17. **Thus also [is] the faith** (the trust, conviction and loyalty): **if it should not continue to have works** (include actions; possess deeds; have employment), **by itself it exists being dead** (or: is lifeless; = is a corpse) **in correspondence to its own nature** (in the sphere of itself).

An example of this is the seed that does not fall into the ground (be implanted) and die: it abides alone (John 12:24), and will not bring forth life, but in time will die. What is loyalty, if you do not stand by your friend? What is conviction, if it does not empower the decisions of you life? What is trust, if you do not live with complete reliance upon the Father? The Seed of His faith may have been sown in your field, but if He has not yet prepared your soil (through burning off the competing weeds, through plowing up the beaten-down path of you life, through adding soil, or substance, to your rocky terrace) will it produce a crop?

18. **Yet someone will say, "You continuously have** (hold) **faith, and I continuously have** (or: possess) **works** (actions). **You at once show me** (exhibit to my eyes) **your faith apart from the works or actions, and I, forth from out of the midst of my actions and works, will show** (exhibit to) **you my faith, trust, conviction and loyalty."**

What does Jacob mean here? We are not certain even where to put the quotation marks – the translations vary. Is this all what this "**someone**" is saying, as I've punctuated it, or is it a statement in the first sentence, followed by Jacob's response with, "**You at once show me**..."? It seems to me that Jacob's straw man is making the point for Jacob in this illustration, the point being that it is the works that demonstrate the faith, and without action faith cannot be shown. It is not a "faith versus works" position. Either reading gives the same point.

19. **You continuously believe** (or: trust; are convinced) **that God is One** (or: that God exists being One; that One exists being God; or: that there is one God). [Deut. 6:4] **You are performing** (doing) **beautifully** (excellently; ideally) – **even the demons** (Hellenistic concept and term: = animistic influences) **continuously believe** (or: presently trust; are constantly loyal; are normally convinced [about this]), **and constantly shudder** (bristle; shiver; are ruffled).

> [comment: in this last phrase Jacob is either making an ontological statement about "demons," or he is using sarcasm, referring in a derogatory manner to the Jews who also believe this; Jesus used the term "diablos" (devil; one who thrusts-through folks) to refer to Judas in John 6:70; He used the term *satan* when speaking to Peter in Mark 8:33; this phrase could also refer to the superstitious mindsets of folks who have believed Jewish or pagan myths, or have accepted animistic influences into their thinking]

This seemingly parenthetical statement is in the midst of Jacob's point about faith needing action in order to be productive, which he was making since vs. 15 and which he continues in vs. 20, then on to the end of the chapter. I suggest that vs. 19 needs to be understood in the context of this ongoing topic.

In other words, "So you believe in one God. Wonderful!" You can almost taste the sarcasm. Both his straw man and the demons have faith! Thus, the very negative aspects of the spirit world even have this kind of "faith." Considered otherwise, with my above comment which I include in my translation, he is referring to the Jews who hold this belief in one God, calling them "demons."

20. **But are you willing to experientially and intimately know and receive insight, O empty person, that the faith, trust and loyalty, apart from the works and actions, exists being inactive** (continues unproductive; [*p74* reads: empty; without contents; other MSS: is dead])**?**

This is saying the same thing as vs. 17, above.

21. **Our father Abraham was not placed within the Way pointed out** (made fair and equitable; put in right relationship; rightwised; made a just one; also: = placed in covenant) **from out of works, when offering up his son Isaac upon the altar!**

Reading this as a factual statement, rather than as a question, seems more consistent with the context. The works were the outflow of His believing God; He was already in the Way pointed out and pointed in the right direction (which is trust and faith). His works did not put Him there, they demonstrated his faith, as in vs. 18, above. This is affirmed by Paul in Gal. 3:6,

> "**just as Abraham, 'trusts in God** (or: believed by God; experienced confidence by God), **and he is/was at once logically considered by Him [that he entered] into a right relationship** (or: and it was counted for him into a rightwised relationship with freedom from guilt, fairness, equity and justice which comprise the Way pointed out).'"

See vs. 23, below.

22. **Are you normally seeing that the faith, trust and loyalty continued to work together with his actions and works, and forth from out of the actions** (or: works), **faith** (trust, loyalty and conviction) **was brought to its goal** (was perfected; was matured; was finished)**?**

Works, living a life of doing mercy and producing love, is the goal of faith, and is the finished demonstration that faith exists in the person. A changed life is evidence that the new birth has occurred – it does not produce the new birth. And vs. 22 explains that this existing faith, trust and loyalty "**continued to work together with his actions.**" Faith produced the actions, then worked with them, and so out of the actions faith was brought to its purpose, its goal, and its intended end. The goal is having Christ formed within so that we – joined with Him – become the New Being, the new creation.

23. **And thus the Scripture was made full, the one saying,**

> **"Now Abraham believed** (or: put trust and confidence) **in God** (or: became persuaded by God; adhered to God), **and he was counted into the Way pointed out by Him** (or: he was considered rightwised by Him; he was reckoned fair, equitable and just in Him; alternately: so it was counted into right relation [= covenant inclusion] for him)," [Ex. 15:6] **and he was called "God's friend."** [Isa. 41:8]

This quote confirms my rendering vs. 21 as a statement rather than a question. It was Abraham's faith that counted him into those who having rightwised behavior, which God has pointed out to them.

24. **Are you folks normally observing** (or: perceiving) **that humanity** (or: a person) **is normally being rightwised** (from time to time being placed in right relationship in the Way pointed out; progressively made fair and equitable; normally justified; = put in covenant) **forth from out of the midst of actions and works, and not only from out of faith and trust?**

Here, rendering vs. 24 as a question flows with the statement in vs. 25. We are told in Heb. 10:1 that the Law **"is not even once able** (or: never has power) **at any point to perfect** (bring to the goal, finish, complete or mature) **those folks repeatedly coming near** (approaching) **by offering the same sacrifices every year, on into the whole length** (or: extended or stretched into the unbroken continuance) **[of its existence]."** The Law is the epitome of "actions and works." So the answer to the question of vs. 24 is, "NO!"

25. **Now in this same vein, even Rahab the prostitute, taking under [her roof] and welcoming the agents** (messengers), **and then later exiting them by a different way, was not rightwised** (placed in right relationship in the Way pointed out; made fair and equitable; justified; or: shown to be righteous; also: = brought into covenant) **forth from out of works.**

You see, she said to the spies **"I know that Yahweh has given you the land... For we heard how Yahweh dried up the waters of the Red Sea..."** (Joshua 2:9, 10). Her faith came from hearing the word. Her faith is recorded in Heb. 11:31.

26. **You see, just as the body apart from a breath-effect** (or: spirit) **is lifeless** (dead), **thus also the faith and trust apart from actions and works** [i.e., the living it out] **is** (exists being) **lifeless** (dead).

The subject here is faith, not works. Faith and trust are kept alive by action, just like breathing keeps the body alive. Faith, like a seed sitting alone on a shelf, can abide alone and eventually die. But in the planting of faith (the seed) a plant is brought to birth. The work of planting did not produce the seed or the plant, but the work of planting was necessary to bring the seed to its goal: a new plant. But the plant came from the seed. Dig all you want to, if there is no seed there will be no plant. But we are co-laborers with Christ (the Seed; the Faith): we go out and sow the Seed in the world.

John Gavazzoni shared with me the following insights in a recent email:
"Note that he says 'AS the body without the spirit is dead, SO faith without works is dead.' Pardon my belaboring it: faith is AS the body. One would usually expect James to connect the spirit (the inner dynamic) with faith, and the body (the outer display) with works, but in his corollary he connects the body with faith, and the spirit with works. Here I see James' affirming with Paul that it is 'God who WORKETH in you both to will and to DO of His good pleasure.'

"I think James finally nails the wonderful dynamic that he is expositing, by bringing the reader full circle to 'the faith of God' being the actions within the body of our faith making our faith effective unto appropriate actions. Each time we become aware of a lack of some action by which faith fulfills itself, we are driven back to patiently waiting upon God who worketh (faithFULLY) in us.

"I've often pondered how it is that God's actions are full of faith, i.e., He is faithFUL He is convinced, assured, confident, persuaded in the inevitability that His Being is the source, means and destiny of all things, and acts out of that assurance. It's His faith working by love, that is, His love is confidently certain. THAT'S what He saw in Abraham that He accounted as righteousness." (end quote)

Chapter 3

1. **My brothers** (= fellow members), **do not continue to become many teachers** (or: stop becoming a bunch of instructors; or: let not many of you folks proceed to be made teachers), **seeing, and knowing, that we shall receive [a] greater effect from the decision**
> (or: will take more intense scrutiny and evaluation; will get a stronger result of the separation; will receive heavier judgment),

The verb form of "**become**" is present imperative, and either middle or passive, thus the varied renderings. He is saying that not everyone should desire to have a place of being a teacher because of the responsibility which that function carries. And although it may be considered a place of honor and preeminence, God has a greater expectation for the performance of this function, and so teachers will experience a "**greater effect from** [His] **decision**" after evaluation of their work – the judgment may be more intense, and heavier, commensurate to the responsibility.

2. **for we all are tripping and stumbling** (= making mistakes) **many times [and] are causing many to entangle their feet, lose balance, and stumble. If anyone is not continually stumbling in word** (or: collected thought; reason; or: = what he says), **this one is a mature male adult** (or: a perfect husband; = complete and finished person), **with power and able also to guide the whole body [as] with a bridle.**

God's fairness will require more from teachers since their mistakes can cause many to become entangled, lose their balance, and stumble. It is the mature person that has both the power and ability to guide what he says. What a teacher says to a group of believers guides that whole body of believers.
> "**So to everyone to whom much was given, much will be sought for from him** (at his side or situation); **and to whom they set much alongside** (or: committed to and put in charge of much), **of him they will more excessively request and demand.**"
> (Lu. 12:48)

From the second sentence of vs. 2, above, we can see that a teacher needs to be a mature person in Christ who does not constantly stumble in what he says. The stable person will be given power from the Spirit, in order to guide the body of believers. We must remember that our words have consequences.

3. **Now if we are thrusting the bridle bits into the horses' mouths to make them continually yield themselves to us, we also continually lead together** (or: change the course of and direct) **their whole body.**
4. **Consider also the ships, being of so great size, and being constantly driven under rough and hard winds. They are continually steered under** (or: by) **the smallest rudder, wherever the impulse of the helmsman** (the one presently guiding straight and right) **continues determining and intending.**

Jacob continues in his illustrations of how something small can have influence upon something big. We should keep in mind that our teaching, what we say and how we say it – though at the time possibly even seeming insignificant – can have a great effect.

5. **Thus also, the tongue is a little member of the body, and yet is continuously making a great boast** [other MSS: constantly brags about great things] **– consider how great a forest a little fire progressively sets ablaze** (or: lights up)!

6. **Well the tongue [is] a fire; [its fuel is] the System of injustice** (or: the ordered and decorated but dominating world of secular culture, religion, politics and government which is unjust; or: The tongue, also, [is] fire: the world of disregard for what is right). **The tongue is placed down within our members, continuously spotting** (staining; = defiling) **the whole body, and repeatedly setting on fire the wheel of birth** (= the cycle of the origin [of life], or of generation; the wheel of genesis), **as well as being continuously set on fire by** (or: under) **the garbage dump** (the depository of refuse; Greek: Gehenna – the Valley of Hinnom).

In vs. 5 and 6 he is showing how important is our tongue – what we say. Our words can start a fire in the congregation, and the problem is that we usually have the dominating system of the world (our culture, our politics, our religion, our news media, etc.) as the source for what we say. He compares our carnal talk to getting its fuel from the garbage dump. The result is the defiling of the whole called-out community (the body), and causing destruction on every aspect of peoples' lives. Our tongue is the match that cause the whole forest to burn.

The phrase "**the wheel of birth**" is a literal rendering. William Barclay renders this, "the ever-recurring cycle of creation." This is enigmatic, and Jacob does not explain it, but I suggest that he is giving a picture of the recurring damage – from birth to death, throughout the whole of life – that the tongue repeatedly causes, as round and round we go, constantly dipping into garbage which we then spew upon others.

7. **For every nature, both of wild animals and of flying creatures, both of creeping animals and of those in the salt sea, is continuously being restrained** (tamed) **and has been restrained by the nature of man** (the human nature).
8. **But the tongue – an unruly** (un-restrainable; other MSS: unfixed; unstable; restless), **worthless** (ugly; bad; malicious; unrefined; harmful; base) **[member], full of death-bearing venom – no one of humanity is able** (continues having power) **to subdue, restrain or tame.**
9. **With it we continuously speak well of** (or: speak a good word about; bless) **the Lord** [other MSS: God] **and Father, and with it we constantly curse** (pray down upon) **those men having been born "according to** (down from and corresponding to) **God's likeness."** [Gen. 1:26-27]
10. **Out of the same mouth is continuously coming forth blessing and cursing. My brothers, there is no need** (or: it is not necessary) **for these things thus to be repeatedly birthed** (or: to keep on happening in this way).
11. **A spring** (or: fountain) **is not continuously bursting forth the sweet and the bitter** (or: cutting and pricking; [*p74*: salty]) **out of the same hole** (or: opening).
12. **My brothers, a fig tree is not able to produce olives, nor a grape-vine figs, neither brine to produce sweet water.**

Vs. 7-12 expand his thoughts on what we say, and how our ability to speak is unruly and what we commonly say is worthless and often contains "**death-bearing venom**" – we are like serpents, and often speak from that source. What an indictment! The world of words in which we live "**no one of humanity is able** (continues having power) **to subdue, restrain or tame**." We are inundated from every side, from local gossip and complaint to international broadcasts.

We are religious, we "bless God," and we are profane, we curse our brothers – all out of our same mouth, from our inner life. But he tells us that "**there is no need** (or: it is not necessary) **for these things thus to be repeatedly birthed** (or: to keep on happening in this way)." Vs. 11 and 12 give two illustrations from nature that such behavior is unnatural. It comes from our alienated selves, our old estranged nature. He is calling us to live from the New Human, the Christ within us, not from the law of sin in our members. It is only the Christ life that can accomplish this.

Vs. 9 shows our spiritual duplicity. As Paul said, we are yet carnal. We fail to see that our fellow human beings (born in God's likeness) are Christ's brothers – and ours – and we neglect them and are vicious toward them. We fail to perceive true identities – of both Christ and humanity.

13. **Who [is] wise and understanding** (adept) **among you? Let him at once exhibit** (show; present to the sight and demonstrate) **his works and actions out of beautiful behavior** (fine, ideal, excellent and appropriate conduct) **in gentleness of** (or: considerateness from) **wisdom.**

Here he calls to the higher being within to exhibit actions from the beautiful and ideal life of Christ, Who is gentleness, wisdom and appropriate conduct. It is only the Christ-life and His Being within us that makes us wise, understanding and adept – from our union with Him.

14. **Yet if you folks continuously have bitter rivalry** (or: jealousy) **and selfish ambition** (or: faction) **in your heart, do not habitually boast** (exult) **and lie** (speak falsely or deceitfully) **concerning the truth or reality** (or: are you not now vaunting against and falsifying the truth?).

I have given the last clause first as a statement, and then as a question. The first is saying that even if you find ugliness in your heart, don't make it worse by lying about it, or speaking deceitfully about the truth of the situation, or about the reality of this life in Christ.

As a question it asks that if you harbor rivalry, jealousy, selfish ambition or faction in your heart, is this not "vaunting [yourself] against" the truth in Christ, and in the end making Christ as the Truth to be false, in you? And yet, it seems that we see this as much in the "churches" as in society, so I suppose that is why Jacob brought this up in his general letter.

15. **This is not the wisdom continuously coming down from above, but rather [is] upon the earth** (or: earthly; terrestrial), **pertaining to or proceeding from the soul** (soulful; having the mind, will and emotions as its source; = natural), **pertaining to, or proceeding from, or having the characteristics of demons** [Hellenistic term and concept; = influences thought of in that period and culture as being animistic or personified].
> [comment: note that the three adjectives "earthly," "natural/soulish," and "demonic" are tied together to this same context, as being of the same sphere of being – or, fruit of the same tree]

So those negative characteristics noted in vs. 14 do not come from heaven (above; figure of the realm of spirit), but rather from the realm of earth. They come from the soul: from our mind, will and emotions, and Jacob goes on to say that the terrestrial and the realm of the soul are also the same realm of what the Hellenistic world called "demonic," which is simply the realm of the distorted; the sphere of corrupted thinking along with unloving attitudes and behaviors. Jealous rivalry, faction and selfish ambition fall into the category of "demonic."

16. **For where [there is] jealousy** (rivalry) **and selfish ambition** (faction; intrigue), **in that place [is] instability** (disorder; an unsettled state) **and every ignoble** (base; vile; worthless) **practice.**

These are simply the fruit of estrangement from God, and alienation from His reign – the unregenerated human condition – and instability, together with base practice, also come under the category of "demonic," giving us a better understanding of that word.

17. **But the wisdom from above is** (constantly exists being) **indeed first** (or: primarily) **pure, thereafter peaceable** (or: peaceful; pertaining to peace and harmony), **suitable** (fair; reasonably lenient; yielding; unassertive; considerate), **compliant** (easily persuaded; receptive; reasonable; willing to yield), **full of mercy** (= practical help) **and good fruits, non-separating** (not discriminatory; undivided in evaluating; unwavering; unprejudiced), **unpretending** (or: not hyper-critical; not judging from a low point of view; not focusing on tiny distinctions; not overly judgmental; not under-estimating of reality) .

It is interesting that Jacob calls these qualities – which we might call character traits – "**the wisdom from above**," which could mean from God or heaven. They are the traits of a person that is in the Way pointed out, who has the qualities of Christ. This could be another list of the "fruit of the Spirit," for such attributes come only from Christ within us.

18. **Now the fruit of fair and equitable dealing** (justice and right relationship in accord with the Way pointed out; the condition of being rightwised, or turned in the right direction; also: = covenant participation) **is continuously being sown in peace and harmony by and for those habitually performing** (making; doing; producing) **peace and harmony.**

This fruit is from the Tree of Life. Again, it is the fruit of the Spirit, which results in equity and fairness, rightwised relationships, justice, and being turned in the right direction – which is the Way that has been pointed out, which is Christ.

The method and the environment of sowing the seeds of this fruit is peace and harmony. It comes from the inner being of those that live in peace and harmony, and make it a practiced way of life. This is another description of the body of Christ, or of the New Being that is within the new creation.

Chapter 4

1. **From what situation** (place; source) **[arise] battles** (or: wars; situations of combat) **and fights** (quarrels; strife; controversies) **among you folks? Are they not from this source** (or: place)**: from out of your sensual pleasures** (enjoyments and gratifications) **[which are] themselves continually performing as soldiers within your members?**

What? You mean it's not from demons? Well, yes they are, if you realize that distorted sensual pleasures are what the Hellenistic culture classed as "demonic." Note that Jacob says that they are operating in their members. This is what Paul described in Rom. 7:23 as a law in his members,

> "**yet I constantly see** (or: observe) **a different principle** (or: law), **within my members, [which is] by the Law** (or: custom; or: [= Torah]) **repeatedly taking the field to wage war against my mind** (or: to wage war in opposition to, and in the place of, the law of my mind), **and repeatedly taking me prisoner and leading me into captivity within the principle** (or: in union with the law) **of the Sin** (the failure; the error; the miss of the Target; the deviation from the goal) **– the one continuously existing** (or: now being) **within my members.**"

Paul uses the same metaphor of a war within each of us, where our alienated self battles against the New Being. It is the law of sin within each of us that creates the battles among us.

2. **You folks are continuously strongly desiring to possess, and yet continuously you do not have; you continue murdering and are repeatedly jealous** (boil with rivalry), **and so you are perpetually unable to hit the mark** (to attain or master [something]). **You are habitually quarreling and fighting.**

> (or: You people constantly have full longing, desire and lust – and still you are not presently holding or possessing – and so you repeatedly murder. You are progressively envious, boiling with rivalry, and yet continue having no power to obtain [your goal], so you are constantly striving and having controversies – even doing combat and waging wars!)

You continue not having [your desires] because you yourself do not continue asking (or: you are not normally asking for yourselves).

Either reading of the Greek text is a sobering criticism. Do we read the "**murdering**" part literally, or figuratively (as John described hate as being murder – 1 John 3:15)? I suggest the latter, as it is tied in with jealousy. Such negative inward attitudes and thoughts are the opposite of hitting the mark: the love of Christ for humanity. Jealousy and rivalry bring conflicts of interest (which are obviously self-centered), and this results in quarreling and fighting since there are divided interests. Paul encounter this at Corinth, as well, where there were factions that each held to one emissary over against another, to the point that Paul said "Christ is divided!" (1 Cor. 1:13a, taking the Greek as a statement, rather than a question. If His body is divided, then the Christ is divided).

The last sentence of vs. 2 leads into vs. 3. First they are not "**continuing**" to ask, and then they are asking for the wrong purpose. For all of these reasons they do not posses their desires. History has shown that these desires were from the estranged and alienated old nature, and they became political – which lead to physical wars and bloodshed, all in the name of Christ. What blasphemy was lived out by those who thought they were doing God a favor. The words of Jesus were truly prophetic, that those who would kill others would think that they were doing God a service (John. 16:2).

3. **You continue asking** (requesting), **and yet are not receiving because you are asking inappropriately** (worthlessly requesting; or: = asking for a wrong purpose) **to the intent that you may spend** (= waste) **it in** (or: on) **your pleasures.**

Again, self-centered and carnal requests that go astray from the heart of God and His purpose in the ages.

4. **Adulterers and adulteresses** (= Folks unfaithful to Christ or God as your husband)! **Have you not seen, and are you not aware, that the System's friendship** (the affection whose source is this world of religion, secular culture, economy and government) **is a source of enmity with God** (or: hostility and active hatred with regard to God; [Aleph reads: exists being alienation to God])**? Whoever, then, may have been made to want** (to intend; to purpose) **to be the System's** (or: world's) **friend is continuing to be established** (habitually set down; progressively rendered or constituted) **[as] God's alienated and hostile person.**

Keeping in mind that Jacob was writing a general letter to those scattered among, and influenced by, other cultures, he may have referred to personal immoral behavior among the called-out communities. Yet, these folks would also be aware of Isa. 1:21, "How has she become a prostitute, a town [= Jerusalem] faithful? Full of [right] judgment [was] Zion. Righteousness, it was lodging in her, yet now, murderers!" (CVOT). Israel committed adultery by turning to the false gods of paganism. This may have been that to which Jacob was here referring.

Through Constantine, the "church" became very friendly with the political System, and then with pagan religious systems, as Christianity became the state religion, and this blending led to the darkness of the Middle Ages. It set up a church system that was at enmity with the love of God, and thus, with God Himself. As codex Aleph reads, it became "alienation to God." The last sentence of vs. 4 applies today as it did back then: friendship with the institutional church, or with a political system, and their systems of control and governmental stratifications demonstrates a lack of being reconciled to God and sets us in a stance that is alien to the heart of God. Instead of the unification that is in Christ, it creates an "us-and-them" mentality and view of humanity.

5. **Or are you supposing that the Scripture is speaking void of effect** (emptily; vainly)**? The breath-effect** (or: spirit) **which housed-down in us normally sets its desire** (longing; affection; yearning) **upon [something], [with a view] toward ill-will, malice, envy and jealousy!**
    (or: The Spirit – which He causes to dwell in union with us – is constantly longing and
    progressively yearning [for us]: to the point of bubbling up zeal and enthusiasm.
    or: Is the spirit and attitude which lives within us periodically longing toward envy?)

My first rendering of the second half of this vs. is saying that our estranged attitude and alienated spirit (i.e., the human condition before regeneration in Christ) leads us toward the negative.

The second rendering takes "the *pneuma*" as referring to the Holy Spirit, and so translates the positive end of the word which has semantic range from "zeal/enthusiasm" to "**jealousy/envy**" (Greek: *phthonos*).

The third alternative reads as a question, and is asking either if our reconciled, born-from-above spirit would be thus longing, or it asks us to search our hearts to see what kind of spirit or attitude is operating in us.

6. **Yet He is constantly and progressively giving greater** (= more abundant; more intense; larger; more frequent) **grace and favor, therefore it is saying**

> **"God continuously sets Himself in opposition[to, and aligns Himself against, those that show themselves above** (the proud; the assuming), **but He habitually gives grace and favor to the low ones** (the unassuming ones; the humble ones; those of low rank)." [Prov. 3:34]

The first clause is an echo of Paul in Rom. 5:20,

> **"But where the Sin** (the failure; the divergence and missing of the target) **increases** (or: abounded to be more than enough; becomes more intense) **THE GRACE** (or: joyous favor) **at once super-exceeds** (or: hyper-exceeded) **over and above, surrounding to excessive abundance and overflow."**

Observe how Jacob sets his first statement in contrast to the quote from Proverbs, saying that this latter is a consequence of the former. Because His grace is sufficient, He sets Himself in opposition to those that might be tested with pride, or to those who show themselves as being above others. Consider the situation with Paul in 2 Cor. 12:

> 7. **And now, in the excess of the unveilings** (or: with the transcendence of the revelations; by the extraordinary amount and surpassing nature of the disclosures), **through this [situation] and for this reason – so that I could not be progressively exalted** (or: would not continue being overly lifted up [in myself or by others]) – **something with [its] point in [my] flesh is given in me** (or: an impaling-stake for the human nature was given for me; or: a thorn to the natural realm, and a splinter by alienated humanity, was assigned to me): **an agent of the adversary, to the end that he** (or: it) **could** (or: should; would) **repeatedly beat me in the face** (or: slap me on the ear) **with his** (or: its) **fist.**
> [comment: this personification of the irritation may well be metaphorical and may refer to his social or cultural-religious situation; this situation calls to mind Job being tested by satan]
> 8. **I called the Lord** [Christ or Yahweh] **alongside for relief, ease and comfort, and entreated [Him] three times over** (or: about) **this, so that he** (or: it) **would** (or: should) **at once stand away and withdraw from me,**
> 9. **and yet He has said to me – and His declaration stands, "My grace is continuously sufficient in you** (or: My joyous favor is constantly adequate to ward [it] off for you), **for you see, ability** (or: the [other MSS read: My] power) **is habitually brought to its goal** (or: finished; perfected; matured) **within the midst of weakness** (or: in union with lack of strength and infirmity)**..."**

I suggest that it was God that was "**continuously set**[ting] **Himself in opposition**" to Paul, in vs. 6 above, through His agent of adversity "**so that [he] could not be progressively exalted** (or: would not continue being overly lifted up [in myself or by others])." And although Paul three times entreated God over this situation, God's reply was that His grace continues sufficient in him, and for him.

7. **Consequently, you must be subjected by** (or: be at once placed and arranged under in; be humbly aligned with and to) **God. So stand in opposition to the [or: your] adversary** (or: take a stand [as in battle] against the one trying to thrust you through [with a weapon]), **and he will flee** (take flight) **away from you!**

Here Jacob draws the logical conclusion: we must be subjected by God, for we all have that seed of pride in our alienated false persona. The question that next arises is, What, who or where is our adversary? If it is those who, as in Proverbs, "**show themselves above** (the proud; the assuming)" then we can simply take a stand in opposition, along with God, and they will take flight. If it is pride within ourselves, then this may only take flight as we align ourselves with the One who sends a goad into our lives, as with Paul. The context of vs. 7 is vs. 4-6. God's adversaries are the friendship with the system, and pride – both of which are within the called-out communities of "the twelve tribes," and within us. These two mindsets and emotions are those things that thrust us through, they are the "devil" within us.

8. **Draw near in God** (or: Approach by God; Be close at hand for God; Be or stay near to God), **and He will draw near in you** (or: be or stay near to you; be close at hand for you)! **You failing folks** (ones missing the target; sinners), **cleanse [your] hands** (= your actions)! **You two-souled folks** (or: double-minded ones; people with split affections and loyalties), **purify** (make of one substance) **[your] hearts!**

Jacob is addressing those of the assembled bodies, and speaking to issues that they, like everyone else, have. They are already in God, or they could not draw near. This admonition also suggests that they can approach God "by God" (the dative case here, with no expressed preposition in the Greek), or approach "for God," that is, to be available for His use, and "to God," that is to be near Him. God makes Himself available as the instrument of our approach to Him, even though we are yet failing, deviating, missing the goal, sinning. Through Him we can cleans our hands (figure of our works and actions), and in Him we can make our hearts (= cores of our beings) of one substance and no longer be "**two-souled**."

9. **You must endure labor and hardships, and be miserable and wretched; you must mourn, and you must cry. Your laughter must be converted into mourning, and joy into dejection with [your] eyes cast down;**
10. **you folks must consequently be made low** (humbled; demoted; brought to a low station) **in the Lord's sight** (= in [Yahweh's, or Christ's] presence), **and then He will lift you up** (elevate you).

In vs. 9 he uses the imperative, which I have expressed using the word "**must**." These adverse conditions are His tool to transform us. Notice the passive voice in the second statement of this verse. This suggests something happening to us. These things need to happen to correct our actions and unify our being, and they are a part of our "drawing near" in Him.

He sums up in vs. 10 what he began in vs. 4. God's making us low, demoting us and humbling us in His presence and before His eyes of fire and feet of burning bronze as He walks among His called-out communities (Rev. 1:14, 15, 20; 2:1), is what does this. When His refining work (Mal. 3:1-6) is finished, then He will lift us up to a higher place.

11. **Brothers** (= believers in God's household) **do not be continuously** (or: stop constantly) **speaking down** (or: gossiping or babbling; wearing someone down by talking; talking a person down) **against one another. The one habitually speaking down against a brother** (= a fellow believer, or, a fellow Israelite; or: = a member of God's household), **and continuously judging** (separating and making decisions about) **his brother, is continuously speaking down against law, and thus keeps on judging** (making separations and then decisions about) **law. Now if you continue judging law, you are not being a performer** (a doer) **of law, but rather, a judge** (one who makes separations and decisions).

Speaking down against someone is not an expression of love. And wearing someone down by talking is also inconsiderate! Gossiping and judging our fellow believers is operating under the Law. It is an expression that is contrary to the Way pointed out and is opposed to rightwised living. It is thus contrary to what even the Law was about, and is also making an evaluation of law (or: what is right). Yet at the same time it is also not doing what the Law says, but rather is elevating the one doing this to the position of being a judge of other people. Paul speaks against this in Rom. 2:1, and in 14:10 asks, "**Why are you constantly judging** (discriminating against;

separating away; making a decision about) **your brother** (= fellow believer)**?**" then in 14:13 says, "**No longer, then, should we continue judging** (making decisions about; discriminating against; separating away) **one another.**"

12. **There is one Lawgiver and Separator** (Decider; Evaluator; Judge)**: the One being continuously able and powerful to deliver** (rescue; heal; save; restore to wholeness)**, as well as to cause loss** (or: bring a condition of utter ruin; or: cause [something or someone] to be lost; or: destroy). **So you, who are you, the one continuously judging the one near you** (repeatedly separating the neighbor; or: presently making decisions about [your] associate)**?**

Judging folks is God's business, not ours. Our doing so is presumptuous and contrary to His instructions to us. What we should be doing is discerning all things by the Spirit of God, or as Paul says in 1 Cor. 2:15,

> "**Yet the spiritual person** (one dominated by and focused on spirit or the realm of the Spirit, and characterized by the qualities of spirit: the Wind which continuously moves across the land) **is, on the one hand, continuously sifting and re-evaluating** (habitually separating and deciding from above on; progressively holding things up for close examination of) **all things...**"

We should be supporting and lifting up our associates, edifying and building them up. Note that the "Judge; Evaluator" is our Savior – continuously able and powerful to deliver and make us whole – and also the One who can cause loss for us and bring us to utter ruin, if His evaluation of our situation leads Him to bring His love to us in this way, for our correction and rehabilitation.

13. **Come now, those continuously saying, "Today or tomorrow we will travel into this or that city and produce** (make; perform; do [something]) **one year there, and then we can trade** (or: conduct business) **and make a profit,"**
14. **– namely, those who are not in the habit of putting their attention upon the thing of tomorrow** (or: who are not normally versed in or acquainted with the morrow; or: are not now standing upon tomorrow). **Of what sort [is] your life? You see, you folks are** (or: exist being) **a vapor** (a mist), **progressively** (or: repeatedly) **appearing for a little while** (toward a little space), **and thereupon continually** (or: repeatedly) **being made to disappear –**

Jacob now turns to their outlook on life and their normal plans for the near future. Vs. 13 gives the natural person's way of life. It is "**today or tomorrow,**" "**this or that,**" etc. In other words, nothing specific – we'll see what happens. He goes on in vs. 14 to say that these are not in the habit of putting their attention upon tomorrow. Next he asks of them this question, "**Of what sort [is] your life?**" – or, What kind of life are you living? Then he answers the question: they are like a cloud that appears for a while, then are continually made to disappear. There is no substance to their way of life; there is no continuity, no focus.

15. **Instead of that, you should be saying, "If the Lord** [= Yahweh, or, Christ] **should will** (or: intend), **we also will live and will do** (or: produce) **this or that."**

Herein lies both purpose and stability: the mind, intent and will of the Lord; the leading of the Spirit. Seeing what the Father is doing, and then doing the same.

16. **Yet now you continue speaking loudly** (boasting; gloating) **in your empty, bragging speech and displays. All such boasting is bad** (harmful; painfully laborious; miserable).

Again, Jacob sees emptiness in the called-out folks – bragging about being the "elect of God," no doubt. Boisterous, yet showing nothing. Proclaiming to have Christ, yet bearing no fruit. This kind of religious boast (evidence of pride) will bring a gush of misery – from God, as He did with Paul lest he become lifted up with pride, or lifted up by others.

17. **So for one** (or: in a man; to a person) **having seen and thus knowing to be continually performing [the] beautiful** (doing [the] ideal; making [the] good; producing [the] excellent), **and**

then not habitually performing (doing) **[it], in him it is a failure** (for him it is error; to him it is sin; by him it is a missing of the target and a deviation from the goal).

Here he returns them, and us, to substance: the outflow of faith – performing the beautiful, doing what is ideal, producing excellence. This equates to feeding the hungry, clothing the naked, visiting the sick and those in prison (Matt. 25).

But having the revelation to do this and having a knowledge that this is what Christ expects of us, and then not by habit performing and doing it is what equates to failure, to falling short of the goal, and to entering into error. It leads to Phariseeism and being classified as a goat (kid – immature one that bounces here and there, accomplishing nothing).

Chapter 5

1. **Continue leading on now, you wealthy folks, burst into tears while continuously uttering cries of distress upon your repeatedly recurring hardships** (difficulties and wretchedness which must be endured).
2. **Your riches have rotted; your garments have come to be moth-eaten.**
3. **Your gold and silver have been corrupted with poison** (or: corroded and covered with oxidation**), and their venom** (or: corrosion) **will be unto you a witness** (or: evidence) **and will eat your flesh** (= the enslaved and alienated self; = the human nature that has been molded by and conformed to the System) **as fire. You folks pile up a treasure hoard in the midst of last days!**
4. **Consider and look to the worker's wage – that having been withheld by you which belongs to those mowing your farms – which constantly utters** (or: shouts) **a cry, and now the outcries and shouts of those gathering in the harvest have entered into the ears of the Lord of hosts** (= Yahweh of Armies)**!**

He now moves to another general category: the wealthy. He prophesies that difficult times are repeatedly coming upon them. Their days of luxury are coming to a close – figured by wealth that has decayed away and lost its value (rotted), by moth-eaten garments, and now even their gold and silver (their horded treasures) are poisoning their lives and bringing sickness to their bodies. Their wealth is disintegrating the estranged self (the flesh) which had conformed itself to the domination System of political, social and economic power in order to gain such riches. This latter could well relate to the church of Laodicea (Rev. 3:17).

The coming last days of which Jacob speaks were the times of the close of the Jewish age with its old, which was done away at the cross, and the resultant coming destruction of Jerusalem, which Jesus prophesied. The end of that world would affect even those that had been scattered away from that City during the times of Acts 8 through 11, to whom he was now writing. Trouble for their area would also come in later years.

Why was this time of judging coming? For the same reason that Yahweh judged Israel in the past – for their injustice and lack of caring for the widows, orphans and the poor. Vs. 4 speaks to their failures and mistakes. They had cheated those who worked for them.

5. **You folks live a soft life in delicate luxury** (or: You self-indulge) **and take excessive comfort and live in wanton pleasure upon the land. You nourish your hearts in the midst of** (or: = fatten yourselves up for) **a day of slaughter!**

We are not told to which day of slaughter he was referring, but the taking of excessive comfort and nourishing their hearts speaks of a lack of care for those in need – a reminder of Matt. 25:42-45, and of the parable of the Rich Man (figure of the Jewish leadership of that time) in Lu. 16. This could also have been prophetic of the slaughter by the Romans which happened in AD 70.

6. **You oppose fairness, equity and justice, while you degrade the way pointed out; you murder the fair and equitable person** (the just one; the one in accord with the way pointed out; the righteous; or: the innocent); **he is not normally setting himself opposed to you** (or: is He not now aligning Himself against you, and resisting you folks?).

This kind of behavior by God's people always brought judgment. The last clause says either that the just person is humbly enduring injustice, or it is saying that God is aligning Himself against the unfair folks to bring them judgment.

7. **Be patient** (long-tempered; long-passioned; slow to rush; or: Have long-term feelings and emotions), **then, brothers, during the continuance of the Lord's** [= Yahweh's, or, Christ's] **presence and His being alongside. Consider! The worker of the land repeatedly receives** (takes out into his hands from within) **the precious fruit of the land, being patient** (slow to rush and with long-term feelings) **upon it during the continuance where it can receive "an early as well as a latter** (or: late) **rain."** [Deut. 11:14]

Jacob calls for patience during this time of the Lord's dealing with the unjust, while His presence continues bringing fairness and equity – reward and pay for what has been done, either way. Take note that God is present and involved with us. He then uses the metaphor of the farmer who is patient in waiting to harvest his crop. The rains of both blessings and judgments (or: corrective measures) must have their seasons. It is the same Greek word *heos* (which I have rendered "**during the continuance**" in both the first statement about the Lord's being alongside them, and then in the analogy of the farmer. As the farmer is present while the crop ripens, so is the Lord also present amidst our situations (as in Rev. 2:1).

8. **You, too, be patient** (be slow to rush while maintaining long-term feelings); **establish** (place supports and make stable; firmly set) **your hearts, because the Lord's** [= Yahweh's or Christ's] **presence has drawn near** (has approached and now exists close to us).

This may be a reference to His presence that was to come upon Jerusalem in AD 70, or to existing situations in the areas of the dispersion. Note the perfect tense "**has drawn near**" – it was an existing situation. He calls for patience during this time, and admonished them to prepare their hearts and give support to one another in preparation for whatever He would do.

9. **Brothers, do not be groaning down against** (or: sighing in relation to; or, may = complaining about or blaming) **one another, so that you may not be separated and have a decision made** (or: be put asunder, scrutinized and judged). **Consider! The Decider** (the Separator, Evaluator and Judge) **has taken a stand, and now continues standing before the doors.**

This sounds like Israel in the wilderness murmuring against Moses when things were hard. Here he is saying that they should not blame their associates or complain that something is their neighbor's fault – they will be evaluated about such behavior, and a decision may be made about their need of purification from such. He calls to their attention that the Parousia (the presence of the Lord for judgment) is close at hand, and in fact has taken a stand. It is a foolish time to act amiss.

10. **Brothers, take the prophets who spoke within [the authority of], and in union with, the Name of the Lord** [= Yahweh] **as an example to be copied: of experiencing worthless responses and bad conditions while suffering from harmful treatment and evil – as well as of patience** (long-suffering; slow-rushing; long-term feelings).

He may be referring to the prophets of OT times, or of recent events of persecution from the Jews (e.g., the stoning of Steven), or from others. These folks had patience during their times of ill treatment.

11. **Consider! We are calling happy and blessed those remaining under** (or: patiently and humbly enduring; or: steadfast and supporting). **You heard [about] the persistent remaining under** (steadfast, patient and humble endurance) **of Job, and you saw the Lord's** [= Yahweh's] **goal** (the end attained by the Lord; the Lord's completion), **because**
> **"the Lord** [= Yahweh] **is great of tender affections** (literally: great of internal organs; full of guts) **and is empathetically compassionate."** [Ex. 34:6]

Paul refers to this as one aspect of the fruit of the Spirit (Gal. 5:22). Job saw only God behind his troubles, so he patiently endured them, seeking God for the answers. He did not speak abusively of satan (God's agent of destruction and persecution), and in fact did not mention satan (which means: adversary) at all, nor even the raiding Sabeans (Job. 1:15). Apparently Job's endurance was a well-known fact. We should also take note that the Lord had a goal in this dealing with Job. Jacob has seen that God had tender affections and empathetic compassions for Job, and thus also does for us.

But these called-out folks are considered happy and blessed because of the Lord's abundance of tender affections and empathetic compassion to them, during their burdensome experiences. We should recall this when afflictions come upon us.

12. **Now before all things** (= above all; but especially; or: before all mankind), **my brothers, do not be in the habit of promising by swearing [to, or, by] either the heaven** (or: atmosphere; sky), **nor the earth** (or: land), **nor any other oath. But let your affirmation continually be, "Yes," and the negative, "No," to the intent that you may not fall under a process of judging** (or: fall by an act of separating for a decision, or by scrutinizing, or by discriminating).

He is saying, "Don't let this practice be a part of your way of life." Don't call upon heaven or earth to back up your promises. Promise from the heart, and simply say "**Yes**," or "**No**." Swearing in this way can lead into a process of judging (either upon yourself, or from you upon others), and it can cause you to fall by evaluating the situation (and then rationalizing about your responsibilities in it), or by focusing on minute details of the arrangement (to see if you can get out of some aspect of what you promised), or by your discriminating against someone in your heart or in your actions (in relation to your agreement). Swearing by the sky or the land implies that there is inadequate integrity within you to do according to your word.

13. **Is anyone among you folks continually experiencing bad things** (misfortune; ugly situations; evil)**? Let him be habitually thinking with a view to ease and well-being and repeatedly speak toward goodness** (or: pray). **Is someone normally cheerful and in good spirits? Let him play a stringed or percussion instrument and make music or sing psalms.**

Along with your patient endurance and remaining under the hard situation to give support, let your thoughts, words and actions project goodness, ease and well-being into the situation. This kind of prayer will have a positive effect. And then, with this creating of a cheerful mood and an uplifted attitude, express this by making music and singing.

14. **Is anyone among you habitually experiencing weakness or normally infirm? Let him at once call to himself the older folks of the called-out community, and then let them speak well-being** (or: pray goodness) **upon him, anointing** (or: massaging) **him with olive oil in union with and in [the authority of] the Lord's** [= Yahweh's, or, Christ's] **Name,**
15. **and then faith's impartation of well-being** (or: the prayer which comes from trust; the desire of conviction) **will deliver** (restore to health; rescue; save) **the one being continuously labored to weariness and exhaustion, and the Lord** [= Christ, or, Yahweh,] **will cause him to rise, and if it may be he has been making mistakes** (performing amiss; doing acts which miss the goal) **it will be forgiven to him** (sent forth for him; let go off in him).

Here there is a call to community: don't try to go through habitual weakness or illness on your own. The older folks in the called-out community will be experienced in speaking well-being, and in doing goodness to you. Let them give you a massage with olive oil while speaking ease to your spirit, in the Name of the Lord.

This brings faith's impartation of well-being, which comes from the group whom you have invited to be with you, which will bring strength and healing, and the Lord will cause you to rise up – and will even cause any mistakes to flow away from you.

16. **Consequently, be continuously confessing fully** (or: openly speaking out similarly about) **your failures** (errors; misses of the target; sins) **to one another, and be habitually speaking well-being over** (or: praying and thinking goodness on behalf of) **one another, in a manner so that you may be cured** (or: would be healed). **A binding need** (or: a petition and an entreaty out of need) **of a person within the Way pointed out** (of a fair and equitable person; of one in right relationship; of a rightwised and rightly aligned man; of a just one) **– which progressively works inwardly and itself continuously creates energy from union – constantly exerts much strength.**

Jacob is advising openness within the community, and the habit of acknowledging to one another our failures and mistakes, and then speaking well-being and goodness over one another.

Next he makes a fascinating statement: either a binding need, or an entreaty that comes from a need, of a person that lives in rightwised relationships with God and others, and who accords to the Way which has been pointed out to us, "**constantly exerts much strength**" from the progressive inward work and the created energy which come from union with God and with the community. The very need creates inward energy and then exerts strength toward its own fulfillment! This comes from union with God, and with His community. The petition (which can be either or both to God and to the community) is an expression of faith with a view to the meeting of the need.

17. **Elijah was a person** (a human being) **of like experiences and emotions with us, and with a thought toward things being well, he spoke toward goodness** (or: prayed) **for it to not rain, and it did not rain upon the land [for] three years and six months.**
18. **And back again he spoke toward goodness** (or: offered prayer), **and the sky** (or: atmosphere; heaven) **gave rain, and then the land germinated and produced her fruit.**

The first point I see here is that the prophet Elijah is considered to be just like us. The next point is that both God's withholding rain and His giving of rain are expressions of goodness (prayer – Greek: *pros-eu-chomai*, "thinking, speaking or acting toward having goodness, and things going well and with ease"). His decisions are always with a view toward our goodness – even if they result in correction.

There is an enigmatic reference to a time period, here: three and one half years. We see this symbolic number in the figures of the Unveiling given through John in Rev. chapters 11, 12 and 13. In ch. 11 there is inference to Elijah in vs. 6. Perhaps Jacob was aware of John's prophecy, and was here issuing a subtle warning of what was to come in Jerusalem in a "time of correction" within the next couple of decades.

19. **My brothers** (= Dear family), **if someone among you may be led astray** (caused to wander) **away from the Truth and reality, and someone should** (or: would) **turn him back,**
20. **continue knowing from experience and realize that this one turning back a sinner** (a failure; one missing the goal; one living in error or under a mistake) **out of [the] straying of his way** (or: from the midst of his path of wandering), **will deliver** (rescue; save; make healthy and whole) **a soul** (= a person) **from out of the midst of death, and "will cover [the] fullness of [his] mistakes** (errors; failures to hit the target; deviations; sins)." [Prov. 10:12]

Jacob ends this general letter with an admonition toward "saving the lost." Here it is for rescuing someone who has been caused to wander away from the new Reality (or: the Truth which is

Jesus Christ) which results in participation in the new covenant. He does not specify a reason or what it was that might cause a person to stray from the Way pointed out, but simply acknowledges the reality that this might happen.

Verse 20 tells us that we should realize that such a rescue of the person making this mistake will deliver that person from out of the midst of death. Not save him from a future death, but rescue him "**from out of the midst of**" death. Here is another definition of what the 1st century writers meant when they spoke of death. A classic example is in the return of the prodigal in Lu. 16:25, where the father said, "**this my son was dead, and is alive again, he was lost, and is found**." It was not speaking of physically being in a grave, but of the separation from the called-out community – from not abiding in the Vine (John 15:6). Turning this person back is the same as grafting him back into the Vine, the source of Life. This is an act of Love, which "**will cover [the] fullness of [his]** errors and deviations."

CPSIA information can be obtained
at www.ICGtesting.com
Printed in the USA
BVHW011918170120
569834BV00003B/159